THE NEW BREED

Books by Andrew Geer

MERCY IN HELL
THE SEA CHASE
THE NEW BREED

THE NEW BREED

THE STORY OF THE U.S. MARINES IN KOREA

BY ANDREW GEER

HARPER & BROTHERS

PUBLISHERS · NEW YORK

904

THE NEW BREED

Copyright, 1952, by Andrew Clare Geer

Printed in the United States of America

FIRST EDITION

K-B

Library of Congress catalog card number: 52-5438

To the memory of the Marines
and Naval Hospital Corpsmen
who died in Korea

Writing a detailed history of men in battle poses the same problem faced by a commander when selections are made for decorations and awards. Many men of great courage are overlooked because their acts of heroism were unobserved or died with the man who would have reported the act. The process of selection and elimination was an unhappy task because the heroic actions of many fine Marines and Naval Corpsmen had to go unrecorded. This will always be the case until each individual can file his own action report.

TABLE OF CONTENTS

Illustrations will be found in a group following page 174.

LIST OF MAPS

FOREWORD

Military history generally deals with campaigns; with the factors affecting the situation; with the decisions of higher commanders; and with an analysis of the results accomplished. The human reactions of the thousands of lesser actors are as a rule painted with a broad brush only. The details are usually left to the historical novel or quasi-historical novel. Yet the actual story is far more convincing than any fictional account. What Andrew Geer has done in *The New Breed* is to picture vividly the real-life, not fictional, Marine, as he fought the bitter battles of the Naktong, struggled with the mud flats and sea walls of Inchon, crushed the enemy barricades in Seoul, and cut his way through a Chinese army from the Chosin Reservoir to the sea. In telling this detailed story, however, Major Geer has not neglected the broad picture. *The New Breed* is a definite contribution to the history of the Korean War.

OLIVER P. SMITH
Major General, U. S. Marine Corps

THE NEW BREED

CHAPTER I

A Fire Starts; the Fire Brigade Is Called

A soft, hot wind whispered over the brown hills of the old Spanish rancho and the summer shrunken streams in the back hills rattled loosely in their oversized beds. As the shadows lengthened and night came on, the wind died away. From rugged Horno Ridge—a ridge cursed and sweated over by thousands of Marines—drifted the mournful cry of a coyote.

It was Sunday, July 2, 1950. It was the second Sunday of a new war, and sabbath routine was forgotten at the Marine base at Camp Pendleton. Marines returning from furlough suspected the division was on an "alert" status when they checked through the main gate and were told that the camp was closed to visitors and liberty had been canceled.

The eight miles from the entrance to the division area seemed longer than usual as they hurried to the club for a quick beer and the latest scuttlebutt on the war in Korea. They saw trucks being loaded at the quartermaster's warehouses and they were certain. "When you get the supply gang working Sunday night it's gotta be serious." At the top of Rattlesnake Canyon they saw lights at division headquarters. Total confirmation came when they found the slop chute deserted and the bar closed. In the squad rooms one glance at the mélange of sea bags, combat packs and new equipment told them more than a written order. They were moving out.

The undertone of tension was as tangible as the build-up of a summer electrical storm in Kansas. To the young Marine there was a definite therapy just in seeing combat veterans going about the job of getting ready. The hash mark and battle star on a ribbon suddenly became a badge of experience to lean on, to follow.

The day the North Korean Army crossed the 38th parallel, a Marine general named Shepherd was motoring through Utah on his way west to take over his new command, Fleet Marine Force, Pacific (FMFPac). By the first available aircraft he flew from Salt Lake City to Pearl Harbor, where he conferred with Admiral Radford, Commander in Chief of the Pacific Fleet. On the second day of July he was in Tokyo and in conference with General MacArthur.

At the conclusion of this meeting a dispatch was sent to the Joint Chiefs of Staff (JCS): ". . . Request immediate assignment Marine Regimental Combat Team and supporting Air Group for duty this command . . . MacArthur." Before final decision was made as to the employment of Marines in Korea MacArthur was to send five more dispatches to the JCS.

In Washington a Marine general named Erskine called on the commandant of the Marine Corps and requested that he be allowed to lead to war the division he had trained for two years. This request was denied because Erskine had already been assigned to a secret mission for the State Department. A general named Smith speeded westward from Washington to take command of the 1st Marine Division.

At Camp Pendleton three young lieutenants, Johnston, Muetzel and Lopez, had received orders transferring them from the division to school at Quantico. They went to their commanding officer and requested their orders be revoked and they be allowed to go to Korea. Their orders were changed.

In Pearl Harbor, Colonel Lewis "Chesty" Puller besieged Headquarters Marine Corps with telegraphic requests for an infantry regiment. After thirty years in the Corps, in which time he had never missed a fight and had picked up seven scars from wounds and four Navy Crosses, Puller felt he rated such an assignment.

In Minneapolis, Pfc. Charles Kaylor, Marine Reservist, helped his wife put their two children to bed. Later they sat on the porch and talked of this new war and how they could get along on a Pfc.'s pay if the Reserves were called. In Tulsa, Reserve Pfc. Albert Collins and his bride of a week, Joan, wondered how many days would be left to them.

The Korean war was a week old. While the 1st Marine Division had received no official orders for deployment the staff, nevertheless, had been working over mounting-out plans from the very inception of hostilities. One thing they did know: in every war since 1775 Marines had been called. Shortly after midnight the expected dispatch arrived:

From: Commanding General (Shepherd), FMFPac
Action: Commanding General, 1st Marine Division
This is a warning order. Prepare to embark . . .

As the decoding officer worked the gibberish into words of meaning, he paused. "As they always say in the movies, 'This is it!' "

When the dispatch was deciphered, it was hurried in to Brigadier General Edward A. Craig, who at that time was the senior officer at Camp Pendleton. Then the staff really settled down to work. Telephone calls were made to homes: "Don't wait up, I'll be here all night."

"What can you tell me?"

"Nothing—just some work to get out."

Once again Marine wives were swept with a hopeless, helpless feeling as they wondered how long "long" would be this time.

In the coffee mess, extra pots of "brew" were set going. The paper facts of war—personnel and equipment figures, ammunition, fuel, rations, transportation and resupply data—had to be compiled for coordination.

By daylight the first rough draft was ready. Time and space factors had been cut to the minimum. A Regimental Combat Team (RCT) could be formed and loaded out in four days and sail in six. The Marines had heard about "push button" warfare, but they had never been issued such an instrument, so they prepared to ship out in much the same fashion as they had for ten major wars and two hundred expeditions.

Normally an RCT would have been commanded by a colonel. When MacArthur requested Marine air to embark with the ground unit, Shepherd felt such a command was too great a responsibility for an officer of that rank. The 1st Provisional Marine Brigade (Reinforced) was activated and Brigadier General Craig was placed in command. Technically a brigade is made up of two regiments of infantry but the Marine organization would have but one rifle regiment with a battalion of artillery and a company of tanks and other supporting units attached.

To form the brigade, the 1st Marine Division had to divide its staff and transfer the 5th Marine Regiment and necessary supporting elements to the brigade; with the peacetime cuts imposed on the Corps, even these measures did not bring the new brigade to combat strength. From 105 posts and stations throughout the United States, Marines from the regular Corps were ordered to Camp Pendleton. They came by plane, train and bus.

Every hour, day and night, brought more Marines into Camp Pendleton. Many had been leading a soft life in recruiting stations and guard companies, and would curse the early days in Korea until they had fought themselves into the physical toughness of the Marine who had assaulted Horno Ridge all summer and been in on amphibious exercise Demon III.

Most of these men had been in Fleet Marine Force (FMF) units before, and while at their various posts and stations had participated in the weapons qualification firing and individual military training the Marine Corps requires of men not serving with field units. All these men required was a short "snapping in" period.

At company level they were fitted into platoons where there was a cadre of seasoned FMF personnel. The attitude toward these reinforcements was to the point: "Snap 'em in right, snap 'em in fast—they may be the guys who'll save your ass."

Ninety per cent of the officers of the new brigade had been in combat; sixty-five per cent of the senior NCO's had been in action against an enemy, but of the corporals and Pfc.'s, only ten per cent had ever been under enemy fire.

From Brigadier General Edward A. Craig, who was to command the brigade, to the regimental commander, Ray Murray, to the battalion and company commanders, few had not faced enemy fire; most had won decorations for bravery in combat. Upon these men was to fall the task of leading the Marine brigade into battle.

To equip the unit for combat the Corps called on their "bank." After World War II, the Marine Corps shipped all the equipment it could lay hands on to their desert supply depot at Barstow, California. Always equipment-hungry from budget "shorts," the Corps jammed this depot with all types of military equipment for reconditioning and moth-balling. To be exact, it must be admitted that much of this equipment was purloined from sister services in a hurry to depart the Pacific after V-J Day. (A coat of paint hid other service insignia.)

From this miser's lair at Barstow came the trucks, DUKW's, jeeps, trailers and amphibian tractors that were to go once more to war. There were more veterans of Iwo and Okinawa among the vehicles than there were among the men who would drive them.

With the assignment of new personnel there were numerous mounting-out details: issuance of weapons and clothing, immunization shots, insurance, wills and pay allotments, along with familiarization courses to be given on new weapons such as the 3.5 rocket launcher and the M-26 "Pershing" tank. Three days before sailing, two Pershings were taken to the range and each tank gunner got to fire two rounds from the 90 mm. guns. The next time the 90's were fired was at the enemy.

In orderly disorder, the brigade began to get its affairs in shape when the blow fell. Headquarters Marine Corps ruled that men who had less than six months to serve and were not going to re-enlist were to be left behind. This would cost all units key men. The cost was not so high as anticipated, however. More than sixty-five per cent of the Marines who could have stayed home volunteered to go along.

"Why not? We'd like to show these Reds what a Marine fights like."

When the brigade was ready to board ships in San Diego Harbor, Craig addressed them.

"Gentlemen, this brigade is going to Korea to fight. We are not the first, nor will we be the last Marines sent to war. In one hundred and seventy-five years Marines have been sent to fight in hundreds of small wars and ten big ones. You have read the papers and have seen the pictures from Korea. You know the kind of enemy we'll meet and what they have done to wounded left behind. As long as there is a Marine alive who can fire a rifle or throw a grenade, we will not leave a wounded or dead Marine on the field.

"It has been necessary for troops now fighting in Korea to pull back at times, but I am stating now that no unit of this brigade will retreat except on orders from an authority higher than the 1st Marine Brigade. You will never receive an order to retreat from me. All I ask is that you fight as Marines have always fought. If you do that I can ask no more."

A tall, slender man with prematurely gray hair now white, Craig had entered the Marine Corps by competitive examination in 1917. In his thirty-three years in the Corps he had built an enviable reputation by his quiet courage, energy and conscientious efforts to perfect himself at his profession. Battle experience had been gained at Bougainville, Guam and Iwo Jima.

A few miles to the north of Camp Pendleton, over the brown hills of the Santa Margarita Range, lies the Marine Corps Air Station, El Toro, headquarters and base of operations for the 1st Marine Air Wing (1st MAW). From here Marine aviation units worked out the problems of close air support with the ground Marines to the south. The 1st MAW would furnish the other half of the team MacArthur requested in his message to the JCS.

When Major General Field Harris received the order to prepare a supporting air group for immediate embarkation to Korea, the wing faced the same personnel and equipment problems as the division. To form a group for immediate employment, leaves were canceled, transfers rescinded and matériel deficiencies were corrected by stripping the wing to provide for the group.

The performance of Marine Aircraft Group (MAG) 33 in forming and loading out was done with a dispatch that matched the speed of the brigade. Alerted on the fifth of July, MAG 33 commenced joining personnel, gathering equipment and loading aboard the aircraft carrier *Badoeng Straits* and two transports. On the fourteenth of July, MAG-33 sailed for Korea.

There is nothing quite like the atmosphere of a Marine unit sailing to war. It is ribald, loud and raucous. Even the families on the dock, for the most part, hide their fears and grief and respond to the carnival spirit. The sailing from San Diego was no different from a hundred others.

The "plank owners" (any Marine not going) were subjected to a barrage of good-natured insults as they stood on the pier. Outsiders were resented and ignored for this was a family affair. The band played all the old marches, then a ruffle of drums quieted them and the commandant of the Corps, General Cates spoke. His talk was short; he had been on too many Marine sailings to be wordy:

"General MacArthur asked for a Marine air-ground team specifically. He probably remembers the 1st Marine Division at Cape Gloucester and the air cover the 1st Marine Air Wing gave his troops at Leyte. He wanted more of you, but you are all we can send—now.

"I didn't come here to wave the flag. . . . I came to say good-by. This is a new experience for me, standing on a dock instead of a deck. Heretofore I've always shipped out with you." Cates paused. "You boys clean this up in a couple of months, or I'll be over to see you."

The Marines grinned. The latest scuttlebutt said they were to make an amphibious landing in the rear of the enemy. Once they got to bashing up the North Koreans' back areas, the front would fold—any boot knew that. Three Tennessee Marines along the railing let out a rebel yell. They knew Cates was from the Volunteer State like themselves.

Cates knew the timber of the Marines at the rail because he knew men and war. He knew that courage is an inconstant trait in man. The degree of constancy obtained in battle is in direct proportion to the training, preparation and leadership troops receive. Marines believe battles are still fought by men. Mountains, rivers, valleys, weather and men are still mountains, rivers, valleys, weather and men despite improvements in weapons and equipment.

One of the imponderables of war is the human element. How will troops react under fire? What is beyond even inspired effort? When can a commander demand no more? These are the warm, human traits a man in command must know. The cold facts of war (transportation, time and space factors and ammunition requirements) are in the book and can be learned in classrooms. The intangibles must be learned in the smoke of battle where courage and terror stalk hand in hand, and the issue is solved by whichever one gains dominance.

The brigade leaders who had been ordered to form and embark in a matter of days knew their commandant was no stranger to their problems. Platoon leader George McNaughton, in the assault on Hill 88 west of Seoul in 1950, paralleled the action of Lieutenant Cates' attack on Bouresches in Belleau Woods thirty-two years earlier. Captain Barber, whose "Fox" Company clung for five days to an exposed Korean hill, had a blood brother in Company Commander Cates of Soissons, who sent a message to the rear:

> I am in an old abandoned French trench bordering on road leading out from your CP and 350 yards from an old mill. I have only two men left out of my company and 20 out of other companies. We need support but it is almost suicide to try to get it here as we are swept by machine gun fire and a constant artillery barrage is upon us. I have no one on my left and only a few on my right. I will hold.

Lieutenant Colonel Cates commanded a battalion defending the International Settlement in China thirteen years before the brigade battalion commanders, Newton, Roise and Taplett, awaited counterattacks near Chindong-ni. Eight years before Murray took his 5th Regiment into the uncertain Pusan perimeter battle, Cates had led his regiment onto another beachhead—Guadalcanal. Five years before Major General O. P. Smith's division assaulted Inchon, Major General Cates led a division onto the bloody beach at Iwo Jima.

Cates knew these men because he had learned the intangibles of war in the friction of battle. He knew that from the first day at boot camp demands had been made on these Marines that could be met only by great physical and moral outlay. The seed of pride had been planted and would flourish in battle and they would perform feats beyond the measures of physical and mental endurance.

Six months later, when these men came off the Chosin Reservoir with "Fourteen Shooting Days until Xmas" painted on their tanks, he was proud but not surprised.

Marines have a cynical approach to war. They believe in three things: liberty, payday and that when two Marines are together in a fight, one is being wasted. Being a minority group militarily, Marines are snobs. They are proud, sensitive and haughty to the point of boorishness with other military organizations. A Marine's concept of a perfect battle is to have other Marines on the right and left flanks, Marine aircraft overhead and Marine artillery and Naval gunfire backing them up.

When the dockside ceremony was over, the band struck up the *Marine Corps Hymn;* lines were slipped, and as the ships slid away there was a great, gusty roar that drowned out the band.

MacArthur's original plan was to have the Marine Brigade and Air Group land in Japan on arrival from the States. Based in the Kobe area, the Marine air-ground team was to have had several weeks for training and rehearsal prior to a projected amphibious landing.

Overnight the situation worsened. The Kum River line could not be held and Chinju was lost. The left flank of the United Nations forces was turned and Pusan was threatened.

Five of the seven UN divisions were nearing exhaustion and an air of panic was sweeping refugee-packed Pusan. The air was full of rumors. The last contradicted the previous, but all were alarming. The question was not "Can we hold?" but "Where will the next breakthrough occur?" Small boat owners in Pusan were asking and receiving exorbitant sums for space aboard their craft in the mass evacuation that was thought to be only a few days away. The most critical days of the Korean war were approaching.

The Pusan Perimeter. *One hundred twenty miles of mountains, plains and rivers to defend. The Marines were ordered to the west of Pusan to protect the southern flank. The enemy was met and defeated when a new threat developed to the north at Yongsan. Within this perimeter the Marine Brigade was to move over three hundred fifty miles in thirty days to meet the enemy at critical points.*

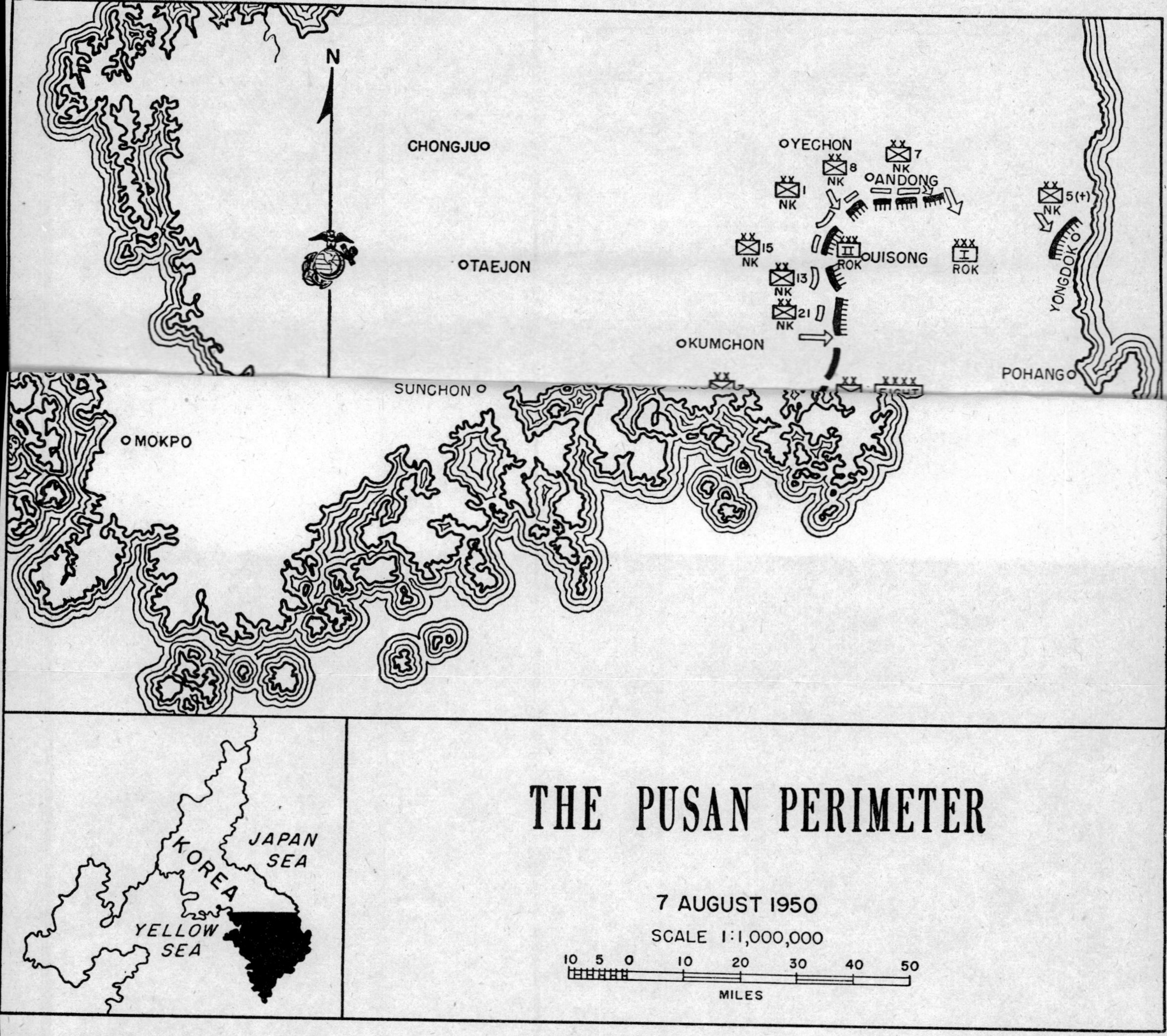

THE PUSAN PERIMETER

7 AUGUST 1950

SCALE 1:1,000,000

Reinforcements had to be rushed in if the defense of the Korean peninsula was to end in anything but disaster. MacArthur ordered the Marine convoy to proceed to Korea with all speed.

Waiting at quayside was General Craig, who had flown to Japan ahead of the convoy. Craig had had the benefit of conferences with MacArthur, as well as General Walker and the Eighth Army Staff in Korea. In addition, he and his staff had made aerial and jeep reconnaissance trips to the left flank where possible employment of the brigade was contemplated.

While he waited, Craig was presented with a bouquet of flowers by Pusan's mayor, Kin Chu Han. The mayor's speech was courtly, sincere and brief. "Thank you for bringing the Marines, General. The panic will leave my people now."

"There are more of us on the way, many more," Craig answered.

Also on the docks to greet the brigade was a South Korean Army band playing their version of the *Marine Corps Hymn*, Korean girls, spies and traitors, and the curious and hopeful. Also at dockside were Marines from the Korean Embassy Guard.

Sergeant Augustus Siefkin shouted to a friend at shiprail, "What'n hell took you so long? This is the end of the line for us."

The twenty-man Embassy guard detail had been in Seoul at the onset of the war. Charged with protecting Ambassador Muccio and staff, the unit was under the command of Master Sergeant John Runch. They had patrolled the chancery area through the early, dangerous days of confusion in the South Korean capital. With the enemy on the outskirts, they had destroyed secret files of the Embassy and escorted the civilian staff and dependents over the glutted roads southward.

The ambassador wrote of them, "I cannot overemphasize the contribution of the Marine guard detachment to the security of the Embassy. Each man is deserving of the highest commendation. . . ."

No group in Korea was happier over the arrival of the Marines than were these Marines.

As soon as the ships tied up, Carig went aboard the U.S.S. *George Clymer*. The regimental and battalion commanders gathered in the wardroom of the *Clymer*.

Craig knew only too well the task facing his small brigade. He had seen the confusion, indecision and demoralization always brought on by defeat and retreat. The training he had received in thirty-three years as a professional Marine gave him a sound, realistic picture of the situation.

On the central front the North Koreans had reached the Naktong River; on the east coast they had captured Yongdok; in the south they were dangerously near Masan, which was only thirty-five miles from Pusan. The Pusan perimeter was taking form. (See map number 1.) A penetration in depth at any point along the line would mean total defeat and a Dunkirk-like withdrawal.

One hundred twenty miles of line were being held by eight under-strength divisions—four American and four Republic of Korea (ROK). The American divisions had been hastily formed from occupation troops and more hastily committed to combat. These units were psychologically and physically unprepared for battle. Defeat and want of will and discipline on the part of many had made fearful ravages in the ranks. The missing in action, the criterion of morale, had reached appalling figures. The ROK's, trained and armed for constabulary service, were hopelessly outclassed.

The enemy order of battle had been identified. Eleven North Korean divisions were in the field. These units were well trained and well armed and many of the commanders and NCO's had gained battle experience while fighting with the Chinese Communist Forces. The North Korean commanders were confident they would be in Pusan by the fifteenth of August.

Craig was cognizant of these factors as he faced his commanders on the ship.

"The situation is serious, gentlemen," he told them. "With the forces available, it is obvious that the perimeter cannot be held in strength. Eighth Army has adopted the plan of holding thinly and counterattacking enemy penetrations to keep them off balance to prevent them from launching a co-ordinated effort.

"At the moment General Walker is undecided in what area we're to be used. We may go north of Taegu and operate on the left flank of the 1st Cavalry Division or we may go west to check an enemy advance along the Masan road. It all depends where the greatest threat develops."

Craig paused. "We are going into battle against a vicious, well-trained enemy in what will be an extended land campaign. Unfortunately, we will have to forget the plan of an amphibious landing. We will miss the vehicles we had to leave behind in San Diego. Much of our moving will be done on foot. We will leave all nonessential supplies and equipment in storage on the docks right here. We'll carry with us two days rations and two units of fire." (A unit of fire is the amount of ammunition a weapon will use in a day of battle.)

Craig studied the faces of his commanders. "The Pusan perimeter is like a weakened dike and we will be used to plug holes in it as they open. We're a brigade, a fire brigade. It will be costly fighting against a numerically superior enemy. Marines have never yet lost a battle; this brigade will not be the first to establish such a precedent. Unloading will begin at once."

At eleven o'clock that night Craig received orders from the Eighth Army to move the brigade immediately to Changwon and be prepared to halt an enemy advance on Pusan in case a breakthrough occurred west of Masan. At six o'clock the next morning the first elements of the brigade were on the move west; at four that afternoon the Marines were astride the Masan-Pusan road. On the seventh of August (the seventh anniversary of the Marine landing on Guadalcanal) elements of the brigade were heavily engaged.

CHAPTER II

The Marines, Air and Ground, Go into Action. August 3-9

While the brigade was preparing to unload in Pusan, Marine Air Group (MAG) 33 was at dockside in Kobe, Japan, where a reshuffling of equipment and personnel was taking place. Major Arnold Lund's Fighter Squadron VMF 323 was to operate off the carrier *Badoeng Straits* while Lieutenant Colonel Walter Lischied's VMF 214 would fly from the decks of the *U.S.S. Sicily*. Major Hunter Reinburg's Night Fighter Squadron (VMF [N] 513) would operate temporarily from Japan.

VMO-6, the observation squadron to be attached to the brigade, caused something of a stir among the Japanese by assembling four of the small OY (Grasshoppers) planes on the dock and taking off from one of the main streets of Kobe. Major Vincent Gottschalk, commanding the squadron, Captains William Parker and "Little Mac" McCaleb and Lieutenant Harold Davis were the pilots who flew the craft from the improvised air strip.

As Davis told the story later, "It was a kick to see thousands of Japs lining the streets to watch us. I thought my wing tips would knock off about ten thousand bugging Oriental eyes as I went down the street for the take-off. We all made it okay but Vince. He tore off a part of his wing on a telephone pole. He couldn't land on the street so he flew to Itami for a new wing. The planes we were flying were horrible junk and crossing Tsushima Straits to Chinhae was hairy, but we made it."

Four weeks later Davis' plane was hit by enemy fire in the Masan area. As he strove to bring it safely down he struck high tension wires. He died of injuries in hospital.

Master Sergeant Herb Valentine, flying a reconnaissance mission with

Lieutenant Melvin Green as an observer, was hit by enemy fire over the flats of Kosong. He made a crash landing in the ocean off the southern coast. Though badly shaken and bruised, both men swam to a near-by island. Later they were picked up by a South Korean Navy tug and taken to Masan. Two days later Valentine was back flying his "grasshopper" armed with "twin thirty-eights"—thirty-eight caliber pistols he and his observer carried.

The honor of drawing first blood from the enemy went to Marines in the air. Two days before the ground Marines went into action, a flight of Corsairs from the *Sicily* were to give the enemy a preview of what was to come from the gull-winged planes.

Major Kenneth Reusser got into the spirit of the occasion on the fifth of August. There being no close support targets at the time, he was assigned the mission of seeking targets of opportunity. Over Inchon he spotted some trucks around a factory building. Leading his flight low, they strafed the area, knocking out most of the vehicles and killing about thirty soldiers in the courtyard.

The flight met with such severe anti-aircraft fire that Reusser became suspicious that the building might house war equipment. Directing his flight to orbit the target at a safe altitude, Reusser went down to see what was inside the building. This he did by going down to fifty feet and flying so near the building he could see in the windows.

The enemy proved sensitive to these peeping Tom activities and opened up on him with everything they had. A second low sweep confirmed what he had seen on the first pass. The building was a vehicle and tank assembly plant. There were six tanks and eight trucks inside. By now Reusser's plane was so badly shot up he had to return to the *Sicily*.

His flight escorted him back to the carrier where he was barely able to land his crippled plane. The rest of the flight refueled and Reusser got into a replacement Corsair armed with napalm bombs and a combination of ATAR and HVAR rockets.

When they returned to the factory building the enemy was waiting. Anti-aircraft weapons opened up on them. Enemy soldiers fired burp guns, rifles and machine guns from the windows. While the rest of the flight machine-gunned and rocketed the area, Reusser in a long, shallow dive fronted the fire and slammed a napalm bomb through a window. The building exploded.

That job finished, the flight continued to Inchon Harbor where they set fire to an oil storage tank. With their rockets and napalm expended, they were about to return to the *Sicily* when Reusser spotted a camouflaged oil tanker. With nothing but 20 mm. ammunition left, he raked the tanker hull from bow to stern from an altitude of ten feet. The ship blew up and also blew Reusser's plane out of control and damaged it badly.

Fighting to keep his plane airborne, Reusser turned toward the haven on the *Sicily*. For the second time in less than three hours, he brought a badly damaged plane onto the flight deck.

Score for the day: six tanks, twelve trucks, thirty to fifty enemy dead, an oil storage tank and a tanker.

Led by Lieutenant Colonel George Newton's 1st Battalion, the brigade moved westward to an assembly area in Changwon. The movement was accomplished by truck and rail. All elements save a platoon of tanks and certain service units were in position by late afternoon. Time was saved and confusion prevented by the extensive use of Marine helicopters by unit liaison officers who used the craft to fly ahead to determine locations before the arrival of the troops.

The first night was not spent in the accepted Marine tradition. Personnel of the band and engineers began firing at imaginary sounds and shadows. Throughout most of the night there was a brawl of rifle fire with the riflemen firing for the comfort the sound afforded. The "trigger-happy" units received a growl from Craig in the morning and the performance was never repeated.

On the fifth of August, Craig was called to the 25th Division Headquarters for a conference with Generals Walker and Kean. A plan for an attack to the west was discussed. "Task Force Kean" was formed of the Marine Brigade and the 5th Army RCT. The 5th RCT was to pass through the 27th Infantry Regiment west of Chindong-ni. (See map number 2.) At the road juction the Army unit was to attack along the right-hand fork of the road toward Chinju. When the 5th RCT had cleared the road junction, the brigade was to initiate its attack along the left fork of the road toward Kosong and Sachon. If the attack was successful the enemy would be cleared from its threatening position on the southern flank of the perimeter.

The following day elements of the brigade began to move from Changwon to Chindong-ni. Until two battalions of the Marines had assembled, the early arrivals were to be under the control of Colonel John Michaelis, commanding officer of the 27th Infantry Regiment. Lieutenant Colonel

Robert Taplett's 3rd Battalion was the first Marine unit to displace forward. Taplett's unit relieved an Army battalion at three o'clock in the afternoon and took up defensive positions.

At 1:30 in the morning (seventh of August) Michaelis called Taplett on the telephone. He said: "Dog Company of the 5th RCT is on the high ground west of Sangyong-ni." He gave map co-ordinates. "They've been under a heavy attack for some time and may not be able to hold. This ground commands the road junction. We've got to hold it or the attack tomorrow can't move. I haven't anything to send to help them. You'll have to send a platoon. I've a guide in my CP [Command Post] who'll take them to the area."

Taplett relayed the information to First Lieutenant Robert Bohn, who commanded George Company. Bohn selected Second Lieutenant John Cahill of his first platoon to contact Michaelis. Cahill reported to the Army commander where he was briefed on the position of the unit he was to reinforce. He picked up his guide and departed.

Rejoining his platoon, Cahill gathered his NCO's about him and briefed them quickly. When he was through he gave his final instructions, "Pass the word to go easy on the water. I don't know how long we'll be up there or when we'll get more."

It was 2:15 in the morning when Cahill led his platoon onto the road to the west. Augmented by a machine-gun squad, the unit moved out in squad column—two files of men burdened with the bare necessities of war, weapons, ammunition and water. A few still clung to ponchos and jackets. Five hundred yards out they were wet with the sweat of exertion and tension.

The moon, in the last quarter and two hours above the eastern horizon, gave off a gray half-light. All about them the night was filled with the sounds of war. Artillery supporting the 25th Army Division was banging away to their right rear. Overhead a flight of planes roared by, and ahead of them they could hear the lighter spatter of small-arms fire that could be the Army unit they were to reinforce or from the 5th Army RCT. It was too indefinite to pinpoint.

The guide spoke to Cahill, "We'll leave the road here, Lieutenant, and work our way across the rice paddies." He pointed to the dark hill mass, gloomy and foreboding in the distance. "That's where we wanta go."

The platoon left the road and began working its way across the dikes intersecting the paddy. It was slow, difficult walking as men slipped and stumbled from the narrow pathways. At the far side of the paddy they came into a corridor of approach to the higher ground. Cahill's judgment of pace told him they had moved about three thousand yards from their initial point.

In bitter, drudging silence the platoon began the stiff climb to higher ground. Upon reaching a clump of trees at the crest and seeing the fall-away of ground on the far side, the guide cursed in dismay and apologized for having taken the wrong road. Everyone was physically spent from the useless climb.

When the guide gave assurance he knew where they were, Cahill passed the order and countermarched the unit off the high ground and retraced his course onto the main road. At the next turning to the right they went into the same valley, but this time on the western flank, and moved along the ditch-bordered road past a village with a schoolhouse in the compound. The high ground loomed over their left shoulders. At this point the guide suggested they wait until daylight because it was impossible to make the climb in the dark. Cahill put his men in defensive positions and said to the radio operator, "Get Lieutenant Bohn on the net. Tell him we're holding up here until daylight."

After repeated efforts they had to give up. Contact with the company could not be made.

The blast of a high explosive shell showered the area with steel splinters, dirt and rocks. The first was followed closely by a second. The only sound which followed was of men slithering to better places of protection.

"Anybody hit?" Cahill called.

"Okay here . . . okay . . . okay."

There was less than an hour of darkness left and the weary platoon stretched out on the hard ground seeking badly needed rest for the climb ahead. As the eastern horizon lightened Cahill spoke to his platoon guide, Sergeant Tom Blackmon and squad leader Sergeant Lee Buettner.

"We can't make this climb tactical. It's too steep—it's grab and hold and climb. Keep 'em closed up. You come with me, Buettner, we'll push right to the top and contact the Army. Let's move out."

Blackmon went along the line stirring the fatigue-drugged Marines. Slowly the unit formed in route column and began the march along the corridor to the sharp rise of ground to the west.

A burst of rifle fire from the left sent them slithering to the ground and into cover.

"Hey, Christ! Knock it off, we're Marines—"

Cahill raced to a point of high ground. "Marines," he bawled. "We're Marines!" The firing died away.

"Anybody hit?"

"Yes, back here."

Cahill ran back along the line to a cluster of men.

"Niemczyk and Wyman—"

Sergeant Jack Macy was bending over Niemczyk and with a knife was cutting off the wounded man's boot.

"Right in the heel."

"Wyman got it in the shoulder."

An Army medical orderly rushed across the open ground between the two units. "We didn't know you were in the area," he panted. "We've got an aid station about three hundred yards from here."

"Send some men back with them, Tom," Cahill told Blackmon. He spoke to the two wounded men. "That's one way of getting out of climbing a hill. See you guys later."

He turned to the head of the column. Macy assigned men to carry the wounded to the aid station. He saw the new rifle the Army corpsman had put on the ground while he worked over Wyman. He looked at his own weapon, a shabby veteran of too many Pacific campaigns. Quietly he made an exchange.

"Okay, let's shove off—"

The platoon began the straining climb up the steep razorbacked ridge. Despite the fact that the men had stripped themselves of everything but the bare essentials, the weight of weapons and extra ammunition came to seventy pounds a man. Men carrying ammunition boxes would swing them upward to the full reach of an arm and using the weight of it as an anchor clamber alongside the box. The climb became a grueling test of physical stamina.

Halfway up, the platoon came under heavy fire from enemy automatic weapons. Because of the sheer slope it was impossible to get into tactical formation and the fire was answered in any manner a man could bring a weapon to bear. Pfc. Bill Tome, held in position on a narrow ledge by Pfc. Melvin Brooks, opened up with his BAR. The enemy fire died away.

Blackmon was severely wounded and a detail of men were left with him to get him down the ridge to the Army aid station where Niemczyk and Wyman had been taken.

Cahill, with Buettner and the Army guide, pushing himself to the limit of his strength, continued to the top. It was eight o'clock when he made the edge of the crest—three hours of tortuous climbing had left him wet and gasping. The plateau was covered with a waist-high pampas grass and brush.

The Army CP was in a concave groove of ground which offered some protection. Cahill made his way to it. He spoke to the weary Army officer sitting in a hole, vainly trying to raise someone over a radio.

"My name's Cahill, George Company, 5th Marines."

"You relievin' me?" he asked.

Cahill shook his head. "Reinforcing you. I've only got a platoon but I'll place squads where you've got platoons."

"We were all right until this morning. I sent my mortars back last night and pulled my men into a tight perimeter for the night and now they can't get back into their day positions." He jerked his head toward an officer near him. "This is Lieutenant Angway."

Cahill nodded to the alert little Filipino.

"How're you fixed for ammo and water?" Cahill asked.

"Short of both."

"Have you requested an air drop?"

"Yes, supposed to be made about noon."

Thirty minutes after Cahill made the top, Sergeant Jack Macy (who was now the senior NCO) brought the platoon over the crest. He reported, "We took three more casualties coming up. Tom Blackmon got it bad. Robinson and seven men stayed to get Tom and the other two back to the aid station. We've got thirty-nine left."

Cahill briefed Macy on the situation and pointed out the defensive positions they were to cover.

"Some of these Army men are bushed. Start feeding Marines to their holes. Richmond, you and Buettner take the right side, Macy, you take the left."

Then Cahill got his radio operator to try contacting George Company CP again. After a time they got through to Bohn.

"We made the high ground," Cahill reported. "We're in contact with the Army and are in position on the plateau. We're under small arms and mortar fire. We took five casualties coming up, but we're okay."

As Macy worked his way through the brush he met an Army sergeant. A heavy growth of beard, lips swollen from heat blisters and lack of water told the story of what the man had been through.

"Christ! I'm glad to see you gyrenes." He made no attempt to hide the tears cutting pathways in his dirt-covered face.

Macy began the placement of the squad. Leaving the main body in the shelter of the low area about the CP, he crawled out with two men trailing and led them to the position they were to hold. Once there, he instructed them as to the positions to be occupied by the others, their field of fire and angles of supporting fire for adjacent positions.

It was tedious, risky work, but he wanted to know exactly where each point of defense was and that the men were aware of the other friendly positions.

At midpoint along the left side was the spot for a BAR. Creeping and crawling, Macy led Tome and Brooks to the location. This was the area facing the peak held by the enemy and would be the strong point of resistance to attack. Lying prone, the three men began to dig a deeper hole when a burst of machine-gun fire hit Tome. Macy grabbed the BAR and returned the fire.

"Help Tome," he told Brooks.

"It's no use, Macy. Tome's dead," Brooks cried.

The enemy fire died away. Macy put his hand on Brooks' shoulder. "They're zeroed in on this spot—I'll move you." As Macy spoke he saw little puffs jerking at the back of Brooks' dungaree jacket as bullets tore through him. Brooks settled across Tome's body.

Brooks died before Macy could get his jacket unbottoned to look at the wounds. From his position to the right Pfc. Lonzo Barnett rose and hurled a grenade as far as he could. The machine gun stopped abruptly.

Macy crawled over to Barnett with the BAR. "We'll hafta leave that hole open. Keep it covered."

Macy returned to the CP area where the last of his men were waiting. The machine gun had become inoperative because of the rough handling up the ridge line. Pfc. John Johnson, the machine-gunner, was working over the weapon when a sniper shot killed him instantly. The death of Johnson, coupled with the loss of Tome and Brooks in less than an hour after gaining the plateau, had a shock effect on the others.

Cahill made an inspection of positions, speaking words of encouragement he did not feel.

"Stand fast and we'll be okay. The colonel says the 2nd Battalion 5th Marines are coming up to help us out."

Throughout the morning the Army-Marine unit was subjected to heavy small-arms and mortar fire which caused three more casualties among the Marines and five to the Army. The Army company commander was wounded and had to be evacuated. Cahill called down artillery fire on the suspected mortar positions but was unsuccessful in silencing the weapons. Of greater concern, however, was the intense heat and the lack of water. The expected air drop did not arrive and, being unable to get information assuring that it would be made, Macy asked for volunteers to go to a Korean village at the base of the hill where a stream of water could be seen.

Pfc.'s David Wilson, Lonzo Barnett and George Paz, with Corporal Arnold Hutchinson indicated they would make the risky trip. Gathering together three canvas waterbags from the Army troops, the five plunged off the plateau and down the cliff toward the village. Almost immediately the group came under long-range fire.

"We're dead ducks if we hold up," Macy told the men. "Keep moving."

Going down as swiftly as possible and picking cover as they went, none was hit. The village had been under sporadic artillery fire throughout the morning and there was a certain amount of concern felt by Macy and his volunteers as they entered the deserted hamlet and plunged into the shallow stream.

Medical rules about the usage of halasone tablets were forgotten as the group drank from the stream. It took some time to fill the five-gallon canvas bags because they had nothing but canteen cups to use as dippers.

Waterlogged and with the added weight of fifteen gallons of water, the unit faced the rugged climb back to the crest with little relish. A half mile from the village Macy met Lieutenant Arthur Oakley, platoon leader from Captain John Finn's company.

"What's up, Lieutenant?" Macy asked.

"We're to relieve your outfit," Oakley answered.

"We'll show you the way," Macy volunteered eagerly.

"We're holding up here until the rest of the outfit closes up."

Macy and his group continued their grueling climb and once more entered the sporadic fire zone. They reached the summit in a state of

---

The Battle of the Crossroads. *The Marines attack to the south. Kosong is captured and Sachon is the next objective when the Brigade is ordered to rush to Yongsan. The Marines meet the enemy at the battle of "No Name Ridge" and the perimeter is saved. Two weeks later the Brigade is once again rushed to Yongsan to stem a second break-through.*

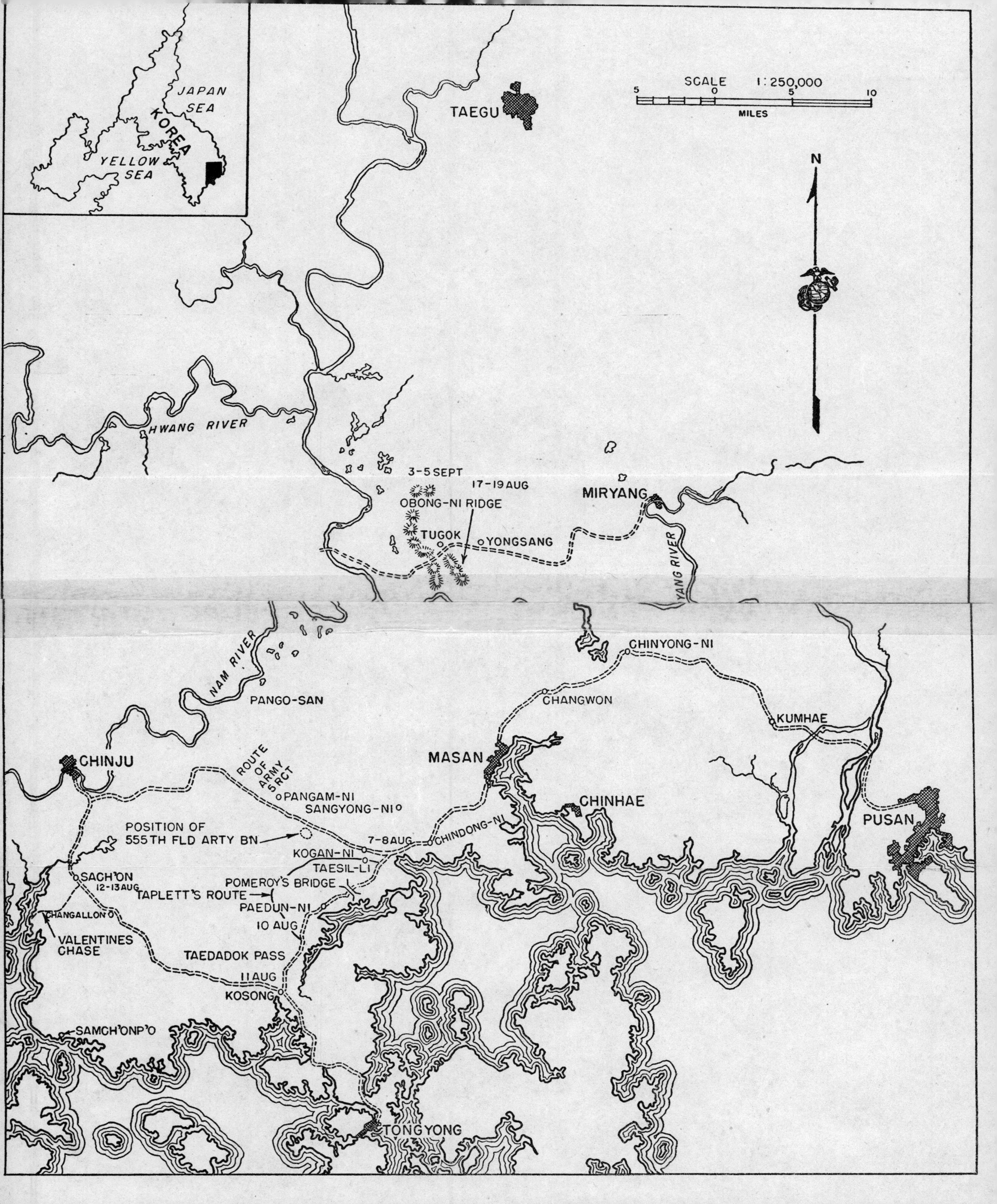
JAPAN SEA
KOREA
YELLOW SEA
SCALE 1:250,000
5 0 5 10
MILES
N
TAEGU
HWANG RIVER
3-5 SEPT
17-19 AUG
OBONG-NI RIDGE
TUGOK
YONGSANG
MIRYANG
YANG RIVER
NAM RIVER
PANGO-SAN
CHINYONG-NI
CHANGWON
KUMHAE
CHINJU
ROUTE OF ARMY 5 RCT
PANGAM-NI
SANGYONG-NI
MASAN
CHINHAE
PUSAN
POSITION OF 555TH FLD ARTY BN
7-8 AUG
CHINDONG-NI
KOGAN-NI
TAESIL-LI
SACH'ON
12-13 AUG
POMEROY'S BRIDGE
TAPLETT'S ROUTE
PAEDUN-NI
10 AUG
CHANGALLON
VALENTINES CHASE
TAEDADOK PASS
11 AUG
KOSONG
SAMCH'ONP'O
TONGYONG

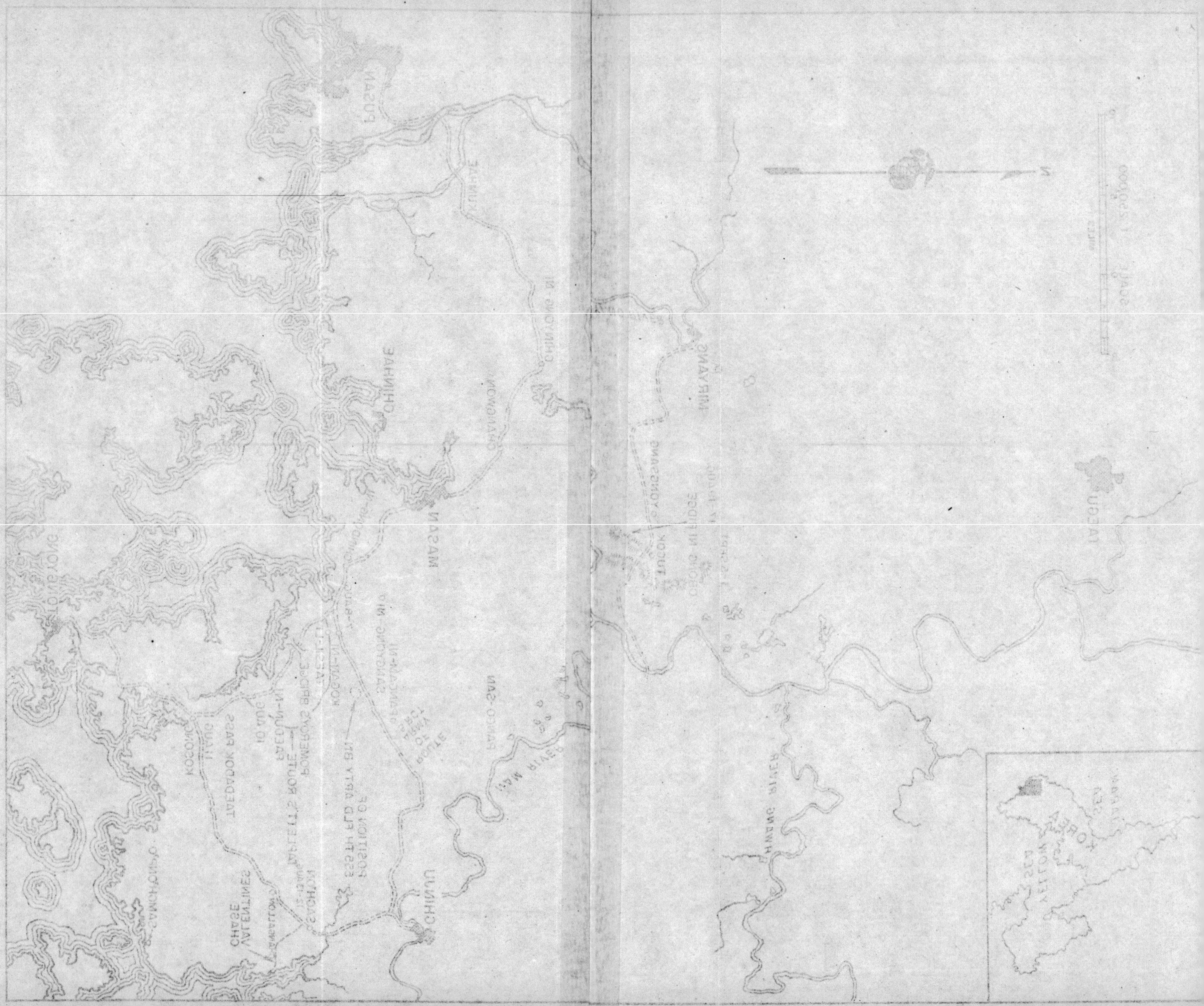

PUSAN
MASAN
CHINJU
TAEGU
MIRYANG
KOREA

exhaustion. The water they carried provided four ounces to each man. Macy told Cahill of seeing Oakley.

An hour after Macy returned from his water detail an Air Force cargo plane circled overhead. The Infantrymen and Marines joined in hoarse shouts of jubilation.

"Right here, buddy!"

"Easy does it. Right in my lap, Mac—don't make me move for it."

The ground troops watched the circling plane with fascination. They saw the bundles tumble from the open door. They saw the parachutes open—and drift away.

"They've missed us."

"Christ Almighty."

"It's goin' to hit the Gooks."

Of the eight bundles dropped, only one fell near enough to the beleaguered unit to be retrieved. Once again Macy led a group from the perimeter and dragged the packet back to the crest. Eagerly they ripped it open and for a moment were shocked into speechlessness.

"Citronella!"

"Whatta those guys think we're fightin'? Gooks or mosquitoes?"

Cahill got Bohn on the radio. "The air drop missed us. We need water and ammo. There's rations enough in the Army dump—water, ammo and medical supplies are what we need."

Bohn told him in return, "I'll get the OY's to make a free drop."

Back at Chinhae, fourteen air miles from Cahill's position, the message of the abortive air drop was received, and two pilots, Master Sergeant Lloyd Britt and Captain William Parker, readied their observation planes for a free drop. Water cans and ammunition were attached to the improvised bomb racks on each wing.

Shortly after three o'clock, Parker came in low over the area and was met by intense small arms fire. He spotted the marking panels set out by the platoon. At stalling speed and thirty feet altitude, he made his drop, hitting the panel. Close behind him came Britt in the second OY.

The water cans burst on landing, but enough was salvaged to give each man a drink.

Britt and Parker returned to the field at Chinhae. In less than an hour they were over Cahill again. The small planes rocked under increased enemy fire and Britt took a head-sized hole in the rudder section, but the plane stayed in the air. The second drop was on the target again.

Later in the afternoon Oakley reached the plateau and worked his way into the CP where he told Cahill that the orders had been changed and that Dog Company was going to dig in on the hill lower down and to the south for the night and the relief would not take place until the next morning. From their positions on the higher ground Cahill could see Finn's men digging in with the mortar platoon setting up on the third hill still further south.

Cahill, accompanied by Angway, who had proven himself a man of courage, and Macy slipped from the perimeter and down the hill to Finn's CP.

"We're going to need some help," Cahill told Finn. "There are less than sixty Army men left and I've had three killed and eight wounded. If we lose our position that'll put you in a bad spot."

"I know that, Blackie, but I've had orders to hold here until morning; we'll relieve you at daylight."

Keenly disappointed, Cahill started back up the hill. Macy joined him. "I talked with one of our corpsmen. Tom Blackmon died. . . ."

Upon regaining the perimeter, Cahill and Macy set about the task of getting the men into position for night defense. Men on the border line of heat exhaustion were placed with those who were withstanding the tension and battle fatigue.

The night passed quietly and there was a certain recovery from the relative coolness. In the early morning hours the men relieved their overpowering thirsts by licking the dew from their rifle barrels. Shortly before dawn the enemy could be heard moving into position for an attack. Every Marine came to the alert and those of the wounded who could move, crawled to positions on the perimeter. The enemy attempt to infiltrate was beaten off after a short, sharp fight and the enemy returned to their former plan of saturating the plateau with small arms and mortar fire. Pfc. Michael Yercich was killed and three Army men wounded.

Once again Cahill talked to Bohn, "We beat them off but we're still under heavy fire."

With this setback the enemy lost their last remaining chance to capture the commanding piece of ground overlooking the MSR (Main Supply Route) and road junction. Thirty-four hours after Cahill's platoon moved out to reinforce the Army company they were relieved by Finn's company. Gathering their dead and wounded they went down the hill to Chindong-ni. Of the forty-eight men who had started out on the night march six had been killed and twelve wounded.

C H A P T E R I I I

The "Advance" to the Southwest. Paedun-ni and Kosong Are Captured. August 9-13

The plan for the "Task Force Kean" counteroffensive went into effect on the seventh of August. The plan called for a thirty-minute air preparation and a ten-minute artillery bombardment to precede the attack. The Army movement forward began promptly at 6:30 in the morning, but soon came to a halt as the enemy made a flanking attack on the Army 5th RCT. Kean then ordered Craig to send a Marine battalion forward to relieve the 2nd Battalion of the Army 5th. By noon, elements of the Army 5th, Michaelis' and Lieutenant Colonel Harold Roise's 2nd Battalion of Marines were involved in the action. There was considerable confusion with the 27th attempting to retract, the Army 5th caught in a flanking attack and Roise's battalion moving forward in a heavily contested area.

General Craig was placed in command of all troops in the sector.

Roise's battalion had boarded trucks and moved from Changwon at two in the morning on the seventh of August, arriving at Chindong-ni three hours later. Shortly after arrival they came under heavy shelling. The enemy troops were using 120 mm. mortars and one man was killed and eleven wounded in Easy Company before counterbattery fire silenced the enemy. Captain George Kittredge, commanding the unit, was wounded and Lieutenant William Sweeney assumed command. At midday Roise received orders to move his unit westward and occupy the high ground in the area where Cahill was beleaguered and to relieve E and F Companies of the Army 5th RCT.

Upon receipt of the orders, Major Morgan McNeely, operations officer for Roise, picked up Captain John Finn commanding Dog Company and Lieutenant Michael Shinka in his jeep and went ahead to contact the Army guide who was to be waiting for them in the schoolhouse compound at Sangyong-ni. Without incident the party arrived at the village where they found an Army sergeant waiting for them.

Behind McNeely and his reconnaissance group came Dog and Easy Companies. Because of the shortage of trucks the two units moved into their zone of action on foot. Before the columns had moved a half mile their green combat utilities were black from sweat and dust.

"Watch that water—cut it down—there's no tellin' when you'll get more—" Water discipline, however, was not good and before the afternoon was over the units would be in desperate straits for lack of it.

At a steady two-and-a-half mile an hour pace the files moved along the dusty road. Four miles west of Chindong-ni they turned off the main road and headed north through a wide valley bordered on the right by rice paddies and potato and bean patches. Paralleling this secondary road on the left was a ditch of running water and beyond the ditch the early rise of ground that led to the heights they were to climb. In the daylight they could see what Cahill and his platoon plodded over and did not make the false turn as he had done in the dark.

With Oakley's platoon at the point, the column negotiated the road into the valley without incident and entered the schoolhouse compound. Second Lieutenant Wallace Reid, in trace, brought his unit into the village area. Emmelman's 3rd Platoon was still on the road when they came under long range machine-gun fire from a village across the valley. Emmelman's unit took cover in the water filled ditch alongside the road while Oakley set up machine guns in the compound to answer the enemy fire.

While this sporadic dueling continued, Emmelman's unit worked its way from the ditch and into the shelter of the village. Finn briefed his platoon leaders on the information received from the Army guide. Oakley's platoon began the steep climb to the objective, which was the plateau held by Cahill.

Oakley's point flushed a small group of enemy who were inclined to make a stand. A small fire fight broke out. The sound of it in the hills was like the handclapping of an eager audience. The column halted.

"Come on," Oakley shouted, "let's clean 'em out."

He led the rush upward and the enemy broke and ran to the north through the scrub pine. Now began the ordeal of scrambling and crawling up the steep hill under a burning sun. When the line stopped men leaned forward, feet spread and would have fallen but for the support of their weapons. Some vomited, others just gagged on the dry air and turned green over their own terrible retching. Pfc. George Mayo of Emmelman's platoon fell and broke his leg. Sergeant Douglas Bell made him comfortable alongside the trail. "There'll be some civilian litter bearers along, Mayo. They'll help you down."

"Okay."

Dog Company continued the climb. Men began to fade and fall out of line. It was during this phase that Macy and his water detail met Oakley.

Leading the way to the crest Oakley contacted Cahill. He reported to Finn that he was on the top and received orders to return to the next lower hill mass where the company was assembling. When Finn reached the round-top hill below the one occupied by Cahill, he reported to Roise and received orders to hold his present position for the night and effect the relief in the morning.

Sullivan placed his mortars on the third crest to the south while the rifle platoons began to dig in. Shinka, in command of the machine-gun platoon, got his guns into position and commenced a duel with enemy guns to the northwest.

Sergeant George Chapman of the 3rd Platoon discarded his carbine and picked up an M1 rifle that had been abandoned by previous troops in the area. With Sergeant Douglas Bell on the binoculars, Chapman adjusted his new weapon. With his rifle zeroed in, Chapman went on a sniper prowl and picked off two enemy despite the fading light.

Sweeney's company had moved out of Chindong-ni in trace of Finn. It was his mission to relieve the Army unit south of Finn's objective. Sweeney's approach was not so steep nor high, and the unit reached night defensive positions without opposition.

Civilian water carriers were able to reach Sweeney but VMO-6 had to be called upon to get water to Finn because of enemy fire and the rugged terrain between his unit and the road on the valley floor. The free drops from the "Grasshoppers" bounced water cans over the round-top. One hit Pfc. Lenerd Mateo on the shoulder, temporarily knocking him unconscious and breaking the stock of his BAR. As with Cahill, enough water was salvaged to relieve the more ravaging demands. As nightfall came on and the heat subsided, men who had dropped out began climbing the hill and rejoining their squads.

The night passed under sporadic long-rang fire: During the early morning hours the enemy attempted their infiltration attack on Cahill's positions. Immediately after this subsided, Emmelman led his platoon into the advance on the plateau.

Shortly before reaching the crest the Marines began to receive trajectory fire which became grazing fire as they came onto the top. Emmelman directed his men to take positions on the left rim of the plateau while Reid took his platoon to the right. As Oakley came to the top with his unit he moved down the center.

The enemy, aware of the reinforcement being made, redoubled their fire which was cutting off the tops of the pine scrub about thirty inches from the ground.

Sergeant Bell, squad leader in Emmelman's platoon, contacted an Army sergeant in the concave hole where the CP was set up. The sergeant volunteered to guide Bell and his men into their positions so that his own men could be relieved. The firing became heavier as Bell and the Army man crawled forward under the cover of the brush and they were constantly being showered by twig tops cut off by the overhead fire.

"Lend me a grenade," the Army man said to Bell. "Maybe we can discourage 'em."

Bell handed the man the explosive. As he rose to hurl it, machine-gun fire hit him full in the chest, killing him instantly. Bell continued forward with his squad at his heels. He got them into position and told them to dig in while he went forward to place an air panel. As he was spreading the marker, a grenade came in and knocked him down. A second one came closer and tore a hole in his side.

His men hauled him through the brush to the rim and turned him over to the evacuation personnel. Midway down the hill Bell and his bearers came on Mayo still in the brush by the side of the trail.

"Haven't they got you down the hill yet?" Bell asked.

"There're other guys hurt worse'n me." Then Mayo added, "It's a good thing I stayed here. A couple a Gooks were slipping in behind us to pick off our wounded coming down. They didn't see me. I got both of them."

The heavy, accurate enemy fire was taking its toll. On the right, Reid was moving ahead of his men to seek out covered positions. As he ran over a bare knob of ground he was hit by machine-gun fire and killed. The platoon held up as the word was passed to the rear to the second in command, Technical Sergeant Sydney Dickerson. Finn came forward with Dickerson to where they could see Reid's body in an exposed position.

"He may be alive," Finn told Dickerson and began to move across the knob. He was hit twice before he reached Reid and it was with some difficulty that he was retrieved for evacuation. Dickerson assumed command of the platoon.

On the opposite side of the plateau Emmelman received a paralyzing head wound and his men dragged him off the hilltop in a parachute. Chapman was killed in the same area where Bell had been hit; Staff Sergeant William Pascoe was wounded and Pfc. Charley Heckman was killed as a dysenteric stomach forced him from his foxhole.

These casualties were received before the unit had been on the plateau an hour.

Upon the evacuation of Finn, Technical Sergeant Reeves went forward from the company CP to check on the air panel placed by Bell. An air strike would have to be called in if the position was to be held. As Reeves passed Oakley's position in the center, Oakley shouted to him, "Stay low, Gunny, they're cutting this brush like a hayfield. I'm going forward to see if I can spot these Gook gun positions."

"Okay."

At the moment Oakley was the only company officer on the plateau. Shinka was below at the schoolhouse compound to act as a guide for reinforcing troops that were supposed to come into the zone before noon; Sullivan had remained below with his mortars and Hanifin, executive officer to Finn, having been overcome by the heat on the previous day, was bringing others similarly affected to the plateau. The only other officer on the top was Second Lieutenant Karl Wirth, forward observer for the artillery.

Reeves could sense the tension building up in the Marines with the sudden loss of officers. Exposing himself fearlessly, he raged at the riflemen for their slowness in getting into position. His remarkable display of courage and anger dispelled the feeling of panic that was spreading.

Determining that the air panel was in the proper position, Reeves began to work his way through the brush to the CP area to get Wirth to co-ordinate the air strike with Lieutenant Manning Jeter, the forward air controller, who was back at Battalion. As he passed the position where he had talked with Oakley a few minutes before, Reeves was told that the platoon leader had been killed as he went forward endeavoring to search out the enemy positions. Staff Sergeant Thomas Crowson was in command of the platoon.

Reeves returned to the CP and informed Wirth that the panels were in position. Wirth relayed the information to Jeter. Immediately Jeter got in touch with the orbiting Corsairs overhead.

"Hello, Playboy, hello, Playboy—this is Rosebush. Do you see the markers? Over."

"Rosebush, this is Playboy," Lieutenant Colonel Norman Anderson answered from his control Corsair overhead. "We see plain and clear. Over and out."

Anderson led his Corsairs onto the target in a rocketing, strafing, napalming attack. So close did they sweep in front of the hard-pressed ground Marines that empty shell casings from their machine guns fell onto the men below. After a thorough working over of the area from the air, enemy fire died away and positions were consolidated.

It should be remembered that the Marine battalions, due to personnel shortages, had but two rifle companies, instead of three. This limited the tactical capabilities of the battalions, but more important it did not allow for two companies in line with one in reserve and caused a physical drain that was constant and deadening to the assault units.

At 0600 on the morning of the eighth of August, Newton's 1st Battalion moved out afoot from Chindong-ni along the road toward the Kosong-Chinju junction. (Roise was on the high ground to the north.) Newton was to follow in trace of elements of the Army 5th RCT to the junction where the Army unit would take the right fork. Newton's 1st would swing out on the southern spur and proceed to the high ground to the immediate front and relieve the 1st Battalion of the Army 5th so that this unit might rejoin its parent organization.

On Newton's arrival at the junction he found that an enemy roadblock had not been overcome by the Army 5th. Murray ordered Newton to pull his battalion back and put them into defensive positions; to by-pass the roadblock and continue to the south was impossible because a rice paddy had to be crossed and the flanking high ground was not secure.

Orders were received from Murray to cross the paddy an hour before midnight. The Army 1st Battalion was instructed to provide guides to lead the Marines to their positions in the hills beyond the rice paddy.

It was a dark, moonless night as the battalion formed and waited. There was considerable firing and activity to the right front (in the direction of the roadblock) but little or no action from the left. There was some consolation in this because this was the direction of the move.

Civilian Koreans told Newton the enemy had the rice paddy covered by snipers and automatic weapons. To add to the threat, it would be impossible to move across in tactical formation. The crossing had to be made in a column, utilizing the dikes as pathways, and the tension mounted when the guides did not appear.

To complicate the situation further, the Army unit withdrew without waiting in position until relieved. There was a display of temper between Newton and the officer commanding the Army battalion over his withdrawal. Newton made a quick decision—cross the paddy at once to get into the vacated positions before the enemy could occupy them. Civilian Koreans volunteered to act as guides.

The word was passed, "Keep close interval and make it quiet—move out."

Like underwater swimmers going for a distance beyond their endurance, the Marines moved out. The only sound came from the rattle of equipment and the shuffle of feet on the narrow dikes. The crossing was a build-up of explosive tension. The rawest boot knew the risk involved. The phrase "sweating it out" was coined for occasions such as this. A pintle pin on a machine gun, swinging to the rhythm of the gunner, beat out a tinkling little tune.

"Stop that God damn bell ringing—"

In an anticlimax, which happens all too seldom in war, the battalion crossed the paddy without drawing fire. It took until four o'clock in the morning, however, before they had searched out the vacated positions and were set up. Thirty minutes later they received orders to attack and seize the high ground to the immediate front.

By this time the 1st had been on the move, afoot, twenty-two hours. Water discipline was not good and canteens were nearly empty. To a man who is working to the limit of his physical capabilities under tension and in great heat, the feel of a nearly empty canteen swinging on his hip is tantalizing torture. The knowledge that a resupply may be hours away only increases the mental turmoil and desire for water.

Shortly after first light, Newton ordered his companies to move along the ridge line to higher ground. After three hours of slipping, crawling, searching, they reached the crest of the dominating terrain. Though little enemy resistance had been encountered the twenty-seven hours of continued exertion and lack of water had the two units completely spent. The bare ridges afforded little protection from the deadly sun, and by noon most of the canteens were empty.

Captain John Tobin, commanding Baker Company, received orders to move onto the high ridgeline to his left. The ridge to be seized was on the flank of the road to Paedun-ni and Roise's battalion would be moving south on this route once the attack got underway.

Tobin got his unit onto the ridge, but it took three hours and left his men completely exhausted. Marines who could stand staggered to defensive positions; others crawled on hands and knees to places of semi-shade and collapsed. Two men in a critical state of overexertion and heat prostration, became temporarily deranged.

Tobin got Newton on the radio, "We're on the ridge, Colonel. No contact with the enemy, but we're in bad shape. We need water and a helicopter to take out two bad cases."

"I'll get a helicopter and water to you as soon as possible," Newton answered.

Captain Bob Longstaff brought his helicopter onto the ridge line in a touch-and-go flight and evacuated the two prostrated Marines. For the first time in the history of war helicopters were evacuating casualties from front line positions.

Captain John Stevens, commanding Able Company, had an easier zone. His line of approach to his second objective took him across a canyon down which flowed a stream of fresh, cool water. The unit was able to refresh themselves and refill canteens.

Roise was scheduled to be relieved so that his unit could lead the Marine advance southward. The relief was to be effected by a battalion of the 24th Infantry. The commanding officer of this unit reported to Craig on the morning of the ninth that he was being held up by a roadblock and was being ambushed on the Chindong-ni–Masan road.

Upon receipt of this information Craig ordered that the high ground to the north of Chindong-ni be seized; Murray assigned the task to Taplett's 3rd.

Captain Joe Fegan began the attack shortly after nine in the morning with the mission of seizing a high ridge commanding the Chindong-ni–Masan road. With Post's unit in brigade reserve Fegan had but two platoons in the attack. William's 1st Platoon led the assault, and slow progress was made against heavy enemy fire. Corporals Ralph McNamara and Lloyd Green fought to the top with seven men; they were driven off by a volley of grenades. McNamara was wounded. Fegan called in an artillery preparation. Staff Sergeant James Davis went forward and placed air panels in position for an air strike. The first napalm attack of the Korean war by Marine Corsairs took a heavy toll. The assault continued with Di Lorenzo's platoon passing through Williams.

It was a slow, grueling advance with the bare terrain affording little or no cover. The original objective was taken and a second assigned some eight hundred yards north-northeast of the road. Once again Di Lorenzo's platoon moved out and met with ever increasing resistance. The leading squad came under heavy automatic weapons fire and was taking casualties when Corporal Melvin James assumed command of the unit. Shouting orders and words of encouragement and disregarding the enemy fire, he got his men into better positions and built up a return fire with BAR's. With a base of fire established, he continued to expose himself by moving into the enemy fire to get six wounded Marines to safety. With James active on the right flank Technical Sergeant Ray Morgan and Corporal Donald Terrio teamed their efforts on the left to destroy a machine gun. Terrio grenaded another gun, putting it out of action.

The attack continued with Staff Sergeant John Wheatley leading the assault. With ever increasing air and artillery support, Fegan got his unit onto the final objective late in the afternoon. Marine Corsairs and artillery took heavy toll of the withdrawing enemy. By 6:30 in the evening Fegan's company had moved over fourteen hundred yards in the face of a determined enemy. This against the most difficult terrain in a manner which was to earn them the title of "The Ridge Runners." For nine hours the assault units had been put to a severe physical test. Fourteen were rendered temporarily noneffective due to heat exhaustion and many others were suffering from overexertion and lack of water.

As the unit was digging in for the night defense of the key ridge line, an unfortunate accident occurred. Staff Sergeant James Davis was repairing a defective grenade when it slipped from his hands. The pin flew out as it fell on the ground near other Marines.

"Grenade!" he shouted and threw his body over the explosive. The blast killed him instantly.

While Fegan was attacking to the north and east, elements of the Army 24th Infantry were fighting to the south. Late in the afternoon the enemy opposition had been largely cleared away and the Army 5th RCT reported their battalions were reaching the crossroads without opposition. When Craig informed General Kean that the enemy opposition had been overcome, the Marine commander was relieved of responsibilities as sector commander and was ordered to make a night advance on Paedun-ni.

The first forty-eight hours of battle in the Korean war had cost the Marines 33 killed and 141 wounded.

With Newton's battalion on the high ground above the south fork of the road and Taplett's battalion patrolling and securing the area at the junction, Roise was ordered to take his battalion along the south fork and to capture and defend Paedun-ni. Upon consolidating, he was to send a motorized element into Kosong.

Roise's battalion remained in position on the high ground until relieved by the 2nd Battalion, 24th Infantry, just before dark on the evening of the ninth. In the operation of succor and relief Roise's battalion had suffered nine killed, and forty-four wounded. There had been ninety-four cases of heat prostration, all of whom returned to duty after a rest. Captain Andy Zimmer came forward from the regimental staff to take command of Dog Company; Staff Sergeant Crowson retained command of Oakley's 1st Platoon, with Second Lieutenant Mike Shinka taking over Emmelman's 3rd. The 2nd Platoon was to be commanded by Second Lieutenant Ralph Sullivan.

Attached to Roise in support was Hofstetter's Baker battery of artillery, First Lieutenant William Pomeroy with a platoon of Pershing tanks and Second Lieutenant Raymond Fields with his 75 mm. Recoilless Rifle Platoon.

Zimmer (Vice* Finn) and Sweeney brought their weary riflemen off the plateau above Sangyong-ni and into the valley. Once again they took the road bordered by the ditch and retraced their earlier route to the assembly area for the night march on Paedun-ni. Despite sixty-nine hours of marching, climbing and fighting, morale was high and the word went around, "Let's beat the Doggies to Chinju."

The plan for the advance was to have a fire team covered by a reconnaissance platoon in jeeps lead off. A mile behind this point would come elements of Sweeney's Easy Company riding on three tanks. The riflemen welcomed the lift.

"It's dirty, rough and noisy, but it beats pounding that road."

"Hey, Mac, get the number of this tank—13."

"Thirteen's my lucky number."

"Well, it ain't mine!"

* "Vice" means "replacing."

Because the night move was to be made under strict blackout conditions over narrow roads, it was necessary for one of the tank crew to precede the vehicle on foot as a guide and by the use of a shielded flashlight assist the driver.

Good progress was made until just before daybreak when the lead tank—thirteen—came to a small bridge. It was a single slab of concrete fourteen inches thick and not much longer than a tank. After inspecting it, Pomeroy decided the bridge would hold the forty-two-ton vehicle. Ordering the "passenger" riflemen to walk across, tank thirteen started over the bridge. The bridge collapsed and the tank crashed through, forming an inextractible wedge between the abutments.

Pomeroy broke his hand as the tank hatch slammed down on it, and a crewman, who was acting as guide, was shot in the foot when the coaxial machine gun was set off by the shock of the fall.

Hastening to get his remaining tanks across in support of the point, Pomeroy clambered aboard tank eleven and ordered it to cross the dry stream bed. Midway across eleven threw a track. Further passage at this point was completely blocked and the following artillery and vehicles of the brigade train had to halt. Sweeney put riflemen on the high ground commanding the bridge for protection of the stalled vehicles.

The engineers, well to the rear of the column, found it nearly impossible to get their dozers and heavy equipment past the other vehicles on the narrow, winding road. The first estimate was a twenty-four-hour delay before a by-pass could be built that would take heavy equipment. Craig and Murray converged on the scene. Civilian labor was commandeered and a fill was made that would take jeeps and light vehicles. With the jeeps across the cut, the rifle units continued the advance.

The riflemen, on foot again, departed the scene with some reluctance: "Christ! The first ride we've had in Korea and it has to fall through a —— bridge."

Embarrassed at the failure of the bridge, the tankmen called to their passengers, "If you see a Good Humor man up there, send him back. From the looks of the old man's face, we can use him."

In four hours a by-pass was constructed which would carry the brigade heavy equipment. Pomeroy got into another tank and with two in trace, took out after Zimmer and Sweeney. Hofstetter got his artillery battery rolling as the two rifle companies were probing through Paedun-ni.

Roise had his battalion in Paedun-ni by eight o'clock. Reconnaissance of the town showed there was no enemy. A platoon of Sweeney's company entrucked and proceeded toward Kosong. Limited by the lack of trucks, the remainder of the battalion continued on foot.

Three miles south of Paedun-ni the point came under enemy fire. The advance party and support deployed to join in the fire fight. From overhead the Corsairs came down and erased strong points from the high ground. Enemy resistance was subdued in forty minutes and the advance element entrucked again for the dash to Kosong.

At Taedabok Pass, nine road miles from Kosong, the enemy had prepared an ambush by placing three hundred troops supported by mortars, antitank guns and artillery on the commanding ground surrounding two cuts of road through the rise of high ground. By the expert use of camouflage, the enemy was in position to deliver maximum destruction to Roise's battalion as they passed through the narrow defile.

Overhead, flying reconnaissance for the point, was Sergeant "Pat" Britt in a battered Grasshopper. Despite the excellent use the enemy made of terrain and camouflage, Britt discovered the trap by flying at less than fifty feet altitude. He warned the battalion and the advance party began to close on the point. Hofstetter's battery of artillery occupied positions to support the attack. At three in the afternoon the battle of Taedabok Pass was joined.

Zimmer (minus Shinka's platoon which had been assigned the rear guard) and Sweeney committed their rifle platoons to the attack of the high ground commanding the road cut. With an excellent employment of ground, air and artillery, heavy damage was inflicted on the enemy. Clearing the pass, however, was slow.

When the brigade moved out for the attack on Paedun-ni and Kosong, Taplett's 3rd had been left behind in the Chindong-ni area to consolidate and secure the high ground north of the village. With that mission completed and the area turned over to the 24th Army Regiment, Taplett was ordered to move into position behind Roise.

Guided by Captain Kenneth Houghton's Reconnaissance Company, Taplett took his battalion over an alternate route which left the main road south of the much-fought-over road junction, and weaving through the hills turned south beyond Taesil-li. By taking this route Taplett was able to by-pass the tank-crushed bridge and the regimental train. Three hours after departure in trucks from Chindong-ni, Taplett had closed on Roise. (See map facing page 20.)

Murray was waiting for Taplett as the commander of the 3rd came down the narrow, gutted road from the hills. Briefing Taplett on the situation, Murray ordered, "Pass through Roise at five-fifteen and continue the attack to Kosong—"

At the designated time, Bohn took George Company through the forward elements of Zimmer's unit. From the hundreds of enemy dead, abandoned and destroyed vehicles, antitank and machine guns it was apparent the enemy had lost the major portion of a battalion in the engagement.

Major Morgan McNeely, executive officer for Roise's 2nd, went forward with a jeep reconnaissance group to oversee the final passage of lines as the 3rd passed through the 2nd. Rounding a bend in the road, the jeep came under enemy machine-gun fire and McNeely was severely wounded. First Lieutenant Jack Westerman of Bohn's unit was injured removing McNeely from the area of fire.

Despite heavy losses, the enemy had not given up its rear guard delaying action and further fighting developed. It was growing dark when McNeely was returned to the 3rd Battalion CP area. The unit surgeon, Navy Lieutenant (jg) Robert Harvey,* in the process of setting up his aid station, was without a blackout tent. An emergency operating room was established in Taplett's command tent. McNeely was evacuated to the Army base hospital at Masan the next morning, but died of his wounds five days later.

After the passage of lines, Bohn's George Company continued the advance and an hour later the unit came under heavy fire from machine guns and mortars. Flank guards prevented forward movement to destroy the guns, and it was too late in the afternoon for air support. Murray issued orders that if the guns were not destroyed and forward movement resumed, Bohn and Fegan were to seize the high ground to the right and left of the road and establish defenses for the night. Shortly after ten o'clock, the enemy positions were overrun. Bohn was preparing for a night approach march on Kosong when he received orders to hold up for the night.

When relieved by Taplett, Roise's unit had been on the move and in action eighty-eight hours. Under the most difficult conditions of terrain and heat, the battalion had moved a distance of nearly fifty miles and, with the assistance of Marine air and artillery, had inflicted over six

* Doctors and hospital corpsmen with Marine units are Navy personnel.

hundred casualties upon the enemy and had captured or destroyed many weapons, trucks and vehicles.

As Roise's battalion set up defensive positions, the exhausted Marines of the 2nd lay in their holes in the red dirt. For the first time since leaving Changwon they had all the water they could drink and field rations could be eaten with some degree of relaxation.

Excessive perspiration had kept their socks and leggings in a constant state of sogginess and the feet and ankles of many men were becoming ulcerated with sores the size of fifty-cent pieces. As fresh socks were distributed by battalion supply personnel the riflemen of Dog and Easy Companies accepted the clothing with eagerness.

"Thanks, Mac. I don't know whether it's sweat or pus, but my socks are wet."

During the night the enemy re-formed and moved machine guns and mortars into position to block the Marine advance in the morning. At first light Bohn and Fegan patrolled the immediate area to insure there had been no night infiltration. An hour later George Company moved out and the point came in contact with the enemy. After a short fire fight the outpost was overrun. Four men were wounded, including Bohn, who remained in action. Displaying an energy that was to earn Bohn's company the nickname of "Gorgeous George," the point moved forward rapidly.

With Corporal Giaquinto of Counselman's 3rd Platoon (Counselman had replaced Westerman) at the point, the advance party and supporting group fell in trace and the move south was on. Behind Bohn were the long lines of men and vehicles of the brigade train. If this column was to move with any degree of speed, halts and deployment of the main body must be held to the minimum. The responsibility rested with the point and flank patrols protecting the point.

The point is the determining factor on how fast the column will move. If it is aggressive and has alert flankers, the long train in the rear will move without undue halts. If it is timid and holds up on suspicion of contact with the enemy, it will be the cause of confusion that always comes with stopping and starting a long military train. The point must go forward until taken under fire.

Thus, in the approach march, the speed of the entire regiment depends on the energy of a young officer and even younger NCO's.

Giaquinto struck off boldly, and with the flanking patrols searching the borders left and right, a two and one-half mile an hour pace was set.

With the rest of his platoon, Counselman followed to the rear of Giaquinto a few hundred yards. Because of the stiff pace the flanking patrols, who had to search and snoop as they went, had to run most of the time to keep abreast of the advance party. Counselman constantly put fresh men on the flanks by jeep, and these men, knowing they would be relieved shortly, gave their utmost. The point kept to its steady, mile-eating pace. Light resistance was offered by enemy outposts as the advance continued and three hours after the jump-off, Bohn had moved nearly nine miles and was in the outskirts of Kosong.

It was during this part of the advance that the Marine air-ground team demonstrated the team work envisaged in their training together. The forward air controller, Lieutenant Daniel Greene of the 3rd Battalion, placed himself in his radio jeep with Counselman's advance party. Overhead Greene had two Corsairs flying a "squirrel cage" advance directly over Giaquinto on the point. Two more close support aircraft were instantly available to assist the first two, if necessary. Advising Greene and searching out ambush spots was Valentine in a Grasshopper plane, flying at brush-skirting altitude.

The approach march from Taedabok Pass to Kosong was made with the efficiency and dispatch that regimental commanders hope for but seldom obtain.

Murray ordered Taplett to seize Red Hill twenty-five hundred yards southwest of the city. While Bohn moved against the new objective, Fegan took his company into the town to insure no enemy strong points remained. Bohn left the road and entered the rice paddies toward Red Hill. As he neared his objective his company came under fire from the right rear flank. Corporal Donald Sowl, leader of the 1st Squad in Duncan's platoon, turned his men to this surprise attack. A bullet broke his right arm. Sowl continued in action and his squad brought the enemy position under fire and quickly neutralized it.

With this obstruction cleared, George Company continued the attack on Red Hill. Light to moderate fire was received from its crest. Bohn called for air support. While the Corsairs napalmed and strafed the high ground, Lieutenant Granville Sweet turned his platoon of tanks on the target. The enemy began a hurried withdrawal and the capture of the hill was effected without further resistance. There was some sniper fire as Fegan's men began to move through the town. One diehard North

Korean was firing an antitank rocket discharger down the street. The house in which he was hiding was burned and the Marines moved on.

Shortly before noon Kosong was secure and Fegan took his company into the lead for the march on Sachon. The rapid advance of the Marines on Kosong caught the enemy in an unprepared state. There were ample signs now that the withdrawal was becoming a rout. The enemy, attempting to retreat to the more defensible area around Sachon, fought a skillful rear guard action until these elements were largely destroyed and Marine air caught a vehicle train of the 83rd Mechanized Brigade hurriedly departing Kosong.

A "turkey shoot" for the Corsairs followed. Twenty-three sorties were flown from the *Badoeng Straits* while the *Sicily* put aloft twenty-seven. With rockets, napalm and 20 mm. the Corsairs turned the withdrawal of the enemy into a confused debacle. The road was littered with dead and wounded, and destroyed and abandoned vehicles as a second regiment of the 83rd was decimated.

On the ground the footsore Marines seized those vehicles still operative (trucks, motorcycles with sidecars, and jeeps) and used them to speed their advance.

Master Sergeant Herb Valentine, who had already made one crash landing in the ocean, was searching and snooping with his OY for targets and concentrations of troops to report. As the Corsairs wrought havoc with the main column, Valentine spotted a jeep racing at high speed toward Sachon. Beside the driver crouched a man with a rifle. In the back seat was an officer sitting ramrod erect with arms folded. As Valentine brought his Grasshopper down to fifty feet over the speeding vehicle, the driver and rifleman cast nervous glances at the plane, but the man in the rear never so much as diverted his rigid front-face position.

"What do ya think?" Valentine asked his observer, Lieutenant Pat Sivert.

"Must be the Gook general."

Sivert reported the fleeing jeep, but there were more important targets along the road and a Corsair could not be spared for a single vehicle.

"Let's get him with our twin thirty-eights," Valentine suggested. Sivert agreed. Both men drew their thirty-eight caliber pistols (the only armament aboard the plane) and opened the side windows. Valentine brought the plane down to brush-skimming height. Flying with one hand he began shooting with the other while Sivert leaned far out for better aim.

The driver of the jeep got even greater speed from the vehicle and nearly hurtled into a ditch as he jerked his eyes from the road to look at the plane. The rifleman alongside the driver began to answer the fire of Sivert and Valentine, while the passenger in the rear gave no indication he was on anything but a Sunday drive.

Valentine pulled up to miss a hill and both men reloaded their pistols. Because of the speed of the jeep and a head wind, Valentine had to throttle back on the plane only slightly to keep directly overhead. On the far side of the hill the running fight was resumed.

Over a distance of twenty miles neither side was able to score an effective hit. Sivert and Valentine had used up most of their ammunition. They wanted to save a clip apiece in the event of an emergency landing behind enemy lines.

As they were about to give up the chase the jeep made a skidding left turn at a road junction and headed toward the ocean. Valentine brought his plane down on a final run and the driver looked up once too often. The jeep hurtled over a steep cliff. As the jeep turned over and over in the air, the officer in the rear seat was still in his rigid, folded-arm position.

While Valentine was playing tag with the North Korean general, the gull-winged Corsairs continued to shoot up the line of advance for the ground Marines. Lieutenant Doyle Cole, flying wing on a strike, was hit by anti-aircraft fire. He coaxed his plane into a long, shallow glide and landed in the ocean a short distance offshore.

General Craig, flying a helicopter reconnaissance mission ahead of the advance, saw the plane crash-land in the water. Piloted by Gus Lueddeke, they went over the water and hovered above Cole, who had gotten out of the plane and was floating in a raft.

With Lueddeke holding his craft a few feet off the water, General Craig lowered a line and pulled the dripping pilot into the glass house of the helicopter. Grinning and happy at his quick rescue, Cole slapped the general on the shoulder, "Thanks for the lift, buddy—" His grin faded as he saw the star on the dungaree jacket. "Thank you, sir!"

"Glad to be of service, Lieutenant."

From the same flight Captain Vivian Moses was shot down and made a crash landing behind enemy lines. Within a matter of minutes, Lueddeke had his helicopter over him, picked him up and returned him to the *Badoeng Straits*.

Score for the day to Marine Air: vehicles (all types) destroyed, 118; supply dumps destroyed, 2; ammunition dumps left burning, 2; buildings housing troops destroyed, 8; southeast section of Sachon set on fire; concentrations of troops south of Sachon, north of Kogan-ni and along route of withdrawal neutralized and dispersed with heavy casualties; one jeep, presumed to be carrying a Very Important Person, destroyed.

Along this corridor of destruction, Fegan pushed his company, overcoming a fanatic rear guard with orders to hold and die. At six o'clock in the evening, Fegan was ordered to halt and set up "all-round" defenses for the night.

The next morning Newton took his battalion through Taplett and resumed the advance on Sachon. During the night the enemy had withdrawn and the Marine advance was made against light and scattered opposition.

A North Korean major was captured. He told his interrogators: "Panic sweeps my men when they see the Marines with the yellow leggings coming at them."

During the short time in Kosong, Harvey, the 3rd Battalion surgeon, set up in the schoolyard. Casualties had been light, but there were heat prostration cases and a large number of men suffering from dysentery. Shortly after Fegan moved out, the word came back that an ambulance was wanted to pick up a wounded man.

Naval Corpsman William "Andy" Anderson volunteered. Despite two previous wounds (he refused evacuation) Anderson could still drive the jeep ambulance. With Sergeant Lamb riding "shotgun" on the hood, Anderson drove forward. Through the files of the supporting group and advance party the jeep moved. As they came to the point an antitank gun opened fire, hitting the ambulance. Lamb was thrown into the ditch wounded. Anderson was killed. Not long after this, Corpsman John Marquez went across a field of fire to get a wounded Marine. He was killed getting his man to a place of safety.

In the action on this day, August 11, two men were killed; both were Corpsmen from the Naval Medical Corps.

On the night of the eleventh of August the enemy, still supremely confident of capturing Pusan, began a series of counterstrokes which would halt the Marine advance, force the withdrawal of the Army 5th RCT and capture Yongsan and Miryang to the north. During the night, the 4th North Korean Division pushed a salient across the Naktong

River; a reinforced regiment advanced along the railline from Pango-San and swung across the MSR (Main Supply Route) of the 5th RCT in the region of Pangam-ni. Here they dispersed the personnel and surrounded the 155 mm. howitzers of the 555th Field Artillery Battalion.

In the early afternoon of the twelfth of August, the fourth day of the attack toward Sachon, General Craig received orders from the Army command to rush a reinforced battalion back to the Pangam-ni area where the 555th (Triple Nickle) Field Artillery had surrounded. With Newton and Roise in the van of the attack toward Sachon, Murray ordered Taplett to report to the commanding general of the 25th Army Division. Reinforcing the battalion for this detached action, were Captain Bill Nichols with his C Battery of 105's and a section of 75 mm. Recoilless guns and 4.2 mortars.

Stripping the brigade of all available trucks, the battalion climbed aboard for the dash to the rear.

"What's th' scoop, Mac?" the riflemen asked one another as the trucks took them over the same road they had fought to take the day before.

"Musta been a breakthrough."

"Must be something if we're getting a ride to th' party! Just when we had it soft an' fat in reserve. We might even of got some hot chow."

"What's that?"

Placing the battalion under the command of his executive officer, Major John Canney, Taplett accompanied Craig to the brigade CP in the Kosong area for further briefing. At Brigade the information on the situation was incomplete. A report from the commanding general of the 25th Army Division was to the effect that the enemy had cut behind the 5th Army RCT and their supporting artillery had been overrun. It was estimated an enemy force of twenty-five hundred to three thousand was astride the 5th's MSR and the situation was critical.

Taplett was directed "to report by helicopter to a liaison officer of the 25th Division at a bridge southwest of Chingdong-ni; the officer was to be in a jeep with a red air panel over the hood of the vehicle."

Lieutenant Colonel Joseph Stewart, operations officer for Craig, accompanied Taplett on the mission. With Lieutenant Bob Longstaff at the controls of the 'copter they took off; in a matter of minutes they found the rendezvous bridge but there was no sign of a jeep. After hovering and searching for a time they discovered a light tank camouflaged in the stream bed. Longstaff landed near by and Stewart and

Taplett contacted the tank commander, Lieutenant Torman, U.S. Army. It turned out to be a fortunate meeting, for Torman, an able officer, commanded the Armored Reconnaissance Company of the 25th Division. He knew the area but had seen no sign of the liaison officer and his sentries posted on the road had seen no such vehicle or officer.

Torman had no communications with the division but there were numerous wires in the ditch alongside the road. After cutting in on several they finally got one connected with the Army division at Masan. Stewart talked with the operations officer and when this staff member was informed the liaison officer was not in the area Stewart was given the vague mission "of attacking to the north."

Taplett asked Stewart to get a clarification of the order; to attack to the north from what point and to what line? It was obvious from further conversation that the division was somewhat confused and had depended on the missing liaison officer to have checked the situation and to issue the necessary orders. Finally Taplett received verbal orders to "look the situation over"; "do what he thought was proper"; "eliminate enemy activity in the area," and to "insure the security of the remaining battery of the 159th Field Artillery."

In addition, Stewart and Taplett were informed Brigadier General G. B. Barth, assistant commander of the 25th Division, would arrive in the area to take command. Upon his arrival Taplett would report to him for further orders.

Stewart and Taplett returned to the helicopter and made a detailed reconnaissance of the area preparatory to the arrival of the battalion. In the dry stream bed south of the road they came over the positions of the artillery unit. There were three six-gun batteries (eighteen 155 mm. howitzers) still in their gun pits with ammunition in orderly stacks and jeeps, trucks and prime movers in place.

"Looks like a kid's toy battlefield," Taplett said.

"Damned expensive one," Stewart answered. "There's a couple million dollars' worth of equipment down there."

In the meantime Canney had the battalion on the road, and using the alternate route to by-pass the tank-crushed bridge the 3rd was making excellent time in their retraction. Taplett and Stewart landed in their helicopter near the end of the column and informed Canney where the debarkation and assembly area would be. Once again the 'copter took off and the two asked Longstaff to set them down in the area of Taesil-li where A Battery of the 159th Field Artillery was located.

At this point, Colonel Daly, commanding officer of the 159th was contacted. He informed Stewart and Taplett that the 555th had been overrun and annihilated with very few survivors. The main enemy force he supposed had struck from the north and were now in the ridges and hills immediately northwest and southwest of his positions. From the information gathered from Daly and his reconnaissance of the area Taplett decided to attack and seize the high ground to the north of the road with the jump-off point being the village of Kogan-ni. Daly readily offered to furnish artillery support until Captain Bill Nichols coula get his battery of artillery into position.

Two hours and fifty minutes after entrucking, the leading elements of the 3rd were in the assembly area near Daly's CP. After a fifteen minute preparatory fire from the Army battery of 155 mm. howitzers, Fegan took his company into the attack. In the meantime Greene, Forward Air Controller, had been calling over the radio for Marine aircraft. The mission of the 3rd had been designed so hurriedly no aircraft were assigned to support the effort. Greene continued his efforts hoping to catch Marine planes returning from search and reconnaissance missions without having expended their armament.

In this regard it was a rule with Marine airmen that they would, when sent on search and attack missions for Eighth Army, always check in with Marine controllers on the ground if their primary mission had proven fruitless and they had ordnance aboard.

Greene contacted a division of Corsairs armed with napalm and rockets, and notified Fegan immediately. With Fegan selecting the targets, the Corsairs supplemented the work of Daly's artillery, and How Company was able to reach the ridge with a rush. On the top there were signs that a considerable force of enemy troops had hurriedly departed the area. At this point Taplett ordered Fegan to prepare night defenses and to move westward along the high ground in the morning.

The remainder of the battalion was disposed in a perimeter defense with the 159th Field Artillery, Nichols' C Battery, Bohn's George Company and the Headquarters and Service Company in a common defense perimeter. While establishing these positions, Daly reported enemy activity in the village across the stream bed; Greene called down strafing runs by two South Korean P-51 planes and the enemy dispersed. Later a Marine patrol found the village deserted.

When General Barth arrived in the area at seven o'clock, Fegan was on the high ground north of the road and the remainder of the battalion was tied in with Daly's artillery to the south of the road. Barth complimented Taplett on the dispatch with which the 3rd had withdrawn a distance of twenty-three miles and gotten onto the high ground; he gave his approval for the seizure of the rest of the ridge in the morning. Upon receiving the report of the abandoned equipment of the 555th he stated that an Army salvage unit would be sent forward to make the recovery and that the area would be restricted from artillery or aerial fire until such recovery could be made.

The next morning the Army Tank Officer, Lieutenant Torman, reported to Taplett that he had been ordered to support the 3rd Battalion. Taplett assigned him to the road from where he could cover Fegan's left flank. In the meantime the morning attack began after an artillery preparation from both the Army and Marine batteries as well as air support from the Corsairs.

Fegan seized the second ridge line which ran east-west while Bohn's unit took the ridge that branched off to the north. The objectives were taken after negligible resistance but there were continuing signs of a hurried withdrawal by the enemy. The high ground commanding the MSR and the area where the abandoned guns of the 555th lay was taken and consolidated by ten in the morning. At this time Fegan received orders to contact survivors of the artillery unit under a bridge southwest of the hill occupied by his company.

Taplett and Torman took a small recon party along the main road and rescued a group of wounded who had managed to slip from the area. Colonel Ray Murray and Major Larry Smith prepared to drop a message to the Army survivors under the bridge alerting them that Fegan was on the high ground to the east and north and was attacking in their direction. The message was put in a 60 mm. mortar canister and a yellow streamer tied to it.

In a helicopter piloted by Lueddeke, Murray and Smith took off. They circled over Fegan's positions and swung off to the south and east toward the bridge. Almost immediately the entire valley floor erupted with small arms fire, and tracer bullets began to streak past the plane. Lueddeke jerked the 'copter into a maneuver not prescribed by the manufacturer and assuring his passengers that "maximum speed had been attained" made it to safety.

It was obvious that the enemy, while not strongly opposing the Marines on the high ground, had designs on the eighteen large howitzers and related equipment in the valley floor.

With Torman's light tanks and Marine rocket teams protecting the left flank from the road, Fegan continued to advance to the west. At the extreme end of the ridgeline they were able to bring the bridge area under small arms fire and the cut-off artillerymen were able to escape to friendly lines. The enemy was making repeated attempts to move the heavy equipment out of the valley and Murray finally received permission from General Barth to destroy, by artillery and air, the vast amount of stores and ammunition as well as the guns.

CHAPTER IV

The Advance Ends in a Tragic Withdrawal. August 13

To the south the brigade, minus Taplett's battalion, continued the advance on Sachon. With elements of Captain Kenneth Houghton's Recon Company forming the point and Tobin's B Company in the advance party, the push west was made against little or no opposition. Along the roadside and low ground on the flanks were the testimonials of the havoc wrought by the Marine Corsairs the day before. Some fifty motorcycles with sidecars and over twenty Ford jeeps were passed. All vehicles were Russian built.

A few foot-weary Marines clambered eagerly into those vehicles still operative and continued the advance in a style to which they were unaccustomed.

"That's the only good thing I know about bein' in the lead, you get first grabs."

Newton's battalion had been assigned the mission of capturing Sachon and passing through the town to continue on and seize the high ground to the north and west. Attached to him for this effort were five Pershing tanks from First Lieutenant Robert Winter's platoon of Houghton's Recon Company, and a detachment of engineers.

Houghton's unit, traveling in jeeps, led from the point about a mile in advance of Tobin's company. With helicopters and observation planes patrolling the flanks, good time was made. Sixteen miles had been covered by one o'clock in the afternoon and Houghton and his men were entering a valley near the village of Changallon. Sachon was three and a half miles to the west. Seven miles beyond lay Chinju.

Though the heat was intense, there were several factors which made the fast move possible. The company water trailer roamed up and down the columns dispensing water, and a stream paralleled the road. When the ten minutes in every hour rest period came, the Marines would plunge into the water and get the momentary refresher of wetting down. Morale was high over the fast move and prospects of the early capture of Sachon.

Everyone in the brigade was imbued with the idea of taking Sachon before the Army 5th RCT captured Chinju. From the road junction west of Chindong-ni, where the Army unit and the brigade had separated, it was about twenty air miles to their respective objectives. Road mileage, however, because of the swing south to Kosong, forced the Marines to move thirty-four miles, while the Army 5th had to cover twenty-eight miles on a more direct route. On such small things is morale raised: the desire to be first. This made the rifleman forget blistered feet, the sun and six days without cooked rations. They were also gaining another asset: the constant fighting and marching was boiling off the fat. The brigade was fast becoming a lean, hard outfit with fewer and fewer succumbing to the heat.

During the night the enemy had withdrawn hurriedly, leaving their dead and much equipment. At Changallon Valley they received orders to make a stand on the high ground commanding the route of approach of the brigade. Reinforcements were sent forward from Sachon. With energy typical of Asiatic troops, they worked the long night through at preparing and camouflaging their positions. The selection of terrain for the ambush was automatic for a trained military commander.

The road the brigade was following ran west from Kosong to Osan-ni. At this point it began to angle northwest toward Sachon. The road entered the valley of Changallon with hills of six hundred feet in height on either side and rice paddies of four to five hundred yards in width between the road and high ground. Directly behind the village of Changallon was another rise of ground which formed a **U**-shaped pocket, with the open end of the **U** the point of entry for the Marines.

By first light the enemy were so well concealed that the low-flying Grasshoppers and helicopters could not snoop them out. The plan of the enemy was to wait until the point, advance guard and supporting troops were well within their interlocking bands of fire before opening up.

Houghton, with his reconnaissance personnel at the point, was suspicious of the pocket because of the obvious terrain advantages afforded an alert enemy. Despite the lack of sightings reported by the "squirrel-caging" planes overhead, Houghton entered the valley with misgivings.

If the enemy was to make a stand before Sachon, this was the place. Beyond Changallon the next defensible ground was northwest of the objective city.

A massacre was prevented only by great good luck and the alertness of Houghton's unit.

As the point was crossing a small bridge on the outskirts of Changallon, they saw two enemy soldiers running for cover toward the village. Of an estimated five hundred enemy in position, two had wandered from their places of concealment. When the point took these men under fire, the North Koreans could still have effected their ambush by remaining silent. Instead, they opened up with a premature fire and the bloody battle of Changallon Valley was on.

Almost as soon as the point deployed and returned the fire, it became apparent to Houghton he could not handle the situation. By now he was under fire from the front, left and right flanks and right rear.

Houghton got Tobin on the radio. "We're taking more than we can handle up here."

"I'll send up Schryver's platoon and two tanks."

As soon as the enemy opened fire, the men of Baker Company deployed to the right and left of the road into the ditches and rice paddies which contained about two feet of water. In the hurried seeking of positions in the water and mud, all but two of the radios on the company net went out. Platoon leaders were forced to rely on runners.

As First Lieutenant Hugh Schryver took his platoon forward, Second Lieutenant "Scotty" Taylor brought his unit up with three tanks to take over Schryver's positions. Because of the ditches and rice paddies, the tanks were restricted to the road and were unable to deploy. The wounded began to come back tired, distressed and unfavorable, as wounded always are, over the outcome.

"They got a —— division up there—an' we ain't even got to 'em yet."

By using the radio on a tank, Tobin got a message back to Newton requesting an air strike on the high ground to the right flank. Tobin sent his runner, Pfc. Milford Pritchard, back to Second Lieutenant David Cowling of the 3rd Platoon with orders to move through the rice paddy and be prepared to assault the high ground on the right as soon as the air strike lifted.

Setting up his CP and aid station, Tobin sent an ambulance and stretcherbearers forward to Houghton. Because there were only two Naval corpsmen to a company, the stretcherbearers were formed from

Marine cooks, bakers and bandsmen. They moved forward with a dispatch and courage that gained them the praise of every man in the line.

It was the practice of the artillery to displace by echelon during these fast moves and Jordan's battery in support of Newton's 1st came into action quickly. The 4.2 mortar crews had some delay in finding a solid base in the rice paddies from which to fire. It was not long, however, before the riflemen on the line had the support of all arms.

Winter's tanks rolled forward taking the enemy on both flanks under fire at 750 yards. They also hit into a group of the enemy attempting to move from the village to the high ground on the right. Maximum casualties were inflicted. The tanks continued forward and contacted Houghton's hard-pressed point. From this position the Pershings were taking all-around fire. Because of the flooded ditches, they were denied maneuverability and were forced to remain in column on the narrow road. During the period of the fire fight, over four hours, the M-26's delivered flank and frontal fires. Twenty houses in Changallon were destroyed by tank 90 mm. guns. While the leading tanks rendered support to the point, Sergeant Albert Keller, acting as battalion intelligence scout, made his way forward under heavy fire and rendered first aid to the wounded and organized the evacuation of wounded by using the tanks at the rear of the column.

With two runners, Tobin started forward to contact Houghton. Less than a hundred yards up the road a machine gun took them under fire and the three scrambled to a place of safety behind a paddy dike. Tobin noticed one of his men jerking and shaking as if suffering from palsy.

"What's the matter?" he asked.

"I'm scared, Cap'n—"

Tobin scowled at the youngster. "Don't you know, lad, Marines are never scared—"

The enemy machine-gunner who had chased them into the paddy got the range and began cutting away the top of the protective dike toward where they lay. Tobin finished his lecture by adding, "I see what you mean. Let's get the hell outa here!"

The three made a dash for it to the far side of the road and worked their way slowly forward.

While Cowling moved his platoon into position for the attack on the high ground to the right front, Newton came forward and ordered Stevens to send two rifle squads and a machine-gun section from Able

Company to take positions on the right flank. From this position they were to lend supporting fire to Cowling. Another rifle squad from Stevens' company was sent to reconnoiter the high ground on the left flank.

By this time all supporting weapons were in position and ready to fire. When the artillery and mortars had worked Cowling's objective over, the Corsairs were called down and napalmed and strafed the ridge line. Machine-gun fire from this area was silenced.

Cowling's platoon reached the high ground without too much opposition, but as soon as the crest was reached, the enemy, concealed on the reverse slope, counterattacked. Outnumbered three to one, Cowling was forced from the crest and halfway down the slope before he could stem the vicious attack. In the fight, Cowling had been shot through the left foot, two men had been killed and six others wounded. Out of radio contact with the company because of the wetting-down the SCR 536's got coming through the paddy, Cowling called Sergeant Branson to him.

"Contact Captain Tobin. Tell him to get artillery and air on the objective again and we'll counterattack and regain the top. Tell him we have two dead and seven wounded."

Branson made his way down the slope and across the fire-swept rice paddy and delivered the message to Tobin. Upon being informed of the situation, Newton ordered Cowling to fall back on elements of Stevens' company. After a twenty-minute artillery and mortar barrage, followed by an air strike, Stevens was to pass through Cowling's platoon and seize and hold the objective. By late afternoon Stevens had accomplished his mission and enemy fire from that flank ceased. Cowling and the other wounded and dead of his platoon were evacuated as the unit rejoined Tobin.

With his right flank secure, Newton ordered Tobin to take the high ground to the left and set up defensive positions for the night. Artillery, mortars and air were again to be employed to soften the enemy before the assault.

At 5:30 in the afternoon, Taylor had his 2nd Platoon on the high ground. As the unit moved over the hill to the forward slope they saw the enemy retreating down a ravine. Quickly Taylor turned to Sergeant "Ski" Lischeski. "If you move, Ski, you can get down there and cut 'em off."

Lischeski set off with his squad and, moving rapidly down another ravine, had his men in position as the retreating enemy unit came from their corridor. The ambush worked perfectly and the enemy platoon numbering thirty-eight men was killed and the officer leading them wounded. The officer was turned over to the South Korean police (a number were attached to each company) to return to the battalion CP for interrogation. The man was dead on arrival and the Marines learned how bitter the feeling was between the Koreans. In the future they would conduct their own prisoners to the rear.

It was ten o'clock at night before Tobin had his company defenses set up and communications with the platoons arranged. Because of radio failures and lack of wire, Tobin had to improvise. There was only enough wire to tie in with the 1st and 3rd Platoons by telephone. Contact with the 2nd would have to be maintained by radio. A single line of wire was laid back to the battalion. In uneasy restlessness the men of Baker Company waited out the night.

This ended the first phase of the battle of Changallon Valley. The alertness of Houghton's point and premature fire from the enemy had saved the battalion untold casualties.

As the forward units tied in their lines for the night, Tobin's company held the high ground on the left while Stevens was in a similar position on the right flank. Houghton's point had been withdrawn to the battalion area and the thousand-yard paddy area between the two companies was registered in by artillery and mortars to deny passage to the enemy during the night.

Marine airmen, on the prowl throughout the day and constantly available for air strikes, were a prime factor in keeping casualties to a minimum once the battle was joined and assaults of the high ground were being made. From their offshore bases, Marine air had mounted over sixty missions of destruction in support of Eighth Army units as well as the brigade. Captain Vivian Moses, who had been shot down the day before, rescued and returned to the *Badoeng Straits* by helicopter, was shot down again and crash-landed in a rice paddy. Moses was thrown clear of his plane and landed face down in the water. Knocked unconscious by the fall, he drowned before Captain Gene Pope could reach him with a rescue 'copter.

In four days the brigade had covered twenty-nine miles by road measurement. This can be multiplied fourfold when the climbing-falling distance over the hills is computed. It was about this time that the Marines came to the decision that there were only two directions in

Korea—straight up or straight down. And two kinds of weather—hot and hotter.

Newton's battalion had taken over the advance at first light on the morning of the twelfth of August. During the next sixteen hours the battalion moved forward sixteen miles, engaged in a bitter four-hour fire fight, and occupied the high ground on both flanks of Changallon. Water had been adequate during the march, but once the high ground was occupied resupply was impossible because of darkness, the proximity of the enemy and lack of personnel. Rations consisted of the packets a few men had clung to during the advance.

Well aware of the condition of Newton's battalion, Murray ordered Roise to pass through the 1st in the morning and continue the advance on Sachon. In the meantime, Craig had received orders from General Kean to withdraw with all speed to Chindong-ni "in order to hold a defensive position and mop up enemy resistance in the zone of action of the 25th Division." So urgent was the retraction of Marines required that Craig was authorized to destroy any equipment which would hamper the speed of the Marines returning to the critical zone.

Upon receipt of the order, Craig detached Roise's 2nd from the 5th Marines to become the brigade covering force during the withdrawal. Newton was ordered to withdraw his unit from the high ground before daylight and to head the return march. Unit commanders were informed they could destroy any equipment which would hamper the speed of withdrawal because of the limited number of trucks available. No equipment which would be of aid to the enemy was to be left behind.

The decision was a difficult one to make. Finally it was decided that galley ranges, C rations and PX supplies were the least vital to future operations. When the troops saw the last remaining chance to get a hot meal being destroyed, they accepted with ironic philosophy.

"What the hell! Why lug the crap around when we won't have time to use it. This is a Purple Heart and K ration war anyway."

At midnight Major Merlin Olson, executive officer to Newton, got Tobin on the telephone.

"We've received orders from regiment to be on the move at six-thirty. Have your outfit on the road and ready to board trucks at that time."

"What's the scoop?"

"We don't have the details, but it's hot. We're going back. Have your outfit ready to move down at 0400. You'll precede Able Company. Two-five will cover the withdrawal."

"Okay."

Tobin put up the phone and looked at his executive officer, Captain Ike Fenton. "We're pulling out at 0630. We'll start moving off here at four."

"What's up?"

Tobin relayed the information he had received from Olson.

Fenton shook his head in dismay. "Twenty-nine bloody, sweating miles down the drain. What a war this has turned out to be!"

At four o'clock in the morning, as the platoons were preparing for the withdrawal, Taylor reported movement on his front and asked for illumination. When Tobin tried to get through to the other two platoons to warn them, he was unable to contact Staff Sergeant Cirinelli, who had taken command of the 3rd Platoon after the evacuation of Cowling. The wire was also dead back to the battalion CP.

Within minutes of Taylor's report two green and one red flare broke over their positions and an enemy counterattack was launched with savage fury. The initial attack was against Taylor's platoon and illuminating mortars revealed the enemy moving into the ravine between Taylor and Schryver. Both platoons and the 60 mm. mortars opened fire to prevent this penetration.

An even larger force hit Cirinelli on the left flank and rolled over two machine guns at that extreme left point. The enemy immediately employed the captured weapons against the rest of the platoon. In confused, deadly night fighting, Cirinelli was forced back about a hundred yards.

Tobin told Pfc. Milford Pritchard, "Tell Cirinelli to hold what he has and I'll put all the supporting fire I can on his flank." Pritchard was killed before he got to Cirinelli; Sergeant Malcolm Budd was killed as he went forward to get Pritchard's body.

As Lieutenant Bob Kiernan, the artillery forward observer, was calling down the artillery fire, a machine-gun burst knocked out his artillery radio. Improvising hurriedly, Kiernan got Stevens of Able Company on the company radio. "We can't get through to the Fire Direction Center. Will you relay our requests—"

With the unit across the rice paddies acting as a relay, the artillery and 81 mm. mortars opened up. In a brilliant display of pinpoint marksmanship they blanketed the left flank. Yet the enemy came on. From the fire being taken by the company, it appeared that the attacking force was all armed with automatic weapons.

When Schryver reported that the force on his front was increasing and he doubted his ability to keep them from getting between his platoon and 2nd, Tobin ordered the company to pull back into Taylor's area to reorganize for a counterattack. Schryver's 1st did the rear guard while Cirinelli and company headquarters pulled out.

Once again the artillery and heavy mortars put on an outstanding display of marksmanship as they walked their fire down the slope to cover Schryver as he pulled out to join the rest of the company.

Before daylight Tobin had his unit consolidated and was preparing to counterattack. In the early half-light, the enemy positions with the two captured machine guns were spotted. Both weapons and crews were destroyed by 2.36 rocket fire. As dawn approached, the fire power of the Marines began to drive the enemy back.

"Okay, Bob," Tobin said to Kiernan. "Get the artillery and mortars to lay onto our front and walk them back toward the point—that's where we're going."

By this time the telephone wire with the battalion had been repaired. Newton got Tobin on the phone. "What's your situation?" he asked.

"We're just getting ready to jump off."

"Hold it. Get your wounded down the hill and bring the rest of the company to the road at once. We'll cover your withdrawal with artillery and mortar fire."

"But Colonel, we've got eight Marines out there. We can get to them in less than an hour. Give me an hour, just one hour—"

"I'm sorry, but I can't. We've got orders to withdraw immediately."

Tobin turned wearily to Fenton. With an effort he controlled his voice. "We've got orders to withdraw at once, Ike. Take what's left of the 3rd Platoon, gather the wounded and dead and get down to the road. I'll cover you with the 1st and 3rd."

"We can drive these bastards back and get those kids on the point in an hour," Fenton protested.

"You heard me ask the colonel—"

"Good God! John, we can't—" Fenton turned away to hide his tears. "Telling Cirinelli and his outfit to pull out and leave those Marines out there is going to be one hell of a job," he said softly.

With the wounded helping the wounded and the able carrying the dead, Tobin brought his bitter men off Hill 202. A final flare of enemy fire hit the first squad of Schryver's platoon on the withdrawal. Master Sergeant Young dashed up the hill from the CP area and taking command of the squad directed the further withdrawal while attending the wounded.

Cursing as only men can curse who are emotionally taut and physically exhausted, Baker Company entrucked and started back. The dust rose thick and red around the trucks and moved with them, each in its own perimeter of dust. The men riding sat in morose, jolting silence, the only sound among them being the spewing and hacking of men who had breathed the dust to the base of their lungs.

They sat on the iron-striped floor holding their weapons among the boxes of ammunition, grenades, water cans and K rations. A feeling of guilt prevented their eyes from meeting. Eight Marines had been left on that hill. God burn the son of a bitch who gave the order!

Though the reason for their hurried withdrawal was explained to them, the riflemen on Hill 202 will never forget that they were forced to leave eight of their number to the violations of a vicious enemy.

In the action of Changallon Valley, Newton's 1st Battalion suffered fifteen killed, thirty-three wounded and eight missing in action.

CHAPTER V

The Perimeter Is Saved. The First Day of Battle for "No Name Ridge." August 17

At 1:30 in the morning on the fourteenth of August, Craig received orders to move the brigade with all possible speed to Miryang. This meant the Marines were moving from the south end of the perimeter to the center. Twenty-six hours and seventy-five miles later the Marines were in the designated city. A British military observer watched the battle-worn rifle companies of the 1st Brigade pass through Miryang on their way west to block the enemy penetration over the Naktong River.

This officer reported to his command in Tokyo:

> The situation is critical and Miryang may be lost. The enemy have driven a division-sized salient across the Naktong. More will cross the river tonight. If Miryang is lost Taegu becomes untenable and we will be faced with a withdrawal from Korea. I am heartened that the Marine Brigade will move against the Naktong salient tomorrow. They are faced with impossible odds, and I have no valid reason to substantiate it, but I have the feeling they will halt the enemy.
>
> I realize my expression of hope is unsound, but these Marines have the swagger, confidence and hardness that must have been in Stonewall Jackson's Army of the Shenandoah. They remind me of the Coldstreams at Dunkerque. Upon this thin line of reasoning, I cling to the hope of victory.

The brigade came out of Changallon physically tough and psychologically hard. The broiling sun, steep hills and long marches had taken from them the shipboard softness of eighteen days at sea. Gone was any idea that the war in Korea was a police action where a few thousand North Koreans would be rounded up and herded back over the 38th parallel. They knew the enemy to be a vicious, skillfully led and well-equipped foe that could inflict heavy casualties in any action. They were prepared to meet with heavy losses and to carry on the attack, and were openly scornful of units unable to face these hard facts of war.

During the advance on Sachon, the brigade had been under the operational control of the commanding general of the 25th Army Division. While the brigade was assembling in the area of Chindong-ni, Taplett's battalion was still in the process of clearing out the enemy roadblock in the rear of the Army 5th RCT and rescuing personnel and equipment of the Triple Nickle artillery battalion. Upon the completion of this assignment, control of Taplett's unit reverted to the brigade.

At this time the brigade was placed under the control of the Eighth Army and General Craig was ordered to move at once to Miryang where the Marines would come under the operational control of the 24th Army Division, commanded by Major General Church.

Twenty-six hours after leaving Changallon the brigade was in Miryang. The long move was made by rail, shuttling trucks and LST. The bivouac area was in a grove of trees on the Miryang River and the troops had time to bathe, get a change of uniform and eat a hot meal—three experiences new to them since leaving shipboard at Pusan thirteen days before. New combat uniforms were essential. Webbing, boots, leggings and uniforms had rotted on their bodies from being constantly wet from sweat and the slime of rice paddies.

During this period (August 7-13) the brigade had suffered 315 casualties; 66 had been killed or had died of wounds, 240 wounded, and there were 9 missing in action. The first replacement draft had not yet arrived from the United States. The rifle companies received replacement by the transfer of cooks, bakers, bandsmen and officers and men from brigade and regimental staffs, as well as tankers and artillerymen into the depleted assault infantry units. Despite these measures, however, the rifle platoons were understrength.

That such transfers could be made without lessening the effectiveness of the rifle companies was made possible because of the traditional Corps doctrine that a Marine is a rifleman first and any specialty he may follow is secondary.

The Miryang River, which swung a dull, muddy coil of water around the town, was the bathtub for a brigade of men. The Marines in the stream were bicolored—tan of face, neck, hands and forearms, the rest of their bodies the white of shark's belly, bleached from sweating and sweating, always sweating. Every now and again the bathers would pause and cock an ear to the voice of the guns to the west. Had the wind changed, or was it closer?

It was closer. The 25th Division had been badly mauled and the enemy salient across the Naktong was deepening with its focal point aimed at Yongsan.

Before midnight on the sixteenth of August, Roise and Taplett had their units east of Yongsan and began the relief of the 35th Army Regiment. Newton was to bring his battalion forward on the second shuttle of trucks. Wood's artillery battalion had five hours before nightfall to get into position and register for the morning shoot on objective number one, Obong-ni Ridge. The movement forward was delayed by the failure of one hundred trucks from the Eighth Army motor pool to arrive.

On the carriers *Badoeng Straits* and *Sicily*, the two Marine Air Squadrons were rearmed and awaiting daylight to launch their first planes to support the battalions moving up for the attack. "Andy" Andeson, Deputy Commander of MAG-33, flew in from the *Badoeng Straits* to co-ordinate the air support missions.

During the past ten days these two squadrons had flown over four hundred sorties in support of the brigade as well as other units of the Eighth Army.

These squadrons, the Black Sheep and Death Rattlers (names carried over from the Pacific war) had napalmed, strafed and rocketed such pathways of destruction through the enemy that the gull-winged Corsairs were becoming psychological as well as actual instruments of warfare.

The 4th North Korean Division had forced a crossing of the Naktong River on the night and morning of August 12-13. In the process the Army 35th Regiment had been badly mauled and had lost considerable personnel and equipment. By the time the brigade arrived from Sachon, the enemy occupied a salient of some five thousand yards square. This re-entrant was manned by over six thousand enemy troops supported by tanks and artillery. Their immediate goal was Yongsan, twenty-five miles west of Miryang. Farther to the north the enemy 29th Regiment of the 10th Division had also crossed the river. This force was a direct threat on Taegu.

The 1st Marine Brigade was thrown across the main road leading from the Naktong to Yongsan. The situation was critical and there was considerable confusion. Accurate information was impossible to obtain. General Church gave Craig the mission of capturing three ridge lines between Yongsan and the river. The last and highest in the area commanded the low ground and the Naktong ferry crossing. Once the third objective was occupied, the enemy would be forced to recross the river. On the Eighth Army front in the attack were to be, from left to right, the Marine Brigade, 9th Infantry, 34th Infantry and the 1st Battalion of the 21st Infantry. There were seven commanding hills in the enemy salient. The Marines were assigned the mission of capturing three—two to the south of the Naktong-Yongsan road and one to the north.

Defending Obong-ni Ridge, objective number one of the Marine attack, was the 18th Regiment of the North Korean 4th Division, commanded by Colonel Chang Ky Dok. Chang was a veteran professional. He had gone to military school in Russia and had received his field training with the Chinese Communist armies in North China. He had slightly more than a thousand men at his disposal for defense, and he placed all three of his battalions in line to repel the Marine counterattack. Chang, from his many spies in Yongsan, was aware of the coming attack by the "yellow legs."

Chang called his battalion and company commanders to a meeting on the night of the sixteenth of August. He told them, "Intelligence says we are to expect an attack by American Marines. To us comes the honor of being the first to defeat these Marine soldiers. We will win where others have failed. I consider our positions impregnable. We occupy the high ground and they must attack up a steep slope. Go to your men and tell them there will be no retreat. I will take instant action against anyone who shows weakness."

Obong-ni Ridge resembled the back of a giant, gaunt snake with six arthritic spurs along the spine while the rib lines formed shallow corridors to the top. (See map number 2.) These "spurs" were numbered according to their height in meters. The one on the extreme right, overlooking the road and flanked by the village of Tugok, was Hill 102; with saddles between came the rest—109, 117, 143, 147—and the highest at the southern end, 153. Midway along the spine a landslide had formed what looked like an ugly red wound. "Red Slash Hill" was the Marines' name for the objective at the time; the correspondents labeled it "No Name Ridge." The facing was of rocky shale and sparse scrub pine. There was little or no natural cover and digging in would take time if an attack stalled on the way up.

To the rear and across a valley from Red Slash was a lower ridge paralleling the objective. From a point midway along this ridge there was a clear view of the valley below and the approaches to the hill to be taken under attack. A narrow, gutted road on the floor of the valley wound through the paddies from the village of Obong-ni and joined the Yongsan-Naktong road where it dipped around the base of Hill 102. The aid stations were set up on the reverse slope of a low hill across the valley from "No Name."

As though on the rim of a huge amphitheater, a parallel ridge offered a clear and unobstructed view of the attack. Waiting in the tension and inner turmoil that faces every commander of troops at such a time, General Craig set up an advance observation post at this point and waited for the action to begin. He knew that the intelligence on the strength and positions of the enemy was incomplete and the reconnaissance of the area hurried, but conditions would not allow more careful preparation. Constantly hampered by the lack of a third company in the battalions and never certain of his flanks, he had been forced to attack with his battalions in column. Instead of attacking objective one with two battalions abreast and enveloping the flanks, he could commit but one battalion frontally because his right flank would be uncovered until the 9th Regiment took the high ground in the Tugok village area, and one battalion had to be placed in a blocking position at his left rear after relieving the 34th Army Regiment.

The plans had been laid and the order given, and the troops were on their way to engage the enemy. It was too late for changes to be made. There was nothing more the brigade commander could do but wait out the time. The battle was in the hands of the regimental and battalion commanders. Once the action was joined even the men of these lower echelons become dependent on the leadership of their company officers. At the hour of attack the commander is alone with his doubts and his God.

Roise's battalion had been assigned to lead the assault. They had departed Yongsan at night by truck and proceeded along the main road to their assembly area. Detrucking, the 2nd continued on foot through the early morning hours and came into an area of death and destruction. The still air was heavy with the sickly-sweet stench of dead that tied knots in the stomachs of the riflemen.

As the half-light of dawn came over the eastern hills, the files of Marines could see the forlorn scene of abandoned dead and equipment littering the surrounding hills and road. They turned away from the stark horror of the Army aid station with the wounded who had been butchered as they lay on their stretchers.

The movement along the floor of the valley was slow and silent save for the shuffle of feet and the creak of web equipment and the muffled metallic sound of weapons. The riflemen in the column carried their rifles as they would for comfort, slung loosely over right or left shoulder or trailing in the crook of an elbow like a quail gun. It was a route column marching in easy fashion.

At their backs, as they marched, the eastern horizon was flaming with gun flashes and the echoes of thunder joined in one continous rumble. Overhead they heard the sighing flutter of shells passing. On their faces they felt the faint breath of concussion. Wood's artillery was going into action.

"I hope this is over early—it's goin' to be hot today—"

"In more'n one way, Mac."

"Why do we always get the crap details?"

"You know how that's decided, don't you?"

"Brief me, wise guy."

"We got three rifle battalions, so when they're figgering these things out, Colonel Murray says, 'I'm thinking of a number between one an' three. What is it?' Some wise guy at Regiment says, 'Two.' So there goes the 2nd."

"What'n hell you guys gripin' about? Didn't we have three hot meals and a night's sleep at Miryang?"

"Cut the yak-yak."

By seven o'clock Sweeney and Zimmer had their companies on the line of departure. Using the red slash in the ridge as a boundary, Zimmer took the area to the right of the marker while Sweeney assumed responsibility for the assault on the left. Sweeney's ridge line had the three rocky spurs—from left to right, 153, 147 and 145—while the three facing Zimmer were 117, 109 and 102. On Sweeney's left flank was to be Second Lieutenant Nick Arkadis' 1st Platoon. The interior platoon, in contact with Zimmer, was the unit led by Second Lieutenant Charles Christiansen. Second Lieutenant Mike Shinka was Zimmer's left flank assault platoon, while Technical Sergeant Charles Crowson (Vice Oakley), would be on the extreme right.

The jump-off was set for eight o'clock. For thirty-five minutes the air and artillery would alternate with a preparatory bombardment.

The Corsairs, staggering off the carrier decks with more than a ton of ordnance, vectored over the target. When the artillery fire ceased on order, the planes came screaming down, rocketing, bombing and strafing. When the Corsairs were through, Wood's artillery came slamming in again. Then it, too, fell silent.

"Okay, let's move out."

From the paralleling ridge to the rear, the watchers saw a thin line of men rise from the ground and begin to move across the rice paddies. Four understrength platoons—one hundred and thirty men—in the assault against a rise of ground of a steepness which would force the riflemen to crawl and scramble.

The valley was silent now save for desultory sniper fire which sounded like distant firecrackers. The only movement was the line of Marines as they cleared the rice paddies and into the oblong patches of stunted cotton and beans. Then the line began to alter as Christiansen's 2nd slowed under fire from the village. A gap came between Shinka's left and Christiansen's right.

The line developed a further curvature as Crowson's platoon on the right came under heavy fire from Tugok village and the high ground to his right rear. As yet there was no fire from the crest. The tension on the observation point lessened. Perhaps the artillery and air had driven the enemy off the top. The thought was more a prayer than a hope, for they were "skinning the lion while the beast yet lived." The ridge line was held by troops under orders to "hold or die."

Bordering Red Slash was a narrow, shallow, rain-formed gulley. At the base of the hill it was some ten feet wide and four feet deep; it narrowed and became shallower at the top until it was scant shelter for a man lying flat.

Shinka directed Corporal Walter Baker, leader of the 3rd Squad, to take his men into this gulley and make the approach from that corridor. The other two squads, twenty men, continued straining against the incline and doing their best to provide supporting fire one for the other.

When the watchers on the observation ridge saw the mortar smoke blossoming in Crowson's lines and machine-gun fire kicking up a devil's dance of dust into the right flank, General Craig said sharply to Stewart, "Contact Division—tell them they'll have to push the 9th Regiment forward—we're taking heavy fire from their zone—"

Shinka reached the top with twenty out of his thirty men. In a panting, sweating rush, the Marines began to jump into the shallow holes dug by the enemy; almost at once they came under heavy machine-gun fire from the right flank. The enemy then came from their holes on the reverse side of the slope and the fighting became a confused, horrible melody of shouting, cursing and the blasting of grenades and mortars.

Corporal Bill McCarver was killed as he attempted to put out an air panel; Mateo, already wounded, killed three enemy with his BAR. In a wild melee Ceniceros was hit just after he took the weapon from Mateo. Lenz was killed as he attempted to place an air panel in position. Shortly after that, Mackison and Mayberry of the 1st Squad were wounded. Baker, snap-shooting from his left shoulder, killed an enemy soldier with camouflaging brush in his helmet as the man tried to crawl into a flanking position.

Without support on his right or left and unable to get his men under cover from the deadly flanking fire, Shinka was forced to order the withdrawal of his men.

"Get the wounded down," he shouted to Reese.

Those who could crawl began the descent; those who were helpless were placed on ponchos and were hauled or carried off the ridge. Midway down, Shinka gathered his men in the gulley and made the wounded as comfortable as possible and saw to the application of field dressings. There were but fifteen men fit for the next attack.

Shinka got Zimmer on the radio. "We can take and hold the top if you'll get that flanking fire off us. I've got fifteen effectives left—give us an air strike and some more men and we'll make it—"

"I can't give you any men. I've just sent Dickerson's platoon over to support Crowson, but I'll get an air strike in right away."

While Shinka and his men went to the top and were forced back, Crowson and his platoon reached a point two-thirds of the way up the slope where they were pinned down by heavy fire from the front as well as the right flank. Crowson saw that one of his squads was in trouble from two enemy machine guns. Moving forward alone he took the enemy under fire with his carbine. Standing in full view of the Marines as well as the enemy troops Crowson methodically eliminated the machine-gun crew one by one; then he turned his fire and attention to a second gun and eliminated that as well.

Hard hit by casualties and without the benefit of a rain gulley, it was nearly impossible to retrieve Marines wounded in forward positions. A system was evolved wherein a Marine would crawl as far upward as possible toward the wounded man. Waiting a time for a lull in the firing the Marine on the rescue mission would throw a poncho to his helpless friend. By dint of great effort and pain the wounded Marine would struggle onto the camouflaged cover. Once he indicated he was in position, the rescuer would inch his way forward and upward until he could reach a corner of the poncho. Then slowly retracting he would haul the poncho and wounded man down the hill.

As this re-forming and evacuation of wounded went on, Zimmer sent Dickerson's platoon to the right flank of Crowson. Roise ordered the 81 mm. mortars and tanks to lay down a fire on the village and ridge to the right and at the same time called in an air strike on the ridge line.

On the left flank Arkadis had pushed his attack through the village and was on the lower base of the slope; Christiansen had failed to develop his attack with resolution. Little or no advance was made in his zone.

On the floor of the valley, corpsmen fronted the fire to bring back the wounded to the safety of a collecting point. From there the ambulances took them and crawled slowly back over the rutted road to the aid station. Corpsman Charles Scribner organized and led a gutty little band of South Korean civilians across the valley and up the slope. On the way up they carried water and ammunition; on the way down they brought wounded and dead. Six times during the first three hours, Scribner and his volunteers crossed the valley floor, six times they brought out wounded.

At the aid station, Navy Lieutenant Bentley Nelson, surgeon for the 2nd Battalion, saw the line of bleeding and helpless rise from three to seven to fifteen to forty—and the ambulance jeeps still came along the road from the valley.

"Get a helicopter in for these two, and loosen the tourniquet every ten minutes until it arrives—"

On and on without pause—Nelson was constantly faced with the decision of who was beyond help, who was operable and who should have priority on the helicopter to reach the life-saving facilities in the rear. From stakes, poles and rifles held upright by their bayonets plunged into the earth, red rubber tubes poured plasma and blood into nearly bloodless bodies. And still the wounded came in and the men bringing them in were getting hurt. Corpsman Billy Leeke received his second wound in a week. He was replaced by John Babbick in Arkadis' zone. Babbick was killed as he went to the assistance of a wounded Marine.

Three other corpsmen, Warren Albin, Alford Green and Herald Williams, were wounded.

There were too many wounded for the small detachment of corpsmen. The wounded helped the wounded, while the poncho-wrapped dead became one, two, three rows along the roadside.

Out in the fireswept valley, Chaplain Otto Sporrer knelt low over a young Marine. "*Per istam sanctum unctio nem—*"

The boy died before the crucifix touched his lips. Covering him with a poncho, Sporrer signaled to his group of South Koreans and led them back up the slope.

Throughout the day the tanks assisted in shielding the evacuation of wounded while fighting a continuous duel with enemy antitank guns on the ridge and giving supporting fire to the assault troops. The Pershings took countless mortar and AT hits, but were not damaged enough to become inoperable. Overhead Captain "Little Mac" McCaleb, in his tiny observation plane swept low over enemy foxholes on the ridge and dropped hand grenades from the open windows of his cockpit.

During the morning a well-camouflaged enemy artillery battery had been causing considerable damage to the rear areas. For hours the artillery had tried to put the weapons out of action without success. Lieutenant Pat Sivert, coming on station in McCaleb's plane, looked the area over. When he was informed that artillery ammunition was low, he requested and got two Corsairs to knock out the enemy guns. When the planes arrived on station Sivert requested the artillery to fire a round of white phosphorus to mark the target for the aircraft.

The marking round was fired and a direct hit was made on one gun, destroying it as well as the ammunition stacked near by and taking a heavy toll on the gun crew.

While all these supporting actions were going on, Shinka and Crowson made preparations for the second assault on the ridge. Roise warned the rifle platoons that an air strike was going to be laid on and then turned to his forward air controller. "Bring 'em down, Jeter."

Jeter began talking to the tactical air co-ordinator orbiting overhead. Within a matter of minutes the Corsairs swooped down on the ridge with rockets and bombs. These pilots knew only too well what was happening to the ground units and their attacks were pushed with the greatest courage and resolution. They wrought heavy casualties on the enemy but the one weapon which would have made the ridge line untenable to the enemy was lacking because of the shortage of napalm tanks.

When the gull-winged planes had done what they could, the two rifle companies went into the assault for the second time.

For the space of two hundred feet the thin line made steady progress against little or no opposition. Then the enemy came from their holes on the reverse slope and rushed into shallow positions on the forward edge and opened fire with automatic weapons, and began rolling concussion and fragmentation grenades down on the climbing Marines. The flanking fire, which had gone silent when the units withdrew to re-form and while the tanks and mortars were firing into the village, resumed again.

In a matter of minutes the thin line of Dog Company riflemen became a scattering few struggling upward. There was nothing that could be done by command. The battle was too closely joined to risk artillery, mortars or air. The battle had to be fought by the lowest common denominator of a military organization—the squad, half squad, two-man fire teams and single men.

From the paralleling observation post, men were sickened at the sight of the thin, depleted line moving into the face of such bitter fire and seeing the wounded falling and tumbling down the steep slope. Now there was no line; there were eleven, then nine gray-green figures still lurching forward.

"Good God!" correspondent James Bell said in a choked voice. "How brave can men be? Pickett's charge on Cemetery Hill must have been like this."

Mike Shinka had started the attack with fifteen men; when he reached the top there were but nine remaining. He led them further along the slope than before and he got his men into positions still occupied by dead enemy. Reese saw some troops in the saddle between Hills 109 and 117. That was Easy Company's zone.

"Easy Company," he roared.

"Yes," came the answer and with it a blast of fire. Then they saw the mustard-colored uniforms and the odd-shaped cloth caps.

Reese was cursing as he poured fire from Mateo's BAR into Easy Company. Shinka considered the situation. He had Reese, Baker and Kennedy from the 2nd Squad; Cedargren, Smith and Hric from the 1st, and two Marines who had sideslipped over from Crowson's unit. He could not remain where he was with the enemy on the reverse slope hurling grenades into his men and the flanking fire still coming in from the village and ridge to the right. If he could clear the enemy off the top, that would open the ascent to Crowson and Christiansen and positions of cover could be taken from the flank fire until it was brought under control. It was either go forward or get back.

The decision was made for him as a burst of fire hit them from the right flank again. Reese was shot through the thigh, breaking his leg, and Hric was shot in the stomach. Shinka crawled to Hric's side and pulled him back into a place of better cover. As he was assuring Hric that they would get him off the hill, a bullet hit Shinka and tore away the lower part of his face. Temporarily he was stunned and unable to breathe because of the strangling blood. He put his head down between his legs in an attempt to clear his throat.

Unable to talk into the radio to inform Zimmer of the situation, he motioned to his men to withdraw down the hill.

Baker crawled to Reese's side. "Okay, Dick, I'll get you down."

Reese shook his head. "I can crawl. You help Hric."

Cedargren and Baker put Hric on a poncho and began to carry him off the hill and into the comparative safety of the gulley. Holding his jaw in place with his hand, Shinka crawled from Marine body to Marine body on the small portion of ridge line his men had gained to make certain no wounded were being left behind. As he finished his tortuous rounds he was hit in the right arm. The shock of it knocked him down and he rolled some distance before he could stop.

Finding it difficult to breathe because of his excessive bleeding, Shinka followed the crawling Reese and poncho-borne Hric down the slope to where the gulley was deep enough to provide cover for what was left of his platoon. A runner came in from Zimmer and told him that Tobin's Baker Company was going to pass through. Shinka nodded. With his left hand he directed the evacuation of the wounded from the gulley and back across the pea patch and rice paddies and to the battalion aid station.

A time comes in protracted assaults when the energy of even the best troops is exhausted, when even the bravest platoon officers and stoutest NCO's shrink from leading another attack into the sacrifice imposed. Arkadis, who had led his platoon with energy and courage, was wounded and his platoon depleted. Zimmer's Dog Company, with Shinka and

Crowson leading their units with rare courage, was so badly cut up as to raise grave doubts about its ability to mount another attack.

Murray, who was with Roise and Newton at a joint battalion OP, ordered Newton to take the 1st through the 2nd and to continue the attack. He also sent a warning order to Taplett to be ready to move out at once.

Upon being relieved, Roise brought what was left of his battalion onto the high ground to the rear of Obong-ni and set up defensive positions. Of the two hundred and forty riflemen who had made the attack, less than one hundred walked out unattended. The 2nd had suffered one hundred and forty-two casualties, including twenty-three killed.

The battle for Obong-ni Ridge had been in doubt seven hours. Roise's 2nd had begun the assault at eight in the morning. It was three in the afternoon before Tobin and Stevens had their companies in relief positions, and objective one was yet to be taken.

Tobin was to relieve Zimmer while Stevens relieved Sweeney. Tobin went forward to contact Zimmer and as they were discussing positions, an enemy machine gun opened up and Zimmer and his radio operator were wounded. As Zimmer was being evacuated, Tobin told him, "You'll be okay, Andy; you'll be playing basketball in a couple of months."

Tobin called in Schryver and Taylor who were to take their platoons into the assault. After he had briefed them on the plan of action and attack they rejoined their units. Tobin then called Fenton forward from the mortar positions. As Fenton walked along the road he came on General Craig.

"Watch yourself, Ike—it's hot up here," Craig called.

"Aye aye, sir."

Fenton joined Tobin in a cut in the road. The two proceeded through the cut and onto a small rise of ground where the company front could be seen. Tobin was explaining the plan of attack when a burp gun opened fire from a clump of bushes across the road. Tobin fell to the ground with his arm and chest laced with multiple wounds.

"Jesus, Ike, I've been hit. Get the map." With his sound arm he tried to get the map from the breast pocket of his dungarees. Because of the shortage of maps it was the sole guide available to the unit; Fenton retrieved the blood-soaked paper and rushed Tobin back to the aid station. Fenton assumed command of Baker Company.

In the assault Schryver took his unit into a draw at the base of the ridge to escape the fire which was still coming in from the village. Re-forming he began the assault on Hill 109. About halfway up his unit was pinned down again by heavy machine-gun fire.

Schryver got Fenton on the radio. "We're catching hell from the village to our right flank. Get the artillery and mortars on it."

"I can't see it from my position," Fenton answered. "You direct the fire by relaying over your 536."

A concentration of artillery and heavy mortars was placed on the village while Sweet moved a section of Pershings forward and opened fire with his 90 mm.'s. After twenty minutes Schryver was able to advance, but the enemy fire from Hill 109 was too intense to attempt a frontal assault. Working around to the slope on the roadside of 102, the 1st was able to seize and hold the first of the six spurs.

While Schryver was maneuvering for the capture of 102, Taylor, denied maneuvering possibilities because of terrain, was finding his advance up the face of the ridge slow and costly. Immediately, when Schryver reached the crest line, the 1st Platoon turned their fire onto the spur to the south to aid Taylor. By five o'clock in the afternoon, Baker Company held 102 and 109 in strength. In the final attack, Taylor was seriously wounded and evacuated. He died of his wounds as he lay beside Tobin in the Army Field Surgical Hospital at Miryang.

To the left of the red slash boundary, Stevens Company was taking heavy casualties in their assault. With Tom Johnston and Sebilian leading their platoons in the attack, they fought to gain 143. Johnston worked his platoon up a shallow corridor to the saddle between Hills 117 and 143. About seventy-five yards from the top of the saddle they were pinned down by machine-gun fire from the higher hill to the left. Johnston placed BARman Camper in position and, borrowing a grenade from Pfc. Billy Lindley, said, "Now gimme some fire!"

Johnston rushed forward. He threw a grenade and went down. As soon as it exploded he was up and charging forward again. As he hurled his second grenade an enemy grenade exploded near him and he was instantly killed. Technical Sergeant Frank Lawson took command of the platoon. Lieutenant George Fox's 3rd Platoon had been assigned to battalion reserve. Stevens requested permission from Newton to commit it. His request was granted and Fox took his unit through the 2nd and pressed the attack on 143, but the enemy was too strong and well positioned to be dislodged before nightfall.

To the right of Johnston's platoon Sebilian was wounded and Staff Sergeant McMullen took charge of the 2nd.

As the day of bloody fighting came to a close, Fenton's company held Hills 102 and 109. Stevens' line tied in with Fenton's on the saddle between 109 and 117. From there it bent back and down the slope. Stevens' platoons were in line in the following positions: McMullen had the 2nd Platoon on the right and was tied in with Fenton's left platoon, now commanded by Lischeski. In the center, facing on Hill 117, was Lawson (twice wounded during the day) with the 1st. On the left flank bending down the hill was Fox's 3rd. To further refuse the left flank Newton formed a unit from Battalion headquarters and service personnel and hooked them to the left of Fox.

In these positions the two units dug in for the night.

The heavy mortars and artillery were registered in on corridors of approach and areas of concentration likely to be used by the enemy. Throughout the night these weapons would continue harassing and interdiction fire and they would fire barrages on call. Wood's artillery was also ordered to maintain fire on the river crossing to prevent reinforcements crossing during the night.

As the two units were digging in for the night, Fenton saw three enemy tanks moving on the road around the base of Hill 102 and headed for the battalion CP and aid station. He contacted Newton by field telephone. "Three enemy T-34 tanks on the road. They're in column and headed for your CP."

"Okay, Ike, don't bother them—we'll take care of them back here."

This was to be the first contact the Marines had with the vaunted T-34 and they prepared to meet it with feverish eagerness. Winter's 3rd Platoon of Pershings were refueling and loading ammunition when the flash came that enemy tanks were approaching. Clambering into his command tank, Winters led off to join with the enemy. Two other Pershings followed him in trace. The 75 mm. Recoilless Rifle Platoon was on the spur road leading down from Observation Post Hill where they had been lending support to the troops on the ridge.

Lieutenant Paul Fields put his section of Recoilless Rifles in position to cover the curve in the road. Charlie Jones placed his section to the rear of Fields in support. In the meantime the rocket section of the antitank assault platoon raced to positions on the right of the road where it curved around Hill 102.

As Corporal Norbert Alvarez got into position and waited with his 3.5 rocket launcher, he shouted to Gilberto Casas on his left, "Betcha a can of beer I stop one first shot."

"You stop him an' I'll blow him," Casas answered.

On the ridge line there was a lull in the fighting with both sides awaiting the outcome of the battle below them. If the raiding tanks were successful in shooting up the rear area and destroying communications and supporting fires, the force on the high ground would be in a difficult situation until Taplett's 3rd could rush in from the left flank.

In the meantime the enemy tanks, two close together and the third a half mile to the rear, came rolling along the road. Three Air Force P-51's sighted them and made repeated strafing runs with no apparent effect. These planes were not under Marine control and Fenton had considerable difficulty calling them from the attack when their fire began to hit into his right flank. Unknown to the Marines at the time, a fourth tank with troops attached was en route to the area to support the first three.

At the curve in the road Alvarez, Casas and the rest of the rocket section waited. They could hear the tank, and over the shoulder of hills they could see a cloud of dust rising. The dust cloud stopped and hung just beyond the shoulder, then they saw the gun of the tank come into view. It moved right and left like the searching tentacle of a giant octopus.

"Now—"

"Wait."

Alvarez settled lower and sighted on the left front tread. The tank was in full view and within a hundred yards before the rocket launcher slammed its load into the track. The tank paused, but came on with all guns firing wildly. Casas scored a hit at the same time that a 75 from the Recoilless rifle struck the machine-gun mount on the right front and tore a large hole in the hull.

Like a badgered animal, the tank halted but continued to fire on the OP. Winters' lead tank scored a direct hit, setting the tank afire. The turret hatch was thrown open and the crew attempted to escape, but a hail of small-arms fire killed them as they spilled out.

The second tank, seemingly oblivious of what had happened to the leader, swung off the road to pass its burning brother. It was hit in the gas tank by a 3.5. When the tank commander threw open the turret to escape, a 2.36 white phosphorus rocket ricocheted off the turret cover and went into the tank, setting it afire.

Because of the narrowness of the road, Winters placed two of his tanks hub to hub, so that both of his 90's could be brought to bear. As the third tank came around the bend, the Pershings slammed into it, putting it out of action. In less than ten minutes the three enemy tanks had been destroyed and the personnel killed.

From the ridge line Fenton's unit gave the Marines below a cheer. The bogeyman myth of the Russian T-34 tank had vanished in the smoke of the three burning tanks at the curve of the road at Obong-ni.

"If you got the guts to wait 'em out, we can knock out any tank," Alvarez reminded the others in his section.

Corsairs destroyed the fourth tank and dispersed or killed the troops with it. The attempted encirclement had ended in failure. The decision would be reached on the crest of Obong-ni Ridge.

Just before dark Casas was killed by a chance shot as he moved into a new position in Stevens' zone. During the day the Marines had taken two hundred and five casualties: one hundred and eighty wounded, twenty-three killed and two who had died of wounds.

Though the 18th North Korean Regiment was still holding four of the six embattled spurs and were resisting with great tenacity, Chang's unit had been hard hit; he had lost nine of his antitank guns by counter-fire from Marine tanks, and replacement guns could not be manhandled to the ridge in time for the second day. In addition, nine machine guns and eleven mortars had been lost to artillery and air bombardment, but of greater importance was the leveling of Tugok Village. Flanking fire from that area would be of no assistance in the future.

During the day he had taken six hundred casualties from all arms, but this did not disturb him too much. Replacements were available from the 16th Regiment. The problem facing him was simple; during the night he would re-form his units, feed in replacements and counterattack before dawn and reoccupy Hills 102 and 109 before day-light permitted use of air attacks to aid the ground troops opposing him.

As Chang made his plans he was constantly fortified by information from his unit commander on Hill 147. This information was accurate and in detail. The 2nd Battalion of Marines had opened the attack and after suffering heavy casualties had been replaced by the 1st

Battalion. Colonel Chang reported this with considerable elation and pride to his division commander, Major General Kim Dok.

The 1st Marine Battalion was the enemy unit now occupying Hills 102 and 109. Less than four hundred troops were in position to oppose him and he knew the exact position where the two companies had joined their flanks. He would force a wedge between them and defeat them in detail. Once they were overcome, the enemy would have only one battalion left to carry on the battle.

Despite the failure of the flank turning tank task force, Chang faced the second day of battle for "No Name" Ridge with confidence as he ordered a counterattack for 2:30 in the morning.

CHAPTER VI

The Battle of the Naktong Bulge Is Won and the Enemy Is Driven into the River. August 18-19

As the sun sank it shone in the eyes of the Marines, but the temporary hindrance to their vision was nothing to the thought of the darkness to follow. With Fenton and Stevens preparing positions for the night, there was no doubt in the mind of either that an enemy counterattack would be thrown against them before daylight.

As Fenton's men dug in he heard a young rifleman singing, "Oh, how I hate to see that evening sun go down." The songster of Baker Company knew only too well what to expect. Five nights before he had dug in on a hill over Changallon, seventy-five road miles to the south and west. What he didn't know was that, brutal and costly as Changallon was, the night attack on Obong-ni Ridge would make it seem a skirmish.

Every precaution was taken to assure that the expected attack would be repelled. Double lines of telephone wire were laid between company CP's and the platoons, as well as back to the battalion. Field telephones of Russian manufacture had been captured and were being used. Made of plastic, they were found to be lighter, easier to handle and just as efficient as that of United States issue. Trip flares were set up and the two companies settled down to await the attack with twenty-five per cent of the personnel alerted to maintain listening watch.

Sergeant Frank Lischeski, commanding Taylor's platoon, was on the left flank and tied in with Stevens' right. At 2:30 in the morning he got Fenton on the phone.

"There's movement on my front, Cap'n. They're getting ready to hit. I've alerted everybody—get plenty of light out here."

Within a matter of minutes a green signal flare went off and the enemy struck Lischeski's left flank where it joined Stevens' right. Employing automatic weapons and grenades, the attackers broke through and turned the flanks of both defending units.

Corporal Jewell Bruce, in command of the left flank squad, re-formed his men to repel the attack.

"Over here!" he shouted. "Set up here—" He placed a BAR in position. Running from position to position and hurling grenades, he placed his men. "Grenades! More grenades—"

Ignoring the enemy fire, Bruce stood silhouetted against the light of the 81 mm. illuminating shells, hurling grenades and encouraging his men. Lischeski brought men to the critical flank and the breakthrough was temporarily halted, though the two companies had been split.

When Bruce was struck down, his close friend, Pfc. Jack Headley, went momentarily berserk, and charging from his hole he hurled grenades, destroying the machine gun and crew that had killed Bruce.

Shortly after the initial assault began, the counterattack was extended to the entire front of both companies. As soon as Fenton learned of the breakthrough, he ordered Lischeski to pull his platoon back toward the company CP and form a company perimeter defense. Before Fenton could form his perimeter defense, however, the enemy penetrated into his CP area. Close in, hand-to-hand fighting ensued. This enemy thrust was thrown back with most of the force being killed. Despite heavy casualties, Fenton had secured his lines.

All along the front, illuminating shells lighted the confused scene with a garish whiteness. Thus the attackers and defenders were held in this fire-rimmed semicircle. For the enemy it would prove nearly as costly to retreat as it was to advance. For the Marines there could be no reinforcements until morning and they wouldn't retreat.

"We'll just hafta take the —— ridge back again if we leave it!"

As soon as the attack started, the artillery and heavy mortars opened fire on prearranged targets, and began pouring their high explosives into the enemy lines as fast as it was possible to fire. While the immediate effect did not alter the situation facing the rifle companies, it did prevent the organization and passage of enemy reinforcements to the attack.

Newton got Fenton on the field phone. "What's your situation?"

"They've turned my left flank and I've pulled the 2nd platoon back. We're under heavy attack all along our lines. We still hold 102 and 109—"

"Can you hold until daylight?"

"We'll hold."

Stevens was in a more critical situation than Fenton. The Able Company commander was handicapped by an earlier tragedy when four rounds of white phosphorus landed in the middle of his 60 mm. mortar platoon and inflicted eighteen casualties, thus denying the use of that supporting weapon. The attack on Stevens' front came from the crest and around both flanks of Hill 117. The main force of the enemy assault hit Lawson's unit. The first thrusts were repelled until Lawson, wounded for the fifth time, had to be evacuated. Denied his courageous leadership, the platoon gave ground and a wedge was driven between McMullen and Fox. Stevens was forced to move his CP to the left where he began to rally and form remnants of the 1st Platoon.

Under the illumination from 81 mm. mortar shells, the enemy method of attack could be seen. A squad would rise and hurl grenades and then rush forward a few yards, firing to their front and flanks with automatic weapons. They would then fall to the ground and the same action would be repeated by another squad. In this manner three penetrations were made in Stevens' lines. Though they took heavy casualties, the enemy persisted in these tactics even when under the light of illuminating shells.

Without abatement, the enemy pressed their attacks until daylight, at which time they took positions on the high ground to dig in against the air and ground attacks full light would bring against them. The attack had gained the North Koreans local penetrations and control of the saddle between 109 and 117, but Fenton held onto 102 and 109.

Upon reorganizing in the morning, the cost of the fight to the Marines could be computed. Fenton had dug in the night before with 190 men and five officers. He now had but 110 effectives remaining for duty. There were only eleven men left of the 2nd Platoon. Schryver was hit on the forehead by a grenade fragment and knocked unconscious. When he regained consciousness he went down the hill and had his wound dressed. The bandage was so bulky he couldn't wear a helmet; he went back up the hill and rejoined his platoon without it.

Stevens, who had gone into the night battle with 185 men, had but 90 remaining who could maintain positions in the line. Badly depleted as the two companies were, Fenton and Stevens began reorganizing and preparing for an attack to seize the remaining spurs on the ridge. Lieutenant "Metz" Muetzel, wounded on the first day as well as the second, left his machine-gun platoon and took command of Johnston's 2nd.

When the flanks of the two units had been penetrated and turned, twelve men from Stevens' company had withdrawn into Fenton's perimeter. With Baker Company furnishing supporting fire from Hill 109, these men under Technical Sergeant McMullen attacked at first light down the saddle toward 117. This attack was co-ordinated with the remainder of Stevens' unit working toward the saddle from their positions.

Pinned down by enemy machine-gun fire, Pfc. Harold Twedt worked his BAR into an exposed position where he could fire on the enemy gun. He silenced one gun with his first clip. He charged the second gun firing his BAR from the hip as he drove forward. Receiving multiple wounds, Twedt silenced the second gun before he died of his wounds.

The platoon gained the saddle and began the assault of Hill 117. Midway they again were pinned down. Stevens called for an air strike on the enemy strongpoint.

"We're held up by heavy machine-gun fire from the east slope," Stevens told Newton. "The co-ordinates are 43.2-86.6. Will you have Smitty bring in an air strike?"

"How far is this from your front?"

"About a hundred yards."

"That's pretty close."

"I can't go forward and it'll cost casualties to withdraw. I'll get the men in holes. I think it's a risk we have to take."

"Right." Newton turned to Lieutenant James W. Smith, his forward air controller and explained the situation.

"Okay, Colonel, tell the troops to get into their holes and stay there until it's over." By radio Smith contacted "Andy" Anderson, the tactical air co-ordinator who was circling overhead in a Corsair.

"Knee-hi, this is Jasper 14. Ground attack held up by machine guns on east slope Hill 117—target co-ordinates 43.2-86.6—friendly troops one hundred yards down slope. Repeat: Friendly troops one hundred yards down slope."

"Will make dummy run; observe and advise."

Anderson circled into position and dived on the target. As he pulled out, Smith told him, "You are on target."

Upon being informed that the proper target had been identified, Anderson spoke to the four Corsairs vectoring over the area. "One

Knee-hi, this is a marking run. Observe mark and attack when in position."

Again Anderson dived on the target, and this time he fired a smoke rocket into the center of the enemy emplacement. Captain "Pat" Kelley saw the marking plume of smoke rise from the rocket and took his Corsair into the dive. He released a five-hundred-pound bomb. It exploded dead center on the target.

Under a shower of rocks and dirt, Fox's 3rd Platoon rose from their positions and rushed the hill. Near the crest they came on the blasted area. Four machine guns had been destroyed and the crews killed. Hill 117 was seized without further opposition. Stevens had requested the air strike at 7:34; nine minutes later the Corsair had blasted the target, and five minutes after the five-hundred-pounder exploded, the 3rd Platoon of Able Company was on the crest.

Throughout the years Marine air and ground commanders had worked out the distance-poundage factors that explosives could be dropped without resultant injury to friendly troops. Roughly, it is that a hundred-pound bomb required one hundred yards between the center of impact and front line troops; a two-hundred-pounder, two hundred yards, etc. The placing of the five-hundred-pound bomb on an enemy strongpoint at slightly more than a hundred yards was a calculated risk that was deemed acceptable under the critical circumstances.

Unfortunately, a Marine rifleman was killed by the blast. This proved to be the lone casualty inflicted on friendly troops by Marine airmen, though they habitually brought their attacks within the closest proximity to the ground forces.

Immediately after Fox's unit seized Hill 117, it moved south against Hill 143. After a mortar barrage and another air strike, the spur was captured. By now it was evident that the main line of enemy resistance had been broken.

While the Newton's battalion was clearing the remaining enemy off Obong-ni Ridge, Taplett passed his 3rd around Fenton's right flank and pressed the attack on objective number two, which was another ridge line a thousand yards farther east.

In the mopping up on Obong-ni, Stevens and Fenton counted eighteen heavy machine guns of Russian and American manufacture, twenty-five light machine guns, sixty-three sub-machine guns, eight antitank rifles, and large quantities of ammunition and grenades. In the immediate vicinity of the company positions, 183 enemy dead were counted. More than 100 were found buried in caves and fox holes.

Basing the casualty rate on the established rule that for every man killed there will be three wounded, Colonel Chang's 18th North Korean Regiment could be listed as no longer being an effective fighting force. This was further confirmed when prisoners and dead from the 19th North Korean Regiment were examined.

Fenton received a shock when a SCR 300 Army radio was recaptured. The radio was in operating condition and was set to the frequency of the 1st Battalion. It was obvious the enemy had been listening in on all conversations between Stevens and Newton and himself during the attack and defense of the ridge. From this source, the enemy had learned the exact spot where the two units had tied in their flanks during the night.

The battle for Obong-ni Ridge had raged for twenty-six hours with few lulls during this period. The 1st and 2nd Marine Battalions had been hard hit by casualties and it was evident the enemy had staked the defense of the Naktong Bulge on their ability to hold that key ridge. When they failed to dislodge Fenton and Stevens with their morning counterattack, the enemy division commander was faced not only with the loss of the commanding high ground, but the loss of his division in recrossing the river. An hour and a half after the counterattack began (four o'clock in the morning) and the Marine companies held, rear elements of the enemy division were ordered to withdraw over the river.

Taplett's battalion, fresh and eager, jumped off with Joe Fegan's company in the assault. As Williams' platoon neared the crest the enemy ran from their holes on the reverse slope and hurled a volley of grenades down on the Marines. The Marines at the point fell to the ground. Williams, slightly to the rear of the leading element, answered by throwing two in return. The Marines in the forward positions tossed resupply grenades back to Williams who in turn would pull the pin and hurl them onto the crest. The enemy became discouraged in the face of this kind of relay and began to withdraw. Corporal Henry Carlton led the rush forward. The next few minutes was a free-for-all shoot.

One hour and twenty minutes after jumping off, Fegan reported he was on the crest of Hill 206. Taplett had set up a forward observation post on Obong-ni. From this position he gave a demonstration of utilizing supporting arms that was to become classic. Air, artillery and mortars worked over the ground ahead of Fegan.

Bohn put his company into the attack on the right flank of Fegan at 11:30. One hour later George Company was on the right side and top of Hill 206. It was evident the enemy was in a demoralized state and they were fighting an unco-ordinated rear guard action. The ridge line was cluttered with abandoned dead and equipment.

With the capture and consolidation of the second objective, Murray ordered Taplett to attack and seize the third and final objective in the brigade zone of action. Objective three was Hill 311 which lay north and west and across the Yongsan-Naktong road from objective two. The usual rice paddy flanked the east side of the road. Atop Hill 311 was a plateau of the general size and shape of a football field. It was thickly covered with scrub pine and the northern end held a clump of trees. From this high point the land mass gradually fell away to the ferry crossing three thousand yards to the west.

The avenues of approach were two razorbacked ridges which built up sharply from the paddy bordered road. The one ridge rose from the vicinity of the village of Shikken-ri and led onto the plateau from the south. This was the ridge Bohn was to take with his unit. Fegan's ridge built up from the road farther to the east. Thus the two units would converge on the plateau from the east (Fegan) and south (Bohn).

The two rifle companies descended from Hill 206 and crossed the rice paddy to gain the road. Fegan mounted his men on Pomeroy's tanks to speed their arrival at the base of his ridge of approach. Bohn's avenue was closer at hand and George Company began the twelve-hundred-yard climb at 3:30 in the afternoon. While the rifle companies were in movement, Taplett displaced the heavy mortars and 75 mm. Recoilless guns forward and these weapons, in conjunction with air and artillery, began to place preparatory fires on the enemy-held plateau. Pomeroy's tanks, after offloading Fegan's unit, furnished supporting fire as How Company began its sharp climb. The plateau became hidden in a pall of fire, smoke and dust.

Two hours after leaving the road, Bohn had his unit under the southern rim of the plateau. The climb had been under moderate resistance, but as the unit approached the top and the supporting fires had to be called off, heavier fire was received. Assault patrols were sent out to secure the sector assigned to George Company.

Fegan, with a longer avenue of approach, went into the assault with

Di Lorenzo's unit moving up the razorback while Post's platoon was echeloned on the right flank slope. Because of the waist high brush the use of machine guns in the attack was precluded. Taylor got his mortars into position of support as Staff Sergeant Dale Stropes led the assault line forward under ever-increasing enemy fire. Carlton, always pushing forward, was killed. Terrio, Fegan's runner, grenaded another machine gun out of action. Fegan attempted an enveloping movement with Williams' platoon moving up to the left of Di Lorenzo. Terrain and enemy fire prevented this. Pfc. Richard Lewry rushed forward with his BAR to lend support. He was killed. Fegan (by radio) asked Bohn to try taking the pressure from his front by enveloping the enemy positions on the crest. Fegan was wounded. Terrio rushed down the hill and brought back litterbearers to carry Fegan out of the zone of action. First Lieutenant Thomas Lennon assumed temporary command. Further fighting developed as the enemy made a final, desperate stand to hold the commanding ground to the river crossing.

In Bohn's unit Cahill was wounded and Pfc. Stanley Merchant and Corporal Bob Robinson were killed in the attempt to encircle the enemy strongpoint. Before darkness brought an end to the hilltop battle, eight others of Cahill's 1st Platoon were wounded. Both companies dug in for the night without having completely erased the enemy from the brush and tree clumps.

The Naktong River had become a death trap and was clogged with enemy dead as Army and Marine artillery and all available aircraft concentrated on the destruction of the routed division. When nightfall forced the Corsairs to return to their carriers, night strafing and bombing attacks continued by Marine night fighters based in Japan. Throughout the night Wood's artillery pounded the crossing lanes.

At first light Lennon sent his unit into the attack and Bohn sent a patrol under Master Sergeant Ryder (replacing Cahill) to contact How Company and assist in wiping out the remaining enemy in the tree clump.

At the first indications of the Marine attack, thirty enemy soldiers slipped from their tree clump strongpoint and were seen running down the western face of the hill and into the village of Pang'o-ri, which lies between Hill 311 and the river. Peterson's 81 mm. mortars burned the village with white phosphorus.

This proved to be the last ground action in the reduction of the enemy salient across the Naktong River. However, Marine air was to have a day unrivaled in the Korean war. In addition to supplying close air support planes for the Marine and Army units in the attack, the Corsairs struck at the enemy endeavoring to cross the river as the general withdrawal began.

Ground patrols were sent to the edge of the river. The sight that met the eyes of the Marines somewhat eased the sorrow over friends who had been killed and wounded in the forty-eight-hour battle. The equipment and dead of a destroyed enemy division were on the plains before the river. The Brigade Ordnance Section recovered thirty-four large caliber artillery pieces, including five Army 105 howitzers and countless small arms and machine guns.

Late that afternoon Craig received orders that the Marines were to be relieved by elements of the 24th Army Division and return to Miryang for an indefinite period of rest and reorganization. During the attack and capture of the three key ridge lines in the enemy salient, the Marines had suffered 258 casualties. Of this number 60 had been killed and 6 had died of wounds. In twelve days of battle in Korea the brigade had taken 643 casualties.

When General Craig returned to Miryang he went to the Army hospital to visit the Marine wounded, and then to the cemetery where the grave-digging parties were still at work preparing places for the poncho-shrouded Marines.

The white crosses with their black lettering were already prepared. Each bore a name, a number, a unit and a date. In the slanting afternoon sunlight they looked clean, chaste and melancholy in their neat piles. Five stacks of twelve. Only the names on the topmost cross could be seen, just as the leading man of a close interval file blocks out the man behind him.

Corporal Jewell C. Bruce, 669078, 1st Battalion 5th Marines; First Lieutenant David S. Taylor, 048493, 1st Battalion 5th Marines; Corporal William L. McCarver, 1078995, 2nd Battalion 5th Marines; HM3 John L. Babbick, Jr., 7908026, U. S. Navy; Corporal Robert E. Robinson, Jr., 670769, 3rd Battalion 5th Marines.

Craig looked at the crosses and the names. As the sun settled in the west he returned to the CP area and sat before his tent and watched the truckloads of weary riflemen move into the bivouac area and then down to the river to bathe away the grime and filth of three days of bitter fighting.

Throughout his career in the Corps, General Craig had shown a kindly, avuncular interest in his men. A senior Marine flag officer summed up Craig's attitude briefly: "I've known Eddie Craig over thirty years. If he has a weakness, it's the inner torment he suffers when his unit takes casualties."

Speaking softly, Craig told his aide, First Lieutenant John Buck, that he would like to talk to the members of 2nd Squad, 3rd Platoon of Dog Company. Buck went down into the bivouac area near the river and searched for the men the general wanted to see.

During the Pacific war, when he commanded a regiment, Craig had long planned to make a pictorial history of a squad of Marines so that, in some way, civilians might know what thirteen men must go through in training and battle. There never seemed to be the time at Bougainville, Guam or at Iwo Jima for such a project. When he received word that he was to command the Marine Brigade in Korea, he knew that his name would be noted in history with the deeds of his command. He could not alter that nor was there a way to plan in history the names of the almost nameless, faceless men of the rifle companies who groveled in the dirt and climbed the hills and died. With death they became a digit in the casualty figures and a telegram to be delivered.

None of these things could be changed, but one small unit could be immortalized, thus immortalizing all such units. Even in the rush and hurry at Pendleton he discussed the matter with the officers of his staff and a plan was evolved. A random squad from a random platoon would be selected. From the time of selection until the brigade was disbanded, a pictorial history would be kept of these thirteen men to show them in the spit and polish of their liberty uniforms, at games during recreation periods and in the grime and dirt of the field. If possible, the camera would follow them into battle—at least catch them as they went in and record it when they came out.

Craig thought that perhaps some moving picture company might take this film and, using background shots of their homes and schools and churches and girls, make a picture that would tell the people what a squad goes through in battle.

There was no search to find or create a "showcase" squad that was highly trained and particularly well led by veteran NCO's. Had Craig or the Marine Corps been trying to propagandize, they could have hand-picked such a squad by assigning proven men to it. Instead, the 2nd Squad of the 3rd Platoon of Finn's Dog Company was chosen.

None of the Marines in the unit had been with the 5th Marines when the Korean war broke out, and as a result had not participated in summer maneuvers; none were veterans of the Pacific war; all came to Pendleton from one of the many posts and stations throughout the nation. They all had one thing in common, however, and that was Marine boot camp and basic infantry tactics with an FMF unit.

To lead the squad was Sergeant Richard Reese. A first-rate mechanic, Reese was at the Marines' desert supply depot at Barstow when recalled to the brigade to take over a squad going to war. Reese was a top athlete in high school. In the Corps, he became a tough, keen sergeant with the know-how to handle any company weapon better than the man assigned to it.

The Corps employs a different organization within its squad than does the Army. The twelve men in the squad are divided into three fire teams. Each fire team is headed by a corporal or Pfc. The task of control for the squad leader is thereby lessened and the fire power (one BAR to each fire team) greatly increased. Leading a fire team is the final schooling before the squad and platoon. In a fire fight, the fire team leader is the "general" of three men and twenty yards of front.

The first fire team was made up of Corporal Walter Baker and Pfc.'s Mateo, Kennedy and Kelly. Baker was a good athlete and captain of his high school football team, where he studied agriculture with the idea that he might take up farming after his Marine Corps days were over. At the time the Korean war began, Baker was a member of the post fire department at Barstow supply depot. When ordered to Pendleton he requested duty with the tanks. He was issued an M1 and told to take charge of a fire team.

Pfc. Lenerd Mateo was an assistant BARman in the first fire team. Of Filipino-Irish descent, Mateo was a sharpshooter with the M1; he was also a good draftsman and was on duty at the Depot of Supplies in San Francisco when ordered to join the brigade. Pfc. Don Kennedy was the BARman. Small, dark and wiry, Kennedy had been an iceman in civilian life. The fourth member of the first fire team was Dick Kelly. He was a good boxer.

The second fire team was led by Corporal Robert Hansler. He was a good mechanic and had requested motor transport duty, but was assigned to line duty where the greatest personnel shortages existed. Hansler's BARman was tall, slender Bill McCarver. McCarver was a fine rifleman who had won prizes with the M1 as well as the BAR and was an instructor on the rifle range. He liked line duty, but wanted to transfer to Marine aviation and take flight training to become a pilot. Pfc. Charles Heckman, a farm boy, was McCarver's assistant. Heckman was an expert with the M1 rifle and had had considerable experience with flame throwers. When the Korean war began Heckman had been chaplain's assistant to Lieutenant Commander Ingvoldstad, Regimental Chaplain 5th Marines. Pfc. Vandal James Mayberry was the fourth member of the 2nd fire team. He had been a telephone lineman and tractor operator around his home town, before joining the Corps.

Corporal William Bushnell was the leader of the 3rd fire team of Reese's squad. He had worked in a grocery store and at textile-pattern making before joining the Marines. A fine rifle shot, he was particularly adept at selecting concealment and cover on maneuvers. His BARman was Pfc. Robert Joseph Skye, a youngster of American-Indian descent. Before entering the Corps, he had shipped out of Seattle with the Merchant Marine. His choice was artillery. Pfc. Phil Lenz was the assistant BARman for this team. Lenz was the youngest in the squad. Small, wiry, with a ready smile, he was liked by everyone. His father was a minister-farmer. Lenz was a good hockey player; he also played the piano. The rifleman for Bushnell's fire team was Pfc. Henry Ceniceros, of Mexican parentage. Ceniceros was a good rifleman and morale builder for the squad with his cocky manner and ready tongue for jokes.

A sergeant and twelve men going to war. Lenz at seventeen was the youngest; Reese at twenty-one was the oldest. Two of them, Kelly and Mayberry, were married. Geographically as well as by parentage, they were a cross section of the nation. In the 5th Marine Regiment there were fifty-four rifle squads and there was little difference between the one led by Reese and the other fifty-three.

The squad didn't understand the idea behind their being photographed by still as well as moving picture cameras and Ceniceros was causing retakes with his clowning. When the other Marines in the company and battalion saw Sergeants Kerr and Frank, from the combat photo section, leveling their cameras on the unit, they came in for considerable joshing. They became known as "Hollywood Marines," amongst other names.

The squad came under fire for the first time as Finn's Dog Company moved up the hill to relieve Cahill and the Army company.

The first intimation they were under fire came when rocks and dust from the road and water from the rice paddy began to kick up on the right. The squad hit the ditch on the left. The fire was from long range and was inaccurate. None was hit.

With some little embarrassment because of their sudden stage fright, Reese got his squad onto the road and led the way into the compound. Mateo had a welt on his leg from a bullet-propelled pebble. Then began the grueling climb. Though men of the platoon dropped by the wayside, Reese bullied his squad into sticking it out.

When Marine pilots made the free drops of water and medical supplies from their Grasshoppers, Mateo's BAR was broken by a falling water can and his shoulder bruised. He rearmed himself with one of the abandoned rifles on the hillside.

As the sun went down, the squad looked at the steepness of the larger hill to their left and knew they would be in for another climb in the morning and perhaps a fight. At first light Emmelman's platoon led off for the top with Reese's squad in the lead. The higher they went the more enemy fire they came into.

On the top of the larger hill the fire was severe and there was the confusion of one unit moving into position and the relieved unit moving out. Emmelman was raging along his line to hurry the platoon into positions when he was wounded. Chapman was killed, Reyes of the first squad was hit and Bell was also wounded.

As yet no one in the 2nd Squad had been hit, but an enemy machine-gunner, an expert with the short burst, was doing a professional job of covering the area. Hansler and Kelly, in the same hole, put an abandoned Army helmet on a stick and held it in the air. The North Korean gunner hit it twice with his first burst of three. Reese and Mateo, sharing a hole, put a K ration box up as a shield against the sun and the cardboard was shot to pieces. As Kennedy finished digging his hole deeper, he put his entrenching tool on the top of the bank of earth and shale and the tool was hit. Bushnell of the third fire team was the first to become a casualty. As he jumped into a new hole which would place him in a better position, a bullet entered from the front rim of his helmet, glanced between the steel and fiber liner, and coming out through the rear, lodged in his back. Shortly after this, Skye, in the hole next to Bushnell, took a bullet through the arm.

This had occurred in the first forty-five minutes after the unit reached the top of the hill.

Because of the hurried, indifferent field rations and the many changes in water since leaving ship in Pusan, many men were suffering from stomach disorders. Heckman was forced to accede to the demands of dysenteric cramps. Combat veterans had counseled the newcomers that the attendant filth be ignored and to gain relief without moving from their foxholes. During the lull in firing, Heckman left his position to care for his needs. He was hit by a three-bullet burst of machine-gun fire and killed instantly.

During the rest of the day and into the next, the squad remained in their positions along the left rim of the high ridge without further casualties. Marine air erased many of the enemy positions and those that were not destroyed became wary of opening fire. When the shortage of water became acute, Ceniceros and Kennedy volunteered to obtain some. Dragging a water bag, they crawled from the top and over the rim and down the steep hill to the same stream that had supplied Macy and his patrol thirty-six hours earlier.

On the return climb, Ceniceros was overcome with the heat while struggling with the heavy container. He was evacuated to the aid station in the valley in a babbling, incoherent state. Kennedy reached the top with four gallons of water to be shared by thirty men. During the night, Ceniceros took leave of the aid station, obtained a weapon and rejoined the squad on the hilltop.

Dog Company was relieved late on the second afternoon and returned to an assembly area near Chindong-ni. From this point the push toward Sachon was to begin. In the reorganization, Second Lieutenant Michael Shinka took command of the 3rd platoon in place of the wounded Emmelman. Reese was transferred from the squad to become platoon sergeant. Baker, who had been in charge of the first fire team, took over the squad.

Because there were no replacements, the fire teams in the squad would all be short men. Hansler took over the first fire team with Mateo on the BAR and Ceniceros as a rifleman and assistant BARman. The second fire team was to be led by Mayberry with McCarver on the BAR and Kelly as the third man. In the third fire team there were but two men, Kennedy and Lenz.

In the move of the brigade south to Kosong and Changallon, the Hollywood squad saw little action. Two weeks from the day they landed in Pusan with the rest of the brigade, the 2nd squad, with the rest of Shinka's platoon, were committed to the assault of Obong-ni Ridge. In an action already described, the unit fought with valor and skill in the face of a fanatical, determined enemy.

Lenz, McCarver and Hansler were killed. Ceniceros, Mayberry, Kelly, Mateo and Reese were wounded. As is always the case, the spirit of the squad was typified by the strongest man in it. From its formation, Sergeant Reese had been the bellwether. Physically tough and psychologically prepared to accept responsibility under the most adverse circumstances, Reese personified the Marine NCO in action. Severely wounded and in grave doubt as to his ability to negotiate a steep hill to safety, Reese waved away assistance and directed that another Marine be helped.

When General Craig sent his aide into the bivouac area to find the remaining members of the 2nd Squad, he knew the casualties among them had been heavy, but he did not know the exact number. Then he saw Buck coming from the river and through the pine trees with four Marines. Craig went down the gentle roll of land to meet them. They had their weapons slung over their shoulders and had bathed in the river, but were still in dirty sweat-packed utilities. The left breast pockets of their utility jackets held letters from home.

Baker, Kennedy, Mateo and Kelly came to attention before their brigade commander. He put them at rest easily. The closer men are to battle, the narrower becomes the line between officers and men. There was little or no restraint; they became five veterans of battle speaking of friends who had fallen. They told him of the death of Heckman in the first battle, and of Lenz, McCarver and Hansler on the ridge and the wounds suffered by the others. The lines in Craig's face deepened.

When they were through he remarked about the letters in their pockets and they told him the news from home was good, and the general smiled when Kennedy told him his wife was going to have a baby. Then the four Marines came to attention and saluted and turned away. Craig's answer to them was more like a benediction than a military gesture.

Returning to his tent, he found Colonel Edward Snedeker, brigade chief-of-staff, waiting for him.

"We've just received orders from Eighth Army. We're to move at once to Changwon and be prepared to counterattack in the 25th Division sector—"

CHAPTER VII

The Enemy Recrosses the Naktong and Miryang Is Threatened. The Central Perimeter Is Saved Again. September 3-5

Without a pause, with scarcely time to pay homage to the Marines who had died on Obong-ni Ridge and the Naktong salient, the brigade entrained and entrucked for a hurried shift to the south to face another threatened breakthrough. Again the depleted rifle companies were assigned personnel from brigade and regimental staffs, artillery and service units. Despite these measures, none of the assault units could be brought to strength.

At one o'clock in the morning on the twenty-first of August, thirty-two hours from the Naktong, the brigade was closing on Changwon and went into positions in the 25th Army Division sector. Wood's artillery battalion was detached and ordered to Chindong-ni, where they went into action.

The first replacement draft arrived from the United States and was joined to the rifle companies. During the next week the Marines conducted patrols behind the 25th Division zone of action, and at the same time held small unit training problems to indoctrinate the replacements.

On the morning of the twenty-ninth of August, members of the brigade who could be spared from patrol assembled on the "bean patch" parade grounds for a ceremony. A bobtailed band had been formed from bandsmen not yet assigned to rifle squads. To the tune of the *Marine Corps Hymn,* with Schryver and Muetzel as platoon leaders, eighty-seven men marched before the reviewing officers. This unit was known as the Purple Heart Company and was commanded by First Lieutenant Robert Bohn. Every man in it had been wounded and returned to duty. Purple Heart medals were awarded by General Craig. Technical Sergeant Ernest

DeFazio received his third such award; Lieutenant "Metz" Muetzel and Corporal Marvin Wells their second.

After the distribution of medals, Syngman Rhee, president of the Republic of Korea, made a speech to the assembled troops. He told them: ". . . you Marines brought hope to my people. You brought us victory when all we had known was defeat. . . ."

The tradition of officer leadership in the Marine Corps was tragically illustrated on this day. Six rifle company commanders brought their units ashore at Pusan on the third day of August. In the next twenty-six days of combat, five of these officers had been wounded; of the eighteen rifle platoon leaders arriving in Korea, nine were wounded and four killed in action in the same period.

Until further replacements arrived from the United States, sergeants would be leading platoons, corporals in charge of squads and Pfc.'s running fire teams.

Marines garnish a regimented existence with rumor. They call rumor "scuttlebutt." By the time the Purple Heart parade was over, their talk was filled with it.

"I got some hot scoop."

"What?"

"Colonel Snedeker flew to Japan."

"Maybe he's got friends over there."

"I'll say he has. The whole God-damned 1st Division's over there."

"The hell you say! Is that straight dope?"

"We're goin' to join the division and make a landing in th' rear of these bastards. We'll be ramming bayonets up their bung holes in a week."

"Two more weeks of this crap an' we wouldn't have enough left to hold another Purple Heart parade."

"They got ships waiting for us in Pusan right now. We go aboard as soon as they're loaded."

"Okay, you guys, shake the lead. We're moving out."

"What's up, Macy? Are we headin' for Pusan?"

"Pusan, hell! We're goin' back to the —— Naktong. There's been another breakthrough."

On the morning of the first of September Craig received orders from General Walker to be prepared to move at once to an unknown destination. To the dismay and consternation of the brigade staff, the movement of heavy equipment to Pusan for embarkation was halted. Further preparation and planning for the Inchon landing were suspended. Wood's artillery was ordered to return from Chindong-ni and rejoin the brigade.

By six o'clock in the evening Craig had established his advance CP at Miryang; at 11:30 that night further orders were received from Eight Army to move the brigade to a position in the rear of the 9th Army Infantry Regiment. With Roise's battalion acting as a covering force, the brigade moved into its assigned positions early the next morning. At 2:30 in the afternoon orders came through from General Walker placing the brigade under the operational control of the 2nd Army Division.

Accompanied by Major Frank Stewart, assistant operations officer, Craig took a helicopter to Kyungjo and reported to Major General Laurence Keiser, commander of the Army unit. A conference was held immediately to discuss the employment of the Marines. In addition to Keiser and Craig there were Colonels Collier and McClain from the Eighth Army staff, and Colonel Tulley, chief-of-staff for the 2nd Division.

Tulley explained the plan of attack desired of the Marines. Craig objected inasmuch as the plan called for the brigade to attack through the 9th Regiment lines in an extended formation against a number of objectives simultaneously.

Craig informed Keiser that he would prefer to execute the attack against successive objectives, taking one at a time and while maintaining depth in the formation of his brigade. Craig's plan was adopted. Collier then requested that the brigade attack at once because the situation was desperate. The Eighth Army staff officer stated that he doubted that the 9th Regiment could hold; that all available troops had been thrown into the line.

Craig opposed the plan of attacking immediately. It was late afternoon and only the forward elements of the brigade were in the area. It meant committing the Marine units hurriedly and piecemeal. Craig told Keiser he preferred to attack at first light with his entire force in hand and the Tactical Air Control Section available to conduct air strikes.

With some reluctance the Army commanders agreed and orders were issued for the Marines to attack on the following morning and restore the former positions of the 9th Infantry.

In the eleven days since the Marines had left the Miryang-Yongsan-

Naktong area, the enemy had once again crossed the river in force against the 2nd Army Division. Obong-ni Ridge was lost and Yongsan captured. A counterattack had cleared the town, but the enemy was on the high ground eight hundred yards to the west. The 9th Regiment had been badly mauled and engineer, tank and miscellaneous troops had been thrown into the line to hold until the Marines arrived. Enemy forces forming this critical salient were elements of the 2nd, 4th and 9th North Korean Divisions.

Craig issued the attack order and Murray set up his regimental CP in the vicinity of the 9th Regimental CP in order to co-ordinate the relief of that unit. He ordered Newton and Roise to move their battalions into position for the relief and to jump off in the attack. At daylight it was discovered that a night attack had driven the 9th Regiment into the outskirts of Yongsan. The Marine attack was delayed as the two battalions fought their way to the line of departure.

As soon as Houghton's Recon Company was relieved by elements of the 24th Division, of guarding the vital pontoon bridge at Susan-ni, Craig sent them to Murray to protect the left flank. Murray dispatched them immediately to Chonni to establish a strongpoint in that area. Taplett's battalion was ordered into position three thousand yards due east of Obong-ni with the mission of establishing local security along the avenues of approach leading into the regimental positions.

For the first time since landing in Korea, Craig and Murray were confident enough of the flanks to attack with two battalions abreast and one in reserve. Heretofore, because flank security was not assured, the attack had been made with one battalion in the assault and the remaining two in column to assure control in depth.

With Newton to the left of Roise, the second battle of the Naktong began. Objective number one was a ridge line west of the line of departure. Intervening was an eight-hundred-to-one-thousand-yard rice paddy. The boundary between the battalions was a road bisecting the rice land. It was the only entrant for the tanks or vehicles.

At 8:55 the Marines started across the open, low ground. Immediately the advancing units were taken under fire from long range small arms. It was not of an intensity to halt the attack. From the battalions' areas 81 and 4.2 mortar fire was placed on the enemy positions and the enemy fire was discouraged though not entirely halted.

Thirty minutes after the jump-off, Fenton's unit came under such heavy fire as to pin it down and stop the advance. Corsairs were called down immediately. Using napalm, the high ground held by the enemy was burnt out and once again the advance resumed. From the time of the request until the Marine airmen unloaded their bombs, only seven minutes elapsed.

Though pinned down intermittently in the crossing of low, exposed ground, through the immediate use of supporting mortars, artillery and close air support, Fenton reported he was on the forward slope and prepared to make the assault on the high ground at 10:55. His unit had negotiated the paddy crossing in exactly two hours. Ten minutes later Stevens had his company abreast of Fenton.

On the right flank Roise's 2nd had a wider paddy to cross. In addition, there were several small hills scattered throughout which had to be secured as the unit advanced. As these were seized, the 2nd came under heavy fire from the village of Myong-ni, as well as mortar fire from Hill 116 to their immediate front. Again Corsairs were called down in conjunction with mortar and tank fire.

With "H. J." Smith (the new commander of Dog Company on the right of Jaskilka's Easy Company) the units crossed over the low ground and through the village and came to the forward slope of Hill 116. With Jaskilka's company furnishing the base of fire support, Smith made the assault of the hill from the north. Air observation reported the enemy retreating from Fenton's and Stevens' assault. Smith's mission was to reach the crest of Hill 116 to cut off this withdrawal.

The initial advance was lightly opposed, but as the Marines reached the northern crest, the enemy rushed reinforcements in from the south and heavy fighting resulted. Depleted by casualties, Smith was ordered to dig in and hold what he had gained.

While Smith was fighting to his objective, Fenton and Stevens were having a race with the enemy defending their ridge line. Evidently caught offbalance by the swift advance of the 1st Battalion, the enemy began rushing reinforcements to the high ground facing the assault of Able and Baker. The Marines won the race by thirty minutes and caught the enemy coming across the rice paddy on the far side. What transpired was a "turkey shoot" in the vernacular of a rifleman. There was a chattering of rifles and BAR's on the mustard-green lines of men running in ragged retreat. Fenton's sweating Marines enjoyed the interval—the time it takes a frightened man to run four hundred yards uphill—as they got into firing positions which pleased them and began to fire as casually as on the range at Quantico.

"Pulled that one a bit—"

There were many casualties inflicted as Marine rifle fire reached out and killed men at four and five hundred yards. Very few of the enemy escaped. Those who did ran into the fire of Wood's artillery. Aerial observers reported, "Excellent results."

During the day, the 1st and 2nd Battalions received 157 casualties, of which 34 had been killed.

As these casualties were being evacuated, the 1st Battalion aid station was receiving sporadic sniper fire, which hampered the work of the staff considerably. Tiring of such activity and knowing the Marine wounded could not receive the undivided attention of Nelson, the battalion surgeon, Corpsmen Melvin Hogan and Jack Richter picked up their weapons and went into the hills. Thirty minutes later they returned with five prisoners. In the hills were two enemy "not returnables." The sniper fire on the aid station ceased.

The Marine air squadrons on the two carriers had worked out a shuttle system whereby one unit was on station while the other returned to refuel and rearm. During the day the Marine airmen delivered four close air support missions (four to six planes in each) to the 2nd Battalion, and three for the 1st. Other Marine aircraft under the control of Klondike (VMO-6) strafed troops, destroyed buildings where the low-flying observation planes detected enemy troops hiding and eliminated sixteen gun and mortar positions. In addition, the Corsairs were over the Army front lines giving them assistance when requested.

Master Sergeant Herb Valentine won the promise of a can of beer from Murray by spotting twelve enemy artillery pieces and some three hundred artillerymen and infantry in camouflaged positions south of Songnigok, a village about two thousand yards northeast of Obong-ni. An air strike destroyed the guns and killed or dispersed the troops. Murray didn't have the beer at the time and payment was deferred, but Valentine appreciated the thought nonetheless.

This was the first time for many of the Army ground commanders to witness the Marine system of close air support. Their enthusiasm was unbridled. Colonel Paul Freeman, commander of the 23rd Regiment on the right flank of the brigade, wrote General Ridgway in Washington:

We must have Tac Air in direct support of infantry regiments just as we have artillery; and communications must be direct and simplified. Infantry can't do the job alone. Infantry and artillery is a good team, but only by adding adequate and efficient air support can we succeed without devastating losses . . . The Marines on our left were a sight to behold. Not only was their equipment superior or equal to ours, but they had squadrons of air in direct support. They used it like artillery. It was, "Hey, Joe, this is Smitty, knock the left of that ridge in from Item Company." They had it *day and night* . . . General, we just have to have air support like that or we might as well disband the Infantry and join the Marines. . . .

After having led his regiment through six months of grueling warfare, Freeman reaffirmed his sentiments on close air support at a briefing at GHQ, Tokyo.

As the battalions tied in their lines for the night they were informed they would have close support furnished them by Marine night fighters. The first night attack was run at 10:15. From the ground the forward controller talked the plane into the target.

"We're getting mortar fire; our position, first ridge line east of rice paddy—enemy on third ridge east of paddy; one thousand yards east of burning village."

"I see three fires," the pilot answered. "Not certain which one. Do you see me?"

"Saw you in the moon, but lost you. Blink your lights—okay, got you now. Will mark target with white phosphorus. You are north of target; watch for WP, on its way—out."

The pilot sees the mushroom of white smoke on the ridge. He shoves the throttle forward and in a thirty-degree dive makes his attack. Oriented now, he repeats his run. The enemy mortar fire stops.

"On the nose—thanks."

Reinburg's VMF(N) 513 was the only unit to fly single engine planes over Korea at night. Obviously the task of control is manifold, but not insurmountable, and the value to the ground troops has been proven.

Dive bombing and strafing at night are not easy jobs. The pilot is about the busiest man ever to fly a plane. He does the work that is normally assigned to eight men in a multiengined bomber. He is, simultaneously, pilot, gunner, bombardier, radioman, navigator, radar operator and aerologist. This squadron seldom missed a night and VMF(N) 513 flew more than two thousand hours of dusk-to-dawn missions in one month.

After a brief time for orientation the Marine night fighters were able to give the riflemen night support by knocking out mortar positions, artillery emplacements and hindering the movement of troops. Armed with nearly two tons of explosives of one type or another, these Marine pilots became expert at selecting enemy artillery flashes and knocking out the gun that made it. They didn't accept the bait the North Koreans put out by making false flashes. The enemy were never able to duplicate the color of the artillery flash with the explosives they used. In a night fire fight it was a comparatively simple task to pick out the enemy strongpoints and destroy them. Another method of indicating the point of desired attack was to have two widely separated machine guns fire tracers over the defiladed target. The night fighters bombed the **X** point where the tracers crossed.

Rockets were found to be too risky for night use. The flashing discharge from the plane temporarily blinded the pilots and they were doing enough blind flying without adding to it by using this weapon. It was soon learned that the enemy heartily disliked these night intrusions and would cease fire as soon as they heard planes overhead. After discharging all their armament, the pilots would cruise about, and by changing propeller pitch would simulate diving attacks.

From ten at night until 5:45 the next morning, Marine night fighters made six controlled attacks and numerous others on a search-and-attack basis. The two forward battalions had a quiet night.

At eleven o'clock that night Murray directed Taplett to pass through Roise, and with Newton on the right to continue the attack. Promptly at eight o'clock, the 1st and 3rd jumped off. Twenty minutes later Taplett reported he had reached his first objective and was preparing to assault Hill 116. This was carried with light casualties. By now it was evident the enemy had withdrawn during the night and was fighting a delaying action. There were indications of the withdrawal becoming a disorderly rout.

In the 1st Battalion zone of action, Stevens and Fenton advanced rapidly. Twenty minutes after the morning attack began Fenton had his company in the enemy's division command post. Tents were still up and equipment was left throughout the area. Two Russian T-34 tanks, unmanned and in excellent condition, were captured. They were turned over to Army ordnance for examination, inasmuch as they were the first enemy tanks to be captured in operable condition.

By 3:15 in the afternoon Newton's battalion was on the high ground less than two thousand yards northeast of the old battle area of "No Name" Ridge. With Taplett and Newton affording one another supporting fire the advance continued with increasing signs of demoralization in the enemy ranks. Before the two battalions dug in for the night they had advanced nearly three miles.

Once again the Marine airmen carried the attack to the retreating enemy. Behind their swift and low-flying strikes they left the roads littered with dead and abandoned equipment. Counterbattery fire by Wood's artillery destroyed nine enemy field pieces and raised fearful destruction in the rear areas.

The night passed quietly until early morning when the enemy threw a heavy counterattack on Bohn's front. It had begun to rain and the enemy was able to obtain close-in positions before the assault. The attack was repulsed quickly. The enemy did not press the attack boldly and it was thought that this was a diversion for the main effort they were to make against the 9th Army Regiment on the extreme right flank. The jump-off was delayed thirty minutes as Wood's artillery turned to support the 9th, and the Marine attack could not be pressed until the attack on the flank was resolved.

Denied close air support because of weather, the 1st and 3rd Battalions jumped off at 8:30. As the zone of action narrowed between the 9th Regiment of the 2nd Army Division and the Naktong-Yongsan road, Taplett was ordered to take his battalion to the left flank of Newton and continue the attack to the south of the road. The advance continued rapidly until midmorning when the battalions began receiving fire from Obong-ni Ridge. Enemy troops could be seen digging in on the old battleground. Newton was ordered to halt his advance until the 9th Regiment tied in with his right flank, and Taplett could sideslip to his right to gain contact with Stevens.

Throughout the day it had been raining hard and aerial observation was impossible. The moisture on the hot, parched earth created a miasmic ground fog which restricted frontal visibility. At 2:20 in the afternoon, Fenton came under a savage counterattack of ground troops supported by tanks. The troops came from the troublesome village of Tugok and the low ground off the road.

The enemy tanks moved eastward along the same road as they had in the first battle of the Naktong. In this case, however, the surprise came to the Marine Pershings. The lead tank of the Marine section had been giving Fenton support fire, and as it came around the bend in the road its 90 mm. gun was trained to the left flank. The enemy tanks took it under fire and destroyed it. The second Pershing had to pass around the first to obtain a field of fire and was put out of action. An Army tank also was destroyed. The crew escaped without casualties. The remaining Marine tanks withdrew to blocking positions where all could bring their fire to bear at once when the enemy came around "death curve."

A 2.36 rocket team from Fenton's unit got into position on the forward slope to the right of the road and took the lead T-34 under fire. It slowed the lead tank, but didn't halt it. Lieutenant Dale Brown rushed forward with a section of 3.5's. They arrived as the 2.36's were firing their last rocket. Corporal Walter Carrow got into position quickly with his rocket launcher. In order to obtain a clear field of fire he had to stand silhouetted against the skyline. Despite heavy machine-gun fire from the tanks, he coolly and quickly got off nine rounds, totally destroying a T-34. With the rest of the rocket section in action, the remaining enemy tanks were destroyed. Credit for all three enemy tanks went to the 3.5's.

In the meantime Fenton was having considerable difficulty containing the pressure on his lines. The ridge he was occupying was oval-shaped and there were a number of blind spots in his field of fire and the enemy was using these as corridors of attack. The continual rain had made his radios inoperable and he could not contact battalion to request mortar and artillery support.

Fenton called Pfc. Bill Wilson to him. "The Army is coming up on our right flank. Contact them and tell them my radios are out; ask them to bring artillery onto my front."

Wilson took off to the north. Running along the reverse slope of the ridge line, he came to the point where Baker Company flank ended and the 2nd Battalion of the 9th Army Regiment was joining in. Quickly he found the company commander and explained the situation. The officer accompanied Wilson to an observation point where the areas of fire could be seen.

As Wilson was pointing out the target area a burst of machine-gun fire wounded the Army commander. Wilson saw the officer evacuated, and picking up the radio gave directions to the artillery. When he had saturated the village and routes of approach, he turned the artillery onto the crest of Obong-ni where he saw the enemy setting up a field piece. He called a third mission onto trucks he saw to the west of the ridge.

Satisfied that he had fulfilled the request of Fenton, he returned to Baker Company.

The fire fight on Fenton's front was becoming a kill-or-be-killed engagement. Groups of thirty to forty enemy attackers would assault along the line seeking local penetrations. In the mist, slime and rain the defender and attacker were locked in a battle that would come to bayonet as Fenton's unit began to run low on ammunition.

First Sergeant Leonard Young was shot through the chest as he moved from position to position on the crest. The litterbearers took him down the hill.

"Don't let 'em fall back, Cap'n," he cried to Fenton as he was borne past. Machine Gunner Leonard Hayworth left his gun to get ammunition for his weapon. There was none. He went back to his position with a bayonet—to wait.

Runners from Fenton got back to Newton's CP and the 81 mm. mortars were placed on the company front. When the fire-for-effect was completed, the mortars had only eighteen rounds remaining. Stevens sent Muetzel and his 2nd Platoon to Fenton with ammunition and grenades.

Muetzel's arrival came at the climax of the battle. The boxes of grenades were torn open and the explosives were tossed forward much in the fashion of a baseball relay from center field, to second base, to home plate—only in this case the catcher, on taking the throw, pulled the pin and hurled it down the slope. Before the attack was repulsed Stevens sent a mortar section and McMullen's platoon across the road. The savagery of the fighting may be judged by the casualties to the Marines. Twenty-three had been wounded and two killed. Of the wounded two were to die later.

With the failure of the tank-infantry assault, the enemy appeared to have accepted the fact that further retirement was necessary. Enemy troops could be seen withdrawing from Obong-ni Ridge and moving westward toward the Naktong. As the Marines were preparing to advance, orders were received to hold present positions and not to prepare too elaborate defenses.

Dave Duncan, *Life* Magazine photographer, confirmed the rumors that began to run along the line. He told Fenton, "Ike, the brigade's going to be pulled out and sent back to Pusan."

"Th' hell you say!"

"I just got the dope at battalion."

With ill-concealed impatience the Marines waited for the relieving units to arrive. By now it was general knowledge that Freeman's 23rd

Army Regiment was to relieve the Marines by midnight and the trip to Pusan for embarkation was to begin.

"Let's get outta here before some other outfit blows a cork an' we gotta go plug it."

"Ol' Pusan 'U,' how I love you! Just keep those ships waiting—we'll be there."

The relieving Army units brought news from the States.

"Did you hear what President Truman said about you Gyrenes?"

"What?"

"He said you guys were nothing but a police force for the Navy."

"If we're nothing but police, I wish to God he'd give us an easier beat. A man can get hurt on this one."

Early in the afternoon of the fifth of September, General Walker directed that the Marine Brigade be relieved by midnight and move at once by rail and truck to Pusan. At two o'clock in the morning, Craig received a message from General O. P. Smith to mount out in accordance with previous plans. Before noon on the seventh of September, the brigade was in Pusan and began loading out. Eight days remained for them to join the 1st Marine Division, brief troop commanders and troops and lead the assault on Inchon.

The second battle of the Naktong cost the Marines 220 casualties, of which 39 were killed in action. During the period from August 7 to September 7, the brigade received 903 casualties. Among these were 22 Navy medical corpsmen who lived, marched and fought with the Marines. Six had been killed in action and 16 wounded while performing their duties of attending the wounded.

BATTLE CASUALTIES

Killed in action	149
Died of wounds	14
Missing in action	9
Died of disease	1
Wounded in action	730
Total	903

The 1st Provisional Marine Brigade, activated on the seventh of July, 1950, was deactivated and joined the 1st Marine Division on the thirteenth of September. While engaged in the battle to hold the Pusan perimeter, the brigade traveled more than three hundred eighty miles in

5th Marine Regiment (1st Provisional Brigade)

Changes in command of rifle companies and rifle platoons due to casualties for period August 7 to September 5, 1950

1st Battalion		2nd Battalion		3rd Battalion	
Able	Baker	Dog	Easy	George	How
Stevens	Tobin WIA Fenton	Finn WIA Zimmer WIA Uffelman* Smith	Kittredge WIA Sweeney Jaskilka	Bohn WIA(2)**	Fegan WIA Lennon* Wildman
1st Platoon	*1st Platoon*	*1st Platoon*	*1st Platoon*	*1st Platoon*	*1st Platoon*
Sebilian WIA T/Sgt. McMullen	Schryver WIA**	Emmelman WIA Shinka WIA Heck KIA	Arkadis WIA Deptula	Cahill WIA M/Sgt. Ryder	Williams
2nd Platoon	*2nd Platoon*	*2nd Platoon*	*2nd Platoon*	*2nd Platoon*	*2nd Platoon*
Johnston KIA T/Sgt. Lawson WIA** Muetzel WIA (2)**	Taylor KIA T/Sgt. Lischeski* T/Sgt. Sallaberry	Oakley KIA T/Sgt. Crowson* Howard	Nolan WIA Christiansen	Duncan WIA S/Sgt. Perez	Post
3rd Platoon	*3rd Platoon*	*3rd Platoon*	*3rd Platoon*	*3rd Platoon*	*3rd Platoon*
Fox WIA** T/Sgt. Bolkow* T/Sgt. Milar	Crowling WIA S/Sgt. Cirinelli Morris	Reid KIA Sullivan WIA T/Sgt. Dickerson WIA Hanifin	Eddy WIA	Westerman WIA Counselman	Di Lorenzo

* Denotes temporary command under battle conditions until replacements could be sent forward.
** Denotes wounds received but the man remained in action.

less than a month while moving to attack positions. Three major engagements were entered into in addition to numerous small unit actions.

From Chingdong-ni to Sachon, to both battles of the Naktong, the Marines fought against a numerically superior enemy, yet they never failed to take their assigned objectives.

In these thirty-one days of battle the Marine Brigade met, defeated and largely destroyed the 83rd Mechanized Brigade, three regiments of the 4th North Korean Division and a brigade of the 9th North Korean Division. Casualties committed on the enemy by ground and air attack were 3,400 killed, 9,600 wounded and 69 captured. In addition, the Marines captured many pieces of heavy artillery, recaptured six U. S. Army 105 mm. howitzers, plus numerous small arms and vehicles. Eight enemy tanks were met and destroyed by various arms demonstrating the effectiveness of American antitank weapons against enemy armor *if properly employed.*

Despite this remarkable record the losses to the Marines in the south had been costly in more than numbers. Among those killed, or so badly wounded that retirement from the Corps would be necessary, were some of the finest junior officers and NCO's in the Marine Corps; men such as Blackmon, Reid, Oakley, Taylor, Bruce, Twedt and Budd are not readily replaced.

Sergeant Augustus Siefken of the Korean Embassy Guard rode with Ambassador Muccio by the Pusan docks as the brigade was loading out.

"I've got a lot of friends in that outfit, Your Excellency," Siefken said.

"I presume you have."

"I'd sure like to go with 'em."

"Yes?"

"What would Your Excellency do if I just took off an' went with them?"

"Why, I don't know, Siefken. I suppose they'd send you back to me for disciplinary action."

"I'd come back soon as the fightin' sort of dies down after the landing."

"I won't encourage you in leaving your post, Sergeant, but I'll promise you this. When you come back, I don't believe you'll be dealt with too harshly."

That night Siefken "joined" the 5th Marines for the Inchon landing.

CHAPTER VIII

The Minute Men of 1950: The Marine Reserves Are Called

After bringing the brigade to strength, the 1st Marine Division had slightly more than three thousand officers and men remaining. In the next twenty-seven days the division would have to form two war-strength rifle regiments, two battalions of artillery, a tank and motor transport battalion, a shore party and other supporting units.

Between July 31 and August 10, the division joined 6,831 men from the 2nd Marine Division, 812 from the 1st Replacement draft, 3,630 regulars from posts and stations throughout the world, and over 10,000 officers and men from the Organized Reserves.

Five days after the brigade had sailed, President Truman authorized the calling of Organized Reserve units. Ten days later, Reserve battalions from Los Angeles and San Francisco and companies from Oakland and Phoenix reported at Camp Pendleton—the Minute Men of 1950.

The Minute Men of 1950—a fine-sounding phrase, but one that was lost on the harried Reserve commanders as they attempted to form their scattered members into a unit, while answering a thousand phone calls and meeting a hundred callers—parents, wives and politicians.

Hardship deferments were requested; some were granted, some were refused and mistakes were made. The orders of mobilization read, "Ordered to extended active duty in excess of thirty days." This did not give a young man starting a new business much to go on. There were a few who tried every means, from political influence to faked medical certificates, to keep from going. More, many more, reported at once (though their pay did not start until the day they entrained), and worked and slept in the armory for a week, packing the unit equipment.

Then there were others who paid their own plane fare across the continent to make it back to the unit in time. There were still others, former Marines who were not in an Organized Reserve unit, who rushed to the closest training center and begged to be taken on. Under the existing regulations, this could not be done. As volunteer Reserves they would be processed individually.

The Los Angeles area had so many volunteers who wanted to go they were called the "Wailing Wall Gang" as they waited hopefully outside the armory for a change in regulations.

Despite a staggered schedule for the arrival of reserve units, facilities at Pendleton were taxed to the utmost as new areas and tent camps were opened. Meals, such as they were, were served on a twenty-four hour, seven days a week basis. Reserves arriving on one train were fed, billeted and turned out to assist in debarking the next unit.

As new arrivals detrained they would contact the first "old timer" they saw on the rail siding.

"What's the scoop, Mac?"

"Ain't had time to find out."

"How long you been here?"

"Thirty-six hours, and no sack time yet."

The housekeeping details were minor in comparison to those of selecting Reserve personnel who would be assigned to the division. It was vital to the individual Reservist, as well as the division, that only those who were qualified by previous training or military experience be included in the organization. This task had to be performed quickly, but with a minimum degree of error; the life of the Reservist as well as those in his unit was at stake if it turned out that he was untrained.

In the classification of the Reserves pouring into Pendleton, two categories were set up: Combat-ready and Noncombat-ready. Combat-ready was defined as "Reservists who had been members of the Organized Reserve two years and had attended one summer camp and seventy-two drills," or "two summer camps and thirty-two drills," or "who were veterans with more than ninety days' service in the Marine Corps." Noncombat-ready applied to all Reservists who did not meet these standards. This latter category was further divided into a Recruit Class for those who had been in the Organized Reserve less than one year or who had poor drill attendance records.

The establishment of these standards was neither hastily arrived at nor lightly considered, but represented the collective judgment of some of the most experienced field commanders in the Corps.

Serving to increase the problem of selecting Combat-ready Reservists was the fact that, while the majority of the Reserve units reported with their records in excellent shape, many either became separated from their records in the hurried movement or were unable properly to prepare them. Inadvertently the records of one Reserve unit were burned.

By itself, this lack would not have resulted in a serious situation but, coupled with the narrow time limitations, it created a problem which had unfortunate repercussions. The margin of error in the selection of Reservists for combat was increased and the payment of some personnel was delayed as much as two months.

To overcome the lack of records, Reservists were interviewed before the decision was made as to whether or not they were qualified for Combat-ready category. In these interviews, Reservists often manifested a strong desire to be classified as Combat-ready, and this desire influenced many of them to present an overly optimistic picture of previous training. Some resorted to outright exaggeration in order to make the "team."

A Reservist's statement that he considered himself qualified was not accepted as proof of his fitness, and his Reserve unit officers were questioned. Any Reservist who felt that he required more training, and so suggested, was at once removed from further consideration for immediate assignment to combat duty with no prejudice.

Approximately fifty per cent of the Reserves reporting at Pendleton were placed in the Noncombat-ready or Recruit Class. Fifteen per cent were selected for duty with the division. The balance was assigned to post and station billets to replace regular Marines who had previously joined the division.

The formation of the 1st Battalion, 7th Marines is an example of the speed of organization required. Lieutenant Colonel Ray Davis reported in to Pendleton on the morning of the twenty-first of August. Two hours later he was assigned command of the 1st Battalion. As yet there were no troops in his unit. All Davis had was a small cadre of veteran officers and NCO's.

Davis got into a jeep and drove down Rattlesnake Canyon past the old Ranch House and onto Basilone Road. Each installation along the twenty-one mile route—Chappo Flats, the rifle range, the artillery impact area, the infiltration course—was a reminder of the work to be done and the training that could not be done because there was no time.

At Tent Camp Two, the row-on-row of empty tents was the final shocking reminder that he was the commander of a battalion which existed only on paper. He called to meeting the veterans already assigned to his command.

"We have a week to form a battalion," Davis told them. "At no time in our careers will we be faced with greater responsibility—sixty per cent of our men will be Reserves. Some of these men will be veterans from the last war, many will be youngsters who have been in Reserve organizations. It is our job to get them ready for combat. If we fail, they'll forfeit their lives. There are only twenty-four hours in a day, but we'll use all of them."

This talk set the tone and tempo for the formation of a battalion which had no superior in Korea. Through every daylight hour the newly assigned men took to the field for instruction and training exercises under the veterans. On more than one occasion the Marines in the 1st Battalion lined up at night to draw equipment and clothing so the daylight hours would be free for uninterrupted training. There were midnight familiarization courses in weapons and afterward squad leaders took their men into the hills for small unit exercises.

First Lieutenant Chew Een Lee wrung a promise from Davis that he would be given a rifle platoon and not be kept at battalion headquarters as an interpreter. Officers of the 1st Battalion still talk about Corporal LeRoy Pearl. A trained radio operator, Pearl convinced Davis he would be more valuable as a fire team leader than as a communicator, and he was so assigned.

Imbuing the other three members of the team with his spirit, Pearl held night courses in familiarization with weapons. When the team had reached the proficiency Pearl demanded, he took them into the hills beyond the camp.

It was 2:30 in the morning when he led his men from the company street, across the dry creek and through the poplars into the black brush beyond. In the moonlight the firebreaks were wide scars in the sterile hills.

"The problem tonight," Pearl told his men, "is a fire team attack on an enemy strongpoint. Now remember the hand and arm signals." He deployed the two riflemen on the flanks of the BARman. Pearl pointed out the "head" on the other side of the creek. "There's the strongpoint."

"You're not kidding, Mac," the BARman answered as the four began to crawl through the brush toward the latrine.

Twenty-seven days later, Davis took his battalion ashore at Inchon.

Colonel "Chesty" Puller had won his fight to fight. Winning a regiment had cost Puller $1,019—$19 for commercial telegrams to the commandant, assistant commandant and General Erskine requesting a regiment, and $1,000 to transport his family from San Francisco to his home in Saluda, Virginia. A portion of this expense was reimbursable, but Puller figured the rest a good investment.

Puller reported in at Pendleton on the fourth of August. He formed the 1st Marines and sailed for Korea ten days later. In the Mediterranean, the 3rd Battalion, 6th Marines was on station with the U. S. fleet in that area. They boarded transports and raced through the Suez Canal, across the Indian Ocean and into the Pacific to join the division at Kobe, Japan. They became the 3rd Battalion, 7th Marines and landed at Inchon.

The true nature of this accomplishment, unprecedented in the annals of military history, becomes increasingly clear when it is realized the 1st Marine Division, with only three thousand as a cadre, reached a war strength in excess of twenty-three thousand officers and men and landed at Inchon in a period of fifty-three days.

Behind these time and space factors are the answers to the questions many families and Marine Reservists are asking. Will it happen again? Why were Marine Reserves so hastily recalled to active duty? Why were they committed to battle so quickly?

To find the answer, a review of the record leading up to the Korean War should be made. It may give the Reservist an answer to events which have affected his life and may affect it in the future. History indicates there will be more Koreas, and Marines will be the first to go to these "international fires" as long as the statement "as the President may direct" remains on the statute books. In the past one hundred seventy-five years Presidents have "directed" the Marines to make more than two hundred landings in foreign countries without benefit of declaration of war. "Police action" appears to be a more modern term.

The Marine Corps never has, and probably never will receive consideration in time and space factors. The picture of Sergeant Quirk and

Captain Flagg brawling for the favors of a girl just before moving into battle (to the strains of the *Marine Corps Hymn*) is for the dreamer, the romanticist and the screen writers. The realist in the Marines, Reserve or regular, is the man who has his will drawn and sea bag packed.

Between the twenty-ninth of June and the twenty-eighth of July, General MacArthur sent six dispatches to the Joint Chiefs of Staff relative to the employment of Marines in Korea. As the military situation worsened, these dispatches became more urgent in tone until the final one demanded the use of commercial shipping to get the Marines to the battle area if government transportation were not available.

For the second time in less than a decade, Marine Reserves were hastily called back to active duty. Fifteen per cent of the Marine landing force at Inchon was made up of civilian Marines. This percentage grew to nearly fifty per cent in the battle of the Chosin Reservoir.

For most of the young Reservists, this was high adventure. War always is to those who have not yet been in one. As one young Marine put it, "I had my summer plans set. I was going to Pendleton with my outfit for two weeks' training. After that I was going to the mountains and sack out on the beach at Tahoe. Then things happened. I went to Pendleton all right, but I kept right on going. I saw a beach—Inchon. I saw mountains north of Hungnam and spent considerable time around a mountain lake—Frozen Chosin. Ten whole months and it didn't cost me a dime. I got two Purple Hearts, a frozen foot and a Chinese bugle. How can you beat a deal like that?"

This was the attitude of the majority of Reserves who had not been in the last war. The call to active duty was greeted with enthusiasm. To a few of the Reservists called for the second time, there was no such virgin enthusiasm but rather some bitterness. The general attitude was, "A big war—okay, I'll go. I'd expect to, but this thing in Korea—I don't think I should be called."

These were the Reservists in the twenty-four to thirty age group. These men had been in the previous war and had been released from active duty in 1946. They were just becoming established in businesses or professions when they had to settle personal affairs in a matter of hours and once again go to war.

From Shelby, Montana, to El Paso, from Boston to San Francisco, the Marine Corps was criticized for its hasty mobilization and early commitment of Reserves. Headquarters Marine Corps was deluged with letters from families, civic groups and members of Congress. Congressmen who voted in favor of the presidential order mobilizing the Reserves, wrote critical letters to the commandant when Reserve sons of constituents were recalled.

In the parlance of an artilleryman, the critics were bracketing the wrong target. The Joint Chiefs of Staff ordered the commandant of the Marine Corps to send a division to Korea and to have it in the battle area on a certain date. At no time prior to the issuance of this order did the JCS ask the commandant his views on the subject.

At the outbreak of hostilities the strength of the regular Marine Corps was slightly more than seventy-four thousand. The Corps was ordered to send a division of twenty-three thousand and an air arm of nearly four thousand. In addition it had to continue to maintain Marine detachments aboard Naval vessels, guard companies at Naval shore installations, Embassy guards, recruit training commands at Parris Island and San Diego and sizable forces at Quantico, Camp Pendleton, Lejeune (to rebuild the 2nd Division) and the El Toro and Cherry Point Air Stations. Obviously this was impossible to do with seventy-four thousand men.

The President authorized the mobilization of the Reserve. Congress sanctioned this authorization. The Marine Corps fulfilled its obligations by organizing, training and sending to the Korean war a hard-hitting mixture of regulars and Reserves which made every fight a winning one.

Had the regular Marine establishment consisted of twenty thousand additional men, the Reserves could have been recalled in planned stages, giving the civilian Marine time to make adjustments at home and to receive refresher training before going into combat.

As it was, the regulars met the first shock. The brigade comprised the raggedy-ass regulars who took the fearful losses in July and August and led the Inchon landing in September.

On July 16, 1941, the commanding general of the 1st Provisional Marine Brigade received an order from the chief of naval operations to "defend Iceland against hostile attacks." Twenty-three days later, the Marines landed in Iceland. In this brigade of Marines, hurriedly assembled from forces on the east and west coasts of the United States, was a battalion commander, Lieutenant Colonel O. P. Smith. In one year less than a decade, Smith (now a Major General of Marines) was faced with the formation of a division for employment in Korea.

A tall, gaunt, gray man, Smith had, for thirty-three years, striven to attain the ideal in his profession. From the first day he entered the Marine Corps he was an indefatigable student. A man of simple tastes and strong religious principles, his methods were direct and systematic. When time allowed, he gave problems exhaustive study; when it was lacking, he was never at a loss for a solution.

He was impatient with dull minds and unrelenting with slothful officers. After a tour of duty in Washington as the assistant commandant of the Marine Corps, Smith was assigned to command the 1st Marine Division. Never happy in the social glitter of the capital, it was with a deep sense of humility and thankfulness that he was finally relieved of the Washington scene to be with troops. Commanding the 1st Marine Division is the most coveted command in the Corps. For Smith this was a return home. In the Pacific war he had commanded the 5th Marine Regiment, and later was chief-of-staff of the old 1st Division. After being promoted to brigadier general he became the assistant division commander and remained with the 1st Marine Division throughout the Peleliu Campaign. Now he was to lead it into battle. He assumed command on the twenty-fifth of July.

Between the second and eighteenth of August there were constant conferences regarding personnel, equipment and ships. On the sixteenth, the advance echelon of the division staff departed by air for Tokyo; General Cates arrived from Washington and Shepherd from Tokyo; Puller's 1st Regiment sailed and Litzenberg was preparing to board ship with his 7th. On the eighteenth, Smith and the rest of his staff left by air for Japan.

Arriving in Tokyo early in the morning of the twenty-second of August, Smith was met by Admiral Doyle, who commanded Amphibious Group One (PhibGrpOne), and was taken to the U.S.S. *Mount McKinley* where the advance echelon of the division staff was quartered. As Smith was freshening up, Colonel A. L. Bowser, Division Operations officer, called on him. Smith was informed that he had an appointment with General MacArthur at 5:30 that afternoon.

It was also at this time that Smith learned that his division was to land at Inchon on the fifteenth of September. Time and space factors were not improving for the Marines. Marsden prepared and landed a brigade in Iceland in twenty-three days; Vandegrift was given thirty-one days' warning to prepare the 1st Marine Division for Guadalcanal, Smith was given twenty-four to prepare for Inchon.

CHAPTER IX

Preparation for Inchon

In April of 1915 the British sent seventy-eight thousand troops and three hundred ships to force the Dardanelles. This ill-fated amphibious operation struck the shoals of improper planning and went down to tragic defeat because the doctrine and techniques of such warfare had never been perfected. The failure of the Gallipoli campaign affected military thinking throughout the world. The general conclusion of all Army staffs and most Naval commands was that the large-scale amphibious operation against a fortified or defended shore was doomed to failure.

As late as 1943, Commodore Roger Keyes, second-in-command of the Naval force at Gallipoli disaster, wrote: "Among the most valuable lessons we learnt from the original landings was the folly of attempting to storm a defended beach in daylight."

The statement of Keyes generally expressed the Naval thinking throughout the world. Army general staffs, being landbound for centuries, have a hearty fear of water and the amphibious landing is considered suicidal.

This thought was slowly changed as a new concept of warfare was evolved. As the Princeton professors Isely and Crowl wrote in their masterpiece on amphibious warfare: ". . . the fact that the United States and her allies were prepared by 1942 and 1943 to launch full-scale amphibious assaults against powerful enemies in either ocean was primarily due to the foresight and planning of the United States Navy and more particularly the United States Marines."

General MacArthur conceived the Inchon landing, but between conception and execution is a chasm that must be bridged by the most detailed network of plans and techniques imaginable. The Navy and Marine staffs under Admiral Doyle and General Smith were forced to work out the details under time and space factors which were alarming to both. The doctrine for such an operation was established, but there were so many missing ingredients for the Inchon site that all concerned had reason to doubt the outcome.

Smith's conversation with Bowser, preparatory to calling on MacArthur, had raised several questions regarding the forthcoming landing. The tidal range in the Inchon basin is one of the most extreme anywhere in the world. The fifteenth of September had been selected as D-day because on that day the tidal range reached plus 31.2 feet; only on this day did the tide reach this extreme. Unless this date could be met, the next tide (thirty-foot stage) would not occur until mid-October.

To further complicate the operation was the time when these favorable tides would be reached during daylight hours. Morning high tide was forty-five minutes after sunrise and the evening high tide twenty-seven minutes before sunset. An additional complication presented itself in that the only suitable landing areas were fronted by stone sea walls constructed to block the entrance of extreme tides into the city. These walls were some sixteen feet in height and presented a scaling problem to the assault troops. Grappling hooks, ladders, cargo nets and lines would have to be used. This meant a delay at the critical point of the landing when troops were first getting ashore.

Because of the restricted waters and extensive mud flats which prohibited all but radar-equipped vessels from making a night passage of the straits, it was impossible to land the entire landing force on the morning tide. The key to the port, Wolmi-do Island, would have to be seized on the morning tide while the rest of the landing force would not come onto the beach until just before sunset.

To Smith the landing, as proposed, boiled down to a few basic factors. The Marines would land over docks and sea walls and attack through a city of 250,000. Because of the tide, the main effort would have to be made late in the afternoon with little opportunity for the rifle battalions to consolidate before nightfall. Puller's 1st Marines and the rest of the Division would not arrive in Kobe until the third of September. At that time all the ships in the convoy would have to be completely unloaded and then combat-loaded prior to sailing for the objective area.

Smith had learned from Doyle that the Navy was not satisfied with the selection of the landing site. It imposed on them nearly insurmountable problems of ship and small boat handling in restricted waters. At the moment the Navy was looking for an alternate place to land where the enemy communications could be cut without becoming involved with treacherous, narrow waters and a large Oriental city.

It was with these thoughts that Smith departed for his meeting with MacArthur. The first officer he met was MacArthur's chief-of-staff, Major General Edward Almond. Following the briefest acknowledgment of meeting, they launched into a discussion of the forthcoming landing. Smith voiced his objections to Inchon as a landing site.

Almond demurred. He told Smith there wouldn't be any organized enemy to oppose the landing; that the difficulties would be purely mechanical; the date was set and could not be changed. With that he ushered Smith into the office of the commander in chief. MacArthur was cordial and greeted Smith warmly. When the discussion turned to the coming invasion he told Smith: "The landing of the Marines at Inchon will be decisive. It will win the war and the status of the Marine Corps should never again be in doubt."

After a lengthy conference Smith returned to the *McKinley* to give the operation further study.

Three months prior to the outbreak of war in Korea, the Corps had sent a Marine Mobile Training Team to Japan. Under the command of Colonel Edward Forney, this team was to train various Army occupation troops in amphibious warfare and related subjects. Each officer and enlisted man on this team was an expert in amphibious landings.

At the time the war broke out, the team had completed the training of three Army Regimental Combat Teams. Early in July, when MacArthur decided upon a landing at Inchon, Forney and his team had been assigned to the 1st Cavalry Division to prepare them for the amphibious assault. By this time, however, the Eighth Army was so hard pressed that the 1st Cavalry had to be sent to Korea. When the X U. S. Army Corps was formed, Almond appointed Forney his deputy chief-of-staff and throughout his Corps staff placed other members of Mobile Training Team. The rest of Forney's team was assigned the task of training the 7th Army Division.

Because of their work on the Cavalry project and their time in the Far East, Forney and his team proved invaluable to the Navy-Marine staff as they began the planning of the landing. In the meantime, Navy

UDT (frogmen) units probed the beaches of Posung-Myon as an alternate site. The report came back that a landing could be made in this area in daylight hours without the risk of tide and narrow waters of the city of Inchon. However, mud flats and limited exits did exist.

When informed that Posung-Myon was more acceptable to the Navy, Almond stated that the decision to land at Inchon was final; that only by its seizure could the capture of Seoul at an early date be certain. For the first time the Marine and Navy commanders became aware of Seoul as a political objective.

Admiral Sherman arrived from the United States and a conference was held at COMNAVFE Headquarters. Attending the meeting were Admiral Sherman, Radford, Joy and Struble; representing the Marine Corps were Generals Shepherd and Smith. Doyle, who was to command the attack force, gave a two-hour presentation on the hazards of a landing at Inchon. Later in the day Doyle made a similar presentation for MacArthur and General Collins, Army Chief-of-Staff. Although no formal request was made to change the target area, Doyle's evaluation im plied the Navy would be happier if a change were granted.

When MacArthur did not alter his plan, Smith instructed his staff to work up plans for the rapid seizure of Kimpo airfield, the crossing of the Han River and the capture of the capital.

The Marine-Navy staff aboard the *Mount McKinley* put in untold hours smoothing out the final scheme of maneuver. Fortunately, many of the officers on this joint staff had worked together before on problems of amphibious landings in the Pacific. Behind them were the lessons of Guadalcanal where shore party control was practically nonexistent, the New Georgia campaign where Marine Raiders were stopped cold because it was found close air support could not substitute for artillery, and Tarawa, the catalyzer of all assault amphibious landings. In a matter of days the plans were drawn for one of the most intricate amphibious landings in the history of warfare.

The Marine staff on the *Mount McKinley* could not place much credence in the assurance that the landing would be "relatively unopposed." Burned into the memories of all Marines are the "mechanical difficulties" of the landing at Tarawa.

"Plan that it's going to be a tough sonofabitch. If it isn't, we're one to the good."

As details were completed plans had to be distributed to widely scattered units; the 5th Marines who were in Korea, Puller's 1st Marines in

Kobe, the Marine Air Wing at Itami, the 7th Marines still at sea (though Litzenberg had flown on ahead with a small staff) and the 11th Marines at Osaka. So dispersed were the units, it was impossible to have a conference of field commanders.

Smith had been assured the brigade would be released from Eighth Army control on the first of September. This would give the 5th Marines two weeks to join replacements, integrate the third company in each battalion, and to rehearse all units on the landing.

When the brigade was ordered back into action at the second battle of the Naktong, Smith brought the issue to the front at the conference the next morning. At the meeting was Almond, Admirals Joy, Struble, Doyle and Generals Ruffner and Wright of MacArthur's staff.

Smith told Almond that as landing force commander he could not insure the success of the operation if the 5th Marines were not made available to him. Almond answered that General Walker felt that to remove the Marine Brigade at this time would be harmful to the morale of the Eighth Army and might prejudice the outcome of the defense of Pusan. Almond said the 32nd Regiment of the 7th Army Division would have to be substituted for the 5th Marines.

This was an alarming proposal, inasmuch as the 7th Division had been stripped time and again to furnish replacements for units already in Korea. Only recently the 7th had joined eight thousand South Koreans to their ranks and were in the early steps of training under a "buddy system" where an American GI took a Korean soldier as his special charge.

Smith reminded Almond that in a complicated amphibious landing such as the one about to be conducted, last-minute substitutions could not be made with untrained troops. If substitutions were made, he would cancel the mission of the 5th Marines and allow Puller's 1st to make the assault with the 32nd following onto the beach in trace. Smith closed his objection by saying that to make a landing on a one regiment front would be going beyond the point of considered risk.

Admiral Joy supported Smith and suggested that a regiment of Army troops in Japan be assigned to the Eighth Army as a floating reserve, thereby relieving the 5th Marines. Almond agreed that this was feasible and that he would present the plan to Walker by telephone. He ordered Wright to see that the 17th Regiment of Infantry was outloaded at once and shipped to Pusan in time to get the 5th Marines out of the line and to Inchon by D-day. An hour after the meeting Smith was informed the

5th Marines would be released by the Eighth Army at midnight on the fifth of September.

It soon became obvious that considerable propaganda value was being attached to the recapturing of Seoul by the twenty-sixth of September—ninety days from its loss to the enemy. As a result, Colonel Ely, who commanded a Special Operations Group, was ordered to land north of Inchon and dash inland and capture Kimpo Airfield.

This group, trained by Forney's team, was designed for back-of-the-lines demolition work and lacked the numbers or skill for such a dangerous venture. The mission of the unit was outlined: Ely's group, aboard a ROK vessel, would move up devious channels north of Inchon, where they would take to rubber boats. From this point they would have to paddle several miles against a five-knot tide. Landing at dusk they were to move cross-country a distance of ten miles at night and seize Kimpo airfield at dawn. The plan, however daring, was a rash gamble, for the requirements must fit the plan if the execution is to succeed.

Smith opposed the plan on several counts: Ely was to operate in the 1st Division zone but would not be under Marine command; the Marines had been given the mission of capturing Kimpo without delay, Ely was given the same mission. Inasmuch as company radios have a range of only four miles the Marines could never be certain where Ely and his unit were and this would hamper naval gunfire and air support. In addition Smith felt that no account had been taken on the effect of the tides on rubber boats. Last, but not least, intelligence indicated there were too many enemy at Kimpo for the small unit to handle.

On these grounds Smith opposed augmenting Ely's unit with Marines from Houghton's Reconnaissance Company.

The second scheme proposed by the X Corps staff was to have a battalion of Marines embark in LVT's at the beachhead and dash for Kimpo in a motorized column. Smith refused this plan on the grounds that such a move was tactically unsound besides being beyond the capabilities of such specialized vehicles which would be required for the later crossing of the Han.

General Shepherd, on his fourth trip across the Pacific since his flight from Salt Lake City at the beginning of the war, arrived in Tokyo and approved the scheme of maneuver for the division though he was concerned over the fact that the two assault regiments would not join lines for the first night. Shepherd also supported Smith in denying Marines from joining Ely.

The 1st Marine Air Wing, under the command of Major General Field Harris, had arrived and headquarters were set up at Itami. Heavy responsibility for isolating Inchon from enemy reinforcements during the day rested with a co-ordinated and detailed air support plan. The Air Support Group of the Attack Force was comprised of the two Marine squadrons from the *Sicily* and *Badoeng Straits* and Navy squadrons from the fast carrier group. Brigadier General Thomas Cushman was designated tactical air commander for X Corps, and he would set up and assume control of tactical air from Kimpo as soon as that objective was seized and declared operational. Air support in its entirety would be furnished by Marine and Navy aircraft.

During this phase of planning there was one Marine unit which was spending every hour of the day and night in a specialized and delicate task. In July when the 1st Marine Air Wing departed California, Major Donald Bush was placed in command of the aerial photo unit which would provide photo reconnaissance for the brigade. Bush, a night fighter pilot with some experience in photo flying, had three pilots in his unit—Captains Ed Ganschow and Ken Dykes, and Technical Sergeant George Glauser. These men had all flown in photo outfits in World War II. The technicians in the unit were all trained men.

The only other photo unit in the Korean area was the team of Captain Dave Booker, and Lieutenants Welch and Crawford on board the *Valley Forge*. When Bush arrived in Japan with his two planes and four pilots they were given the immediate job of photographing the marshaling yards in Seoul. The Navy made the request at noon on the first of August. Covered by Air Force fighters, Bush made his photographic runs and had the results in to the Navy in time for an air strike the following morning.

What had started out to be a unit to cover the requests for a brigade turned into a photo section for the Eighth Army in the southern fighting and later for X Corps. With two F4U-5P's and four pilots, all the photos of the Inchon sea wall, mud flats, surrounding islands and beaches were made by Bush and his men. On one occasion the two planes flew thirteen sorties in four days to get the pictures so badly needed by the G-2 Section of the division.

Serious delays occurred when a typhoon struck the Kobe area. Considerable equipment was lost to the water which flooded the docks, and several ships were damaged. The greatest loss, however, was time. For twenty-four hours it was impossible to continue with the loading of ships in the convoy.

At eight o'clock on the fifth of September, a conference was held at which all unit commanders were informed that loading must be speeded up and that the vessels would sail whether completely loaded or not. The deadline sailing dates were given:

	From Kobe	From Pusan
APA's and AKA's	0150 on 12th	1000 on 13th
First Tractor Grp.	1000 on 10th	0200 on 12th
2d Tractor Grp.	1045 on 10th	0315 on 12th
Wolmi-do Grp. (Taplett's 3d)		0140 on 13th

The key to the defenses of Inchon was the island of Wolmi-do, and it was a plan of calculated boldness to take it early in the morning and then to depend on naval gunfire and close air support to deny enemy reinforcements from pouring into the city. General Smith dismissed the even greater hazard of attacking the island and city simultaneously at daylight because the troops in the Inchon assault would have to traverse a narrow, tortuous channel in the pre-dawn hours while exposed to close, enfiladed fire from the island.

Murray had selected Taplett's 3rd to make the assault on Wolmi-do at 6:30 on the morning of the fifteenth. At 5:30 in the afternoon, Newton and Roise, landing abreast, would begin the direct assault on the city. Over on the right flank, Puller would land his 1st Marines at the same time and push forward in an encircling movement to cut off the enemy in the city and deny reinforcement. Puller had selected Lieutenant Colonel Allan Sutter's 2nd and Lieutenant Colonel Thomas Ridge's 3rd to lead his assault on Blue Beach. The attacking Marines would have ninety minutes of daylight to establish their lines in a heavily populated Oriental city.

To insure that the defenses of Wolmi-do would be destroyed before the troops landed, the Navy ordered four destroyers to approach the island within close range to bombard and draw fire if there were enemy guns. It was a calculated risk the Navy was willing to assume to flush out strongpoints in advance.

A holiday spirit prevailed at headquarters in Tokyo; a landing was to be made and the North Korean Army would be crushed and the war would be over. There was little security as the coming battle was fought over the bars at the GHQ Officers' Club and the Correspondents' Club. Everyone at GHQ attempted to find an excuse to make the excursion. It would be an occasion to get out of the heat of Tokyo and have a little outing.

A second typhoon caused further delay, and some of the ships already en route to the target area came to trouble in the heavy weather, but all made it safely. Just before the *McKinley* sailed, nine general officers from the Tokyo GHQ staff descended on the ship for transportation. Accommodations aboard the command ship were severely strained and room was made by shifting the Navy-Marine working staffs onto cots in the lower deck alleyways. The amphibious assault upon Inchon was on.

To lead his infantry regiments Smith had three able commanders who inspired confidence and delighted in responsibility. Puller of the 1st Marines believed in direct action and carried out his orders with a determination and singleness of purpose that stunned the enemy and was a constant source of surprise to the Army staff at X Corps. A student of war in general and the campaigns of Stonewall Jackson in particular, Puller was fast becoming a legendary figure in the Corps.

Litzenberg of the 7th Marines had considerable staff background and it was reflected in the handling of his regiment. His manner was quiet, scholarly and convincing. He was constantly abreast of the tactical situation and fought his regiment with magnificent results. Extremely loyal to his men, they answered by naming themselves "Litz's Blitzes." The performance of the 7th at Yudam-ni was sufficient to insure Litzenberg's place in history as one of the fine regimental commanders of the Corps.

Murray of the 5th Marines was the junior of Smith's three commanders. Normally the 5th would have been commanded by a colonel, but Murray, still a lieutenant colonel when the war broke, was in command of the 5th and the Corps saw no reason why they should replace him with a senior officer. He more than justified the confidence placed in him and his handling of the 5th Marines throughout the Korean campaign was exemplary.

The 1st Provisional Marine Brigade was disbanded on the thirteenth of September and the 5th Marines became an organic part of the 1st Marine Division. Other units, such as the artillery battalion and tanks, joined their parent units with the division. Craig became assistant division commander to Smith while the officers of the brigade staff were absorbed by the division.

Upon being relieved by the 23rd Army Regiment at midnight on the fifth of September, the 5th Marines made a night foot march of eight miles to the entrucking area and thence fifty miles to Pusan. Between the sixth and the thirteenth the Marines in Korea were reorganized, joined replacements and made plans for embarkation and an amphibious assault on Inchon.

Taplett's 3rd was to be under control of the division during the Wolmi-do phase and would revert to regimental control as soon as the main landing was made on the city itself. When the rifle companies of the 3rd were told of their assignment the news was received with some misgivings.

"Here we go again—old 3/5's goin' to be the sacrificial hog. If we take this island, the rest'll land in time for dinner. If we get clobbered, it can be called off an' the rest go back to Tokyo."

Red Beach, assigned to Murray's 5th, posed several problems. The beach was fronted by a sea wall and at How-hour the top of the wall would be four feet above the ramps of the landing craft. Ladders had to be hastily constructed when light, aluminum models were not available in quantity. Constantly improvising and calling on the experience of numerous landings in the Pacific, the Marines prepared for the assault.

Because of the narrow beach, Newton and Roise would be forced to land their battalions in a column of companies. Newton was assigned the mission of seizing Cemetery and Observatory Hills while Roise was to take the buildings on the right and the high ground in his portion of the regimental zone of action.

It was going to be a race against darkness to land and secure assigned areas between the landing time of 5:35 and sunset at 6:42. There could be no rehearsal of scaling the sea wall by the 5th Marines for no such feature, natural or manmade, could be found in South Korea.

Puller's 1st Marines landed in Japan on the third of September and began their planning. Blue Beach, south of the Wolmi-do causeway, was also fronted by a sea wall, but beyond the wall was a sparsely settled sector with a scattering of factory buildings and open fields. Puller's mission was to land and push along the southern outskirts of the city and circle northward thus cutting off the ingress or egress of enemy troops.

Planning of the 1st was hampered by the dispersal of the battalions in Japanese campsites; two battalions were located sixty-five miles from the regimental headquarters. These two battalions, Sutter's 2nd and Ridge's 3rd, were able to get in a week of training and rehearsal. The sea wall on the Kobe waterfront provided a rehearsal area to try out the makeshift ladders.

Despite the fact that Inchon had been occupied by American forces at the end of World War II, no accurate maps were available of the city or its waterfront. Also lacking was detailed information as to the number and types of enemy troops defending Inchon and Kimpo Airfield. The accumulated knowledge of the enemy's military tactics consisted, for the most part, of the enemy in the offense. Inasmuch as the Eighth Army had fought a continuing withdrawal, there had been no opportunity to appraise the North Korean Army's defensive tactics.

The Marine Brigade had discovered the enemy to be bold and tenacious to a point, but, forced to retreat, order failed and withdrawals became routs. This information was too uncertain, however, to forecast the enemy's reaction to a penetration into the heart of his newly won domain.

Defending the Inchon-Kimpo area were elements of the 18th North Korean Division, one regiment of the 9th North Korean Division and odds and ends of service and training units. This force totaled approximately five to seven thousand. While the waterfront area was honeycombed with prepared defensive positions, Bush's daily aerial photographs indicated many were unoccupied.

The Inchon landing was to be made in the face of many uncertainties and mixed feelings prevailed that it might be another Tarawa or Iwo—or a push-over.

CHAPTER X

The Inchon Landing and Penetration to the Han River

The assault on Inchon was a Navy-Marine operation both in planning and execution. During the softening-up period aircraft from the fast carriers (*Philippine Sea*, *Valley Forge* and *Boxer*) under the command of Rear Admiral Ewen would pound away at the enemy defenses. Teaming with this force would be Marine aircraft from the *Badoeng Straits* and *Sicily*.

Two days before the landing, three Navy destroyers moved in and anchored within "spitting distance" of Wolmi-do. From these positions they began to rake the island with five-inch shellfire. The desired effect was achieved—enemy guns hidden in caves on the island opened fire. Spotting aircraft overhead located the camouflaged positions and they were destroyed. The calculated risk had paid dividends. Although the destroyers were hit on the exchange, no serious damage or casualties were inflicted and the enemy lost gun emplacements which could have been of serious consequence to the Marines of Taplett's battalion. Marine and Naval air exploded ninety-five thousand pounds of napalm on the island.

Colonel Ely called off his pre D-day expedition when he and his group could make no headway against the sweeping tide. They could get their rubber boats no closer than a thousand yards off the shore, and

The Inchon Landing. *The enemy is caught by surprise as the Marine-Navy team storm in from the sea. With Puller on the right and Murray on the left, two regiments of Marines cross the mud flats and scale the sea walls of Inchon. The city is captured and the Division drives eastward toward Seoul.*

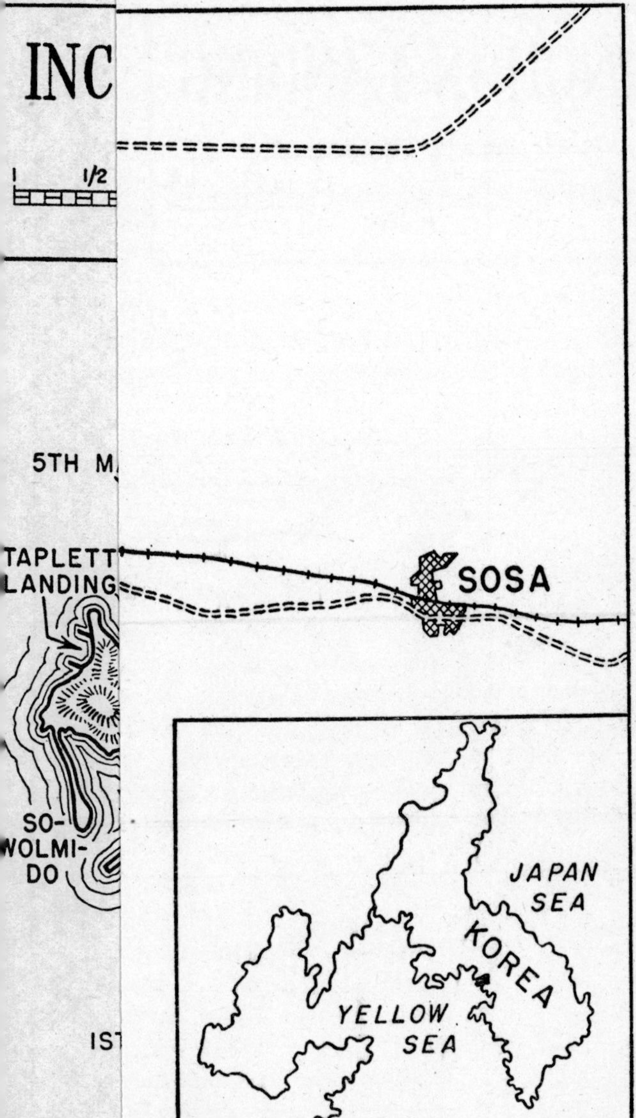
INC
1
1/2
5TH M
TAPLETT LANDING
SO-
WOLMI-
DO
IST
SOSA
JAPAN SEA
KOREA
YELLOW SEA

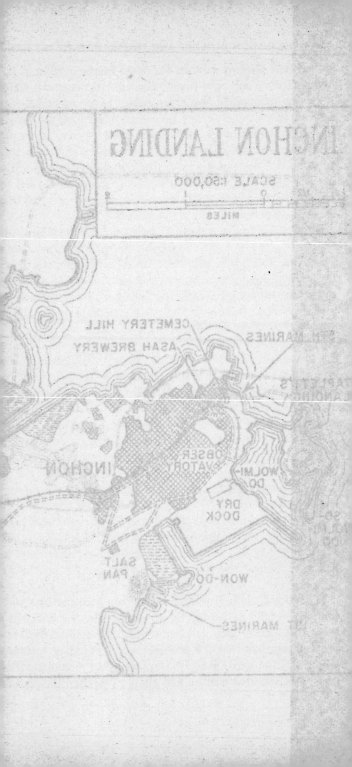

gained that position only by the most frantic paddling. It is fortunate hydrographic conditions denied the unit their suicidal effort.

As one member of the group said, "Every night for the rest of my life, I'm going to get on my knees and thank God for that tide."

Much to the surprise and dismay of the Navy, an amphibious operation was attempted by Eighth Army the day before the landing at Inchon. Without informing Naval sources of the mission or objective, seven hundred eighty ROK guerrilla troops were loaded onto a ROK LST and sent fifteen miles north of Pohang to land in the rear of the enemy and destroy enemy communications.

Without a beach reconnaissance or a hydrographic survey having been made, the LST came to trouble almost immediately in a twenty-five knot wind and heavy surf. The ship broached and was taken under fire by enemy antitank guns. Later, machine guns and mortars were added to the armament against the stricken ship. Many ROK troops drowned in the surf and those who had gotten ashore soon became demoralized and suffered severe casualties from enemy fire.

An urgent request was made for Naval assistance. Air support arrived and the enemy fire lessened to a degree. The battleship *Missouri*, the cruiser *Helena* and six destroyers were withdrawn from previously assigned shore bombardment schedules designed to support the landing at Inchon. They lent every assistance to aid in withdrawing the LST and beleaguered ROK's from the beach.

Tugs were dispatched from Pusan in an effort to withdraw the broached ship. This proved impossible and the LST was lost. For the next five days every attempt was made to withdraw the ROK troops from the shore, but the heavy surf was the cause of many losing their lives. Finally a relief LST arrived and collected the wounded and dead. The small ROK unit had suffered 60 dead, 110 wounded and 32 missing. By the time this mission of succor and rescue was completed, the Marines had landed at Inchon and were preparing to cross the Han, but had been denied the support of the big guns from the *Missouri* and *Helena*.

D-day for Inchon was clear, but with a high overcast and the prediction of rain later in the day. Smith went to the flag bridge of the *McKinley* with General Shepherd before daylight. A loud-speaker system had been arranged so that the people on deck could be informed as to the progress of the battle. At 5:30 Captain Sears, in command of the attack transports, reported that he had safely negotiated the tortuous channels and was in position to land the troops on the island of Wolmi-do. Fifteen minutes later air and naval gunfire began the final bombardment. Thirty minutes after this, three LSMR's (Landing Ship Men Rockets) laid down a shattering rocket barrage.

MacArthur came onto the flag bridge as the voice over the loudspeaker announced, "Landing force crossing line of departure."

There was a buildup of tension during the time it took the landing craft to negotiate over a mile of water. Two minutes before the troops hit the beach, Naval gunfire lifted and Marine Corsairs began strafing the beachline until the ground units were but fifty yards offshore.

"First wave a hundred yards offshore . . . no enemy fire. . . ."

"First wave ashore! Moving inland rapidly."

The site selected for the landing was the bathing beach on the northern arm of the island. The scheme of maneuver was to have Bohn's unit penetrate a short distance across the arm and then turn sharply to the right. While Counselman's platoon seized the high ground, the other two, O'Connell and Peard, would secure the western shore and seal off the causeway to the satellite island So-Wolmi-do. Wildman was to push his unit directly across the arm and then he too would make a right turn and seize the village and seal off the causeway leading into Inchon. From there his unit would push along the eastern shore past the Standard Oil storage tanks to the southern tip. At this point he would tie in with Bohn's unit in the vicinity of the gas works.

The first wave hit the island beach at 6:33. Bohn's boat, on the extreme right, struck an underwater obstacle a short distance from shore and hung there. Ordering the coxswain to lower the ramp, Bohn, followed by Jaworski, his executive officer, and the radio operator rushed forward. All three men disappeared from view. The other members of the boat slid to a halt on the ramp.

Divesting themselves of their equipment, Bohn and Jaworski surfaced and made it ashore while the boat backed off and came in farther down the beach. In the meantime, the other craft in the wave had unloaded Counselman's platoon and the turn was made, and the race was on for the high ground where the radio towers and botanical gardens were located.

McMullen brought his unit ashore in trace of Wildman and pushed across the island toward the causeway. As Wildman did a right turn, McMullen drove across and sealed off the causeway leading to Inchon and the caves in the northern end of the island. Thirty-one minutes after landing the high ground was seized and the American flag raised.

Sweet's platoon of tanks came ashore from an LSD (Landing Ship Dock) and were divided into three sections to support the ground units in mopping-up operations.

There were a number of caves holding enemy troops who refused to surrender, and the dozer tanks were used to fill in the openings. It is estimated more than one hundred enemy were entombed in this manner. One hundred thirty-six enemy were captured and one hundred eighty killed. Later in the morning, Corporal Beauchamp of George Company, supported by three tanks, took a squad onto So-Wolmi-do and made fast work of securing this adjoining island. An enemy platoon was destroyed in this action.

When the flag was raised, MacArthur went below to his quarters and wrote a dispatch to Admiral Struble: "The Navy and Marines have never shone more brightly than this morning."

The critical period began when the tide began to fall and all activity ceased until late in the afternoon. "The first time we've ever staged an amphibious landing in two acts. I hope our friends don't counterfeit a lot of tickets and crash the gate during intermission. . . ."

To prevent reinforcements, Marine and Naval air joined in isolating a twenty-five mile zone encircling the seaport. Air support and co-ordinating fires were directed from the *McKinley*. This was to prevail until six o'clock in the afternoon of the twenty-first (D plus 6) when the Tactical Air Control Section moved ashore.

Naval and Marine air, flying more than three hundred sorties from the carriers, were successful in cauterizing the infested area, and the enemy, seemingly stunned by the magnitude and speed of the operation, made no attempt to get reinforcements into the city. During the late afternoon it began to rain, which hampered the air operations, but Naval gunfire took over the task of sealing the approaches.

At 3:30 in the afternoon the assault troops began loading into landing craft and proceeded to the rendezvous area. During the approach to the beach, the Naval ships laid down their final, intense bombardment. Immediately prior to the landing, LSMR's fired a two-thousand-round rocket barrage on the landing area.

The scheme of maneuver for both regiments was to land two battalions abreast with each battalion in a column of companies. In Newton's zone on the extreme left, Stevens was to lead off with McMullen and Muetzel landing abreast with their platoons.

Using portable equipment from his landing craft, Lieutenant J. W. Smith, Forward Air Controller for Newton's battalion, called down an air strike on Observatory Hill while moving in on the beach. Two minutes behind schedule, the 1st and 2nd Battalions of the 5th Marines fronted the sea wall. The first waves threw their makeshift ladders onto the parapet and hooked them into position and began clambering over the wall.

"Up and over, up and over—get moving."

"These God-damned ladders don't fit—"

"Up an' over—"

"Move out."

Through a combination of tide, faulty visibility due to smoke from burning buildings and lack of rehearsal, Navy coxswains brought troops to wrong beaches. The first wave, following guideboats, made the approach in an orderly manner, but the succeeding boats, sent in without guides, brought their units to the wrong beaches and platoon and company commanders had a difficult time forming their organizations.

Further confusion was added when a "trigger-happy" LST ran up on Red Beach and began to spray the area with 40 and 20 mm. cannon shells. It was some time before the commander of the vessel could bring his excited crew to order and the firing ceased.

Muetzel, landing to the right of McMullen's platoon, was fortunate in finding the sea wall breached by Naval gun fire. He ran his boats into the openings and his unit dashed ashore. In a few minutes they had captured or killed the enemy troops occupying the fire trenches immediately behind the sea wall and moved briskly across the railroad tracks and into the town proper. Cemetery Hill was on his flank and the Asah Brewery on his front. He seized the brewery and reported to Stevens. The 3rd Platoon under Second Lieutenant Baldomero Lopez came under heavy fire from the trenches and bunkers behind the sea wall. One bunker was overcome and Lopez was about to hurl a grenade into a second when he was hit in the shoulder and chest by machine-gun fire. Knocked to the ground, the grenade fell from his hand.

"Grenade!" he shouted in warning.

He made two futile grabs for the explosive, but his wounds hampered his movement. In desperation he hooked the grenade in the crook of his elbow and pulled it to his body where it exploded. He was killed instantly, but none of his men were injured. First Lieutenant Fred Eubanks, executive officer of Able Company, took temporary command of the unit.

When Stevens informed Muetzel of the fighting that had developed on the left flank, the 2nd Platoon commander pulled back and assaulted Cemetery Hill from the southeast. Twenty-two minutes after landing, Stevens fired an amber star cluster signifying his unit had seized his first objective. Though of short duration, the left flank fight had been costly to Stevens. Eight Marines had been killed and twenty-eight wounded.

Upon landing First Lieutenant Poul Pedersen's company passed to the right of Cemetery Hill and the brewery. Crossing the second set of railroad tracks in the direction of Observation Hill, an enemy machine gun set up in a church pinned down the unit. Technical Sergeant Max Stein rushed through the enemy fire and tossed two grenades into the church. The fire from within the building ceased and Pedersen's unit occupied a portion of the hill.

Newton ordered Fenton to take his company forward and seize the remaining portion of the hill. Fenton attained the objective. By midnight he was tied in with Pedersen on his right and Peters to his left. Fenton had taken six wounded and Pedersen five. Total casualties for Newton's 1st Battalion were eight killed and thirty-nine wounded.

In Roise's zone of action, Jaskilka's company landed to the right of Stevens and pushed swiftly forward. Forty-one minutes after landing, Jaskilka had his unit on the first objective against light resistance. Twenty minutes later the second objective was seized, and five minutes after that the third was occupied.

At this juncture "H. J." Smith took his company through Jaskilka's lines to secure the high ground forward of the regimental objective. After a brief fire fight, Smith had his unit in position. By ten o'clock that night Jaskilka and Smith had tied in their lines with Peters who in turn was in contact with Fenton.

The most serious casualties suffered by Roise's 2nd Battalion came from the LST on the beach. One Marine was killed and twenty-three wounded.

In Puller's zone (Blue Beach), Sutter's 2nd Battalion and Ridge's 3rd Battalion were making the assault. As with Murray's 5th, the first waves landed on the assigned beaches, but from then on there was considerable confusion. The only exit from Blue Beach was blocked by a rock and earth slide caused by Naval gunfire and the assault troops were forced to climb over a fifteen-foot sea wall. Landing with the first waves were platoons of engineers who began immediately to improve the landing site by installing cargo nets over the wall and breaching sections of it with explosives.

It began to rain in the late afternoon and continued into the night, which was inconceivably black. There was much stumbling, falling, clawing and cursing as the companies sent outposts and patrols forward. By two o'clock in the morning Puller's regiment was on its first four objectives.

Total Marine casualties for the day were twenty killed and one hundred seventy wounded.

At 6:30 the next morning Jaskilka passed his company through Peters' and carried on the assault with orders to make contact with Puller's 1st Marines. Contact was made an hour later; the door was closed to any North Koreans escaping the city. Behind the advancing Marines was a regiment of South Korean Marines who captured large numbers of prisoners and Communist sympathizers in the city itself.

During the night the enemy moved six T-34 tanks and a small infantry task force from Sosa into the outskirts of Inchon. At daylight, this force was spotted by an eight-plane flight from Lieutenant Colonel Walter Lischeid's squadron. The Corsairs went into the attack. Six five-hundred-pound bombs and two napalm tanks were dropped. The escorting infantry scattered. One of the tanks went up in flames from a direct hit by napalm; a second had its tread blown off and a third became inoperative. When the first flight had expended its armament a second flight of eight Corsairs came on station and continued the destruction. Two T-34's were destroyed with one napalm tank. The remaining tanks were damaged and deserted by their crews.

On pressing home his third and final attack on the enemy armor Captain William Simpson's plane was hit. Simpson was killed when the Corsair crashed and exploded a short distance from the burning armor.

On the ground Puller pressed the attack and before nine o'clock a penetration of over four thousand yards had been made.

Houghton's Reconnaissance Company moved to the right of Puller's 1st with the mission of protecting that flank as the attack was pressed toward Kimpo and Seoul. By nightfall on the sixteenth both regiments had seized the Force Beachhead Line and the assault phase of the operation was concluded. On the following morning the exploitation phase would begin.

With the consolidation of the beachhead Smith was now ready to launch an attack which would capture Kimpo Airfield and Seoul. Murray was to advance to the northeast, capture Kimpo, cross the Han and attack Seoul from the west. Puller was to advance directly on Seoul along the main highway and rail line. (See map.) Before Puller could enter Seoul, however, the city of Yongdong-po would have to be subdued and captured and a crossing of the Han effected.

Kimpo was sixteen road miles from Inchon, Yongdong-po twenty. An advance of that distance with but two regiments involved a calculated risk with respect to exposed flanks and the possibility of counterattacks. Litzenberg's 7th Marines, en route from the United States, would not be available until the twenty-first of September.

With the assault units moving eastward, the dock area became a jam of trucks, ships and men unloading the supplies necessary to maintain the fighting units. Press boats and sightseers began coming ashore. One boat inched its way through the smoke from burning buildings in search of Charlie Pier. As the boat moved in slowly toward the sea wall, a Marine Pfc. rushed to the water's edge.

Cupping his hands about his mouth, he shouted, "Lay off, you stupid bastard. We're gonna blow the joint!"

The boat turned away. Vice Admiral Struble smiled at Russell Brines, Associated Press correspondent. "I wonder which one of us that Marine was yelling at?"

A section of the sea wall disappeared in a blast of TNT as the engineers began blowing holes in the wall to permit a more speedy unloading of the ships.

Smith went ashore in the afternoon and was met by Craig. The division CP was opened in the southeast outskirts of the city in what had once been a barracks area for occupation forces. The buildings were Quonset huts with dirt floors. The flagpole had been shot down but was soon erected. About the time the national colors were raised, Smith notified Admiral Doyle that he was ashore and would exercise command from there.

The enemy had shown little ability to defend the routes of approach to Kimpo and the Han River. Except for elements of the 18th North Korean Division and even smaller units of the 9th and 17th, the rest of the defenders were a heterogeneous mixture of supply, administrative and training organizations. Large numbers were captured and many deserted to the Marines.

During the night of the sixteenth, a counterattacking force of six T-34 tanks and two hundred fifty infantry was formed from experienced personnel of the 2nd Battalion, 1st Regiment, 18th North Korean Division. Their mission was to strike the 5th Marines in a dawn attack, stem their advance on the airfield and to hold until reinforced.

"H. J." Smith's Dog Company made the sighting of the enemy task force at 5:45 in the morning. The company was in a strong position on the high ground commanding the road which wound through a rather narrow pass. Three enemy tanks were first seen in the miasmic mist of early morning. The three tanks grew into six, accompanied by infantry, and could be seen in the approach march along the road.

Corporal Okey Douglas of the D Company bazooka team saw the tanks bearing down on his position and waited confidently. He knew what the 2.36's and 3.5's had done to enemy tanks on the Naktong. He was convinced he could improve on the record. Backing him up were other tank busters. Pomeroy was there with his platoon of Pershings and Jones' unit was in position with 75 mm. Recoilless Rifles.

The lead enemy tank was but seventy-five yards from Douglas when he opened fire with his 2.36 rocket launcher. His first shot set the tank afire; he assisted in the kill on the second. By this time all weapons in the area were being registered in and a "turkey shoot" followed. The six T-34's were destroyed and more than two hudred of the enemy infantry killed.

About this time MacArthur, Struble and Almond landed at Charlie Pier. Smith met them and took them to his CP. After a briefing session, the group made a tour of inspection. En route to Murray's regiment, the cavalcade passed the six tanks which had been knocked out by Lischeid's squadron the day before. They were inspected and the party continued to the CP of the 5th Marines.

Murray took MacAarthur and the party forward to the scene of the enemy counterattack. The tanks were still burning and the enemy dead littered the area. MacArthur expressed his pleasure at the sight of the destroyed armor and one of his staff officers observed wryly, "You damn Marines always manage to stage everything to your advantage, even a visit by the general!"

Unfortunately, MacArthur and his staff were unable to be in two places at once. At very nearly the same time Douglas was in action with his 2.36, Pfc. Walter Monegan (in Puller's zone) took on six tanks on the outskirts of Sosa-ri with his 3.5—with results as devastating as Douglas's.

The normal procedure for infantry units at this time upon consolidating for the night was to establish roadblocks which consisted of antitank mines in the road and approaches to the positions. Antitank weapons (rockets and 75 mm. Recoilless Rifles) were emplaced to cover these roadblocks.

Behind these positions a tank platoon was emplaced in a defiladed position with unrestricted field of fire. If possible, terrain was selected so that the Pershings could bring fire to bear on the roadblock at five hundred yards. Infantry protection was provided for the tanks on the high ground to the flanks and rear.

It was in such a position that Pfc. Monegan found himself at daylight on a slight rise of ground just off the main road between Seoul and Inchon. Allowing the leading enemy tank to come within fifty yards of his position, Monegan sighted in his 3.5 launcher and fired. He set the T-34 afire; when the escape hatch flew open and an enemy crewman tried to escape, Monegan picked up his carbine and killed him. While this was transpiring Monegan's loader, Pfc. Robert Perkins, had reloaded the weapon.

The second enemy tank was now in position and Monegan took up his rocket launcher, hit and stopped it. By now all weapons in the area were bearing on the enemy armor. Six T-34's were destroyed.

During this phase, a spirit of competition prevailed among the men of the rocket sections. Puller's Marines had heard of the exploits of Casas and Alvarez and the other "rocketeers" in the southern fighting and all were convinced they could and would do better. The antitank section men, armed with the 3.5 rockets, wagered considerable sums on who could make the high score on the Russian T-34 "caviar cans."

Throughout the operation the Marines experienced little difficulty with enemy armor. The Russian-made tank was destroyed by air attack from Marine Corsairs; they were knocked out of action by 2.36 and 3.5 rockets and by the Pershings. The Marines developed a disdainful attitude about the enemy's efforts to employ armored counterattacks.

Defeat at arms always brings forth tales of great hordes of enemy or new and devastating weapons. The weapons to destroy the enemy armor were at hand if the men could be found to employ them properly. In the battle from Inchon to Seoul, fifty-three enemy tanks were sighted; forty-eight were destroyed and the remaining five were found abandoned. Men with the moral stamina of Monegan, Douglas, Casas and Alvarez did more than prove that we had the weapons to stop the enemy.

To avoid confusion the action will remain with Murray's regiment until Kimpo has been captured and the approaches to the Han River uncovered. Once Murray is in position for the crossing the action of Puller's unit will be taken up and carried to the outskirts of Yong-dong-po.

After the enemy tanks were destroyed by Douglas and company, Roise sent the battalion down the road in a column of companies. Jaskilka led off with Easy Company. The march continued slowly as pockets of resistance were met along the way. Supported by English's Able Company of tanks, the attack proceeded until faulty maps caused delay in searching out the proper roads.

Pomeroy's 1st Platoon of tanks missed a turnoff, and after some delay retracted. After further searching, they joined another road which led them to a faulty bridge. The engineers, with the help of native labor, repaired the bridge and the tanks moved across. At this time Pomeroy was joined by Winter's 3rd platoon and both proceeded to Kimpo Airfield and joined up with Roise's 2nd Battalion in time for the assault.

Jaskilka with Pomeroy's tanks in support, was assigned the mission of seizing the south portion of the field and the buildings at the end of the strip. Smith's Dog Company with Winter's tanks in support had the north portion of the field to secure. Peters' Company, in reserve, would take positions at the west end of the airfield. The attack began at six o'clock in the evening. While Jaskilka was moving to the buildings at the eastern end of the strip with two platoons he directed Deptula to seize a road junction to the northeast.

It was long after dark before the buildings had been searched out and the battalion began to set up night defenses. Jaskilka (with two platoons) set up to the south of the East-West runway; Peters emplaced his unit to the west of the field while Smith took positions to the north of the East-West runway.

In the meantime Deptula had secured the road junction but was out of radio contact with the battalion. He ordered his platoon into defensive positions. Shortly after two o'clock an enemy force was heard approaching from the east. Maintaining excellent fire control Deptula's platoon allowed the enemy point and advance party to approach at close range before opening fire. Heavy casualties were inflicted.

About an hour later another force was heard approaching but this time the sound of tanks added a more ominous note. With neither the strength nor weapons to withstand a tank-infantry attack, Deptula came to a hurried decision to withdraw to the airfield.

Jaskilka's concern mounted as the hours passed without contacting Deptula. He sent a patrol under Technical Sergeant Robert Barnett to determine what had happened to his "lost platoon." Barnett made a thorough and exhaustive search but the maze of roads was too much to overcome in the dark and the patrol returned.

Just before daylight troops were heard approaching Jaskilka's lines from the northeast. The Marines in the line were cautioned to hold fire until complete identification was made. Without further incident Deptula and his platoon entered the friendly lines.

Shortly before daylight Jaskilka's unit received a company-sized attack on their front and right rear. Sergeant Marvin Eggersgluss directed the fire of the mortars from an exposed position with excellent results. Corporal Russell House rose to the occasion when his platoon was pinned down by heavy fire. House rushed forward hurling grenades. He continued to expose himself as he readied a 75 mm. Recoilless gun for point-blank firing. He was killed as the attack subsided and the enemy began to withdraw.

At the same time Jaskilka was under attack a squad of enemy engineers attempted to destroy an underpass in the sector defended by Peters' Company. Sansing's 1st Platoon wiped out the enemy unit. During the early morning the villages near the airfield were cleared of enemy and the area secured.

While Roise's 2nd was advancing on Kimpo, Newton's 1st which was in trace, continued on to seize a range of hills east of the airfield. Stevens' company, in the lead, advanced against little or no resistance. In the Ascom City area Muetzel was seriously wounded. He was evacuated to the aid station where his friend, Navy Lieutenant (jg) "Hogan" H'Doubler saw at once that Muetzel's right leg would have to be amputated.

Muetzel was the last of the young triumvirate who had besieged headquarters in July for a change in orders that they might go to war.

The favors of fortune ofttimes desert the man who woos too fervently.

In the case of these three this was true. Johnston was killed on No Name Ridge. Lopez gave his life to save men of his unit; Muetzel, wounded for the third time, lost his leg.

Forty-eight hours after landing at Inchon, the 5th Marines were on the airstrip at Kimpo. Lieutenant General Shepherd, piloted by Captain Vic Armstrong in a helicopter, was in the first friendly plane to land on the air strip. The 1st Marine Air Wing began operating from the newly won field on the twentieth.

First Lieutenant Jack Hanes from the *Badoeng Straits* was the first pilot to land a high performance plane on Kimpo. The area was not secure at the time nor was the field open, but Hanes, returning from a close support mission, thought he would like to be the first. He made an "emergency" landing. As he taxied to the buildings at the south end of the field, he thought there was something vaguely familiar about the officer directing him into a parking position. Closer inspection, to Hanes' embarrassment, revealed it to be General Field Harris.

Too old a hand to be taken in by such a flimsy "emergency" excuse, the general posed for pictures with Hanes under strained circumstances.

Shortly after this, preloaded flying boxcars began arriving from Japan with supplies and equipment for field operations. VMF 212 and VMF(N) 542 arrived before sunset on the nineteenth. These squadrons combined with carrier-based planes flew one hundred thirty-one sorties the next day. By the twenty-eighth of September the wing had three squadrons operating from Kimpo, two squadrons from the carriers *Badoeng Straits* and *Sicily* and one night-fighter squadron operating from Japan.

The Grasshoppers and helicopters of VMO-6 got into early action. With two observation planes flying from carrier decks until fields ashore could be established, the rest of the squadron went aboard an LST. Shortly after 6:30 in the morning on D-day, the first reconnaissance flights by helicopter were made over Wolmi-do and four hours later an artillery observer flying with Captain Vic Armstrong directed an artillery firing mission for the 11th Marines. In the meantime, Englehardt had rescued a downed Naval pilot from the harbor while the other "choppers," flying from the decks of an LST, did fourteen missions during the day. VMO-6 was back on its job of dawn-to-dusk reconnaissance-rescue-evacuation-artillery spotting flights. In the next twenty days the pilots of this squadron were to fly more than five hundred ten hours.

With Kimpo secure, Murray's 5th began the seizure of the high ground overlooking the Han River.

When Roise swung his battalion to the left of the Inchon–Yongdong-po Road to attack and seize Kimpo, Newton continued forward to capture the high ground in successive stages between Kimpo and Yongdong-po. Hill 99 (about two and a half miles due east of the airfield) was seized by Stevens' company and the positions were later reinforced by Fenton's company. Pedersen placed his unit on Hill 60 to the north and commanding the road.

At dawn Fenton saw enemy troops to his left flank advancing on the airstrip and attacking Roise's 2nd. Fenton opened fire with small arms and machine guns while Newton brought artillery and mortars into the enemy flank and rear. At the same time Pedersen was ordered to attack with his unit to cut off the retreat of the enemy force. The co-ordinated fire of the 1st and 2nd Battalions forced the enemy into a hurried withdrawal and heavy casualties were inflicted.

Newton's battalion continued toward the east, the next objective was seized and patrols to the river were sent out. A number of prisoners were taken and a large amount of medical supplies was captured in an abandoned enemy aid station. All these supplies were of American manufacture, having been taken by the enemy in earlier fighting in Korea.

On the morning of the nineteenth, Newton was ordered to advance and seize Hills 80 and 85. These two hills were just south of the Han River and were the last two prominent terrain features before the city of Yongdong-po.

At first light, however, an enemy force crossed the rice paddy in front of Pedersen's positions and began an attack. As Pedersen held up the advance of the enemy with heavy fire, Fenton brought his unit around in an enveloping movement onto Hill 118. Over one hundred enemy troops were killed without loss to Fenton's men.

Approximately five hundred troops were committed by the enemy to this attack and over eighty per cent of the force suffered casualties. Marine casualties were two killed and seven wounded.

One of the wounded was Sergeant Joe Ward, squad leader in Magness' platoon. As the attack developed an enemy grenade was hurled into a position held by two of Ward's men. Ward, seeing it fall, pounced on it and threw it back at the enemy. It exploded as it left his hand. Ward received severe wounds in the hand and arm.

The attack continued with Pedersen's company in the assault. Second Lieutenant Harold Dawe led his 3rd Platoon along the highway and, supported by tanks, machine gun and mortar fire, seized Hill 80. An hour later Corbet's 1st Platoon was atop Hill 85. Shortly after the seizure of these positions the Marines were subjected to a heavy barrage of artillery, mortar and direct tank fire from enemy positions in Yongdong-po.

To avoid heavy casualties, both platoons withdrew from the crest and occupied positions on the reverse slope.

While Murray's 5th was occupied with the capture of Kimpo, Puller was pushing his regiment along the road toward Yongdong-po. During the night of the eighteenth, Sutter's 2nd Battalion had received rather heavy mortar fire from an undetermined enemy position and two Marines were killed and three wounded. Shortly after six o'clock Puller's Marines were in the attack and by nine Ridge's battalion had passed through the town of Sosa. By 11:30 Ridge had seized his objective, fifteen hundred yards east of the town.

During the middle of the afternoon Ridge began receiving heavy fire from mortars and artillery. Marine air was called in as well as artillery fire, but the enemy guns could not be located. The fire came from the southeast and continued periodically throughout the day.

Just before the attack began on the nineteenth, Ridge's unit was again subjected to heavy mortar fire. The advance began on schedule with the 3rd making a rapid advance in its zone.

Sutter's 2nd ran into a well-organized center of resistance immediately after the jump-off, which grew progressively strong as the day wore on. The Seoul highway was heavily mined and two tanks had treads blown off. The infantrymen had to proceed through the rest of the day without tank support. Limited gains were made.

Puller was concerned about his right (south) flank. Since the landing his flank had been exposed save for Houghton's Recon unit, which had covered that area during the early advance. Houghton's unit, however, had to be used now for the early reconnaissance of the Han at the point where Murray's 5th was to cross. Almond assured Smith that elements of the 7th Army Division (the 32nd Regiment) would move onto the high ground to the east and south of Yongdong-po.

Shortly after noon on the nineteenth, the 32nd Army Regiment came into the zone from Inchon and relieved Hawkins' 1st Battalion of the mission of mopping up on the division's southern flank. Upon being relieved, Hawkins was to entruck his unit and sideslip laterally a distance of eleven miles to take positions then held by Newton's battalion.

In the next few hours, time and space factors were paramount in the operations of Hawkins' battalion. The trucks to transport his unit were late in arriving. It was dark before the leading element (Barrow's Able Company) arrived on Hill 118. Inasmuch as the crossing of the Han River by Murray's 5th was already in progress, Newton had been given a time limit as to when he would have his battalion at the crossing site. Additionally, Newton's unit would have to move on foot to the ferry crossing. In view of this, relief in position on Hills 80 and 85 could not be made.

Utilizing various routes, Newton's unit began movement to the Kimpo area. It was two o'clock in the morning before the last elements of his battalion was in the Kimpo area.

During the night and early morning the enemy crossed the rice paddy between the outskirts of Yongdong-po and the rise of ground to the west and occupied the two key terrain features, Hills 80 and 85. At first light a company-sized enemy counterattack was made in an effort to recapture Hill 118. The attack was beaten off with no particular difficulty. The enemy, upon being repulsed, retired to Hills 80 and 85 thus reinforcing those positions.

With Bland's Baker Company on the southern shore of the Han and in position to cross Kalchon Creek by the battered cement bridge, Wray's company began the movement to occupy the two hills to his front. Captain Charles Cable, commander of Fox Battery of 105 howitzers, placed a preparatory fire on the objective. When he lifted his fire and the ground troops did not go into the assault he requested and received permission to fire another preparation. After the second the infantry went into the assault.

With Lieutenant John Guild's 1st Platoon on the left of Lieutenant Henry Commiskey's 2nd, the assault was made up the steep rise of ground. Preparatory fires and aerial strikes had taken a toll of the enemy defenders, but had not weakened the resolution of the remainder who were well entrenched.

In a courageous example of small unit leadership, Guild charged the hill. Despite heavy fire from all types of automatic weapons and grenades, the 1st Platoon commander directed his men in the assault while continually exposed. The fighting became close and Guild killed two of the enemy with his pistol and was getting his men into position when he was severely wounded. Despite his wounds he continued to direct the final stages of the attack, refusing medical treatment or evacuation until the men in his unit had been cared for. Finally, he became unconscious from pain and loss of blood. He died a short time later.

On the right flank of the assault, Commiskey's 2nd was having an equally difficult task. The first to reach the crest, the commander of the 2nd Platoon came to hand-to-hand fighting with the enemy. Jumping into an enemy machine-gun emplacement, he killed four of the enemy with his pistol. Out of ammunition, Commiskey grappled with the fifth member of the machine-gun crew and disposed of this man with a weapon one of his men shoved into his hands. Hill 85 was secured shortly thereafter.

Early in the morning of the twentieth, as Hawkins was preparing for the assault on Hills 80 and 85, Sutter's battalion received its second tank-infantry attack in a period of three days. Sutter had his unit astride the main road between Inchon and Yongdong-po. The latter city was four thousand yards to the east. First Lieutenant John Carter's company was on the high ground north of the highway with Captain Welby Cronk's unit to the south. Between Cronk and Carter was a cut through which the road made a slow **S** turn. Also south of the road but east of Cronk's position was the zone covered by Captain Corey Groff's unit.

Enemy armor was heard moving about in the general direction of the city shortly after midnight, but the force did not begin its attack until four in the morning. The word was flashed that an armored force was approaching. Taylor was alerted to bring his platoon of Pershings forward to meet the threat. In the darkness Taylor's lead tank went off the road and bogged down in the mud, blocking the passage of those in trace. The defenders would be without tank support.

Cronk's CP was on a shelf of rock protruding from the high ground over the cut. From this position the approach of the enemy task force could be seen. In the dim half-light of early morning the vehicles were no more than shadows. The lead vehicle was a truck closely followed by four T-34 tanks. Behind the armor was a troop carrier with troops on foot bringing up the rear.

Cronk's unit took the enemy under fire and the tanks opened up with their machine guns and high velocity cannon. The foot troops behind the tanks deployed to the south of the road and rushed across the low ground toward the Marine positions. Pfc. Mario Yedlewski (Cronk's runner) rose from his hole and hurled a grenade. It landed in the lead truck and in a moment the entire scene was lighted by a terrific explosion. The shooting light was better yet the Korean infantry continued their assault.

Lieutenant Howard Foor, commanding the 2nd Platoon, yelled, "Okay, you Leathernecks, fix bayonets and start sticking the bastards."

Corporal William Cheek awakened when he heard the enemy tanks open fire. The area of battle was over three hundred yards from where Cheek and his bazooka team were dug in. Cheek ran to Groff and asked permission to take a rocket launcher down the hill and engage the tanks. Groff granted Cheek his request after warning the squad leader that the mission was one of great hazard.

Cheek called to Monegan and the gunner joined him. While Pfc. Perkins was unpacking additional ammunition, Cheek and Monegan ran down the hill toward the enemy tanks. Cheek was carrying three rounds. Monegan took a firing position on a knoll. Due to the darkness he was unable to sight in and his first shot was a wild miss. Monegan told Cheek that they'd have to go further forward.

The two men displaced forward until they were within a hundred yards of the tanks. Loading the weapon in the cover of a water tank Monegan stepped from cover. As he was sighting the weapon Yedlewski's grenaded ammunition truck lit the scene.

"I've got it in the cross hairs," he shouted.

"Fire quick," Cheek directed.

The shot was a direct hit on the third of four tanks in the line. Enemy small-arms fire began to saturate the immediate area around the water tank. Perkins joined Cheek and Monegan with more ammunition and took over the job of loading. Once again Monegan stepped from cover to aim at the tanks; once again he scored a direct hit. One of the remaining tanks began to turn around and Monegan yelled at Perkins to reload at once.

As Monegan was sighting in for his third kill, the enemy opened fire with automatic weapons. Monegan was struck down. Cheek and Perkins got him under cover of the water tank and Perkins ran for a corpsman. As Cheek was dressing his wounds, Monegan died.

By this time it was light enough for Carter's unit north of the highway to join in. The last enemy tank in the column tried to turn around and back off the road and bogged down in the mud. From this position it was impossible for the tank to bring its gun to bear; the crew were killed as they tried to escape.

Under the blistering fire from Cronk's unit the enemy attack became demoralized and panic among them spread as the Marines met their rush with bayonets. Three tanks were destroyed and the fourth captured in operable condition. The enemy foot troops were annihilated. Foor kept his bloody bayonet fixed to his carbine for several days.

During the early phase of the Inchon-Seoul operation, enemy resistance was dictated by the circumstances in which they found themselves. It was apparent that the enemy had not expected a landing in the Inchon area and they were weak in manpower for the immediate defense of the port. Many of the troops captured were recent conscripts without the benefit of training; some lacked any military training, and their arms and equipment were poor.

Because of these factors the North Korean commander was forced into fighting, as best he could, a delaying action to the Han River. Ordinarily he would have made his stand under the favorable defensive conditions afforded by Wolmi-do and Inchon.

However, it was obvious the enemy commander was improvising and delaying as best he could while preparing to make his stand before and in Seoul. This became more evident as the two Marine regiments advanced. Each succeeding day brought them in contact with stiffer resistance conducted by troops with better training and equipment.

Smith was convinced that Seoul would not be taken without a bitter struggle.

CHAPTER XI

Seoul: Part 1. The Battle for an Entrance to a City

While Puller's 1st was seizing commanding terrain prior to the final assault on Yongdong-po, Murray's 5th was preparing to cross the Han. This maneuver would uncover river-crossing sites permitting the division to move against the city of Seoul proper.

Murray's CP at Kimpo was subjected to a carnival spirit as the area was overrun with newspapermen and a new category of personnel, VIK (Very Important Kibitzers), from Tokyo. Every plane brought more of these intruders into the area. With no reason or right to be in Korea, they demanded time of Marine personnel when time was running out. In this turmoil Murray and his regimental staff attempted to make their plans for the crossing; finally it was necessary to exclude all newspapermen and kibitzers from the CP in order that battalion and company commanders might be briefed on an operation that was to begin in a matter of hours.

Murray had selected the Korean ferry-crossing site northeast of Kimpo as the point from which he would send his regiment to the northern banks of the Han. The width of the river at this point was about two hundred fifty yards and on the opposite bank lay the town of Haengju. The exit from the town was an indifferent road leading northward for some twelve hundred yards where it joined the main road and rail line into Seoul. To the north of Haengju and bordering the river was a high piece of ground commanding the crossing and immediate terrain inland. This feature (Hill 125) would have to be seized early in the operation to cover the crossing of other units and to allow a penetration inland.

Murray's CP was in the basement of the Kimpo Airfield administration building. The upper stories of the building had been torn and battered by the shelling and bombing and the only intact portion of the structure was in the basement. In a large, dark room lighted by Coleman lanterns meager arrangements had been made to seat those immediately concerned with the river crossing. The room was littered with C ration cans, bedrolls and stretchers which had been used as cots. The utter lack of effort to provide for physical comforts was evidence that the use of the space was considered transitory.

It was 3:30 in the afternoon when the three battalion commanders and the two assault company commanders (Bohn and McMullen) began to gather at the regimental command post for briefing and orders. The occasion gave many Marines a chance to meet friends from other units and the room was soon filled with small talk and smoke.

The line commanders looked with some awe and envy at the clean appearance of the "pogues" from division and Corps headquarters. There was the usual good-natured bantering with unit commanders telling their more fortunate friends on the staff: "Take a day off and come up and see how we're fighting this war."

Bohn, McMullen and Houghton sat together; of all the officers in the sprawly room these three would be the ones most intimately affected by the crossing. They waited. Bohn told his companions he thought the room looked like a World War I movie set and Houghton answered that he "wished the hell it was." They saw an erect, gray-haired man enter through the blackout curtains at the rear door and make his way to an out-of-the-way corner and stand patiently by while the final preparations were made for the briefing to begin.

"Who's that?" Bohn asked.

"General Lowe," Houghton answered. "He's President Truman's observer out here. He wants to swim the river with me tonight but General O. P. wouldn't let him."

"Th' hell you say. He must be nuts."

Murray moved to the front of the room and began to speak. He reminded the assembly that this was the first river crossing the Corps had made in combat in a good many years; that the time for planning had been short, but that neither was there cause or excuse for alarm. He closed his short talk by saying that the mission of the regiment would be accomplished regardless of what happened.

With no dramatics or further fanfare he introduced the regimental intelligence officer, Major William Esterline. The situation on the northern side of the river was vague and there was considerable doubt as to just what effort the enemy could put forth to oppose the crossing and subsequent advance on Seoul. Pictures taken of the area in the past day had not been delivered as yet. A POW had reported the exit road from Haengju was heavily mined. There were so many qualifications to the intelligence evaluation that the assault commanders had the feeling of having sat down to a feast only to have it withdrawn after the first mouthful.

Major Charles Brush, regimental operations officer, followed Esterline. Brush was limping badly from a wrenched knee and he was in considerable pain as he leaned on a cane to give the order. He gave the disposition of friendly troops and supporting arms and brought looks of dismay to the unit commanders when he told them there would be no artillery support until after the crossing had been made. The mission of the 5th Marines, he told them, was to cross the river and seize and hold certain objectives. Houghton's Reconnaissance Company would cross in advance initially by swimming with later reinforcements arriving by LVT's. This unit would seize and hold three objectives, clear one road of mines and plant mines on a second.

Taplett's battalion would cross the river at four o'clock in the morning, pass though Houghton's unit and seize and hold the final two objectives inland on the main road to Seoul. Roise's battalion would cross two hours after Taplett's and pass through and press the attack in the direction of Seoul. Newton's battalion was to remain in regimental reserve and cross on order; tanks and regimental weapons to cross on order; radio silence until "H" hour excepting for Houghton's unit.

As soon as Brush was finished there was a great rush as commanders hurried to their organizations to brief them and to get them to the assembly areas before dark. Bohn and McMullen returned to their units and, gathering up their platoon leaders and key NCO's, hurried to the high ground overlooking the ferry site. From here the company commanders briefed their subordinates on the plan.

Hill 125 is a bald, detached knob of land rising sharply from the north bank of the Han. The town of Haengju lay to the west on a shallow spur of the hill. The high ground and the main part of the town was joined by a scattering of buildings. Under the western shadow of this key piece of terrain was the exit road bordered by dikes.

Houghton selected ten of his best swimmers from among his enlisted personnel to make the swim. Second Lieutenant Dana Cashion and an interpreter, Lieutenant Horace Underwood, USNR, were to make up the balance of the party. Underwood had been born in Seoul and spoke the language and knew the area as well as the natives. Ensign Jack Seigle, a Navy Public Information Officer, had talked Murray into letting him make the trip. Seigle was to be armed with a tape recorder so that the historical crossing could be recorded as it transpired.

The night was clear and the moon, in the last quarter, would not be too revealing. The party gathered on the near shore of the river and took to the tepid, polluted water at ten minutes of nine.

"If the enemy opens fire, which is better? Stay on the surface and get hit or go under and get typhoid?"

Swimming the breast stroke in order that no ripples or splashing would occur, the swimmers formed a unit front and began stroking easily, softly for the enemy shore. Weapons and ammunition were towed in rubber boats as was Seigle's recording instrument.

Fifty minutes of swimming brought the party to the enemy shore where they crept silently onto the beach, collected their weapons and began to reconnoiter the village and high ground to the right of the landing site. Cashion led a small group into the darkness to snoop through the village and search the high ground above it. One hour and twenty minutes later Houghton gathered his small force on the river's edge and listened to the reports of his "prowlers." No enemy had been contacted in the village or on the exit road. Cashion's group did not, however, reach the military or topographical crest of Hill 125. When they came to the ridge line joining the village and the hill it was thought, in the confusion of darkness, the crest had been reached.

With that Houghton signaled the far side of the river for the balance of his unit to begin crossing in LVT's. Nine amphibious tractors (commanded by First Lieutenant Gerald Anderson) bearing the men and equipment of the Recon Company began the crossing. Midway over, the enemy, well entrenched on the hill, opened fire with machine guns and mortars. The fire became so intense that the tractors were ordered to turn back. Four of the amphtracks drifted downstream and became stuck on a sand bar. In the meantime, Houghton and his

---

The Approach to Seoul. *The enemy recovers from the initial shock and the fighting becomes heavier with each day as the Marines press forward to recapture the South Korean capital. Murray captures Kimpo and crosses the Han River. Puller seizes Yongdong-po and drives through the heart of the capital city.*

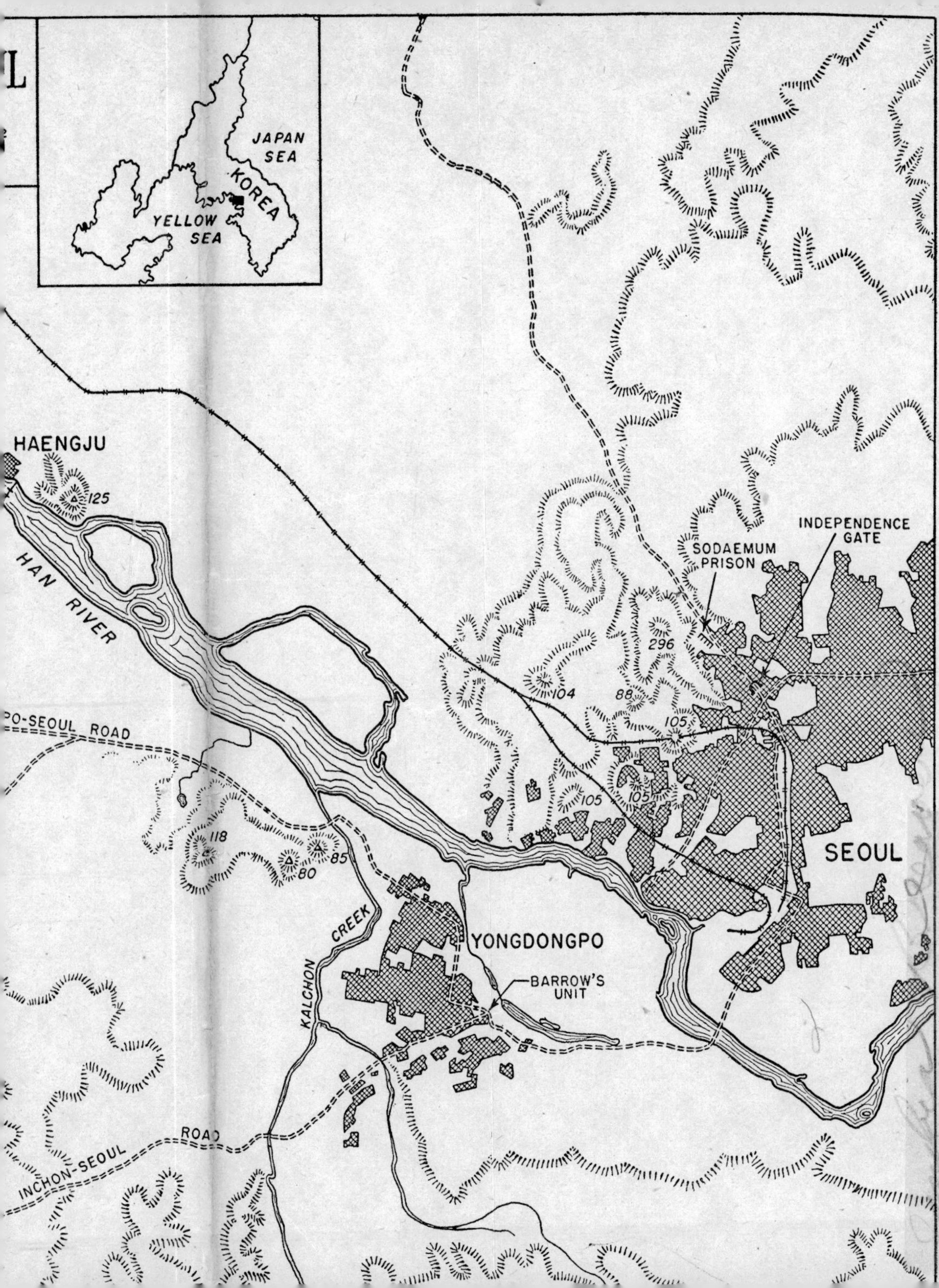
JAPAN SEA
KOREA
YELLOW SEA
HAENGJU
125
HAN RIVER
PO-SEOUL ROAD
118
80
85
KALCHON CREEK
YONGDONGPO
BARROW'S UNIT
INCHON-SEOUL ROAD
SODAEMUM PRISON
INDEPENDENCE GATE
296
104
88
105
105
105
SEOUL

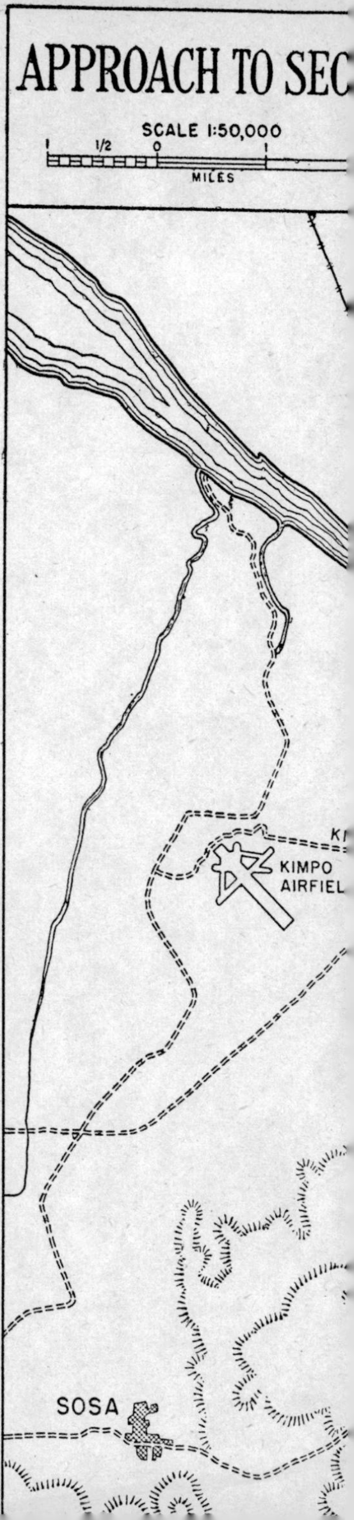
APPROACH TO SEC
SCALE 1:50,000
1 1/2 0 1
MILES
KI
KIMPO
AIRFIEL
SOSA

men were coming under increasingly heavy fire on the beach. With no hope of immediate reinforcement, the order was given to return to the friendly side of the river. Houghton struck off for the tractors on the sand bar to assist in retrieving them.

Excess equipment and the rubber boats were hidden on the enemy shore and the swimming party began the return through water that was being sprinkled by small-arms fire and churned by mortars. With some reluctance, Seigle hid his recording instrument on which he had nearly half an hour of on-the-spot descriptions of the crossing and search of the far bank.*

The swimmers became separated on the return, Houghton was injured by a near miss of a mortar in the water and drifted downstream; Corporal James Morgan, swimming near by but unhurt, went to Houghton's rescue and swam him to safety. The Recon commander had a badly strained back and double vision from concussion; three others suffered wounds. By 4:45 in the morning the party had returned. The original plan of a night crossing had to be abandoned. Murray ordered an assault landing by Taplett's battalion at daylight.

Because of the hurried alterations in plans and a breakdown in communications, the hastily planned artillery preparation for the crossing was inadequate and poorly placed. Rather than wait for an adjustment of fire, Murray decided that Taplett should cross at once. With McMullen's Item Company in the lead, the crossing was made under light to moderate enemy fire. Directly behind McMullen was Bohn's unit with the mission of driving directly inland to the Kaesong-Seoul road and to seize the high ground beyond.

McMullen landed and swung his unit through the village and onto Hill 125 to the right.

There was a certain amount of milling about and confusion as the men of McMullen's unit spilled from their amphibian tractors and began the assault of the high ground. The enemy, reinforced since Houghton had been there earlier, were well positioned and committed to the task of holding at all costs. McMullen's unit began to take casualties as the bare slopes afforded little or no cover. The 60 mm. mortar section came under heavy fire as it attempted to set up to support the assaulting riflemen. Three were killed from the section in

* Seigle retrieved his recorder later, but someone had found it before his return and his historic account was erased by several choice stories which had nothing to do with crossing the Han River.

as many minutes; the machine-gun section from the Weapons Company raced into position to take the fire from the mortar crews. Sergeant James Guffey, in charge of the machine-gun section, was wounded. Corporal Marvin Prince and Pfc. Howard Chancey moved their machine gun into position and opened fire. Prince was killed and Chancey took over the gun. Chancey was killed. Pfc. Charles Fattaig, ammunition carrier, took over the weapon and continued the fire which relieved the exposed men in the mortar section. Fattaig was wounded in the arms and legs. He refused evacuation and continued to operate the weapon.

At the same time Pfc.'s Blanchard and Coley got their machine gun into action to support the advancing infantrymen. The enemy turned their fire and Blanchard was killed; Coley took his place and continued fire with the weapon. Coley was wounded three times in the next few minutes but refused evacuation.

Then, suddenly, the enemy will to resist evaporated; Item Company surged to the top of the hill and that phase of the river crossing was over.

Bohn's unit ignored the brisk fire fight going on to their right and, remaining in LVT's, pushed inland. Along their route they passed a convoy of burnt-out trucks, jeeps and T-34 tanks, which had been destroyed by Marine air. Pushing inland to a distance of twenty-five hundred yards, Bohn's company debarked from the LVT's and after a sharp fire fight seized the high ground.

As the enemy broke and ran, Master Sergeant William Callow called down artillery fire on the fleeing troops. VT (aerial impulse) fuses inflicted heavy casualties, Marine Corsairs further developed the panic in the enemy battalion.

The crossing and drive inland by Bohn's company had been nearly due north. Once his unit had seized the high ground northeast of the Kaesong-Seoul Railroad Wildman's company would pass between McMullen and Bohn. This maneuver would turn the direction of the attack from north to east.

By 1040 Bohn and McMullen were on their objectives and Wildman was moving east. Forty-three casualties had been suffered by Taplett's battalion as Roise's 2nd crossed and passed through to continue the attack.

Few operations have been viewed by so many officers of high rank as the 5th Marine Crossing of the Han River. Murray had set up his observation post on the high ground above the old ferry-crossing site at Kolhwa-ri. From this coign of vantage the deployment of the Marines across the river could be seen without the use of binoculars. Shortly after daylight Marine Generals Shepherd and Smith were joined by Admiral Struble, General Almond and members of their various staffs. Swelling this number was a large coterie of newspapermen.

Under these critical eyes Murray's 5th acquitted itself with an efficiency and dispatch which drew the unqualified praise of everyone; shortly after MacArthur had been informed the crossing was a success he went to Kimpo where he enplaned for Tokyo.

The day after the Han crossing by Murray's 5th, Puller sent the three battalions of his 1st Marines into the attack on Yongdong-po. Bland's company of Hawkins' battalion was positioned north of Hills 85 and 80. On Cable's recommendation, an eighteen-hundred round artillery preparation was fired before they crossed Kalchon Creek and entered the town from the northwest. The network of dikes in the western portion of the city was heavily manned by a tenacious enemy and progress was slow and costly.

By two o'clock in the afternoon the 1st and 3rd Platoons of Baker Company had fought across the first dike and into the factory area in the outskirts of the town. Shepherd, commanding the 1st, had been wounded before midday; Hollingsworth of the 3rd went out with wounds two hours later. First Lieutenant Chester Farmer, Company Executive Officer, went forward to take charge of the reorganization. The two units were formed into one and Staff Sergeant Frank Quadros placed in command.

Forty-five days from the day he had left Tulsa, Oklahoma, Pfc. Albert Collins was in the attack with Quadros' combined unit. Pinned down by heavy fire from the enemy behind a second dike, supporting fire was necessary before the Marines could negotiate the barbed-wire fence and the concrete ditch between them and the dike. The machine gun Collins was serving furnished this fire until the ammunition was depleted. Collins ran across a fire-swept area where a supply of belted ammunition had been stored. Picking up two boxes he began his return. Forty yards from the gun he was struck down by enemy fire. He crawled the rest of the way to the now silent gun. Upon gaining the position he found the other members of the crew had been killed or wounded. Despite excessive bleeding Collins loaded the weapon and opened fire on the rim of the dike. He died of his wounds as he fired the last of his ammunition.

Badly depleted by casualties, Quadros' unit was forced to withdraw.

On the right flank of the attack Sutter's battalion came under heavy fire from artillery, mortar and automatic weapons positions outside the 1st Marines' zone of action. Groff's company entered heavy action in the low hills south of the Inchon-Seoul highway. As so often happens in battle it became a case of "I know where I am but where th' hell are you" between commanders of adjacent units.

Sutter was in constant contact with the commander of the 2nd Battalion, 32nd Army Regiment by radio but definite agreement could not be reached between them as to what hills were occupied by their troops. The Army leader was certain and insistent that he occupied the hills about the village of Kuroi-ni; Sutter was equally certain that the hills in question were being fought over by Groff's unit.

Reluctant to push his unit into Yongdong-po without taking the high ground to his right, Sutter finally gave the order for Groff to withdraw. Puller asked for and received permission to fire artillery onto the hills as Groff's unit withdrew. At the same time Puller requested Corps to assign a liaison officer to settle boundaries and decide who held what piece of real estate. Groff got his unit from the high ground without further incident but Carter's company was pinned down by heavy fire from the same area. Unable to extricate his unit without suffering heavy losses Carter requested an air strike.

First Lieutenant Norman Vining, forward air controller, stood on the crossroads north of Kuroi-ni and brought a flight of Corsairs into action; closer and closer he brought the gull-winged planes to the front lines of the Marines. The last strike was within thirty yards of friendly lines. Carter was able to move his unit out and onto the road and the battalion began the advance that would take them to the Sachon Tributary, a southeasterly branch of Kalchon Creek.

Just when it appeared that the attack might stall with further heavy fighting indicated for the next day. Captain Robert Barrow's Able Company drove deep into the middle of the Yongdong-po and the enemy defenses were shattered.

When Barrow received the attack orders from Hawkins on the morning of the twenty-first, his unit was on Hill 118. Moving south behind the masking of Hill 52 he formed his skirmish line behind a high dike which joined Hills 52 and 43. With the dike serving as a place of concealment as well as a departure line, Jones' 2nd Platoon and Swords' 3rd were to form the assault line with McClelland's 1st to Swords' left. Across the dike from Barrow's unit was a rice paddy witht the rice nearly chest high. In perfect formation the company crossed the dike and plunged into the rice. It was soon apparent that the enemy did not expect an attack from this direction (due west of the city) and Able Company crossed the paddy without drawing fire.

Crossing Kalchon Creek was a simple matter for Jones' unit on the right, but Swords' platoon ran into some difficulty when they came into waist-deep mud. Another high dike on the far side of the creek formed yet another shield while Swords' unit was pulled from the mud and formed to move into the city. A final check was made and Barrow's unit spilled over the dike and began a rapid push along the city streets.

It was very nearly as though the unit was passing through a ghost city. To the left they could hear the racket and roar of the fight Baker Company was having and to the right rear there was the heavier smashing of Sutter's battalion, but Able Company was passing through a military vacuum. It was soon discovered that the radios were undependable with the buildings and wires forming barriers, but by constant use of runners Barrow kept control of his platoons. Advancing over six hundred yards without opposition, Jones' platoon came upon elements of enemy troops moving along the broad concrete highway which connected Inchon and Seoul. These troops apparently were hurrying westward to reinforce the enemy facing Sutter's battalion and did not appear to be aware of Barrow's unit until taken under fire.

Barrow shifted McClelland from left echelon to the right and the 2nd and 1st Platoons destroyed or dispersed this enemy force. On the left Swords' unit had not come to action. Barrow reported to Hawkins that he was seven hundred yards inside the city and neither flank was in contact with friendly troops. Hawkins instructed Able Company commander to continue his advance.

By eleven o'clock in the morning Barrow's unit was through Yongdong-po and had taken positions on a thirty-foot dike on the top of which was a hard top road. (See map.) To the immediate rear of the unit lay the civic center of the city with the courthouse, township office and a five-story building filled with American medical supplies. Between the medical supply building and the roadway-dike was a smaller building with large quantities of enemy ammunition stacked about it. While these buildings were being checked, Swords, on the left flank, had set up his machine guns and was taking enemy troops under long-range fire to the northeast. It appeared that the troops under fire from Swords' unit were withdrawing from the sector facing Bland's company.

In McClelland's area an enemy 76 mm. gun was set up in the street. The crew was destroyed. Pfc. Lavern Altenburg rushed out to the gun to see if it were operable. He was hit by an antitank bullet. McClelland and Corporal George Decker ran into the zone of fire and brought Altenburg to safety. Company Corpsmen David Smith, Fred Johnson and Richard Showstead utilized the plasma found in the captured medical supplies in an attempt to save Altenburg's life but it was a hopeless task. By this time the unit had taken twelve wounded and supplies in the captured building continued to amplify the stock carried by corpsmen.

Barrow was finding it difficult to contact the battalion CP by radio. After a time he got Major David Bridges, operations officer for Hawkins, on the net and attempted to describe the exact location he held in the city. There was some difficulty due to the fading condition of the radio. About this time McClelland's platoon was flushing out a small enemy force in the vicinity of the dry kilns. A grenade was tossed on the other side of a large pile of coal and set off an ammunition dump. The resultant explosion shook the area and tossed an atom bomb mushroom of smoke and dust into the air.

Barrow asked Bridges, "Do you see that explosion?"

"Yeh, it looks like an 'A' bomb. Didn't know you had one with you."

"That's our positions. I'm seventy-five yards north of there."

The radio faded out completely and Barrow was unable to restore contact. The enemy had recovered from their initial surprise at Barrow's fast sweep through the city and there was increasing enemy activity to the rear and flanks of the unit. Barrow put his unit in an all-around defense utilizing a portion of the thirty-foot dike bordering the city. Digging in on the manmade ridge was not difficult and by late afternoon Able Company was in position on both sides of the dike with the plateau of the top covered by fire. The wounded (seven) were moved from the civic center area to the mid-line of the perimeter on the western side of the dike where they were put into positions of cover. Eighteen prisoners captured by the unit were also placed here.

The portion of dike which Barrows had positioned to defend ran generally north and south. Along the thirty-foot sidewalls two-man positions were staggered high and low for a hundred and fifty yards on either side. The men on the western side of the embankment looked into the city and down upon the civic center while the units on the east commanded the low ground and small airfield between them and the Han River. The end positions looked to the north on more of the city and the clay pipe factory. The southern end commanded the township office and Eitohe grade school.

As night approached it became apparent neither the right nor left friendly units would penetrate the area to a depth permitting a tie-in with Barrow. This isolation, however, did not affect the morale of the unit as it prepared to meet enemy counterattacks.

The first of five enemy attacks to drive Barrow's unit from its positions came at dusk. Five enemy T-34 tanks formed in the city and proceeded to the civic center. Between the dike positions and the medical supply building was a secondary road which paralleled the Marine lines by a distance of seventy-five feet. The enemy tanks, in column, moved from the civic center and, making a left turn, began their run across the face of Marine positions.

As the lead tank was making the turn, Corporal Francis Devine hit it with 3.5 rocket and knocked the turret off. It slowed, turned off the road and disappeared behind near-by buildings. The other four tanks, their guns at right angles, ran the length of the perimeter firing armor-piercing shot into the embankment.

Barrow attempted to contact battalion again; for a short space of a few seconds he talked with Bridges and told him of the tank attack and requested an air strike. It was too late in the day for air support. The radio faded again as Barrow told Bridges not to worry.

Fortunately for the Marines the enemy had used armor-piercing shells on the first run and these shells penetrated the soft dirt of the dike with little or no damage. Barrow was concerned that they use high explosive shells on the next attack. The four tanks swept by on the return trip; again they used armor-piercing shells. A second T-34 was crippled and left the line. Once again the enemy armored vehicles turned and swung across the front; a third was crippled and limped out of action. On the final attempt there were but two tanks and both were hit as they returned to the point of origin behind the medical supply building. That was to be the last of the tank attacks.

The next action to be experienced by Able Company was at the southern end of the line in McClelland's sector. In the dark, enemy were seen and heard attempting to remove ammunition from the low building directly to the front. Because of a shortage of ammunition only selective fire was brought onto these people. With daylight twenty-seven dead ammunition carriers were counted in this area.

At the opposite end of the elongated perimeter, in Swords' 3rd Platoon sector, the enemy could be heard forming for an attack and there was considerable loud talking as a leader could be heard exhorting his men. Again, because of the shortage of ammunition, the Marines allowed the enemy to approach within ten yards before opening fire. It was apparent the enemy were creating noise in order to draw fire and reveal positions but the Marines waited with commendable patience.

A green flare was the signal for the attack which came from the northwest side of the road. Shouting "Manzai, Manzai," the enemy skirmish line came slowly forward behind the marching fire of automatic weapons. The attack was beaten off with heavy losses and the enemy retired to the opposite side of the road under the cover of buildings in the outskirts of the city.

Once again the Marines heard much talking and gradually they were able to distinguish one voice above the others as it became obvious that this was the leader. Another attack was launched. Again the Marines of Swords' platoon beat the enemy back. Once more the dike-road defenders heard the North Korean officer delivering his morale building talk. The enemy moved across the road and initiated the third attack from the same direction as the first. For the third time the attackers were beaten off with heavy casualties. While the Marines were preoccupied with the third attack an enemy officer among the prisoners made a run for it. He escaped under a hail of fire.

Shortly afterward an interpreter with Jones' platoon reported him shouting "don't attack . . . they're too strong . . . don't attack. . . ."

Outranked or outshouted by the other leader the enemy formed and made a fourth attack on Swords' positions. On this occasion Corporal Billy Webb, in charge of the 2nd fire team of the 3rd Squad, was forced to withdraw a few yards into the light-machine-gun positions. The enemy was repulsed from here. For the fifth time the Marines listened to the enemy officer exhort his men for still another attack.

By this time Webb had lost patience with the situation and decided on direct action. Telling his fire team not to fire on him when he returned, Webb slipped from his foxhole in the direction of the voice. Moving across the road used by the tanks, he entered the city streets with the enemy officer's voice acting as a beacon. In the shelter of a building Webb found his man, giving a stirring lecture. Taking careful aim he stopped the voice in mid-sentence. Webb raced back to his position. As Swords said later, "That Gook literally talked himself to death."

With the death of their fiery leader, the fifth and last attack was spiritless and was beaten off easily. When daylight came the members of Barrow's company found over fifty automatic weapons in the immediate area and over two hundred and fifty dead were seen on both sides of the road. Countless other enemy dead were later found in the buildings bordering the attacking area; the tanks were also found abandoned.

During the rest of the night and early morning the enemy withdrew and the battle for Yongdong-po was virtually over.

For purposes of orientation the positions of Puller's 1st and Murray's 5th should be noted. On the twenty-third of September Puller had cleared all resistance south of the Han and received orders to cross the river and begin the assault on the capital.

Murray's 5th had crossed the Han on the morning of the twentieth. Before darkness on that day Taplett's battalion had taken its assigned objectives, as had Roise's 2nd. The Engineer Battalion had constructed a pontoon ferry and ramp and twelve tanks were across the river.

On the morning of the twenty-first, after repulsing an enemy counter-attack of one hundred fifty troops, the attack toward Seoul was continued. By 10:30 in the morning Taplett's 3rd had seized Hill 165. With Newton and Taplett abreast, the attack was carried on. Through the twenty-second and twenty-third, the 5th was engaged in a series of bitter battles for the commanding ground west of Seoul.

The ships bearing Litzenberg's 7th Marines were in position for unloading at Inchon later in the afternoon on the twenty-first. By ten o'clock that evening Hinkle's 2nd and Roach's 3rd Battalions were nineteen miles northeast of the port city. The speed with which the 7th unloaded and moved into its zone of action was the cause of many favorable comments. Activated as a regiment on the seventeenth of August in California, the 7th Marines were in the area of Kimpo thirty-five days later.

By design General Smith assigned Litzenberg's unit to flank security and patrolling in the zone on Murray's left flank. It was Smith's desire to give the unit all the time possible for training and orientation before committing them to battle. The burden of the street fighting through the heart of Seoul would fall on the 1st and 5th Marines.

The positions, then, of the Marines at sundown on the twenty-third was this: Puller's 1st was preparing to cross the Han; Murray's 5th was engaged in one of the most costly fights in the Korean war; Litzenberg's 7th was to cross the Han and into a zone of action in rear of the 5th.

In the nine days since landing at Inchon the Marines had suffered 1,149 casualties of which 145 had been killed in action, 20 had died of wounds and 5 were missing in action.

The enemy had been heavily reinforced in the days since the landing at Inchon by bringing units south from Pyongyang as well as from the east coast of Korea. From ground of his own choosing the North Korean commander decided to make his stand in the hills to the west of the city. Before the Marines entered the capital a number of key hills had to be taken. At the upper, or northern end, was Hill 296; next in line to the south toward the Han River, was 105 (north), 105 (middle) and 105 (south). To the east of the southern 105 lay Hill 79. Fifteen hundred yards west of the northern Hill 105 lay a horseshoe-shaped land mass which was to serve as the first redoubt in strength—Hill 88.

The defensive positions held by the enemy on Hill 88 had been prepared with great care. Weapons were emplaced in mutually supporting positions with both the military and topographical crest manned and defended. Groups of emplacements on the crests and forward slopes of the ridge were formed around heavy machine guns with each group having one heavy machine gun and two light machine guns supported by a squad of men armed with rifles or automatic weapons.

Twenty-three hundred troops from the 25th North Korean Brigade defended the area; the unit was largely commanded by NCO's and officers who had seen duty with the Communist forces in China. The bulk of these troops remained in position until dug out and killed by the Marines.

Concrete caves held ample supplies. Individual foxholes were undercut to provide maximum shelter against artillery and aerial bombardment. Smokepots were used extensively to hide positions from Marine airmen. Before and during World War II, the area had served as a training site for the Japanese Army. It was later taken over by the South Korean Military, and, since the fall of Seoul to the North Koreans, it had been utilized by the enemy as a recruit training site. As a result every position was known and plotted for retaliatory fire in case of loss.

The opening battles for these key terrain features began in earnest on the twenty-first, the day after the Han River crossing. After repulsing a light counterattack in the early morning, Murray's regiment began the attack toward Seoul. Newton's 1st and Taplett's 3rd were abreast with the 1st on the right or southern flank. By midmorning Taplett's 3rd had seized several outlying hills and Bohn's company drove eastward to capture Hill 104.

During this attack Master Sergeant Ryder, Mortar Platoon Leader Jaworski and Forward Observer Callow were wounded. When the zone of action was changed Bohn turned the hill over to the 2nd Battalion, Korean Marine Regiment and Taplett continued to the northeast to capture the high ground west of Hill 296. Bohn was wounded by mortar fire as he inspected his platoon positions and had to be evacuated. First Lieutenant Charles Mize took command of George Company. The battalion set up defenses here for the night.

Newton's battalion began the twenty-first in route march formation to objective "Dog." Following the railroad tracks leading to Seoul the unit pushed along at a fast rate. After an air strike and artillery preparation, Stevens and Fenton co-ordinated their maneuvers to capture Hill 96. Pedersen's Charlie Company, in trace of Stevens' unit, swept to the left and captured Hill 68. Fenton continued the attack and Hill 40 was taken. These hill masses were stepping stones to southern Hill 105.

During the day Newton's 1st, though under moderate small-arms and harassing sniper fire, suffered light casualties. Two were killed and seven wounded. First Lieutenant Fred Eubanks, executive officer to Stevens, was wounded and evacuated. That night a shell hit the house Murray was using for a CP and his regimental executive officer, Lieutenant Colonel Larry Hays, was wounded severely in the legs and had to be evacuated. Murray received lesser wounds and remained on duty. Lieutenant Colonel Joseph Stewart, assistant division operations officer, took over Hays' billet.

With the rail line serving as a boundary between Newton's 1st and the ROK Marines on Hill 104 to the north, the plan for the morning of the twenty-second called for an attack by all three battalions in line—Taplett to the left and north, the ROK Marines in the center and Newton to the right and south.

The morning objective facing Newton was the southern Hill 105. Stevens' company was to advance to the base of the hill while Pedersen's company was to envelop the objective from the right. Fenton's unit was to furnish fire support from his positions on Hill 40. Technical Sergeant McMullen led off the attack with his 1st Platoon. By midmorning McMullen had captured the high ground around the radio station. As the 2nd and 3rd Platoons were moving into position for the final assault they were pinned down by heavy automatic and small-arms fire. First Lieutenant Nathaniel Mann, leader of the 2nd Platoon (formerly commanded by Johnston, Lawson and Muetzel) was killed and First Lieutenant Joe Schimmenti, leader of the 3rd Platoon, was severely wounded. Technical Sergeant Bolkow took over the 3rd while Technical Sergeant Johnson assumed command of the 2nd.

In the case of Schimmenti's wound the medical officers of the battalion and regiment came to the decision it was one of those miracle wounds which happen in war. A rifle bullet had entered one side of Schimmenti's neck and passing directly through came out on the opposite side. From front to back the bullet passed midway between the esophagus and spinal column. After being hit Schimmenti walked nearly a mile to the aid station.

The doctor told him, "If I practiced for ten years I couldn't pierce your neck where that bullet did without killing you. Son, you're just plain lucky."

Later in the day a mortar dropped in the aid station area and the battalion surgeon, Lieutenant (jg) "Hogan" H'Doubler, was wounded; a few minutes later he was wounded again by another mortar blast. Receiving wounds at the same time were Chaplain Tennant and Chief Medical Corpsman Douglas Austin.

Upon the evacuation of H'Doubler and Tennant, Austin, though wounded in the face and ankle, assumed responsibility for caring of the wounded coming into the station. With the assistance of Corpsmen Boyle and Thronal, Austin treated over fifty wounded Marines until Lieutenant (jg) Danny O'Toole could be sent forward from division.

Throughout the day heavy fighting developed for Newton's battalion on southern Hill 105. Corbet (1st Platoon) and Magness (2nd Platoon of Charlie Company) swung their units into position for a co-ordinated attack with Fenton's company. After an intense artillery and mortar preparation, Pedersen and Fenton's units assaulted the hill. At 5:30 in the afternoon the objective was secured.

During the day the 1st had suffered twelve killed and thirty-one wounded.

While the 1st was fighting on the southern flank, the ROK Marines in the center of the line found it impossible to advance in the face of extremely heavy fire from Hill 88. This unit took heavy casualties throughout the day.

To the north Taplett's 3rd went into the attack on Hill 296 at seven in the morning. The objective was assigned to Wildman's company and was seized two and a half hours later against moderate resistance. During the morning the enemy began to build up strength on the eastern slopes in an effort to retake the lost ground. Supported by fires from Winter's tanks, Wildman's company attacked down the slopes and forced the enemy to withdraw. A number of prisoners were taken.

Throughout the remainder of the day the 3rd continued extensive patrolling.

With the failure of the ROK Marines to advance in the center, Murray ordered Roise to move the 2nd Battalion through their lines and continue the attack. "H. J." Smith and Peters took their units in the assault. The 2nd pressed the attack from Hill 104 to the southeast in the direction of northern Hill 105.

Midway between Hills 104 and northern 105 lies the horseshoe-shaped land mass previously described. Upon this ground the enemy had positioned seven hundred troops. The southwestern toe of the horseshoe rested on the Sinuiju railroad. From this point the ridge line rose to a height of two hundred fifty feet in the next thousand yards, where it swung eastward forming the heel. From here it turned south again until the eastern toe rested on the rail line five hundred yards removed from the western. The mission of Smith's company was to seize a foothold on the western toe and clear the ridge line from that point to the eastern toe.

With Jaskilka's company in possession of Hill 104, Smith moved his unit along the road to the south, across the rice paddies and the Sha-sen River. Little resistance was met until Heck's 1st Platoon came under heavy fire from the slopes of the objective. Several casualties were taken. Heck was seriously wounded and died a few hours later. The company tied in for the night on the northern slopes of Hill 56 about five hundred yards from the rise of ground leading onto the horseshoe ridge line—88. Staff Sergeant LeRoy Dodge took command of Heck's platoon.

During the night the Marines heard the enemy moving about with considerable physical and vocal energy. At first light on the morning of the twenty-fourth First Lieutenant George McNaughton, commanding the 3rd Platoon, took his unit into the assault on the objective. Because of a heavy morning fog the Marines were denied the assistance of air and artillery support. McNaughton's platoon, numbering thirty-six men, crossed the low ground between their night positions and the approaches to the enemy-held ridge line without incident. To the left were the burning houses of the village at the base of Hill 56 and the dikes bordering the narrow road leading into the rice paddy. Shortly after the climb began, Sergeant Newby's squad came unexpectedly onto the enemy positions. Because of the limited visibility due to the fog and smokepots the Marines and enemy were within grenade range before either was aware of the others' presence. A grenade fight developed. McNaughton was wounded in the shoulder from flanking fire but stayed on the line.

McNaughton sent Sergeant Robert Smith and his 3rd Squad to the right, around a nose on the hill to the eastern slope, in an enveloping movement. This unit was struck by an overwhelming force and in the space of a few minutes seven of the squad including Smith were killed and four were wounded. Corpsmen James Egresitz rushed to the assistance of the wounded and was killed. Pfc. Hintow Johnson, assistant BARman, was the sole member unhurt and able to rejoin McNaughton. With this success the enemy sent a platoon-sized force along the eastern slopes in an effort to envelop the remaining positions occupied by the rest of McNaughton's platoon. This threat was held off by machine guns sent forward by First Lieutenant Karle Seydel, commander of the machine-gun platoon.

The machine-gun section was in charge of Corporal David Kiene and he was killed shortly after the guns got into action. Corporal Kenneth Stewart took charge. The machine guns were receiving a heavy concentration of enemy fire and the casualties to the gunners continued to mount as man after man was killed. It was imperative that the guns be kept in action and the men of the section replaced their fallen members without hesitancy. Staff Sergeant Frank Greene came up the hill to assist Stewart with the machine guns.

Pfc. James O'Toole manned the gun on the right of McNaughton's positions. He was wounded and slid down the slope and had his wounds dressed. He refused evacuation and returned to his gun. Shortly after his return he was killed.

With further losses occurring to the 1st and 2nd Squads, McNaughton contacted Smith by radio and requested assistance. Smith committed Lieutenant Lee Howard's 2nd Platoon. McNaughton went down the hill a short distance and met Howard and briefed him on the situation. Howard took his men along the left slope and was stopped by a withering fire; casualties began to mount in the 2nd Platoon.

The fog was lifting and as visibility cleared the enemy began to pour fire into the Marines from three directions—north, south and southeast.

While McNaughton and Howard were seeking defiladed avenues over which to close with the enemy, Smith set up his CP and aid station in a revetment at the base of the slope. After getting heavy machine guns into firing positions to support the assault troops from the west, Smith went up the slope to contact McNaughton. In the meantime Seydel was ramrodding ammunition up the hill to keep the two machine guns and riflemen supplied. In this task he made five trips across the bullet-swept low ground and up the hill.

With visibility improving, Lieutenant Karl Wirth, artillery forward observer, began to bring in artillery and air support. Howard was wounded as he sought to observe the fire and assist Wirth in selecting targets. Staff Sergeant Crowson was severely wounded as he carried a wounded Marine to cover. Smith ordered Sergeant Richardson's squad from the flank on the south of Hill 56 to the line with McNaughton and then contacted Roise by radio. He explained the situation and asked for instructions. Upon being informed that the objective had to be taken, Smith directed McNaughton to form the men left in his platoon with those of Howard's 2nd and Dodge's 1st into one unit for the attack.

McNaughton had nine effectives left; there were but ten in Howard's unit; Dodge had eleven. Second Lieutenant George Grimes, in charge of the mortar platoon, came up the hill with Wirth. Grimes informed Smith that he was out of mortar ammunition anyway so he might just as well go into the attack with the rest; Wirth was of the opinion he could observe better on top so he would also go. Joining the volunteers was Sergeant Roy Dunmire, forward observer for the 81 mm. mortars. By utilizing ammunition carriers, machine-gunners and company headquarters personnel forty-four men were available for the assault. Smith notified Roise and requested an air strike preparatory to the jump-off.

McNaughton crawled forward to a vantage point where he could observe the bombing and strafing runs. Smith was down the slope a short distance with his radio.

"How close?" he shouted to McNaughton after the first strike.

"Hundred fifty yards. Bring it in."

Smith spoke into the radio and the air controller at the battalion observation post directed the orbiting Corsairs. The next run was even closer to the Marines lines. Further up the hill, on the crest, other planes were napalming and bombing.

By this method of indirect direction McNaughton and Smith brought the air attack within fifty yards of the Marine positions. When the Corsairs were through the time came for the assault.

In any small unit battle the outstanding behavior of a few men is always discernible over the others. The moral balance which decides a hotly contested battle is a delicate thing. On the one side is flaming courage and victory; against this are irresolution and defeat. The scale is tipped by the few—by the ten per cent—who rise to the heights where the enemy and death can be met without a hesitant step.

When the final assault was ordered, the Marines of Smith's company knew what was facing them for they had been through the battle of Sangyong-ni. They had seen their ranks depleted and their leaders (Finn, Oakley, Reid and Emmelman) become casualties. Ten days later they had faced the initial assault on "No Name Ridge" where Shinka and Zimmer and half their number were casualties.

The fortunate few who survived these battles carried into the ranks of the replacements a fatalistic spirit which was a halter to morale. There were none who thought the attack could be carried off with success; all were certain that death was reward for the charge upward.

Of the forty-four men available, thirty-three would form the skirmish line while the remainder came on later with machine guns and ammunition. Thirty-three men deployed along a hundred yards were to make an assault on ten times their number.

The signal for the attack was to be the second of two dummy runs by a Corsair. As the gull-winged plane swooped down the first time the riflemen began to shout and yell for the encouragement it gave themselves and one another; their shouting reached a hysterical pitch as the plane passed over for the last time.

Smith sprang from his hole. "Okay, let's get 'em," he roared. No man in the line hesitated or sought a coward's hole; thirty-three men began to run forward and upward. Well in front of any man in the line, Smith was hit and killed. McNaughton rushed forward and led the charge.

Staff Sergeant "Swede" Larsen had taken position on the right flank of the skirmish line while Sergeant LeRoy Dodge performed the same duty on the left. Pfc. Vincent Pascarelli was wounded in the foot but continued forward; Larsen was wounded and stayed with the line; Pfc. Hill, company runner was wounded and kept lunging upward. Pfc. Floyd Harris hosed the hillside with his BAR as he ran; Kelly of the "Hollywood" squad was in the line.

In the face of the shouting, cursing Marines the enemy reacted in various manner. It was apparent the attack was unexpected; many fled, some pretended death in their holes, others fought, all of them died.

The thin line reached the burnt-out plateau and caught the enemy running down the northeastern slope. It became a free-for-all shoot until McNaughton called it off because of the scarcity of ammunition. A stray return shot killed Harris.

Twenty-six of the thirty-three Marines made it to the top of the hill.

In the reorganization necessary before defensive positions were taken, McNaughton asked for a show of hands on various grades because there were men from all the units of the company on the hill.

"How many staff sergeants?"

Two hands rose. (Dodge and Larsen with the latter wounded.)

"How many sergeants?"

Four hands came to view. (Sypniewski had been killed.)

"How many corporals?"

Four Marines raised their hands.

Eighteen men indicated they were privates first class.

When McNaughton began to give instructions Grimes interrupted. "Hey, George, aren't you interested in second lieutenants?"

That was the first laugh the members of Dog Company had had all day.

When McNaughton asked for volunteers to return and clear any of the enemy from by-passed areas, Sergeant Willie Smithee responded with four other men. Grimes went along to assist and was wounded in the leg.

McNaughton reported to Roise that the crest had been reached and was in his control. Seydel, who had missed the attack because of the ammunition detail, came to the top and being the senior officer present assumed command of the company. When all available personnel were assembled from ammunition and litter carriers and company CP personnel there were fifty-six Marines to defend the hill. Twenty-six of these had been wounded but refused evacuation. Dog Company held their ground against an enemy counterattack later in the day and the enemy main line of resistance into Seoul was broken.

During the engagement Smith's unit suffered 176 casualties of a total strength of 206. Thirty-six had been killed, 116 had been wounded and evacuated, 26 had been wounded but remained on duty.

The next morning Jaskilka's company jumped off in the attack with the mission of taking Hills 72 and northern 105. Supported by Sweet's platoon of tanks, Deptula's platoon moved forward against moderate opposition. Epley's 3rd Platoon in trace of Deptula and in echelon to the right met stubborn resistance in the village of Shinchon to the north of the railway tracks. This area was commanded by the ridge line taken the day before by Dog Company. Epley cleared the enemy from Shinchon and Deptula readied his platoon for the assault on Hill 72.

Korean terrain posed a constant problem of determining positions in view of the fact that the maps were not accurate. In the case of Jaskilka's advance on Hill 72 there was some doubt at the battalion OP as to where he was and if he was moving onto the right target. Visibility was hampered by intervening hills, distance and haze from enemy smokepots. The battalion operations officer, Major Walter Gall, contacted Jaskilka on the radio.

"What's your position?"

"I'm a hundred fifty yards south of the rail line. Four hundred yards to my front is Hill 72. Between me and it is a built up area and a dike."

Gall was not completely satisfied for that answered the description of a number of hills in the immediate area. "Describe 72."

"It looks like Nellie's teat."

"That's it . . . you're on target . . . proceed."

Deptula took his platoon into the assault and by ten o'clock had seized the objective.

In the meantime Taplett's battalion was moving southeast along the spur of Hill 296 and furnishing supporting fire to Roise's unit from that commanding ground. Seydel had Dog Company in the attack early and following the horseshoe-like contour of the ridge had seized the rest of Hill 88 by midday. With the continual use of artillery and air support, Jaskilka prepared for the assault on the final objective—Hill 105. Shortly after noon the attack began with Epley's platoon on the left and Eddy's to the right. At 3:45 in the afternoon Jaskilka's unit had seized Hill 105 and the final enemy stronghold had been overcome.

Over two thousand enemy troops were killed in their stand-and-die defense of the western approaches to the city of Seoul.

The assault and capture of the high ground on the western flank of Seoul had been costly to Murray's 5th. The 5th Marines had been in Korea forty-nine days. During this period, five of the six company commanders who had landed with the brigade at Pusan had been founded and evacuated. At this time Stevens of Able Company was the sole remaining rifle company commander from the brigade. Of the eighteen platoon leaders who led their units into action in southern Korea, four had been killed and thirteen wounded. Of the twenty-four officers involved, twenty-two were casualties before fifty days of combat had been completed.

Tracing the change of command in Dog Company of Roise's 2nd Battalion should prove of value to the members of Congress when extra-hazardous duty pay is next discussed for servicemen. Finn took Dog Company into action on the seventh of August and was wounded on the morning of the eighth. Zimmer replaced Finn. Zimmer was evacuated with wounds on the seventeenth of August. "H. J." Smith then took command of Dog Company. Smith was killed on the afternoon of the twenty-fourth of September.

About this time officers and men who had been wounded in the early days of the southern fighting began to return after a period of convalescence in Japan. Westerman and Cahill rejoined George Company and Jack Nolan returned to Easy. Westerman continued to have indifferent luck. He was wounded and evacuated within three days of his return; friends told him that his pay account was apt to be checked for unnecessary transportation between Japan and Korea. Technical Sergeant Frank Lawson returned to duty with Stevens' company. He had to talk his way out of the hospital because the multiple wounds received at Obong-ni Ridge were scarcely healed.

CHAPTER XII

Seoul: Part 2. The Battle of Buildings, Roadblocks and Barricades

While Murray was battling for the high ground west of Seoul, Puller had secured Yongdong-po and prepared to cross the Han in the shelter of southern 105 which was occupied by Newton.

There was some delay at the crossing site while enemy mines were cleared and the LVT's were assembled. Sutter's battalion assembled before dawn and the first elements began to cross at 7:45. The crossing was unopposed and and only light, long-range sniper fire was experienced by the rifle companies as they moved inland (north) three to four hundred yards and then turned east.

Hawkins' battalion followed in trace of Sutter and once this unit was formed Puller directed Hawkins to pass through Sutter and capture Hill 79. There was some discussion over this maneuver and Hawkins reminded Puller that Sutter was in movement forward. Puller responded that he was aware of the situation and that all Hawkins had to do to complete the passage of lines was to move forward faster than Sutter.

Hawkins' unit took off at a "high port." When Barrow and his unit came charging up on the heels of Easy Company, Carter yelled at Barrow, "What'n hell's going on here?"

Barrow answered, "Take it easy, Johnny. This constitutes a passage of lines."

On one of the rare occasions in modern military history one battalion passed through another with both units moving forward. With a speed and dispatch that drew praise from Puller, Barrow captured Hill 79 and raised the American flag over a schoolhouse.

Upon hearing about the flag-raising Murray's men cried "foul" and pointed out the fact that neither regiment had penetrated the city to a depth to warrant raising the national colors. From that time on a spirited rivalry existed between these two units as to which one would reach the heart of the city first. In Puller's zone were the French and Russian and American Consulates as well as the DukSoo Palace. Murray's route through the city would take him to the South Korean capital building, Changdok Palace.

Each unit obtained a supply of flags and the race was on between two regiments who had great pride in their achievements past and present.

Puller's initial attack had been to the east. Once Hill 79 was secure the direction of the advance had to change to the north.

Puller passed Ridge's 3rd Battalion through Sutter's 2nd and tied in with Hawkins on the right. This difficult maneuver turned the direction of Puller's attack ninety degrees to the (north) left. In order to make this shift possible, Hawkins' 1st had to withdraw slightly in order to pivot on its left flank. The maneuver was completed successfully without loss of momentum and the attack continued at seven o'clock on the morning of the twenty-fifth.

The course before Puller's 1st now lay directly through the heart of Seoul, while Murray's 5th would drive through the northwest quarter.

At daybreak Williams was directed to take two platoons of Pershing tanks to support Puller. Departing the river-crossing site the tanks moved eastward. In the gap between Murray and Puller the tanks were suddenly attacked. The battle broiled heatedly and was in doubt until a flame-throwing tank worked into position where it could turn its stream of fire onto the enemy. Short bursts of flame drove the North Koreans from cover while the other tanks opened on them with machine guns.

Fifteen of the enemy threw away their arms and surrendered. When the remainder saw their comrades walk into the tank lines unharmed, the rest stampeded to give up. Score for the twenty-minute fight: 150 dead North Koreans, 131 prisoners.

The column of tanks and prisoners proceeded into the zone of Puller's regiment. While the tankers were herding their prisoners to the POW stockade, Williams went to report to Puller. The tank commander, jubilant over the success of the venture, was effusive in his report.

Puller was unimpressed. Speaking crisply around the stem of his pipe, he said, "I'm not interested in your sea stories, young man. You're forty-five minutes late. Get your unit into position."

Despite heavy resistance and extensive use of mines by the enemy, the 1st Marines moved into the attack. Aerial and artillery bombardment dislodged the enemy from the rail embankment, but a fanatical enemy continued to fight savagely from roadblocks and rooftops. By nightfall Puller's 1st had advanced into the city to a depth of nearly two thousand yards. That night as they tied in their lines shortly before dark, plans were made to co-ordinate the morning attack with the 5th Marines to the left.

Convinced by enemy action and questioning of prisoners that the North Koreans would defend Seoul to the utmost of their capabilities, Smith was certain the only manner of seizing the city was by assault. This view was not held by General Almond and his staff. It was their opinion that Puller should be sent around to the southeast and attack Seoul from that direction. Smith objected to this plan because he was certain Murray would require assistance in the attack from the west. As events proved, it was too much to ask of one regiment, and before the city was secure it was necessary for Smith to bring Litzenberg's 7th into the battle.

The difference of opinion between Smith and Almond at this time was the result of their training and past experiences with Asian soldiery. Almond, whose combat experience had been against European armies, believed the defenders of Seoul could be maneuvered from the city. Smith was convinced that the North Korean Army was committed to defend the capital house by house and street by street, with all the determination of an Asian soldier when given the order to stand and die.

A number of field commanders in Korea were to learn that decisions based on doctrine arrived at on European battlefields were not always sound against Oriental armies.

When Smith objected to sending Puller around to the southeast, Almond ordered the 32nd Army Regiment across the Han and onto South Mountain in the eastern outskirts of Seoul. The crossing was unopposed and the objective taken with little or no resistance. This move was made on the twenty-fifth. From this land mass the 32nd looked down into the city, but were unable to move into the capital because they would have to cross the lines of fire and advance of

Puller and Murray. The North Korean commander ignored the occupation of South Mountain as he placed the bulk of his forces in the heart of the city to delay the advance of the Marines.

The atmosphere at X Corps Headquarters at this time was tense because of the desire to capture Seoul by the twenty-sixth. Smith and his commanders were in accord with the early seizure of the capital, but did not wish to promise or hang their plans on a date. Puller and Murray had their regiments in position and plans laid for a coordinated attack on the morning of the twenty-sixth. Neither commander held hopes of passing through the city in one day.

At 8:09 that evening the division received a dispatch from Corps to the effect that the enemy was fleeing to the north and was under heavy air attack. The message further directed Smith "You will push attack now to the limit of your objectives in order to insure maximum destruction of enemy forces. [Signed] Almond."

When Colonel Al Bowser, division operations officer, received the order he questioned the accuracy of intelligence based on night air identification. Bowser was certain the "fleeing enemy" were civilians attempting to clear the city and escape the fighting that would ensue within its boundaries. Bowser was fortified in his evaluation of the situation by the fact that heavy street fighting had gone on until night fall when the 1st and 5th had tied in their lines for the night. In addition, Taplett had been counterattacked at dusk and at the moment his left flank was receiving tank fire. When Bowser was directed to carry out the order, he informed Smith who in turn got the X Corps chief-of-staff on the telephone for confirmation. General Ruffner directed Smith to proceed as ordered.

A night attack to a depth of over three miles in an Oriental city without preparation or reconnaissance posed several serious problems. Smith called Puller and Murray personally and directed that they coordinate the attack carefully and that no effort be made for a rapid advance, and to concentrate along streets which could be identified at night. A fifteen-minute artillery preparation was to precede the advance.

When Murray received the order and relayed it to his staff, Stewart said, "I'm afraid we'll have to delay pursuit of the fleeing enemy until we see if Tap can beat off this counterattack."

In Puller's zone Ridge's battalion had had heavy going all day.

Sitter's company on the left of the battalion zone had been unable to seize an enemy street barricade because of the strong defenses both in width and depth. Corley's company on the right of the zone advanced only after heavy fighting but found itself in advance of flanking units. As night came on the rifle companies were withdrawn to more defensible terrain and First Lieutenant Joseph Fisher had to take his unit forward to assist Corley in making the retraction. All three companies were placed on the Main Line of Resistance with emphasis placed on the road passing through the left flank positions where a roadblock was established.

Ridge assigned Major Edwin Simmons to assist the rifle company commanders in setting up their defenses for the night. The roadblock was manned by two rifle squads, a heavy machine-gun section, a rocket squad and a section from the 75 mm. Recoilless gun platoon. This group was commanded by First Lieutenant Harold Savage. Simmons established his forward CP with Sitter in the cellar of a house on the high ground.

When Ridge received the night attack order he directed Simmons to send a patrol three hundred yards to the front to contact a similar patrol being sent out by Taplett's battalion on the left. Corporal Charles Collins was to command the eight-man unit with Pfc. Kenneth Van Kurin acting as the guide through the mine fields facing the block. Three native guides accompanied the patrol. Collins spaced his men at close interval and they moved out, stumbling and fumbling along the dark and unfamiliar streets. Without warning they came upon the enemy in the final stages of preparing for a large tank and infantry counterattack. The North Koreans opened fire on the patrol. Collins yelled to his men to get back and report while he covered the withdrawal.

In the meantime, Puller had set the jump-off time for 1:45. The artillery bombardment was not to his liking and he ordered another fifteen-minute preparation when a flash came from Ridge's 3rd that the force Collins and his patrol had stumbled upon was attacking the roadblock.

At the roadblock a full-scale battle was developing. Simmons heard the fire fight begin which told him Collins' patrol had come to trouble. While preparing for the jump-off the riflemen of the three companies heard the sound of tanks some five to six hundred yards to their immediate front. Simmons gave a flash warning to Ridge and as he was giving instructions to Savage at the roadblock the enemy tanks opened fire and Pfc. Julius Vargo, radio operator, was killed. A blistering fire of high velocity and small-arms fire began to sweep the positions held by Sitter's company and the roadblock.

Simmons informed Ridge of the situation and got in contact with the artillery liaison team. Within a matter of minutes a heavy concentration of artillery fire was being delivered on the advancing enemy.

At the roadblock the first two enemy tanks to approach were taken under fire by the 75 mm. Recoilless rifles, 3.5 rockets and heavy machine guns. One was hit and disabled and the second withdrew. Savage was wounded and Sergeant Robert Caldwell took charge.

Simmons estimated the attacking force to be of battalion size supported by twelve tanks or self-propelled guns. Enemy activity and fire increased to its preassault peak and Simmons ordered the artillery to shorten range until the shells were barely clearing the high ground occupied by Sitter's unit. Assisting the artillery were the 81 mm. mortars firing at minimum range. With Corley and Fisher's units firing from the flanks the enemy attack was stopped.

For nearly two hours the Marine artillery had been laying down barrage fire and Simmons was informed that if such fire was to continue the tubes of the howitzers would be burned out. As soon as the artillery fire slackened, however, the enemy began their tank attacks again. The area before the Marines was well lighted from burning buildings set by the artillery. Three tanks could be seen approaching the roadblock but due to a curve in the road Savage's men could not see them.

Simmons directed the fire of a battery of 155 mm. guns on the tanks. This fire, while it did not destroy the enemy armor, did neutralize their fire. Each time, however, that the artillery ceased firing the tanks would resume. This kept up until 5:30 in the morning. There was a critical period when the rifle companies began to run out of ammunition and Ridge sent an urgent request for machine guns, 3.5 rocket and 75 mm. Recoilless ammunition. By utilizing all available jeeps and trailers, the ammunition was delivered under fire.

The fire of the artillery and mortars set a record for the Korean war. The four battalions of artillery expended all their on-position reserves as well as all the shells in a near-by Army dump. The 4.2 mortars fired

326 rounds, the 81 mm. mortars 650 rounds and the heavy machine gun 120 boxes (30,000 rounds).

Daylight showed the carnage in front of Puller's lines. Three T-34 and one T-70 tanks had been destroyed, as had the two dual purpose 76 mm. and 8.45 mm. AT guns. More than two hundred fifty enemy dead were counted. Daylight also brought the return of Collins who had remained behind to cover his patrol. Hiding in a house, he had dressed in white Korean civilian clothing and made his way in this garb back to friendly lines. Ridge's unit had to be relieved because his men had burned out the barrels of their weapons with prolonged, heavy fire. When newsmen asked about the "fleeing" enemy Puller told them, "All I know about a fleeing enemy is there's over two hundred out there that won't be fleein' anywhere—they're dead."

On Murray's front the counterattack was repulsed by 4:45 and Taplett sent a patrol under Second Lieutenant Lawrence O'Connell to the east to contact the 1st Marines. Upon entering the built-up area O'Connell took his men into a court surrounded by a group of native houses. While prowling about the area O'Connell fell into a hole used for the storage of night soil. For the rest of the patrol O'Connell was a man who "walked alone." Contact with the 1st was not made as Puller's unit was still occupied and there was an enemy force of some strength on the high ground over the railroad tunnel.

It was nine o'clock in the morning before Puller and Murray were able to resume the advance through Seoul. Taplett's unit, on a spur of Hill 296 which tapered off into the outskirts of the city, was assigned the mission of clearing the spur and entering the city proper. With McMullen's unit on the left and Mize on the right the attack began. Almost at once the assault units came under heavy fire from the city.

McMullen took his first two platoons into the attack with First Lieutenant Melvin Snow's platoon to the left of the unit under the command of Staff Sergeant Magnus Schone. At the same time Mize was in the assault through a populated area on the low ground off the spur. McMullen's advance had not proceeded to any depth before the right flank squad under Corporal Robert Salsbury came under heavy fire and was separated from the rest of the platoon. Snow was severely wounded; two Marines were killed and four wounded. Salsbury was also wounded in the shoulder, but was able to continue in action. Taking a position whereby he could defend the others, Salsbury stayed with his wounded and dead members.

McMullen, having lost contact with Snow, committed Peterson's platoon to the assault. As the Marine attack swept forward Salsbury found himself behind the lines but in an exposed position. He killed two enemy infiltrators and was finally relieved several hours later.

The objective was obtained but not before McMullen was wounded (for the sixth time) and Schone was killed, as were four other Marines. Snow had joined the unit as a replacement but forty-eight hours before being wounded and evacuated. Thirteen others had been wounded in the bitter fight. First Lieutenant Wallace Williamson assumed command of Item Company.

To the right of the spur, Mize had found the enemy tenacious and strongly entrenched. Although George Company cleared the area to the streets of Seoul they were still under heavy fire as night came on. Counselman was wounded (for the fifth time) as was Macy.

Progress was slow and required close co-ordination between the rifle squads, mine engineering teams and supporting tanks. The enemy was defending and fighting for every street intersection from behind road-blocks of rice bags manned with antitank guns, machine guns and tanks—all this armament behind a liberal planting of mines.

As the Marines moved into the heavy going of bitter street fighting, X Corps announced that the majority of the city was under United Nations control. For this was the twenty-sixth.

As the riflemen of Sutter's battalion looked down Mapo Boulevard with its barricades every few hundred yards, they were unconvinced.

Puller's instructions to his battalion commanders were based on speed and drive. "Keep your troops moving. All these buildings along our route are filled with Reds. If you keep moving you'll by-pass most of the snipers and rooftop mortars and you'll take a lot fewer casualties. Let the Korean Marines coming in behind you do the mopping up. Keep your troops moving."

Sutter passed these instructions on to Groff and Captain Norman Stanford of Easy Company. Carter had been wounded the day before. Groff was to lead off along the boulevard and clear an intersection of streets known as Kung Hua Noon Circle, some five hundred yards to his front. Once the circle was clear he was to take the left-hand street and push to the railroad station. Following in trace was Stanford. When Groff had passed on to the left Stanford's unit would take the street to the right. Four hundred yards beyond the plaza the two units would co-ordinate their jump-off on the assault of DukSoo Palace.

A hundred yards from the road junction Groff ran into heavy resistance. The first heavy fire fight of the morning began as sniper and antitank fire filled the air and crashed into the masonry of the buildings lining the street.

Groff reported to Sutter, "The 1st Platoon has been hit hard . . . we're held up."

The circle was a litter of stones, bricks, timbers, antitank gun mounts and enemy dead. The buildings around it were on fire and the black, turgid smoke cut down visibility to a few hundred feet. Wounded of the 1st Platoon began to drift back and there was the cry for "Corpsman" heard over the slamming of shells and ricocheting whine of bullets. A shortage of stretchers developed and Chaplain Otto Sporrer tore metal shutters from street windows and utilized these as litters.

With Fox Company held up, Stanford also had to bring his unit to a halt. Stanford went forward with his runner, Pfc. Edward Cavanaugh, to make a reconnaissance of the circle. It might be possible for him to get his unit into the proper street without waiting for Groff's unit to make final clearance, but it was a dangerous maneuver which would expose his left flank to enfilade fire from the enemy opposing Groff.

Unable to contact Sutter because his radio was out, Stanford made his decision; he directed his tanks and assault platoon forward along the left-hand fork. Easy Company passed through the dead and wounded and hard-hit platoons of Fox and carried on the attack.

After a sharp fight the enemy broke and ran. Many were killed. Stanford, who had been with his unit but two days, was wounded in the final assault, and twenty other men were casualties; but the momentum carried on as Cronk's company went into the attack. Captain Charles Fredrick took command of Easy Company.

There were more barricades, more delays as engineers sought out and exploded mines. Marines, unable to stand the heat of burning buildings, dashed forward on the heels of others. Casualties mounted and Corpsman Jimmy Donaghue went forward again and again. When stretchers were no longer available, more shutters were torn off the buildings. Sutter's battalion dug in for the night one hundred yards from the French Consulate.

The next morning at 6:30 Sutter's battalion went into the attack with

Cronk's company leading the assault. Lessons learned in the previous days of street fighting were utilized in breaking through the barricades. A pattern had been evolved. An air strike was called on all barricades and with the tanks employing a rotating relief system the infantry at the point always had two Pershings with them.

Good time was made. The national colors were raised over the French Consulate at 1057; the Russian Consulate was next by midafternoon. The colors went over the United States Consulate at 1537.

On the right flank of Sutter's unit was Hawkins' battalion moving through parallel streets. Wray and Barrow took the railway station and came in for some heavy fighting.

While the 1st Marines was advancing through its zone of action, Murray's 5th was fighting through barricade after barricade toward Changdok Palace. After repulsing the enemy counterattack on the morning of the twenty-sixth, the 5th moved deeper into the city with Taplett's 3rd hooked to Puller's left flank.

Mize, who had replaced the wounded Bohn, fought through his zone of Seoul. George Company was in visual contact with Stanford and Groff of Sutter's 2nd as they cleaned out parallel streets. The barricades became more imposing structures as the middle ground of the capital was reached. Stretching from one side of the street to the other, they were composed of fiber sandbags five to eight feet thick at the base.

The process for overcoming these roadblocks was tedious, efficient and costly. Riflemen gained what points of vantage there were in the streets, from windows and roofs of buildings, and built up a base of fire as the engineers moved forward searching out the mines.

"Fire in the hole!" would come the warning yell as the engineers made ready to set off the mines. Then there would be a series of close-packed explosions and the tanks would begin to move forward, and the enemy behind the roadblock would run wildly for the next barricade to the rear.

Then it was that the tanks and the riflemen and BARmen from windows and on the roofs and along the street would take deadly toll. All this while the Pershings were being pelted, as though by hail, with fire of all kinds. It was not long before radio antenna, external phone boxes and periscope heads had been shot away.

The average time to break through such a barricade was forty-five minutes. Three or four hundred yards along the street, the process had to be repeated. The work of breaking through the hurdles of Seoul would have been much slower and more costly had it not been for Marine and Navy Corsairs. Strafing and rocketing one or two intersections ahead of the ground troops, a heavy toll of enemy personnel was taken before the approach of the Marine tanks and riflemen.

Not directly measurable, but of great importance, was the shattering of enemy morale from these low-flying gull-winged planes. Plainly shaken by the aerial machine-gunning, enemy officers in charge of the roadblocks found that even their command by terror was not sufficient to hold men to the breastworks.

As Mize pushed George Company along toward the palace they hit a roadblock being defended with fanatic resolution. Because it was at a turn in the street it was impossible to get Marine air to hose it with fifty-caliber slugs before the engineers began blowing the mines. It had to be a ground action.

Counselman's platoon, now commanded by Staff Sergeant Arnold, was in the assault. With his riflemen taking positions where they could protect the engineers, Corporal Bert Johnson, in charge of the machine-gun section attached to Arnold, was wounded as he tried to cross the street to set up his weapon.

Exposed to enemy fire, Pfc. Eugene Obregon rushed into the street and dragged Johnson to shelter. As Obregon was bandaging Johnson's wounds the enemy broke across the barrier in a screaming counterattack. Obregon threw his body in front of Johnson and opened fire on the charging enemy with his carbine. His bold action was sufficient to cause the North Koreans to waver and hesitate long enough for other riflemen to beat off the attack. Johnson was rescued but Obregon was hit with a burst of machine-gun fire and killed.

By midafternoon Taplett's 3rd was in the courtyard of Changdok Palace and there was a great, exuberant rush to tear down the Red flag and replace it with the national colors. Technical Sergeant Harold Beaver, machine-gun platoon leader of George Company, took charge of getting the halyards straightened and replacing the Red flag overhead. There was something of a snarl in the lines. With Beaver on the top of a three-man ladder, he reached the halyards and brought down the Red flag and attached the American. With a shout from the men, the flag went up.

While Beaver was fighting the halyards, Taplett, anticipating such a delay, sent another flag to the dome of the building. By three o'clock

USMC Photo, by Sgt. Frank C. Kerr

Marines Moving Out of Pusan to Chanwon

USMC Photo, by Sgt. John Babyak

Hills and Heat

USMC Photo, by S/Sgt. Michael McMahon

VMO 6 Evacuating Wounded from the Front Lines

USMC Photo, by Sgt. Frank C. Kerr

No Name Ridge. All That Remained Were Enemy Dead and Destroyed Weapons

USMC Photo, by Cpl. R. J. Laitinen

Enemy Tanks After a Corsair Attack

USMC Photo, by S/Sgt. Walter Frank

Second Lt. Balmomero Lopez Leads His Platoon Over the Inchon Sea Wall

USMC Photo, by Sgt. John Babyak

Seoul: Burning Buildings, Barricades and Snipers

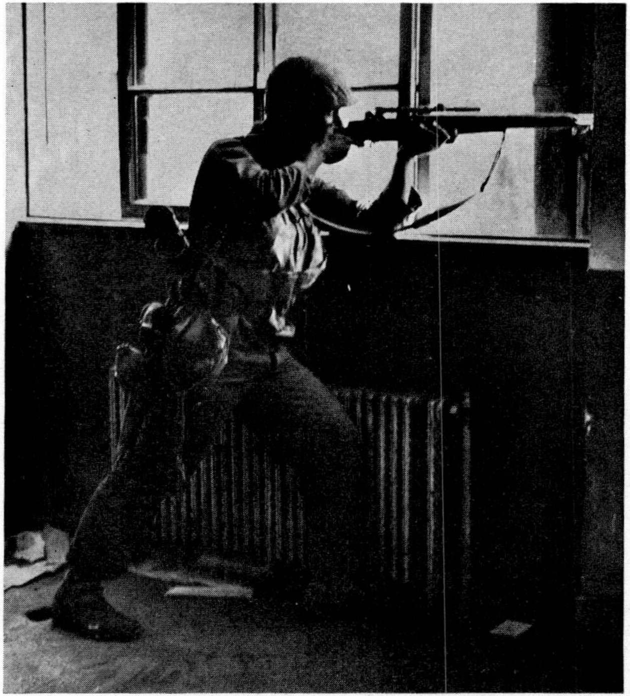

USMC Photo

A Marine Sniper Keeping the Rooftops Clear as Ground Units Advance Through City

USMC Photo, by Sgt. John Babyak

Pfc. Luther Leguire Raises the U.S. Flag Over the American Consulate in Seoul

USMC *Photo*

An Aerial View of the Tortuous Road to the Reservoir

USMC Photo

An Air Drop to the Marines at Yudam-ni

USMC Photo, by Sgt. Frank C. Kerr

In Subzero Weather the Marines Prepare to Fight South from Yudam-ni to Regain the Perimeter at Hagaru

USMC Photo

While Marines at the Point Fight to Overcome a Roadblock, the Men Not Engaged Seek a Few Moments Rest

USMC Photo

Only the Wounded, Frostbitten and Dead Ride

USMC Photo, by Sgt. Frank C. Kerr

South of Hagaru Marine Ground Troops Wait While Corsairs Wipe Out the Enemy Strongpoints

USMC Photo, by Sgt. Frank C. Kerr

Another Roadblock, Another Wait

USMC Photo

The Bridge Is Out and Must Be Rebuilt

USMC Photo

The Bridge Is Rebuilt and the Column Moves On

USMC *Photo*

Frozen and Starved Chinese Surrender

USMC Photo

The Road Is Open and the Ridge Is Cleared of the Enemy. The Marines Advance to the Sea

in the afternoon the capital had been flagged twice and the event entered in the official log of the 3rd Battalion.

In the meantime Puller's 1st was driving through their zone of action. Having started the flag-raising custom in the Seoul battle, the 1st Marines were not to be outdone by anyone. At 10:30 in the morning they hoisted an American flag over the French Consulate; at one o'clock another was placed atop the Russian Consulate. Great cheers greeted this event. At 3:27 the American Consulate was reached and the third American flag was run up by the 1st Marines.

"Damnedest flag-raising contest I ever saw," Technical Sergeant Max Stein remarked. "It looks like the Fourth of July around this burg."

The credit for the official flag-raising in Seoul went to Puller's 1st Marines for raising the flag over Ambassador Muccio's residence. Of course this point will be long discussed and hotly disputed by Murray's 5th, especially Taplett's 3rd. As one of Almond's staff growled, "Ever since that flag-raising picture of Iwo Jima got published, I'm convinced a Marine would rather carry a flag into battle than a weapon."

To which Puller answered tersely, "Not a bad idea. A man with a flag in his pack and the desire to put it on an enemy strongpoint isn't likely to bug out."

It was obvious to Smith that Litzenberg's 7th would have to be brought in to carry on the attack to the north. Orders were issued that the 7th would cut across the front of the 5th north of the capital buildings. The terrain in this area was rugged and would have to be crossed on foot and Litzenberg would have to commit his regiment to action through a pass in the mountains.

In a move that brought a commendation from Smith, Hinkle's 2nd moved through the gap and was in position by four o'oclock in the afternoon of the twenty-sixth. Roach's 3rd came into position in time to join the 2nd in the attack early in the morning of the twenty-seventh.

In the meantime, Captain Richard Breen's Dog Company of Hinkle's battalion, was assigned the mission of contacting the 5th Marines and provide supporting fires and protection on the left flank of Murray's regiment as it drove through the capital city. Breen put his company in a column of platoons with First Lieutenant Edward Seeburger's 2nd at the point; in trace was First Lieutenant Paul Sartwell's 3rd

Platoon. Then came Breen's march CP, the machine guns and mortars. Lieutenant Paul Mullaney's 1st Platoon brought up the rear.

To obtain the assigned positions Breen's unit moved southeast along the Pyongyang-Seoul highway. On the right hand of the company was a heavily vegetated area and the gradually steeping ground to Hill 296 which had entered into Taplett's earlier objectives. To the left of the marching Marines were an extensive orchard area, a school building of some size as well as apartment houses. A bridge along the roadway had been bombed out and this was to affect the operations of the unit at a critical period of the coming engagement.

The unit began to enter the built-up area of the city itself and its route passed by the high walls of the Sodaemun Prison. (See map.) Opposite the prison the main body of the company came under flanking fire. The point came to a halt as it met with heavy fire along the street from the archway known as Independence Gate.

Breen directed First Lieutenant William Goggin, commanding the machine-gun platoon, to get guns forward to the point to support Seeburger. Goggin shouted to Staff Sergeant Robert Bowen and ran forward. Goggin's detachment came under heavy fire at an intersection; Bowen rushed a gun into a native house to the left of the street while Goggin and a fire team answered the enemy fire from under a wrecked truck in the street.

Shooting the machine gun from his hip, Bowen blasted a hole in the side of the house to provide a firing aperture. He got the gun into action and began firing along the street in the direction of Independence Gate. The fire fight by this time was general along the length of the company with all units engaged. Breen had been shot in the arm and it was broken; he continued to direct his unit. Goggin was wounded and Pfc. Alvin Neustadt was killed as they fought back from under the truck. Bowen was wounded but continued in action; squad leader Sergeant Richard Harris was killed.

Breen directed Sartwell to take his platoon into the assault on the prison grounds. The unit was hard hit and progress was slow and costly. Staff Sergeant John O'Neill took his machine-gun section in support and was killed. O'Neil was forty-three years old and had refused the opportunity of remaining in Pendleton as an instructor. Sartwell was wounded but stayed in action; he was wounded again. Breen directed Seeburger to send two fire teams forward toward Independence Gate in an effort to break up the frontal fire. Corporals Francis Brennan and

Joseph Montileone advanced with their teams. It was slow work as the enemy was using automatic weapons fire from the upper stories of the buildings lining the streets. Breen called for tanks but the armor was unable to reach the area because of the destroyed bridge.

Breen's company had come to grips with the enemy at 8:30 in the morning; at noon the fighting was still heavy and the unit had been unable to push into the city.

Litzenberg contacted Breen by radio: "Do you want us to come in and get you out?"

"No, sir," Breen answered. "We're okay, Colonel, if we can move back to the high ground."

"Okay, pull back and we'll see about getting tanks in to you."

Mullaney's 1st Platoon moved back along the road and took positions on the high ground to the north of the road. The withdrawal of the rest of the unit was a slow, orderly displacement as the wounded and dead were collected and taken back before the general withdrawal was ordered. By midafternoon the company was in an all-around defense and the forward observer, First Lieutenant Eugene Brown, brought down air and artillery on the prison grounds. Still later in the afternoon an air drop resupplied depleted ammunition stocks.

During the night the unit was subjected to sporadic mortar fire and Breen was wounded for the second time but continued to direct his unit. Dog Company had suffered forty casualties of which thirteen had been killed. Five (Breen, Goggin, Mullaney, Sartwell and Goodman) of the seven company officers had been wounded. During the night Lieutenant (jg) Edward Burns, regimental surgeon, took three jeep ambulances into Breen's lines and evacuated eighteen wounded. Captain Milton Hull took command as Breen went to hospital.

The following morning Dog Company moved out and made contact with Taplett's battalion at ten o'clock.

While the 2nd and 3rd Battalions of Litzenberg's 7th were occupied with attacking across Murray's front and pressing on to the north, Davis' 1st was assigned the mission of protecting the ferry crossing. Davis ran into a brisk fight as an enemy force attempted to recapture this area. Moving down from the north, the enemy endeavored to penetrate a gap between Banks' Able and Wilcox's Baker Companies. The fight did not last long as the Marine firepower soon built up and forced the attacking force to retire with heavy casualties. At the conclusion of this battle Davis moved north and joined in the rest of the regiment.

The performance of Litzenberg's 7th in its first engagements was to draw the praise of Army, Marine and the United Nations observers and earn for it the nickname of "Litz's Blitz's." Composed of over forty per cent Reservists and organized as a regiment only forty-one days before, the men of the 7th were conducting themselves like veterans in their first fire fights north of Seoul.

On the night of the twenty-eighth Sutter's battalion occupied Hill 132 overlooking the Women's Medical College in the northeast outskirts of the city.

Second Lieutenant Lamar Crawford's platoon of Fredrick's (vice Carter and Stanford) company was located three hundred yards forward of the MLR (Main Line of Resistance) established by the battalion. Pfc. Stanley Christianson and Pfc. Alfred Walsh were manning one of several listening posts which covered the approaches into the platoon area. Shortly after four o'clock in the morning Christianson and Walsh heard an enemy force approaching.

Christianson whispered to Walsh, "There must be a hundred of 'em. Get back and warn the outfit—I'll hold them off."

Walsh slipped away and Christianson opened fire. The enemy were armed with automatic weapons, rifles and grenades made from partially filled bottles of gasoline. Christianson held off this force until sheer weight of numbers forced them over his position. Later, seven enemy dead were found in close proximity to Christianson's body.

While the enemy was being delayed, Walsh returned to the platoon and the unit was alerted. Forty-eight more of the enemy were killed and three captured.

Back at X Corps Headquarters the staff was preparing for the entry of General MacArthur and President Syngman Rhee into Seoul. This event was set for the twenty-ninth. Many calls were placed on the division regarding honor guards and bands. The division's band instruments were in Japan and most of the bandsmen had been assigned to duty with line units. When General Ruffner called a conference of battalion commanders to discuss the guarding of the routes of approach, Smith was forced to remind the Corps chief-of-staff that a war was still being fought and that battalion commanders could not be called away from their units.

Much of this high-pressure planning went for nought when MacArthur vetoed all honor guards and cut the ceremony to the minimum.

Nonetheless, the safety factor involved in moving a large party of dignitaries through the streets with safety posed a problem which largely occupied the efforts of one Army and five Marine battalions.

There was an uneasiness among the Marines over the ceremony. Smith, charged with the security of the city, would be much happier when all visitors departed. Snipers were still plentiful.

The ceremony was held in the assembly hall of the capital building at 11:45. Because of the number of visitors and high-ranking officers from Tokyo, the Eighth Army and United Nations, the Marines were limited to five. Generals Smith and Craig attended with Murray and Puller. Litzenberg had his regiment in an attack to the north and was unable to attend. There were a number of speakers, including MacArthur, President Rhee, the head of the United Nations Commission and Ambassador Muccio. Twice during the ceremony vibrations from the artillery supporting the 7th Marines in their drive northward loosened glass from the shattered skylights and it fell into the assembly room. No one was hit.

At Inchon the 7th Marines had been "joined" by a Navy man named John Taylor. Seaman Taylor had taken midnight leave of his tug in Inchon Harbor and having scrounged a Marine uniform made himself at home with Captain Richard Breen's Dog Company. The Marines enjoyed Taylor because he was a fine fighting man; Taylor got along well with his adopted service and lived in terror of being shipped back to the tug with nothing to do but huff and puff ships into position along the Inchon piers.

The Navy, however, takes a rather narrow view of its members transferring into the Marine Corps in this manner. As much as the 7th Marines would have liked to keep Taylor, there came a time when he had to be sent back to the tug before he could be charged with desertion. It was a sad day when the 7th finally had to send Taylor back to his ship.

When the Inchon landing cut enemy communications and released the pressure on the Pusan perimeter, the Eighth Army broke from the southern area and advanced rapidly to the north. Elements of the 1st Cavalry Division contacted the 7th Army Division at Suwon on the twenty-sixth.

With the Eighth Army and X Corps in contact, efforts were made to deny the escape routes to North Korean units retreating from the southern battle area. The Corps set up blocking positions in a rough semicircle. Beginning at Inchon, the line went south through Suwon and crossed the Han River about thirteen miles east of Seoul. The northern rim of these positions was ten miles from the capital where it turned back to the coast at Inchon again.

All along the main approaches to this line, blocking positions were set up from five to ten miles in advance. The 1st Marine Division was assigned the area north of the Han while the 7th Army Division and the 187th RCT were to the south of the river. Within the city of Seoul itself was the 17th ROK regiment which provided security within the city.

These positions had been occupied by the last day of September; the following day Corps issued the order for the Marines to seize and occupy Suyuhon and Uijongbu. Taplett's 3rd was given the job of taking Suyuhon. This assignment was completed by the second of October and the main route leading to Kaesong was closed to the retreating enemy forces.

Litzenberg's 7th, reinforced by Parry's 3rd Battalion of artillery, Chase's D Company of tanks, Turner's Company of Engineers and Captain Kim's C Company of the 5th Korean Marine Corps, was ordered to advance on and seize Uijongbu.

The enemy, realizing that Seoul was lost, made the decision to make a determined rear-guard defense of the Seoul-Uijongbu corridor. From the outset the 7th met with well-entrenched enemy troops supported by artillery, mortars and tanks.

In a column of battalions, the attack on the new objective began. Davis' 1st Battalion was to move out in advance of Roach, clear the high ground and make a broad feint to cover the entry of Roach's unit into the defile through which the 3rd had to pass.

Davis' battalion moved out swiftly and had secured the objective by 10:30. Roach had his unit on the road thirty minutes later but the advance was held up while engineers cleared the road of mines. Against sporadic small arms fire, the advance continued until south of Nuwonni. In mid-afternoon it was halted by heavy enemy fire.

At this time Davis launched his feint on either side of the defile, simulating the attack of a regiment on a broad front. It soon became obvious the enemy had orders to stand and hold without thought of cost and heavy fire was received from all types of weapons. The feint did not succeed and Davis moved his unit back into the defile behind Roach. Both battalions halted for the night.

The following morning, with Roach on the left and Davis on the right, the attack began at 6:30. The initial advance of the 3rd was rapid, but began to slow as the rifle companies came under heavy artillery, mortar and small-arms fire. Excellent concentrations of artillery and aerial bombardments failed to dislodge the enemy. When Chase's Tank Company attempted to advance to assist Roach, mines in the roads prevented their forward movement. Small-arms fire was so heavy as to deny the engineers access to clear the road.

Total advance during the day was but three hundred yards for Roach's 3rd. In the meantime Davis crossed the stream to the east of the defile and seized Hill 228 by late afternoon.

The following morning the attack was continued with Davis to the east of the road and Roach to the west. Sawyer's 2nd (Hinkle had been wounded and evacuated on September 28) moved along the road between the 1st and 2nd. The advance was rapid and it soon became evident that the enemy had been badly mauled and discouraged the day before. The attacking Marines began to overrun heavy artillery pieces and supply dumps.

By five o'clock in the afternoon of the third of October Sawyer was in the town of Uijongbu. The code word for the operation was "Blitz." When Sawyer got into the city he contacted Litzenberg by radio and reported, "This is the Mayor of Blitz speaking." Roach was on the high ground to the west and Davis to the east. During the advance and seizure of Uijongbu, the 7th Marines had been opposed by the 3rd, 4th, and 5th Battalions of the 31st North Korean Regiment in addition to elements of the 3rd Regiment of the North Korean Division. These ground troops were supported by a battalion of tanks of which Marine air destroyed four and two were captured by Roach's 2nd. Large numbers of enemy artillery pieces and anti-aircraft guns were captured and destroyed.

This ended the Marine action in the Inchon-Seoul battle. The fight for and capture of Seoul proved to be one of the most difficult in the history of the Corps. The division suffered 2,430 casualties, of which 414 were killed or died of wounds. Of these casualties, 1,064 were sustained in the five-day period when the Marines were fighting in the outskirts and streets of Seoul. Murray's 5th suffered the heaviest losses with 1,038 (177 killed). Puller's 1st sustained 769 (92 killed), while Litzenberg took 368 with 72 killed in action.

Losses inflicted on the enemy were by far the greatest he had suffered since the beginning of hostilities. In a fifteen-day period (September 15 to 30) the division captured 4,792 prisoners and committed in excess of 13,000 casualties on the North Korean forces. A vast number of weapons and stores of all types were captured, as well as large amounts of U. S. Army material recaptured and returned to Army sources.

With the Eighth Army moving northward and in position to relieve the X Corps, the future employment of the X Corps came in for considerable speculation. Would the X Corps retain its identity and continue to operate independently or would it be absorbed by Eighth Army? The question was answered on the thirtieth of September when General Smith was summoned to the Corps headquarters where the amphibious landing at Wonsan was proposed.

The plan required the division to retract from its present positions to Inchon, load out in a period of four days and land at Wonsan on the fifteenth of October. From Wonsan the Marines would cut across the mountainous waist of Korea to the Communist capital of Pyongyang. Smith was directed to prepare and submit loading plans by the third of October. The division commander thought the request unrealistic because the Navy had not yet announced the ships that would be available for mounting out.

"It's like shadow-boxing in the dark," Lieutenant Colonel Gus Banks of the 1st Service Battalion remarked when informed of the directive.

Commandant Cates and a small party of officers arrived on an inspection tour from Washington. By helicopter and jeep, he visited all units and tendered his congratulations for the excellent performance of the Marine air-ground team. Ambassador Muccio and General Cates discussed the case of one Sergeant Augustus Siefken who had "joined" the 5th Marines at Pusan. Siefken had been joined by another "joiner" from the Embassy Guard in the person of Sergeant Edwin Wright. Muccio was of the opinion that such spirit should be nurtured rather than destroyed by disciplinary action. Cates was of the same opinion. Shortly after the commandant returned to Washington orders were written making the transfer of the two sergeants to the division legal. Even as General Cates made his rounds, the Marines were in the process of withdrawing; Murray's 5th was relieved by the Army 1st Cavalry and Litzenberg was being relieved by the 2nd ROK Corps.

While the division was loading out, a memorial service was held at the United Nations cemetery. After the invocation by Chaplain Schwyhart there was a talk by General Almond. Flowers and wreaths had been flown in from Japan for the ceremony. Almond placed a wreath on the grave of an unknown ROK soldier. There being no unmarked or unknown Marine grave, General Smith placed his wreath on the cross of Corporal R. C. Matheny of the 5th Marines.

The 1st Marine Division was aboard ship and prepared to land at Wonsan by the fifteenth of October.

CHAPTER XIII

Marine Air Power over Inchon-Seoul: A Classic Demonstration of Close Support

To depart the Inchon-Seoul scene without a deeper study and report on the action of the 1st Marine Air Wing (MAW) would be a disservice to the aerial half of the Marine air-ground team.

During the planning phase for the Inchon landing, Marine officers on General Almond's staff proposed that air support be furnished by squadrons organic to the X Corps—in other words, by planes under the direct control of the ground commander which could not be diverted to other employment by a higher echelon.

Almond readily agreed with the plan and used his authority as chief-of-staff to MacArthur to have it put into effect. A Tactical Air Command (TAC) was formed and placed under the command of Brigadier General Thomas Cushman. VMF's 212 and 312 and night-fighting squadron 542 were en route from the United States and would arrive in the theater on the fourteenth of September. General Harris, commanding the 1st MAW, assigned these flying squadrons to Cushman's TAC. These units, though untested in Korea, were at a high state of efficiency. Personnel shortages had been made up by calling members of the Organized Reserve to active duty.

The two veteran squadrons from Korea (214, 323) were still aboard the carriers *Badoeng Straits* and *Sicily*. Pilots from these units went into action over the Inchon area on the seventh of September. A total of one hundred twenty-two sorties were flown in the next three days. Rail lines, rolling stock and bridges north of Seoul were the primary targets.

On the tenth of September the Marine pilots turned their attention to Wolmi-do Island. Fourteen planes from the two carriers made their first strike on the island shortly after daylight. Approaching from the north the attack was placed on the east (Inchon) side of the island. Napalm was the primary armament used.

The smoke became so intense from the results of the first strike that following planes had to orbit for some time before the designated target area could be seen. Succeeding strikes met with heavy antiaircraft fire from Inchon. By 10:30 in the morning the island had suffered its third aerial attack and was aflame.

When the Marine carriers returned to Japan for replenishment the softening-up program was carried on by Ewen's fast carrier planes and destroyers and cruisers from the Navy. Wolmi-do was under attack again on the thirteenth and fourteenth by Navy surface and air. Ewen began to call the hard-hit target "Cinder Islands."

The Marine carriers were back on station on the fourteenth of September where both squadrons flew combat air patrol missions. After each flight when the four planes were relieved on station they strafed Inchon installations until all armament was expended. Then they returned to the carrier.

On D-day, as Taplett's battalion was moving in on Wolmi-do, an eight-plane flight from 323 bombed the high ground of the island; seven of eight five-hundred-pound bombs landed right on target. The same flight caught an armored car on the causeway between Inchon and the island. It was destroyed. When Bohn and Wildman hit the beach Marine Corsairs were strafing fifty yards to their front.

Wolmi-do was garrisoned by five hundred enemy troops. That the ground Marines were able to capture the island so swiftly and with a minimum of casualties can be attributed to the efforts of Marine and Naval air before and during the assault. The will to resist and fortify gun positions had been destroyed from the air.

During D-day Marine and Navy pilots concentrated on preventing the enemy from rushing reinforcements into the city. While flights of Corsairs ranged the area from Seoul to Suwon searching for troops in movement, others continued to soften up the Inchon defenses. Observatory Hill was hit by five five-hundred-pound bombs and thoroughly saturated with rockets; the breakwater and beach defenses were napalmed and strafed with 20 mm. shells.

The first four waves were ashore and the attack progressing rapidly before darkness forced the Corsairs to return to the carriers.

On the second day of the Inchon landing the two carrier-based units flew seventy-two sorties ranging from close support to deep interdiction. The discovery and destruction of the six T-34 tanks, in which action Simpson was killed, has been recounted. During the next two days there was a lack of close support targets and the Corsairs were forced to seek targets of opportunity and deep interdiction strikes. This phase, however, quickly changed as the ground Marines began to push on Kimpo and Yongdong-po. Puller's regiment called on close air strikes time after time as the 1st moved along the Inchon-Seoul highway.

Ample evidence was being built up that the presence of the gull-winged planes in the sky was enough to blight the aggressive spirit of the enemy. On one occasion First Lieutenant Norman Vining (TAC), tactical air controller with Sutter's battalion, contacted a flight of Corsairs to make a strike on enemy positions which had Groff's company pinned down.

The planes, however, had just completed a mission and were without armament. Nonetheless, the Corsairs began making dummy runs on the enemy just as though they were armed. The volume of fire from the enemy dropped off until it could be termed sporadic. The unarmed planes continued this maneuver until a flight of armed Corsairs came on station. The sudden change from dummy to lethal runs apparently demoralized the enemy and Groff resumed the advance.

Elements of VMF 212 and VMF(N) 542 arrived on Kimpo on the nineteenth of September. Both squadrons launched their first strikes the next day. With two squadrons aboard carriers, four squadrons were available for close air support of ground units of X Corps.

Throughout this phase close air support operations were conducted according to war-tested Marine Corps techniques. All flights, both carrier- and shore-based, reported in to the Tactical Air Control Center at Kimpo for instructions upon arrival in the operating area. From here they were passed on to the Tactical Air Control Party with either the 1st Marine Division or the 7th Army Division.

When these planes reported on station over a battalion they were under the control of the battalion commander through his FAC (Forward Air Controller). Working on the theory that close air support must be immediate if it is to be effective, the Marines have simplified their method of control. If air support is not available when the target develops, it may disappear or cause heavy casualties during the waiting time.

Such operations are not without cost. On the twentieth of September, while on a close support mission, Major Bob Floeck from VMF 214 was shot down over Seoul.

The next day Navy Lieutenant Thomas Coleman was shot down behind enemy lines. VMO-6 was notified. Lieutenant Art Bancroft took his helicopter in search of Coleman. Bancroft's plane captain went along because the report indicated that Coleman was jammed in the cockpit.

As other planes circled the area strafing belligerent North Koreans, Bancroft set his 'copter down. He stayed at the controls to keep the engine running and ready for a quick getaway as the plane captain went to assist Coleman. The fighter pilot could not be extracted alone. Bancroft went to the assistance of his plane captain. Because there are certain difficulties in restarting helicopters Bancroft left his turning slowly. Just as Coleman was freed a gust of wind turned the 'copter over and it beat itself to pieces.

Now there were three men down behind enemy lines. The orbiting planes put in another call. Lieutenant Bob Longstaff was in the area and responded. He set his 'copter down and took on the three men. Somehow Longstaff got the "egg beater" airborne with his excessive load and staggered back to friendly lines.

Bancroft got into a new plane in time to return behind enemy lines and rescue Ensign R. R. Sanders from the *Boxer*.

On the same day Major John Beebe, with Technical Sergeant Kludt flying as intercept operator for him in their F7F "Tigercat," led a flight in support of the 1st Marines in the battle for Yongdong-po. Puller's men had taken heavy casualties and air support was in constant demand. Visibility was poor because of the smoke from burning buildings in the city. Knowing the heavy losses being inflicted on the ground Marines, Beebe repeatedly pressed his attack at an extremely low altitude to insure hitting the enemy positions. On his fourth low-diving strike his plane was hit by enemy anti-aircraft fire and crashed a few hundred yards from the front lines.

The twenty-first proved to be an eventful day for the observation Grasshoppers. Second Lieutenant Ed Gaudette was piloting Captain Robert McClean over Yongdong-po on an artillery-spotting mission when their OY was hit by enemy fire. Both men parachuted to safety behind Marine lines and were returned to Kimpo by jeep. Both received minor injuries from their jump.

Marine pilots were now calling Seoul "Flak Alley."

On the twenty-second the Marines were in the air early and flying missions over Taplett's battalion on Hill 296. In the first twenty minutes of the strike the planes from 212 blasted the enemy-held ridge with sixteen two-hundred-sixty-pound bombs, forty-five rockets and twelve hundred rounds of 20 mm. cannon fire. When these planes had expended their ordnance carrier-based planes from 323 were on station.

Captain James Johnson led his six-plane flight against an enemy strong point; two napalm tanks and four five-hundred-pound bombs neutralized it. Johnson then led his flight against a concentration of enemy troops to the north. Thirty strafing and rocketing runs were made. Taplett moved his battalion onto the ridge against light resistance.

On the twenty-third, Captain Vic Armstrong went behind enemy lines nearly ninety miles to rescue Lieutenant Commander L. W. Chick of the carrier *Philippine Sea*. Under enemy fire Armstrong set down and rescued Chick who was injured. Armstrong flew Chick to the hospital ship in the harbor for treatment and then out to the carrier. Admiral Ewen was so impressed by Armstrong's performance that he ordered the galley on the *Philippine Sea* to bake the "biggest damned cake it had ever turned out."

The next day Armstrong received from the Navy a six-layer, thirty-pound cake that was three feet square.

On the twenty-fourth Lieutenant Colonel Walter Lischied's squadron (212) set a Korean record. Operating only during daylight hours twelve flights flew forty-six sorties against a variety of targets. To illustrate the type of mission a Marine pilot is apt to receive during a day's work the following record is presented.

VMF 212

Flight Number	Type of Mission	Target
1	Close support	Gun emplacements
2	Search and attack	Enemy troops
3	Combat air patrol	Suwon airfield
4	Search and attack	Railway cars, trucks
5	Search and attack	Trucks
6	Close support	Troops and barracks area
7	Close support	Troop positions
8	Close support	Troop and gun positions
9	Miscellaneous	Surrender-leaflet drop
10	Close support	Troops and gun positions
11	Search and attack	Targets of opportunity
12	Close support	Troops and gun positions

Also on this day 323 spotted four T-34 tanks in Roise's zone of action. Technical Sergeant Truman Bunce (the Marines have many enlisted pilots) destroyed the first with a direct hit by a five-hundred-pound bomb; napalm destroyed the second, and rockets damaged the third. A second flight from the same squadron came on two more T-34's. Captain William Longfellow hit it head on with a napalm tank. None of the crew escaped. The second tank was destroyed by a combination of fire.

Of the ten planes participating in the attacks on the two groups of tanks, five were damaged by anti-aircraft fire.

When the Corsairs were grounded because of darkness, the night fighters (542) took up the task of searching out artillery and mortar flashes and bombing and strafing these positions. This discouraged the enemy from employing night-harassing fires and gave the ground Marines a period of rest. When daylight came the squadron continued with interdiction and close support attacks. One correspondent labeled them the "night and day fighters."

On the twenty-fifth Squadron 214 suffered a serious loss. Lieutenant Colonel Walter Lischied, who had led his unit in over three thousand hours of combat, was shot down west of Seoul. It happened that Floeck (killed on the twentieth) and Lischied had been flying Corsairs numbered "13" when they were killed.

Captain "Jimmy" Thach, commanding the *Sicily*, ruled that no planes in the future would carry those numerals.

Lieutenant Colonel Max Volcansek, commander of VMF(N) 542, was forced to bale out at low altitude when an auxiliary fuel tank smashed into his right wing. He landed safely seconds after his parachute opened. On the same day Lieutenant Colonel Richard Wyczawski, squadron commander of 212, had just taken off from Kimpo with a full load of bombs and ammunition when he noticed his engine was throwing oil. He turned for an emergency landing as his plane caught fire. Nearly suffocated by the flames and smoke, Wyczawski jumped from the plane as it rolled to a stop, but collapsed near the burning fighter. Disregarding the danger of exploding bombs and napalm, Navy Corpsman Charles Stalcup ran to Wyczawski and dragged him to safety just before the plane and bombs exploded.

On the twenty-ninth tragedy struck VMO-6. Six miles north of Seoul an OY was shot down and the aerial observer, Captain E. E. Rives, was killed. Second Lieutenant T. D. Odenbaugh, the pilot, landed safely. The accident was reported to division immediately by fighter planes in the vicinity.

When word of the crash came through Engelhardt and Bancroft were with Major Jim Cupp, Division Air Officer. Both men volunteered to go to the rescue but Cupp vetoed the idea until exact information was at hand as to the plane's location. In a few minutes word came from Davis' 1st Battalion in the Uijongbu area that an observation plane had crashed to their right front. Davis gave the position and Bancroft and Engelhardt flipped a coin to see who would go. Bancraft won and took off with Engelhardt tailing him about a half mile.

Bancroft sighted Odenbaugh's plane and began to settle down when his 'copter blew up and disintegrated. Engelhardt called in a "Mayday" (emergency) for fighters and stood by to go in if there was any sign of life. The fighters went low over the area and reported that Bancroft had been killed. It was later reported that Odenbaugh had been taken prisoner.

The first Marine Reserve pilots to become casualties in Korea were Lieutenants Robert Crocker and Bernard Ross. Crocker was shot down and killed on an armed reconnaissance mission on the third of October near Kycha, Korea. Ross crashed on a rocket run north of Inchon three days later.

The daily risks Marine airmen take to assist the Marine on the ground are the direct result of *esprit*, training and indoctrination. The Marine aviator believes the chief reason for his existence is to furnish assistance to the rifleman on the ground. By "close" the Marines mean the immediate area of the front lines.

As a result of continual association and training, Marine air and ground personnel have worked out a system designed to deliver "customer satisfaction," the customer in this case being the rifleman. Marine airmen have made many new and happy customers in the United Nations forces in Korea.

One Army infantry captain wrote in the *Combat Forces Journal*, "Our tactical air arm should spend a few months with the Marines. I don't know what causes the difference, but it is there. The Marine pilots give us the impression that they are breaking their hearts to help us out and are as much in the show as we are."

To illustrate the importance of air support at the right time and place, we return to the scene on the morning of the eighteenth of August when the costly struggle for Obong-ni Ridge was being waged. Marine ground forces had already suffered two hundred and sixty-seven casualties. Fenton and Stevens, with two depleted companies, held a precarious foothold. Throughout the night they had barely managed to fight off strong enemy counterattacks.

Continued penetration of the enemy's lines was essential. At seven o'clock Stevens resumed the attack to dislodge the enemy on Hill 117. Despite heavy supporting fires from mortars and artillery, the assault unit was pinned down by a nest of four machine guns on the eastern slope.

Further assault by the Marines of Able Company would have been extremely costly and there was some doubt that even a resolute attack would be successful. Stevens asked for an air strike. Overhead the orbiting Corsairs were briefed and the target marked. Within minutes, a five-hundred-pound bomb was placed on the enemy position and the guns were obliterated.

From that moment, the issue was no longer in doubt. The enemy began to withdraw; the withdrawal became a rout under the combined assault of ground and air. Before the day was over, the enemy was driven across the Naktong and the river was clogged with the dead.

From September 16 to October 7 VMO-6 made 643 flights totaling 515 hours. One hundred thirty-nine severe casualties were evacuated from the front lines and division doctors estimate that in excess of one hundred of these Marines would have died had they had slower, rougher transportation. Twelve pilots were rescued from behind enemy lines including a night flight and rescue from the Han River by Armstrong.

During the thirty-three day period (September 7 to October 9) the five Marine squadrons flew 2,774 combat sorties. The vast majority of these were in direct support of ground troops. Flying from the *Sicily*, VMF 214 flew 484 combat sorties; VMF 323 from the decks of the *Badoeng Straits* put 784 sorties into the air. Flying from Kimpo Airfield, VMF 212 flew 607; VMF(N) 542 got in 573 combat strikes, while VMF 312 (the last to arrive) flew 288 sorties in ten days.

CHAPTER XIV

Wonsan: A Guerrilla War and a New Enemy

The amphibious assault on Wonsan Airfield had been scheduled for the twentieth of October. While the 1st Marine Division waited on board ship for the Navy to clear Wonsan Harbor of mines, the 1st ROK Corps swept up from the south and captured the city on the eleventh. On the thirteenth, Major General Field Harris flew to Wonsan. Harris decided that air operations could begin from the field immediately. The next day Cole's VMF 312 flew from Kimpo to Wonsan and began operations in support of the ROK's that same day.

Reinburg's VMF(N) 513 was ordered into Wonsan from Japan and arrived on the sixteenth, while Volcansek's night-fighter outfit 542 remained at Kimpo to lend support to the Eighth Army.

The division had a prolonged period of inactivity on board ship. There was a feeling that the war was going to leave them behind. This was largely confirmed when Bob Hope and Marilyn Maxwell landed at Wonsan airfield by plane and put on a show before the Marines were able to land. It was a new experience for the ground Marines to have Marine air in operation and USO shows going on before they arrived on the scene. Army personnel attached to the 1st ROK Corps added another verse to the *Marine Corps Hymn.*

Those tough and fighting Gyrenes
Wherever they may go,
Are always bringing up the rear
Behind Bob Hope and the USO

Northeastern Korea. *Mountainous and barren and with a poor network of roads, the enemy and terrain and weather hamper the actions of the widely dispersed Marine units.*

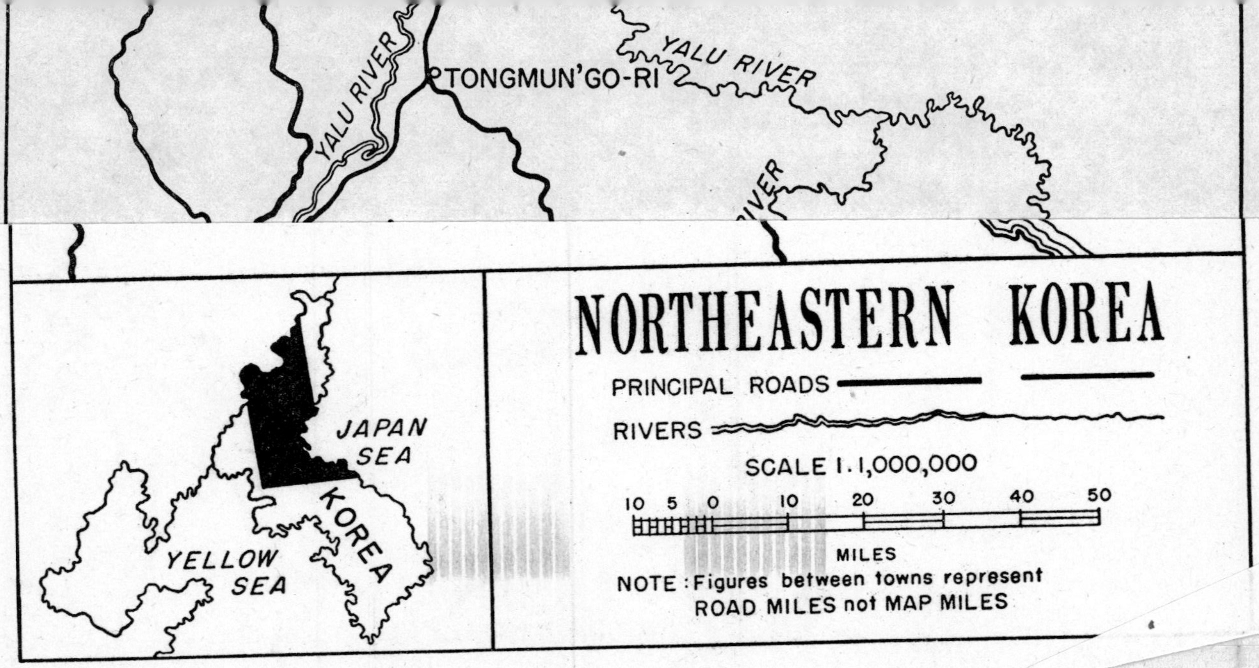

TONGMUN'GO-RI
YALU RIVER
YALU RIVER
RIVER
NORTHEASTERN KOREA
PRINCIPAL ROADS
RIVERS
SCALE 1.1,000,000
10 5 0 10 20 30 40 50
MILES
NOTE : Figures between towns represent
ROAD MILES not MAP MILES
JAPAN SEA
KOREA
YELLOW SEA

When plans were initiated for the Wonsan landing, the X Corps order called for the 1st Marine Division to load out in a period of three days. This meant that nearly twenty-eight thousand Marines and ten days of supplies were to be put aboard seventy-one ships from a harbor where the tides were a constant source of delay to the Navy. It soon became obvious that such a schedule could not be met and the Dog Day landing was progressively set back to a tentative date of the twentieth of October.

Scarcity of maps and intelligence prevented the division and regimental staffs from beginning their planning for the assault landing until October 6. To supply the lack of badly required maps and photographs, Major Donald Bush and his photo section from MAG (Marine Air Group) 33 began the difficult task of photographing fifteen hundred miles of roads and all possible landing beaches. A short time later, this same section performed the nearly impossible task of making a two-thousand-square mile mosaic map of the Hamhung-Wonsan sectors. With only three Corsairs and six Tigercats equipped for photographic work, Bush's small unit flew a total of 239 hours in a fourteen-day period exposing 23,160 feet of film and 97,200 feet of Sonne print paper. The photo laboratory printed over 100,000 nine-inch prints.

The photo laboratory for the unit was headed by Master Sergeants George Brown and Mario Osimo. To keep up with the pilots, Brown and Osimo and a staff of twenty-two worked overlapping shifts of fourteen hours a day. When the mosaic was completed, X Corps requested twenty prints from each negative made of a large area. Brown and Osimo, with their technicians, worked thirty-three hours without stopping. At the end of that time 14,675 nine-by-eighteen prints had been finished. They filled a truck that hauled them away to Corps headquarters.

From these maps and pictures, General Smith and the division staff were able to plan the assault on Wonsan. By the fifteenth of October it was obvious that ROK Army elements would arrive in Wonsan before the division could effect an assault landing. At this time X Corps changed its directive to the Marines. Upon making an administrative landing at Wonsan, the division was to move overland across Korea and seize an objective northeast of Pyongyang, the North Korean capital. At this point it would effect a juncture with the Eighth Army which was advancing northward from the Seoul area.

Upon receiving this new order, the Marine staff began the planning for the advance across the waist of Korea along the Wonsan-Yongdonk-

Pyongyang Road. This new objective for the Marines was one hundred and twenty-five miles from Wonsan and over a narrow, tortuous route. In several places the road twisted over passes in the mountains nearly four thousand feet high. The staff decided the division would move in a column of RCT's. The shortage of vehicles in the 1st Marine Division made obvious the fact that this moving about would be done by many Marines on foot. Lower echelons promply labeled the enterprise "The Long March into Upper Slobovia." About the time this plan was perfected, the whole thing was nullified by the Eighth Army's advance northward and capture of Pyongyang.

It gave considerable relief to Smith and his staff when this mission of a long overland move was canceled.

When MacArthur designated new boundaries between X Corps and the Eighth Army, with the Corps to have its zone of action in northeastern Korea, the Marines were assigned to the southern area. Again another plan was formulated by the division staff and sectors of responsibility were assigned to the three regiments. Removal of the restrictions for the operations of United Nations forces to the north also revoked this plan.

All this time the planning was done at sea. It became a point of ironic humor with the division staff to greet one another upon returning from the "head" with the query, "Any changes since I've been away?"

The division had a name for the proceedings; they called it "Operation Yo-Yo."

On the twenty-sixth of October the division received an order from X Corps in which the Marines were assigned a multifactored mission. The 1st ROK Corps was to be relieved in the Wonsan, Majon-ni and Kojo area. These sectors were to be defended and the routes to the west patrolled; one regiment was to be sent to Hamhung without delay, to advance rapidly northward to the Yalu River. Additionally, a battalion was to be prepared to land at Chongjin (a few miles south of the Yalu), and Marine engineers were to assist an Army engineering group and ROK's in repairing the Yonghung-Hamhung Railroad. The Chongjin operation was canceled later.

Smith received these orders with grave misgivings. In them he read the dispersion and loss of integrity of his division. From Wonsan to Kojo was a distance of thirty-nine miles; Wonsan to Majon-ni twenty-eight miles; Wonsan to Hamhung seventy-eight miles, and from Hamhung to Majon-dong twenty-two miles. The zone of action assigned to the Marines at this time measured three hundred road miles from north to south and sixty miles from east to west.

To execute this order, Smith assigned Puller's 1st to the Wonsan–Kojo–Majon-ni area while Litzenberg's 7th would move north to Hamhung, continue northward to the Chosin Reservoir and on to the Yalu. Murray's 5th would follow in trace of the 7th. At Oro-ri the 5th would take the right fork in the road, and push to the northeast to determine if there was a road to the Fusen Reservoir.

Inasmuch as Litzenberg's assignment, initially, meant an independent operation, the 1st Motor Transport Battalion was attached to him to insure his mobility and logistic support. The Marines, continually short on motor transport, were to feel an even greater pinch when X Corps detached the 7th Motor Transport Battalion from the division and assigned it to the support of Corps troops. This unit, attached to the 1st Marine Division at the direction of General Shepherd in anticipation of an extended land campaign for the Marines, was to see little or no service with the division, and as a result the loss of this unit was a constant source of concern to the division.

At daylight on the morning of the twenty-sixth of October (twenty-three days of inactivity), battalions of the 1st and 7th Regiments began moving ashore. Murray's 5th would follow. The first move to be initiated from the assembly areas about Wonsan was to be made by Hawkins' battalion. This unit was ordered to entrain for Kojo upon landing and to take over and guard a large supply dump in that sector.

As the Marines came ashore they were met with the new battle slogan "Home by Christmas." The Army–Air Force newspaper, *The Stars and Stripes,* published in Tokyo was enthralled with the 187th Airborne paratroop drop north of Pyongyang. General MacArthur was quoted as stating, "This war is definitely coming to an end shortly. With the closing of that trap there should be an end to organized resistance."

Not many Marines believed they would be home in time to enjoy Christmas but there was talk of early rotation and signs began to appear in the division sector: DRIVE CAREFULLY—THE MARINE YOU HIT MIGHT BE YOUR RELIEF.

X Corps intelligence section added to the optimism by stating that little organized resistance could be expected and that the North Korean remnants planned either to withdraw into Manchuria or to make a last-ditch stand in the mountains to the north. This section admitted that the Chinese or Russians might send assistance to the defeated North

Koreans, but this seemed unlikely at the time and there were no developments that indicated such a move.

Litzenberg, however, was not convinced. Gathering his officers and staff NCO's together he warned them that on the drive north they could expect to meet with Chinese Communist troops. For the benefit of the group he reviewed the political situation in China and dwelt at some length on Chinese troops and their leaders. He closed his forty-five minute talk by saying: "If there is anyone here who expects an easy walk to the Yalu River, erase it from your mind now. We are faced with a winter campaign and we're going to have to fight. It's important to win all of our battles, but it's most important that we win our first one when we meet the Chinese."

There was one Marine who cared little about rotation, Christmas or where the division went. Corporal LeRoy Pearl, who had prevailed upon Davis while at Camp Pendleton to transfer him from communications to being a fire team leader, had led his unit with distinction and energy throughout the Seoul campaign. During the long period aboard ship Pearl had found time passing slowly. To keep in practice he would go to the radio shack and transcribe radio messages. Unfortunately he was seen by the division communications officer; there was a critical shortage of trained radiomen. Pearl lost his job as fire team leader. Once again he became a communicator.

In the interval between shipping out at Inchon and the landing at Wonsan, other changes had transpired. Summer was over and it was not long before the Marines were to remember the heat-laden days around Pusan and Seoul with a certain nostalgia.

The day the Marines began going ashore was bright and clear but there was a bite to the wind. The following morning they were to see their first ice in Korea as the rice paddies were lightly frozen over. Old China hands in the division wondered how long and how far north they would advance. They recalled the military maxim handed down from the days of Genghis Khan: "To embark on a winter campaign in the land of the Mongols is to invite disaster."

By two in the afternoon of the twenty-sixth of October, Hawkins' 1st was aboard gondola cars at the rail siding not far from the airfield. Two hours later the unit was in Kojo. The Marines were pleasantly surprised with the clean seaport town, its white beaches and clean water. The war had left it relatively undamaged. Hawkins and his staff received a further surprise. The supply dump they had rushed south to guard did not exist. It had been removed by ROK forces.

Surrounding Kojo is a flat plain some five thousand yards in diameter. From the outskirts of the city to the rise of hills which encircle the seaport was a solid pack of flooded rice paddies. The ROK unit being relieved was a happy-go-lucky outfit which had evidently enjoyed its duty in the area. The officers assured Hawkins that no organized enemy units existed. They had "pushed patrols many thousands of yards in all directions" and found but few stragglers. The enemy had made a few infiltration attacks for food and clothing and some of the local women had gone back into the hills with these marauders, but that was all. When questioned about the large number of young men seen in Kojo and the adjoining villages, the assurance was given that they were North Koreans only too happy to be out of the war.

The night of the twenty-sixth passed without incident and the following day the 1st Battalion moved into positions of defense. The supply train returned from Wonsan and a motor convoy passed over the thirty-nine miles without interruption. When the train was unloaded the ROK unit boarded with their women, children, pigs and chickens for movement northward. The Marines saw considerable humor in the manner in which their allies went to war. They labeled the train the "Okie-Arkey Special." Some of the older Marines said the ROK's put Coxie's Army to shame. The younger Marines wanted to know who the hell Coxie was.

Hawkins placed Wray's company, with two platoons (Jones and McClelland) of Barrow's company, on a long ridge of high ground to the northwest of the city. This ridge ran in a southwesterly direction from the point where it rose from the beach. First Lieutenant Francis Carlon's platoon was positioned on the extreme end of the ridge to be covered and was separated from the other two rifle platoons of Charlie Company by a ravine and road. Swords' platoon was assigned positions on a hill which rose abruptly on the eastern outskirts of Kojo.

Belli's platoon of Captain Wes Noren's company took up positions on Hill 109 which was east of the railroad and twelve thousand yards south of Kojo. These positions faced the ocean and overlooked two villages (Pangdong-ni and Habongdong-ni) and an extensive rice paddy. While Belli's unit was digging in, it was visited by civilians from the villages who brought the Marines gifts of fresh eggs. Noren set up his company CP in the sector covered by Master Sergeant Matthew Monk's

3rd Platoon. Monk's positions were nine hundred yards south of Belli, on the same side of the rail line and overlooking the village of Tongchong which had been the headquarters for the retreating enemy's army.

As Monk's platoon moved through Chanchon-ni to assume positions, an old woman shouted warnings that the young men in the area were enemy soldiers disguised as civilians. ROK interpreters assured the Marines that the woman was crazy and to disregard her. Noren's 2nd Platoon under First Lieutenant George Chambers moved onto a cone-shaped hill twelve hundred yards north and west of the company CP. This land mass (Hill 185) was connected with the main road by a dike which crossed the rice paddy in the vicinity of the railway bridge.

Hawkins placed his CP on the beach north of Kojo. In this area was Kaufer's platoon of 4.2 mortars, Harmon's engineers and a detachment of the 1st Medical Battalion. Throughout the movement into positions there was no enemy opposition offered, though Monk's platoon was subjected to sporadic, inaccurate sniper fire from the hills to the west.

The night promised to be cold and the order was passed that one man in each of the two-man foxholes could remain in his sleeping bag. Under no circumstances were the bags to be entirely closed by the zipper. By trading off, one man would be on the alert while the other gained some comfort by the cover. With no particular uneasiness over the situation, because of the general air of "the war's over," the troops on the perimeter settled down for a long, cold night.

The first indications that the enemy had not given up the area entirely came at dusk when a truck was fired upon and abandoned on the road below Noren's CP. A fire team patrol led by Corporal Clarence Smith went down to inspect the area and to intercept Marine supply vehicles en route from Kojo. Pfc. Robert Montgomery accompanied Smith with his radio. Smith reached the area and came under heavy fire and a sniper bullet knocked his helmet off. Behind the ROK truck was the radio jeep of First Lieutenant Paul Vnencak, communications officer, who had been forced to abandon his vehicle because of the enemy fire and the roadblock made by the truck.

Under close-range fire Smith and his fire team pushed the truck into the ditch and brought the jeep into the company positions. The truck and jeep incidents occurred in the late afternoon. As darkness came on the 60 and 81 mortars were registered on the hills to the right flank of Monk's positions. At nine o'clock a bull cart was taken under fire by the heavy machine guns and the cart and ox clattered over the hill to safety. There were reports that the cart was accompanied by troops but this was not verified.

The first phase of an extremely well–co-ordinated attack by the enemy occurred when heavy assaults were placed on the two Marine flanking units—Belli's platoon to the south and Wray's company to the northwest.

On Belli's front the enemy, working over terrain familiar to them, crept silently into close positions. With the suddenness of an avalanche, they launched their attack. In a wild confusion of bursting grenades and the raving of burp guns, Marines clawed frantically at zippers to release themselves from sleeping bags that became death jackets as the slide openers jammed. Men in position fought back savagely, but the sheer weight of numbers proved too much and the flank was turned and positions overrun.

Sergeant Clayton Roberts took command of the right flank. Shouting to his men to withdraw and reorganize in new positions, he manned a machine gun to cover the withdrawal and protect the wounded. Despite the number of enemy who fell before his gun, others sprang forward. When they closed in to a range where his weapon was no longer effective, he left it to meet the swarming enemy in hand-to hand combat. Corpsman Dorin Stafford heard the cry "Corpsman" and went forward as the Marines were being driven back.

Once the enemy assault opened, further attacks were directed by bugle calls, whistle blasts and signal flashes from flashlights.

While Belli's platoon was in its life-and-death struggle, Wray's company was under heavy pressure on the northern flank. The first assault by the enemy forced a local penetration which killed Corporal John Brooks and wounded three men in his squad. Pfc. Donald Gilligan, also wounded, took command, and redeploying the unit got the machine gun into a position where its field of fire would be more effective, and stemmed the initial assault. Refusing evacuation, he saw to the care of the wounded in his sector and continued to direct the fire and movement of his men.

Throughout the rest of the night the enemy continued to exert pressure on Wray's front, but no further progress was made against his lines.

To the south Noren called Monk on the telephone at 10:30 and informed him that Belli's unit had been overrun and that a withdrawal might be necessary.

The enemy then began to make a series of probing attacks along

Monk's positions. With tenacity and skill, the enemy moved along the thinly held line searching for the flanks and weak spots. At 11:30 the enemy found the extreme left flank and drove in sharply. Sergeant Paul Cassidy reported that he had been forced to give up three positions. Knowing the enemy were by now aware of his strength and remaining positions, Monk notified Noren that he was doubtful of being able to hold with the enemy in possession of the flank. The Marines began receiving heavy machine-gun fire from this sector.

Noren requested permission of Hawkins to withdraw. This request was granted. Monk conducted a slow, position-by-position, withdrawal with cover fire always available for the men in the forward positions.

With Lieutenant Chester Farmer, company executive officer, at the point and Noren at the rear to supervise the disengagement, the platoon came from the high ground to the railroad tracks and moved slowly northward. In the meantime Noren had contacted Chambers by radio and directed him to withdraw from Hill 185 and join forces where the dike intersected the railway. As the unit came abreast of the positions formerly held by Belli's platoon, four Marines who had been killed along the road were found. At the dike-railway intersection, Farmer came upon Staff Sergeant Robert Fisher of Belli's unit who had remained behind with five men to act as a guide for any Marines who had been cut off when leaving Hill 109.

Chambers had not yet reached the intersection when the 3rd Platoon arrived. Directing Farmer to continue the move north, Noren remained at the dike to wait for Chambers and to assist in the later joining of the two forces. Sergeant Edsel Edson had charge of the squad on the point and led the column along the tracks. Slightly north of Chonchon-ni they came upon a number of troops. In the darkness the Marines were challenged in English. As Edson was about to give the password the point came under heavy fire. The platoon deployed to both sides of the tracks and the fire fight became general along the flanks as well as the point.

While Farmer went back to contact Noren, Second Lieutenant Robert Tobin went forward with Technical Sergeant Marlink to assist Edson in evacuating the wounded. Only by the greatest resolution was it possible to get the three wounded Marines to the rear. Pfc.'s Kenneth Evans and Ernest Corin were killed. Interpreters reported the voices on the flanks were saying, "Let's attack them again."

With the arrival of Chambers from Hill 185, Noren consolidated his unit by withdrawing Monk's platoon from their area of contact with the enemy and formed a perimeter defense on either side of the railway tracks. The enemy attacked from the south (rear) of the unit and five Marines were wounded and Pfc. George Bauerfeind, who had accompanied Farmer, was killed.

During this phase of the withdrawal Noren had been out of contact with Hawkins because the two radios were inoperative. In the earlier patrol with Corporal Smith, Sergeant Sawochka had had the antenna shot off his radio; Montgomery's radio was also out of action. While the unit was setting up defensive positions, Sawochka and Montgomery traded parts and got one radio to work. Noren reported to Hawkins.

After an all-around defense was set up, Noren and Tobin made radio contact with the 4.2 mortars on the beach to the north. For the next two hours the mortars fired on the village west of the Marine positions. Enemy activity slackened under this mortar barrage and the rest of the night was spent in comparative quiet.

At daylight Noren organized litter details to carry the wounded. There were seven men who had to be carried. Ponchos were used inasmuch as there were no stretchers available. It took six men to carry one. The unit left the tracks and began the slow, tortuous move across the flooded rice paddies. Barrow's company, minus Swords' platoon, moved south from the city to meet and assist Noren's unit.

An enemy force numbering several hundred, moved from Kojo at this time and were taken under air attack as well as fire from Noren's mortars and machine guns. The enemy unit suffered heavy casualties and was generally dispersed. Stragglers made their way across the paddy and into the hills to the west. Marine Corsairs practically erased the town which had housed the forces attacking Belli's platoon.

Captain George Farish flew his helicopter in from Wonsan and evacuated the more critically wounded directly to a hospital ship in Wonsan harbor.

Through information received from friendly civilians and captured North Koreans, it was evident by this time the enemy was capable of placing several thousand armed men into an attempt to recapture Kojo. The North Korean unit in the immediate area was the 5th North Korean Division.

With the situation building into what might become a major engagement, Puller ordered Sutter's 2nd Battalion south with supporting arms.

The 2nd went aboard the U.S.S. *Okanogan* and were to be landed on the twenty-eighth. Puller flew into the area by helicopter and assumed command.

Upon landing, Sutter sent his battalion through Kojo and a house-by-house check was made for enemy personnel. The earlier attacks by Marine air had largely destroyed the city and no enemy units were found, though a few snipers were killed and stragglers captured. While Sutter was moving through the city, Wray sent a patrol to the area where his unit had been engaged during the previous night and the dead were recovered.

The following day Farish began scanning the area for signs of beleaguered Marines from Belli's unit. He was rewarded when he saw the word "help" spelled out in rice straw alongside a straw-stack. A lone figure beside the stack waved to him. Farish brought his 'copter onto the ground near the man.

"Hiya, Marine, going my way?"

Pfc. William Meister clambered into the plane. "I don't know where you're going, but I'm going with you."

Meister had made his way off Hill 109 during the confused fighting and hid himself in rice straw.

Later in the day, Farish rescued Pfc. Richard Graham and Corporal Donald Pluim. Upon his return to the beach area on this mission, Farish was notified a Corsair had been shot down west of Kojo. Directed by orbiting Marine fighters, Farish flew to the location.

As he brought his helicopter down, the surrounding hills erupted with small arms and automatic weapons fire. In the face of the enemy opposition, Farish hovered a few feet over the cockpit of the crashed Corsair. It was obvious the pilot was dead. The enemy fire increased as the hovering plane assumed a nearly stationary position. It was impossible to retrieve the body and Farish was forced to regain altitude. The next day a ground patrol entered the area and recovered the body.

On the afternoon of the twenty-ninth, Noren led a patrol south along the tracks and onto Hill 109. The body of Sergeant Roberts was recovered with fifteen other Marines who had died with him. Seven of the dead had been trapped and killed in their sleeping bags.

Noren's patrol continued south and into the village of Tongchong where they came under sniper fire. Marine air was called in and suspected houses were destroyed. Upon its return, the patrol had a brisk fire fight with an enemy platoon caught trying to get into the western hills. Sixteen of the twenty enemy were killed.

By now the casualties suffered by the 1st during the night of October 27-28 could be computed: twenty-seven had been killed, thirty-nine wounded and three missing.

One of the missing men was Corpsman Dorin Stafford who had refused to leave the Marine wounded and remained with Roberts. Interrogation of North Korean prisoners revealed that a "Marine medical man" was a prisoner and had been put to work attending enemy wounded. This report was never fully confirmed, inasmuch as the prisoners were reporting from hearsay. Stafford is still listed as missing in action with Private Jack Fischer and Pfc. Anthony Marcatante.

With the arrival of Sutter's battalion and the continuation of aggressive patrolling, the enemy gave up the idea of recapturing Kojo. Aerial sightings reported large bodies of enemy troops moving through the hills to the north. Smaller units, however, continued harassing and guerrilla operations, and the rail line between Kojo and Wonsan was blown in several places. Hawkins' battalion, upon its return to Wonsan, was halted by a blown-out track. The unit went into perimeter defense for the night and continued the next morning.

While the 1st and 2nd Battalions were engaged in the Kojo area, Roise's Battalion of the 5th Marines had been attached to Puller's task group. This insured the protection of Wonsan inasmuch as Ridge's 3rd Battalion had been ordered twenty-six miles inland (west) to occupy and clear the Majon-ni sector of enemy. Additionally, Ridge's unit was to establish blocking positions at the north-south and east-west road junctions through which numerous North Koreans were passing to the safety of the northern mountains.

Reinforced by a battery of artillery, a platoon of 4.2 mortars and a platoon of engineers, the 3rd began the move onto Majon-ni in two march units. Tanks were available to Ridge, but the road was too narrow at the crest of the three-thousand-foot pass for the Pershings.

It is twenty-eight road miles from Wonsan to Majon-ni; by air it is fifteen. From Wonsan northward to Togwon and on to Yonggang-ri it passes through the alluvial plains surrounding the seaport city. At Yonggang-ri the road turns west and upward. From that point it conforms to the Marine description of the Korean landscape. "It's either straight up or straight down—nothin's on the level."

In a distance of five air miles between the sea-level town of Yong-gang-ri to the top of the pass at Masing-Nyong, there is an altitude differential of three thousand feet. Excavated from the sheer walls of barren mountains, the road has awesome thousand foot drop-offs bordering the outboard shoulders. Truck drivers viewed these shoulders with apprehension. The Marines labeled the road "Ambush Alley."

The village of Majon-ni is in a Y-shaped valley fifteen hundred feet below the pass. It housed less than four hundred and the people were as poor as the soil they worked to gain a living.

The defense of the town posed many problems and while most of the battalion was still on the treacherous road, Ridge and his operations officer, Major Joseph Trompeter, made a thorough survey of the area before setting up the plan of defensive positions to be assumed. To the south of the village the road forked, with the right hand passing through the settlement and on to Pyongyang, while the left branch continued south to Seoul. The road followed the general course of the Imjin River, which also split into north and south tributaries east of the village.

It was impossible to establish effective outposts because of the height and distance of the commanding terrain from the village. Ridge decided on a perimeter defense with each of the three companies assigned a sector. Because of the extensive front to be covered the rifle units would be spread too thin for safety. To meet this danger provisional platoons were formed by personnel from the Headquarters and Service Company, engineers, and by stripping the artillery battery to the barest minimum required to operate their guns.

Three roadblocks were established; one on the road leading into the village from Wonsan and each fork was blocked to the north and south of Majon-ni.

Major Edwin Simmons, commanding the battalion weapons company, was assigned the responsibility of constructing and manning these blocks. Strohmenger's artillery battery was faced with the problem of being able to fire in all directions and at extremely high angles because of the nearly perpendicular hills surrounding the village.

As the perimeter forces were digging into positions, the engineers established a water point and began to survey the area for a landing strip which would take observation planes. To obtain sufficient runway space, the river bed would have to be graded and the western end would project beyond the perimeter borders. First Lieutenant Mitchell Duffy's engineers, with the help of indigenous labor, had the strip completed and the first plane landed five days later. Because of the sheer cliff bordering the runway, it would be ticklish work for the Grasshopper pilots to set down and take off.

An additional problem facing Ridge was the control and supervision of the native population inasmuch as the village was inside the perimeter. Because the area had been occupied by Russian forces after World War II and large quantities of Communist literature had been found in public buildings, the sympathies of the natives were suspect. Ridge formed a civil affairs unit of twelve men under First Lieutenant Donald Holmes. From then on he was known as "sheriff."

In turn, Holmes formed a village council and appointed a mayor. Through this body he transmitted the rules of curfew, the conduct of the population and the procedures to be taken by the civilians to insure that health and sanitation measures were observed during the occupation.

With Majon-ni astride the east-central corridor of escape, the roads were clogged with fleeing refugees and thousands of enemy soldiers in civilian clothing. An interpreter was placed at each of the three roadblocks and all persons appearing at them were interrogated and searched for weapons. Further screening was done by Holmes' section. Civilians were escorted to the exit route they desired while military personnel were locked up in the prisoner of war stockade. The civilian populace was moving, in general, from west (Pyongyang) to east (Wonsan), while the military were moving northward. At one time there were nearly seven hundred prisoners in the compound. Over four thousand civilians were processed and released.

It was well Ridge took such elaborate precautions, for the succeeding days would test his unit to the utmost as the enemy made a concerted effort to recapture this road-junction town and open a corridor of escape for units of the North Korean People's Army.

The Marine landing at Inchon isolated the enemy army on the Pusan perimeter and was the cause of its collapse. The safest routes of escape for this beleaguered force were along the central and east coast roads. The west coast escape route was sealed off early by the capture of Seoul and the break-out of the Eighth Army.

The east coast route of withdrawal became increasingly dangerous as the Marines occupied Wonsan. It was then that the enemy turned to the vast, central corridor extending from the Naktong River northward through Andong, Yong-ju, Wonju, Chunchon, Dumhwa and Ichon and along the Imjin River to Majon-ni, and on northward to the designated assembly and rallying point at Kanggye.

Many of the North Korean units broke up into small bands of ten to a hundred, and donning civilian dress made their way to the north, pillaging and robbing as they moved. It will never be known how many enemy troops escaped in this manner. Not all of the enemy units broke up; the 5th, 2nd and 15th Rifle Divisions were held together by strong leaders and, though understrength, retained their integrity throughout the long retreat.

It was the North Korean 5th which tried to recapture Kojo from Hawkins' 1st Battalion. When this effort failed, the unit continued guerrilla operations while moving northward. These raids, in the main, were to replenish rations. Once above the 38th parallel, many individuals, upon returning to their native villages, assumed positions on the local police force or in civic organizations where they could hide out until the People's Army was re-formed and assistance arrived from China.

Early in September the North Korean soldiers had been informed by Kim Il Sung that their Chinese allies had crossed the Yalu and were moving south to launch a counteroffensive. The Marine landing at Inchon hastened the movement of Chinese across the border.

With the enemy's 5th, 2nd and 10th Divisions moving northward for an assembly at Huksu-ri deep in the mountains northwest of Hamhung, the 15th Division, under the command of Major General Pak Sun Chol was committed to the task of opening the road junction at Majon-ni. Armed with rifles, submachine and machine guns, grenades and mortars, this enemy unit was capable of mounting four thousand men into the attack.

By nightfall on the first day, Ridge had his plans for the defense and occupation of the crossroads town well underway. His perimeter defense units were dug in and both telephone and radio communications with company CP's established. Ridge had chosen a Russian-type schoolhouse as battalion CP. The first night passed uneventfully and on the following morning two motorized patrols were made. Foot patrols were also sent out, but no contact with the enemy was made.

Late in the afternoon a supply convoy arrived from Wonsan and reported an uneventful trip. A number of enemy soldiers appeared at the roadblocks and surrendered. They also reported there were in excess of a thousand more in the hills who were hungry and cold and wished to surrender too. Ridge requested Puller to have an air drop of surrender pamphlets made. Despite this sanguine picture, Ridge further consolidated his positions by having barbed wire obstacles constructed and further minefields laid.

The unit settled down to the dull task of manning the perimeter, policing the village, interrogating people arriving at the roadblocks and sending out motor and foot patrols to determine if the enemy was making any attempt to gather for an attack. An air drop of surrender pamphlets was made and the mortars and artillery began a series of harassing and interdiction fires as a further incentive to surrender.

Captain Dave Swinford added to the growing list of prisoners in the stockade. Flying an armed reconnaissance mission, he had knocked out three trucks and an armored car in the Kanggye area. Upon his return he flew over Majon-ni to have a look at Ridge's unit, and by radio was informed that a small house on a ridge line to the south of the village held snipers; Swinford spotted the house and gave it a burst of 20 mm. cannon fire. From the doors and windows tumbled about twenty guerrillas. They began to wave white cloths and bow deeply to the circling Corsair. Slowly Swinford got the idea across by mock strafing runs and began herding the group off the ridge and down to Majon-ni. Ridge sent out a patrol to pick up Swinford's "prisoners."

The treacherous road between Wonsan and the outpost was a source of concern to Ridge. A practice air drop was requested and delivered with success. Satisfied that his unit could be supplied from the air if the road was cut, Ridge went into the fourth day of occupation without having contacted the enemy. It was upon this day that General Pak set the forces of his 15th North Korean Division into a series of maneuvers designed to sever the road to Wonsan and to drive the Marines from Majon-ni.

Corley's How Company was assigned to make the patrol along the southern road on this day. The patrol, led by Lieutenant Harvey Gass was reinforced by machine guns, mortars, an artillery observer and an air liaison section. The unit moved through the southern roadblock and took the winding, mountain-walled road toward the village of Tonyoni-ni. To the east lay another valley and the village of Kumdong. The patrol continued south with the Imjin River to the left of the road and a sheer wall of rocks and boulders rising to three thousand feet on the right. As the small force left the valley of Kumdong, a narrow gorge developed with the mountain of Maam-San rising sharply on the left.

The vehicles of the point entered the gorge which was slightly more than two miles in length. It was not until the main body was in the defile that the well-concealed enemy opened fire from the high ground to the right and left of the road.

The Marines spilled from their vehicles and hastily took positions along the river bank. It soon became evident the enemy had fire superiority as well as occupying positions which were virtually unassailable. To complicate the situation further, the gorge was so narrow the vehicles could not be turned to make a withdrawal. While First Lieutenant Lawrence Simmon, FAC, was informing Ridge of the situation and calling in Corsairs, Pfc. Donald Hofstetter, jeep driver in the mortar section, managed to get his vehicle turned around. Second Lieutenant Kenneth Bott jumped into the vehicle and the two ran the gauntlet of fire. Both were wounded.

By the time Bott returned to the perimeter area, a relief force of the remaining platoons of Corley's company was mounted on artillery prime movers and ready to move out. The artillery had swung their tubes around and were waiting for fire missions. Bott and Hofstetter guided the reinforcements back to the battle area.

The enemy's fire superiority and positions prevented the Marines from more than holding and waiting. Corley, at the head of the relieving force, was faced with the problem of conducting his supporting fire in such a manner that it would not endanger his gorge-bound unit. He set his heavy machine guns up so they fired parallel to the road. In this manner he pinned the enemy down on the west side of the road while a platoon was sent in an enveloping maneuver on the opposite side of the gorge. Mortar and artillery fire was added to that of the heavy machine guns and the enveloping platoon moved out to scale Maam-San.

Suddenly the enemy gave up the fight, withdrew hurriedly into the hills and the patrol was relieved. Five were killed including Lieutenant Richard Smith, artillery forward observer, and sixteen wounded in the short, bitter fight.

By the time the wounded were evacuated from the ambush area and attended to, it was nearly dark. Navy Lieutenant R. J. Fleischaker, battalion medical officer, made the decision that one of the wounded Marines would have to be evacuated immediately to the hospital ship

Consolation in Wonsan Harbor if the man were to live. The request was made by radio.

Technical Sergeant Wayne Kerr volunteered to make a night flight in a Grasshopper. Inasmuch as light observation planes are not equipped with instruments for night flying, such flights entail considerable risk. Additionally, the approach to the Majon-ni airstrip had to be made through a canyon between Obong-san Mountain on the north and Suchin-pong on the south. The distance between these peaks was less than twelve hundred yards. At the base where the hastily built seven-hundred-foot strip extended into the stream bed, the two mountain walls narrowed to less than two hundred yards.

Kerr took off from Wonsan airfield and set a compass course by the light of a flashlight held in his right hand as he guided the plane with his left. After a time he picked out two mountain peaks outlined against the sky. Kerr decided the pass must lie between them. He was correct and below him he saw the strip illuminated by the 3rd Battalion trucks. The landing was made without incident. The doctors and corpsmen placed the wounded Marine in the observer's seat. Take-off meant heading for Tokkok-san Mountain at the western end of the runway. Once the plane was airborne, a sharp bank to the right had to be made to escape the mountain and enter the canyon, which would allow altitude to be gained.

An hour after leaving Wonsan, Kerr was back with the wounded Marine. Forty-five minutes later the Marine was on the operating table of the U.S.S. *Consolation*.

While the patrol was being heavily engaged a supply convoy escorted by the 2nd Platoon, under Second Lieutenant James Beeler of G Company, departed Wonsan. Before the pass was reached the unit came on a section of road that had been blow away. When the convoy halted it was taken under heavy fire. Five trucks and two jeeps were destroyed. A flight of six Corsairs came in and the enemy was dispersed from the commanding ground. A relief force with supporting tanks was organized and the convoy was able to return to Wonsan.

Throughout the day the enemy had shown considerable skill in selecting ambush areas and had waited with patience for the main body of troops to be in their sights before opening fire. With the road to Wonsan cut and the enemy giving every indication of his ability and desire to attack, Ridge requested an air drop of critical supplies.

Captain Don Carlo Blasingame had his Air Delivery Section set up on Wonsan airfield. When the message was received to supply Ridge by air, the section packaged artillery, mortar and machine-gun ammunition as well as six cases of hand grenades. With rations, gasoline and antifreeze, the load came to forty-three thousand pounds and it took one hundred fifty-two parachutes to carry the drop. Lieutenant Colonel Bruce Prosser commanded the flight of planes. Four hours from the time Ridge made his request, the packages were tumbling into the Majon-ni perimeter.

In the meantime, the more seriously wounded were evacuated by helicopters and observation plane. Valentine crashed on take-off from the little strip, but walked away from the OY uninjured. Three days later First Lieutenant William Lucas crashed on take-off when his engine failed. In neither crash, however, was pilot or evacuee passenger injured.

Barrow's company was assigned the mission of getting a forty-five truck convoy through to Majon-ni. Reinforced by a platoon from Captain Lester Harmon's company of engineers, 81 mm. mortars under Technical Sergeant Shelly Wiggins and a section of 75 mm. Recoilless rifles under Second Lieutenant Harold Coffman, the long vehicular train departed Wonsan at 2:30 in the afternoon. With McClelland's platoon on the point and the engineers well forward, the train crossed the plains and entered the mountains. Overhead a Grasshopper was circling and snooping in an effort to detect an enemy ambush; in addition there were two Corsairs on station for aerial support.

The first roadblock was encountered on a sharp hairpin turn below the pass; a section of the narrow road had been blown out. McClelland deployed his platoon and Harmon brought his engineers forward to repair the roadbed. The enemy made no attempt to prevent the repairs. After a thirty-minute delay the convoy moved on. A half mile further on the second roadblock was discovered; the task of repairing the road took another thirty minutes. Four such blocks and delays were encountered as the hours slipped away.

The fifth roadblock was covered by enemy fire and McClelland pushed his platoon aggressively to the front. Two of the engineer trucks were damaged as well as two from motor transport. The enemy was achieving its purpose of fractionalizing the train by destroying trucks along its length.

McClelland attempted to close with the enemy but was pinned down by superior fire from the higher ground. Jones tried to envelop the enemy positions by moving up on the right of the road. Little progress was made on this maneuver because of the inability of the Marines to scale the mountain wall. An air strike was called for by Barrow but control was poor because a forward air controller was not with the unit. The procedure struck upon to direct the Corsairs became rather involved: the unit commander would shout instructions to the radio jeep operator who in turn would transmit the word on to the OY plane circling overhead; the Grasshopper pilot would then talk to the pilots of the Corsairs.

A strike was laid down but poorly placed because of the incomplete information reaching the pilots. Finally the target area was marked by 60 mm. mortars and the Corsairs made their strafing runs and the enemy fire subsided somewhat. With night approaching, however, the unit was soon denied further use of air support.

Barrow was faced with several problems as darkness came on. He could not move forward because of the heavy enemy fire on his front platoon. If he set up a perimeter defense for the night he was certain he could hold his position but in the process he would lose more of the soft-skinned vehicles bearing badly needed supplies for Ridge. Arriving in Majon-ni with a company of men on foot and without supplies would only increase the problems of the beleaguered battalion.

Barrow called his officers together and explained the situation to them. He decided that the unit had to admit temporary defeat and would have to return to Wonsan. He made the decision with considerable reluctance.

By now darkness had come on and in the moonlight the Marines could see the enemy moving into flanking positions along the ridges above them. The order was given to turn the trucks about and for McClelland to disengage with the enemy and the withdrawal started.

This order posed a problem for the truck drivers. The roadbed at this juncture was no wider than thirty feet; on the left was a mountain wall, to the right a drop-off of thirty to a hundred feet. Marine Corps trucks of the type then being used have an over-all length of twenty-three feet. The turning radius of these vehicles, according to the manual, is thirty-four feet eight inches to the right and thirty-five feet six inches to the left.

With much shouting, cursing, shoving and hauling every truck in the long line was turned without accident. Swords' platoon, which had been the rear guard, now became the point and McClelland, as soon as he was able to disengage from the enemy, became the rear guard.

The change in direction was accomplished and the wounded were collected and placed in trucks. A short time after movement to Wonsan commenced a truck went over the cliff taking the driver and twenty men with it. Quickly a human chain was formed by other Marines and the painful task of lifting the injured from the gorge to the road began. The personnel in the truck were largely from Staff Sergeant George Morgen's assault section attached to Barrow's unit for the operation. Sixteen of the twenty men in the truck were injured in the sixty-foot drop. After the rescue was affected the train began movement once again. To forestall further accidents of such nature Barrow gave the order that the vehicle lights were to be turned on. The convoy returned to Wonsan without further incident. Eight men had been wounded, sixteen injured and five vehicles lost.

Barrow reported to Puller. When he was finished, Puller asked, "What do you need to make it through tomorrow."

"Four hours of daylight and an air controller."

The next morning at 8:30, with Jones' platoon at the point, the convoy started out on the second attempt to open the supply route to the 3rd Battalion. The procedure for the move was altered in that Jones' platoon was sent forward of the main body a distance of several thousand yards and on foot. The idea behind this deployment being that the riflemen would approach and possibly overcome a roadblock before the train of vehicles came to the obstruction.

The point fire team was led by Pfc. Robert Kozelka and through aggressive tactics a stiff pace was set and the convoy proceeded without interruption until about six miles into the hills above Wonsan. As Kozelka's team came about a sharp turn in the road it came upon a platoon-sized group of the enemy resting and eating about a blown-out section of road. Caught by surprise the enemy force was killed and dispersed.

It was deduced that the enemy had been waiting to ambush the vehicle train but had depended upon hearing the truck engines grinding up the steep grade before getting into position. The Marine riflemen, far in advance of the trucks, had surprised the enemy and the first block was overcome with such swiftness that further obstructions were successfully overcome without delay. Barrow brought his unit into Majon-ni by early afternoon.

The Marines at Majon-ni gave the new arrivals a hearty cheer; Ridge gave them a place in the perimeter defense between How and George companies.

X Corps had received information that the enemy was using the copper mine area near the mountain of Turyu-San as an assembly point for North Korean troops. X Corps ordered Ridge to investigate the sector.

Turyu-San, one of the highest mountains in the area, is nine miles northeast of Majon-ni. To reach it a patrol would have to traverse a winding, narrow road and pass through three villages before reaching the base of the four-thousand-foot peak. The area was rife with positions of ambush. Intelligence reported there were five to seven thousand enemy troops in this sector. If this estimate was correct, any patrol Ridge was capable of mounting could run into considerable difficulty.

Though it seriously depleted his perimeter defense at Majon-ni, Ridge sent two companies of riflemen augmented by elements of the Weapons Company, on this reconnaissance in force. It was commanded by Major Reginald Myers. To sustain the defense of the village upon the departure of the motorized force, every able-bodied man was placed in provisional platoons and put into the line. When final deployment was effected the battalion reserve consisted of a records clerk, the first sergeant and a runner.

The patrol made its way to the mining site and returned without incident capturing over eighty prisoners on the way. By now the stockade within the perimeter had six hundred forty-three prisoners of war. In a short time they would outnumber the Marines.

The next morning at 1:30 Corley's How Company reported trip flares and booby traps exploding on its front. By 3:30 the entire perimeter was heavily engaged. No penetrations were made in Corley's lines, but the fighting was general, with grenades, mortars and artillery joining in with the rifles and machine guns to make the hill-banked valley roar.

The battalion OP was on a steep lift of sheer hillside west of the village and at a point where the flanks of How and Item Companies tied in. The observation post, manned by one officer and four men, heard enemy infiltrators working into their position and requested illumination. A small enemy force had succeeded in slipping between the flanks of the two companies and were moving in on the OP. Shortly before daylight, out of ammunition, the small OP group was forced to withdraw.

The fighting continued with little abatement on the whole of the perimeter front as a fog-shrouded dawn lightened the scene. The enemy could be seen prowling the high ground in the vicinity of the OP and one exultant officer kept exposing himself and shouting "Banzai! Banzai! Banzai!" He was promptly named "Tarzan" and just as promptly driven to cover by the direct fire of artillery.

With the rifle companies engaged, it was imperative that the high ground be retaken from "Tarzan" and his force. A platoon was hastily organized from cooks, clerks and supply personnel. Under the command of Second Lieutenant Charles Maddox this heterogeneous unit began the assault of the high ground. Because the normal route to the enemy-held position would be exposed to a blistering fire, Maddox led his men to the vertical facing where there was a cover of scrub pine and rocks.

While the platoon made a mountain climbing approach to seek the enemy, the artillery and mortars continued to blast at the summit. By 6:30 in the morning Maddox had his men on top and the retiring enemy received a full chorus of "Banzai yourself, you bastards!"

Breakfast that morning was delayed because of the additional duties suddenly thrust upon the cooks, bakers, and messmen.

Barrow was finally released from duty with Ridge's battalion at the conclusion of this engagement and directed to return to Wonsan. The mission of Barrow's unit on the return trip was to escort six hundred nineteen prisoners from the Majon-ni stockade to the prison camp on the coast. Puller felt a certain anxiety over having two hundred Marines escort three times their numbers through the enemy-infested mountains. To forestall any mishap, Fredrick's company was sent out from Wonsan to meet Barrow. This unit, however, ran into an ambush and only after a heavy engagement was successful in beating the enemy off. The ambush cost Fredrick twenty-seven wounded and eight killed.

In the meantime Barrow had loaded his trucks with the prisoners and covered the open body of the vehicles with tarpaulin which was lashed over the enemy soldiers so that the cargo could not be determined from hillside viewers. With Swords' platoon at the point the unit negotiated the twenty-eight miles without incident and delivered its live cargo safely. Barrow's company was replaced by a KMC (Korean Marine Corps) battalion.

That same afternoon in Majon-ni the civilian population began a mass evacuation of the village. Upon being questioned, it was learned that an attack of "extermination" had been ordered by General Pak; the Marines were to be killed to a man. The people were ordered back to their houses and a strict curfew enforced while the perimeter force was alerted.

The attack developed shortly after one o'clock in the morning. After a series of probing attacks the enemy placed his main effort on the section held by the KMC battalion. Another effort was made to seize the battalion OP. The attack was thrown back and heavy casualties inflicted on the enemy. By this time the rifle companies had the routes of approach so thoroughly covered by fire and mines and trip flares that the enemy attack was thrown back with heavy losses.

With this failure General Pak gave up the idea of taking Majon-ni and ordered the remnants of his division to move northward and gather in the area of Kuksu-ri.

Following this phase the battalion settled down to patrolling, both by vehicle and foot, and manning an alert perimeter at night. Mail arrived by helicopter, wounded were evacuated within minutes of being hit. When the convoys failed, Blasingame's Air Delivery Section kept the unit supplied. On one drop a coil of barbed wire crashed through the roof of the schoolhouse and into First Lieutenant Robert Foyle's room. Fortunately Foyle was out at the time.

On the Marine Corps birthday the cooks prepared a huge cake from various ingredients. Strawberry jam was spread on heavily in place of frosting. By rotating personnel from the perimeter to the company CP areas each Marine received a piece of the sweet.

Ridge's battalion was relieved by the 15th U. S. Infantry on the fourteenth of November. In the eighteen days of occupation of Majon-ni the 1st had repelled the attacks of three battalions of enemy troops. Casualties to the enemy numbered 525 killed, 1,750 wounded and 1,395 prisoners.

Despite the success of their detached operation, the 3rd departed the river-fork village with no regrets or backward glances. By now it was known that Litzenberg's 7th Marines had met and destroyed a Chinese division to the north.

CHAPTER XV

The New Enemy: The Communist Chinese

The hard core and traditions of the Chinese Communist Forces were built by a small group of men who broke with Chiang Kai-shek in 1927. Defeated at Nanchang and later at Swatow and Canton by the Nationalists, the rebel army was faced with a withdrawal to the North. Ninety thousand men began the "long march" from Kwangsi province in South China to a refuge in northern Shensi; before them lay twenty-four rivers, eighteen mountain ranges and six thousand miles. Loading supplies and machines on carts, donkeys and the backs of men and women the "long march" began on the night of October 16, 1934.

Living from the land and drafting over fifty thousand civilians to serve as porters and supply carriers, this army moved to their new capital of Yenan west of the Taiyuam mountains. Stragglers and deserters were rounded up by a close-knit regular unit bringing up the rear. Those who could continue were sent forward in the main columns. Those who fell by the wayside were executed or left to die by the trail. Barefoot or shod with straw sandals, this scarecrow army wormed its way westward across the breadth of China to the river of Golden Sand. Here it turned northward into the stern mountains of Szechwan where sixteen thousand foot passes in the great Snowy mountains had to be crossed. It crossed the Tatu River west of Chungking after the way was paved by the heroics of the "Noble Thirty" at the bridge of Liu. The army continued across the great grasslands. A circuitous route was necessary to avoid the armies of the Nationalists.

It was a march of survival and only the strong survived; twenty thousand of the original ninety thousand made it to Yenan. With the Taiyuam mountains a shield to the east and the great wall and Russia at their backs (north) the men of the Ch'ang Cheng (long march) could compute what had been done. They had passed through twelve provinces and had seized and occupied sixty-two cities while fighting fifteen major battles. During the march two hundred thirty-five days and eighteen nights were spent in movement. The daily average was seventy-one *li*, or nearly twenty-four miles.

For the next sixteen years the People's Liberation Army knew nothing but war. They fought the Nationalists. They made an alliance of convenience with the Nationalists to fight the Japanese, and for the first time they were armed with modern weapons; having no arsenal, the lend-lease arsenal was kind to them. Further supplies came to them with the collapse of the Japanese armies in China. Still more supplies fell to them when they drove the armies of Chiang Kai-shek from the mainland. After thirty years of warfare and thirteen after the "long march," the men who led that army now led China.

Through the lives of the twelve men who guide the political-military destinies of China today runs a pattern of association, education and training extending over most of a lifetime. All are nearly the same age save two. Chu Teh, the oldest, was born in 1886 while the youngest, Lin Piao, was born in 1908. The other ten were born in the years between 1893 and 1900.

Four came from average middle-class families, six from the upper middle class, one from a family of wealth and one from poor peasant stock. Kao Kang, the northerner, and Ho Lung are the only two who had no formal education; both of these men gained their military education in the school of banditry. Nine of the twelve met as youths in grammar or military schools. Seven of them spent time in France and Germany and were expelled for subversive activities in those countries. Except for Mao, Kao and Ho, all have studied in Moscow.

All but two of these men were in positions of command before and during the Long March. These two, Kao Kang and Ch'En I, were in league with the others, but were involved in other duties. Kao Kang was the head of the Communist party and the army in Shensi province at the time the others were on the march to reach a sanctuary in his territory. Ch'En I remained in Kwangsi when the others departed to conduct a guerrilla war against the forces of Chiang Kai-shek.

Chu Teh, the eldest of the group, was in charge of military tactics for the Long March; Mao Tse-tung was the political commissar for Chu's 4th Red Army. This association began in 1927 and in 1931 Chu was appointed commander in chief of the Chinese Communist Armies. This position he still retains. P'eng-Teh-huai, now deputy commander to Chu, commanded the 3rd Army Corps which formed the vanguard on the Long March. Liu Shao-Ch'I has been associated with Mao since 1922; during the Long March Liu was political commissar for P'eng Teh-huai. Chou En-lai, educated in the finest schools in China, Japan, France, Germany and Russia, was to become first assistant to General Bleucher, a Russian advisor to the Whampoa Military Academy. Chou had many of the present military leaders as students. Chou was on the Long March as a deputy to Chu Teh.

The same cross-threads exist in the lives of the others: over a period of thirty years we find a small group of men planning, fighting and killing to bring communism to China and Asia. Steadfast in purpose the grueling, bitter years have bound these men into a hard, solid unit.

There is a Chinese proverb concerning the military to the effect "You don't use good metal for nails; neither do you use good men for soldiers."

This was largely true of China in the war-lord days when the male Chinese peasant sold his services for a few coppers and a bowl of rice a day. With no feeling of nationalism or pride of unit, the Chinese soldier lived in a state of confusion, disease and starvation. Fighting for one side and then the other, at the whim of his general, the Chinese soldier had but one ambition—to come across enough loot to buy a few square yards of land, get a wife and insure himself a good funeral.

Chu Teh and his companions of the Long March changed most of this. The political instructors took over and all hands were exposed to a four-hour daily educational program on the benefits and principles of communism; defecting Nationalist troops were carefully screened and put through an intensive course before being allowed to join the ranks of the People's Liberation Army. All units were generously staffed with informers and anyone heard speaking thoughts contrary to the doctrine laid down by the political instructors was isolated for an intensive training period. If this failed, a pistol shot in the back of the head would cure the man for all time.

More important to the future, however, was the plan set in motion for the youth of the land. Cadres of military schools were started. Enrolled in these schools were young men and women of seventeen to twenty-three years of age with the requirements of "pure ideology and good health, with Junior High School and higher elementary school education." During the period of training, varying from eight months to two years depending on the branch of service, the student is clothed, housed and fed.

The Chinese Army of the future will be supplied by the young people from these cadre schools. The Korean war and time will gradually eliminate the old guerrilla-trained Chinese soldier.

Chu Teh and his staff knew the capabilities of the North Korean Army for many of the officers and men had trained and fought with Chu's forces against the Nationalists. When the United Nations made the decision to support the South Koreans with men and arms, the Chinese military were aware of the defeat facing their allies. They must have been surprised by the early victories the North Koreans won over American forces.

The paucity of transportation facilities and distances being what they are in China, Chu Teh gave the order for his troops to move into Manchuria and prepare to cross the Yalu when the Korean war was but a few weeks old. Elements of the 4th Field Army were training in Manchuria when the war began, but the main body of this force was in and around Shanghai. The 3rd Field Army was in the south near Amoy and Foochow where it was preparing for an amphibious assault on the island of Formosa. It is eighteen hundred miles as a land-bound crow would fly from Amoy to the Yalu.

Shortly after the mid-August defeat of the North Koreans on the Naktong River, the 3rd Field Army began movement northward. The shifting of thousands of men placed a serious strain on transportation and supply facilities. The Marine landing at Inchon and the resultant collapse of the North Korean Army speeded the movement and preparations were hastened to place the Chinese "volunteers" in action against the advancing United Nations forces. The political commissioners began to tell their troops about the sorry plight of North Koreans in their attempt to hold off the imperialistic aggressors. The Americans, the Chinese soldier was told, were bent on conquering Korea and then invading Manchuria and China.

While this preparation of attitude was going on, supply agencies were having troubles outfitting the 3rd Field Army with winter uniforms. Entire villages in the staging areas north of the Yalu were commandeered for the task. The government furnished the cloth, matting and other materials and thousands of men, women and children began sewing. By this means the "Chinese People's Support Army" was literally sewn into winter uniforms as it went to battle. With the rapid advance of the Eighth Army after Inchon, elements of the Fourth Army were rushed across the border with orders to block and hold until the Third could get into position for a counteroffensive.

The critical area at the time was along the west coast of Korea and the main body of reinforcements was sent south from Antung. Three divisions from the Chinese 13th Army Group—the 124th, 125th and 126th—were, however, assigned the task of blocking and holding south of Chosin Reservoir.

During this time the 1st Marine Division was at sea between Inchon and Wonsan and the Chinese command was at a loss to determine the intent or target of the Marines. As soon as the Marines were identified as being on the east coast, the critical area for the enemy shifted from the Eighth Army front to the X Corps front. When Litzenberg's 7th met and destroyed the 124th CCF Division the enemy was forced to hurriedly realign forces. The 9th Army Group was withdrawn from the 3rd Field Army forces preparing to strike a counterblow against the Eighth Army and under forced marches crossed the Yalu at Chian. With the 20th Army Corps in the vanguard, the enemy began a series of night marches over the mountain trails of northern Korea. Under the most exacting conditions the enemy made the crossing of the Yalu and traversed over one hundred and fifty miles of mountainous terrain in a period of twelve days.

The 9th Army Group was under the command of quick-tempered, capable Sung Shih-lun. Born in 1910, Sung studied at Whampoa Military Academy under Chou En-lai. Later he fought under the leaders of the Long March; he commanded a regiment during the epochal journey. At forty years of age Sung had been handling troops in combat since he left Whampoa Academy at seventeen. He is judged a sound tactician and a master of guerrilla warfare and his courage in battle has stamped him as one of the three bravest men in the Chinese forces.

To accomplish the mission of destroying the 1st Marine Division and recapturing Hungnam and Wonsan, Sung had at his command three Army corps—the 20th (58th, 59th, 60th and 89th Divisions), 25th (73rd, 74th and 75th Divisions) and 27th (79th, 80th and 81st Divisions). These organizations had a strength in excess of one hundred thousand men. Because of the rapid deployment of his force over unfavorable terrain, Sung was forced to leave the bulk of his artillery across the Yalu.

Sung's 9th Army Group had gained another weapon new to Chinese armies—pride and tradition. The Chinese Communist 3rd Field Army traced back to the guerrilla bands which remained in the south of China while Chu Teh and the rest made the Long March to the north. In the years of 1934-37 these bands, held together by Yeh Ting, fought a hit-and-run war against Chiang Kai-shek. Incorporated into the New 4th Army they crossed the Yangtze River and went into the Kiangsu-Shantung border area to fight the Japanese. Following the defeat of Japan they turned once again on the Nationalists.

By this time the new 4th was known as the East China People's Liberation Army. Later they were designated the 3rd Field Army. In the civil war years following the Second World War, this army won victories at Hsuchou, captured Nanking and Shanghai. It had never met with defeat. Sung's 9th Army Group, one of four such in the 3rd Field Army, was rated the most effective employed in Korea.

In the school of tactics these Chinese leaders are sound. Battle-wise and trained in the hard school of want, while facing an enemy (Chiang) who outnumbered them, the Chinese Communist leaders had resorted to infiltration, double-envelopment, isolation, and piecemeal annihilation. Once an enemy unit has been enveloped, either by flanking or infiltration, the position is chopped up by further isolation of smaller units.

"Human sea" frontal assaults are rare and are ordered as a last resort when the necessity for victory dictates such a high cost. Newspapers have reported "human sea" attacks on United Nations positions on many occasions. Actually there have been few such attacks made by the Chinese forces in Korea. Such tactics were reported as an excuse for the defeat suffered by United Nations troops. It was simply an extension of the "invincibility" of the T-34 tank device.

Chinese leaders are wary of launching an offensive unless their forces outnumber the enemy by three to one. Once they are convinced this condition prevails they will order the attack during the hours of darkness where probing attacks will reveal enemy positions; once the positions have been disclosed every effort is made to isolate small units from the main force.

Influenced by the vast expanse of China, the Chinese leader will seldom attempt to establish a static defense line as is the practice for Western armies. Chinese defensive tactics are based on a mobile defense, withdrawal when the situation is unfavorable and the use of guerrilla forces to harass the rear and flanks. They make every attempt to strike an enemy unit while it is on the move. They will leave an avenue of escape open so that movement is possible—the theory being that "a cornered rat will fight fiercely; if it is provided a limited avenue of escape and kept on the move it can be gradually worn down with only slight damage to the attacker."

The men in command of the Chinese armies are professional in theory as well as practice. They are thoroughly acquainted with the principles of war as written by Napoleon Bonaparte and Clausewitz, to which they have added the modifications of Sun Tze to conform to the mass of land and peoples at their command.

At the fighting level the Chinese soldier has the Asian stamina and mental fortitude to withstand the harshest demands of command, conditions and climate. "Battle fatigue" is not recognized in the Chinese armies because it is a symptom of failure unacceptable to the Oriental mind. The average Chinese soldier fighting in Korea has a low standard of education, but he has been taught a blind obedience to orders which will make him attempt to carry out an order regardless of the consequence.

This seemingly fatalistic obedience stems from two sources: a new arrogance and reckless aggressiveness built on a long succession of victories and the stern, uncompromising demands made upon them by their leaders. Each unit has its informers and when an action is closed and the unit withdrawn, a critique is held. Men who have done poorly are exposed in a kangaroo-type of court.

There are three forms of punishment the unit commander can mete out depending on the seriousness of the charges. The lesser of the three would mean extra duty in the unit until the next battle, at which time the accused would lead the attack; the second degree of punishment would entail extra work, and a notification of cowardice sent to the man's village; anything more serious than the first two is remedied by a shot in the back of the head from the unit commander's pistol.

Constantly hampered by the lack of a central system of manufacture or supply of ordnance, the Chinese have been forced to employ weapons of Japanese, Russian, English and American design. To overcome the problem of mixtures, weapons of a certain manufacture and design are assigned to specific units. Under this system the three rifle regiments of a division might be armed with three different types of rifles and machine guns. This, however, is being corrected as quickly as possible by a standardization program.

Further supply problems are eased by the Spartan diet of the Asian soldier and the simple manner of preparing food. Each soldier carries, in a loop over his shoulder, a cloth roll filled with rice or the more common Korean fare of rice, millet seed and dried peas ground into a powder. Such a roll is supposed to last the individual soldier a minimum of five days; he cooks and prepares it himself when there is time and a fire. When neither of these is available it is mixed with cold water and eaten.

Resupply of food is simple and basic. When a unit is in action there is little time for food and the man must live from the food roll about his shoulder. When a unit is behind the lines and in a static position, each company will send men on a "rice run." Men in disfavor are given the task of returning to a central supply area and bringing back rice for the unit. These trips are made at night and distances of twenty to thirty miles are covered by food parties in one period from dusk to dawn. One man will return with enough food to last ten comrades five days. Further supply problems are lessened by the minimum usage of radio and telephone equipment. Control during battle is maintained by bugles, whistles and flashlights.

Battle-wise and confident, General Sung's 9th Army Group moved into position to battle the Marines. Through his political commissioners he told his troops: "Soon we will meet the American Marines in battle. We will destroy them. When they are defeated the enemy army will collapse and our country will be free from the threat of aggression. Kill these Marines as you would snakes in your homes."

With General Lui Fei's four division corps in the vanguard, the movement south began with the crossing of the Yalu at Chian. Six miles northeast of the pontoon-crossing area is the city of Manp'ojin. From here to the south the troops had the assistance of a railway and a roadway which follows the Tongnogang River. Because of the proximity of Manp'ojin to the Yalu and the bomb lines established, this rail terminus was free from interruption. The crossing of the river was made at night not through fear of interruption but as a security measure.

The distance from Manp'ojin to Kanggye is forty miles and another twenty-eight to a second junction at Mupyong-ni. This distance was usually made in one night. During the day trains would hide in tunnels or in deep cuts. The personnel would leave the cars and take to the hills where they would cook their meals and rest until dusk when they would regain the train to take up their interrupted journey southward.

Despite continual daylight bombardment from the air, rail traffic continued with only slight interruptions. Direct hits on open railbeds took but a matter of an hour or less to repair; when bridges were destroyed a shuttle service was installed whereby the personnel and supplies on the north side of the bridge were transferred to a train which had backed up to the southern bank. This expediency continued until the bridge was repaired.

At Kanggye, Chung's Army Group split its avenues of approach to the Chosin Reservoir. Lui's 20th Army Corps was to continue on the Manp'o main line to the next southern junction at Mupyong-ni. At this point Lui's troops would leave the assistance of the rail line and take the narrow, twisting road eastward to Yudam-ni. The distance to be covered in this phase was fifty-five miles with several intervening mountain passes of heights to nearly four thousand feet.

To ease the traffic on the main line, which was also transporting troops to face the Eighth Army on the west coast, the Army Corps of General Nieh Feng-chin was sent eastward from Kanggye to Tong-mun'go-ri at the head waters of the Changjin. This crossing of mountains would be supported by a narrow-gauge railway. From this point the troops moved on foot southward following the eastern shore of the reservoir waterway until Kobyoru-ri was reached. Here elements of this army were sent to the eastern shore of the reservoir to take up positions opposite Yudam-ni.

General Sun set up headquarters at Paemyangji-san about ten miles north of Yudam-ni.

Only by the most prodigious effort and energy typical of Asian troops was this move made possible. Horses, oxen and camels were used to augment the transport of man-packed supplies. In a period of less than fourteen days Chung moved his Army from the Yalu and had the major elements in position to begin the counteroffensive on the twenty-seventh of November in conjunction with the attack on the Eighth Army on the west coast.

While moving into positions against the Marines the political commissioners circulated considerable information regarding the enemy Marines they would be meeting in the frozen mountains of Korea. The following was circulated by pamphlet and lecture to the 9th Army Group: "The Bloody Path," by Captain G. Doidzhashvili, USSR Navy.

When in the summer of 1950 the American imperialist marauders, the newly appeared pretenders to world domination, provoked the bloody holocaust in Korea, the Wall Street house-dog General MacArthur demanded that the American so-called "Marines" be immediately placed at his disposal. This professional murderer and inveterate war criminal intended to throw them into battle as quickly as possible for the purpose of inflicting, as it seemed to him then, a final blow on the Korean people.

In putting forward such a demand, MacArthur proceeded from the fact that US "Marine" units have been trained more than any other types of American forces for the waging of the unprecedently brutal and inhuman, predatory war against the freedom-loving heroic Korean people.

It was precisely to US Marines that the Ober-bandit MacArthur addressed the words: "A rich city lies ahead of you, it has much wine and tasty morsels. Take Seoul and all the girls will be yours, the property of the inhabitants belongs to the conquerors and you will be able to send parcels home."

The events in Korea have shown graphically that the Marine Corps stalwarts did not turn a deaf ear to the appeal of their rapacious ataman. They have abundantly covered Korean soil with the blood and tears of hundreds and thousands of Korean women, old people and children. . . .

This is how the American monsters are behaving today in Korea. This is how they behaved dozens of years ago, also. The Wall Street bosses and the supreme American military command publicize in all possible ways the "combat services" of the US Marine Corps, cynically calling them sometimes "our idol" and sometimes "our assault force." The process of surmising the true motives of such enthusiastic references does not present any great difficulties. The crux of the matter is that the American imperialists and the supreme military command of the USA consider the American Marines (and not without foundation) to be the most criminal elements in their armed forces and to be the most capable of discharging the gendarme-police functions of slaughterers and despoilers. This is clearly attested by the bloody trail of crimes against humanity which has been blazed over a period of many decades by the US Marine Corps.

The US Marine Corps was formed in 1775 on the lines of the British "Marines" and its disciplinary manual which came into force a little later was based on the corresponding manual of the British armed forces, which have pursued a course of colonial oppression and violence in many countries of the world, i.e., it was formed for the very same purposes and with the very same functions as the forces of the British colonial empire.

The American "Marine Corps," more exactly the corps of professional murderers and despoilers, is now composed of 485,000 men. The corps is led by a well-known reactionary General Clifton Cates.

Already 80 years ago, i.e., in 1871, units of the US Marine Corps carried out their predatory attack on Korea, encroaching on its freedom and independence with a view to seizing the rich and fertile lands of Korea and enslaving the Korean people. . . .

Seventeen years later US Marines disembarked in Korea for the second time. This was on June 19, 1888, during the insurrection of the Korean people against foreign oppressors. . . .

Six years later the American government again, already for the third time, tried to take over control of Korea by sending a Marine detachment to repeat the disembarkation of a landing force and the campaign against the Korean capital.

In 1904 at the orders of its government the American Marine Corps disembarked for the fourth time in Korea, pursuing the very same aim—the seizing and enslavement of Korea.

However, the four failures of the attempts to conquer Korea did not benefit the American militarists. In the summer of 1950 they undertook on a wider scale and in a more monstrous form their bloody, filthy offensive against the Korean people. But there can be no doubt that on this occasion also they will not achieve their predatory aim here.

US Marines participated directly also in the bloody raid on, and in the annexation of the Hawaiian Islands, in the seizure and colonial enslavement of the Philippines, in the forcible wrenching of Panama away from Colombia, etc. . . .

The US Marines have played and continue to play at the present time an exceptionally ignominious, gendarme-police role in the suppression of the revolutionary movement in many countries of the world. . . .

In their own country the fascist stalwarts of the Marine detachments are guilty of excesses against their own people. They even adopt a haughty and scornful attitude to American soldiers and sailors who are not Marines. . . .

The officers, corporals and privates of the US Marine Corps have always been noted in their operations for their brutality and cruelty against defenseless peaceful population and a weak enemy. But they, like the Hitlerite warriors, quickly lose their combat fervour as soon as they meet with a worthy rebuff.

To a certain extent this explains the shameful fact that in the Second World War, of the 485,000 men in the Marine Corps only 3 divisions (like 1st, 4th, and 5th) took an insignificant part in the battles against Japan, the remaining divisions altogether took no part in the war and were only stationed on conquered territory as a gendarme-police force. Thus, the "combat exploits" of the US Marines in the Second World War bear witness not to military valour, not to boldness and fearlessness but only to the fact that in the person of the Marines the US imperialists have a pack of despoilers, called upon to exterminate the peaceful population of towns and villages.

At the present time when American predatory imperialism is preparing to plunge mankind into the abyss of a third world war, the Wall Street monopolists are rearming their experienced gendarme-police force, the Marines, for better fulfillment of the role of stiflers of small states and peoples. . . .

CHAPTER XVI

The "Advance to the Yalu"

While Puller's regiment was occupied in blocking the movement of North Korean troops northward and mopping up in the Kojo–Majon-ni areas, Litzenberg and Murray were moving their units to the northwest. This was all a part of the X Corps plan of advancing to the Yalu River.

As Smith had feared, two weeks after landing at Wonsan, units of his division were spread out from Kojo to Hagaru—a distance of one hundred sixty-five road miles. He voiced his concern to Almond over the tactical deployment of the Marines on several occasions. On the fifteenth of November he wrote a letter to Commandant Cates in Washington in which he stated, in part: "I do not like the prospect of stringing out a Marine Division along a single mountain road from Hamhung to the border. . . ."

Four days after unloading at Wonsan, Litzenberg had his regiment in position near Hamhung to begin the relief of the 1st ROK Corps and advance to the Chosin Reservoir. A report had been received that a regiment of enemy troops was in the Huksu-ri area. This was dangerously close to the left flank of the 7th Marines as they moved north.

To fully understand the precarious position of Litzenberg at this time the map should be studied. On the right (east) the closest friendly troops would be the 7th Army Division and ROK forces pushing north along

---

The Battle of Sudong. *Litzenberg's Regiment meet a Division of Communist Chinese in battle. The enemy is defeated and the Marines push onto the plateau of Koto.*

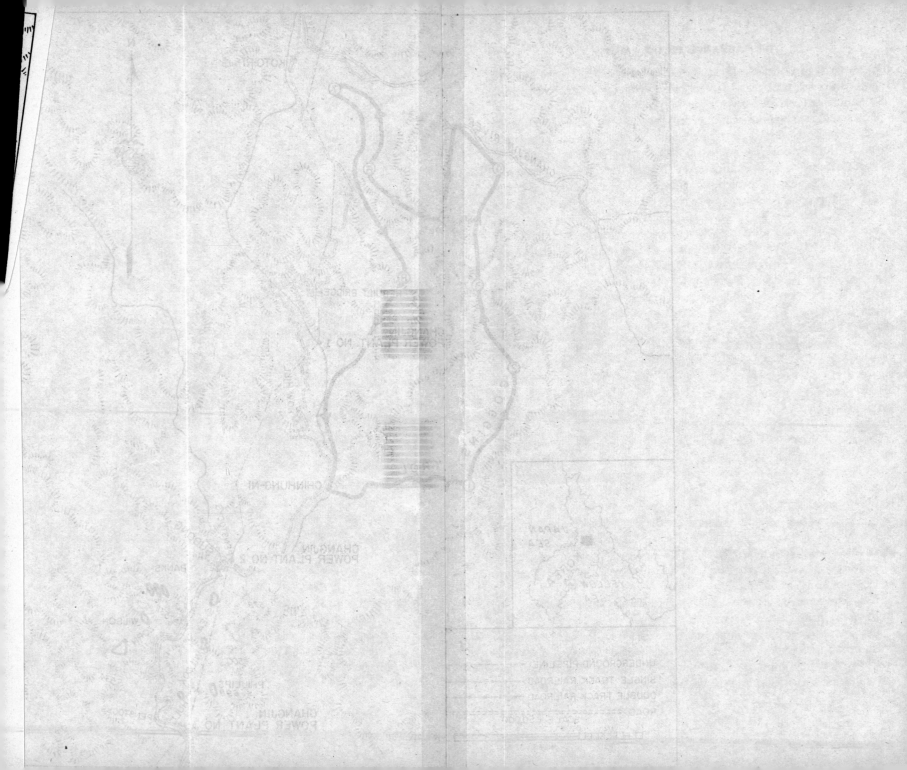

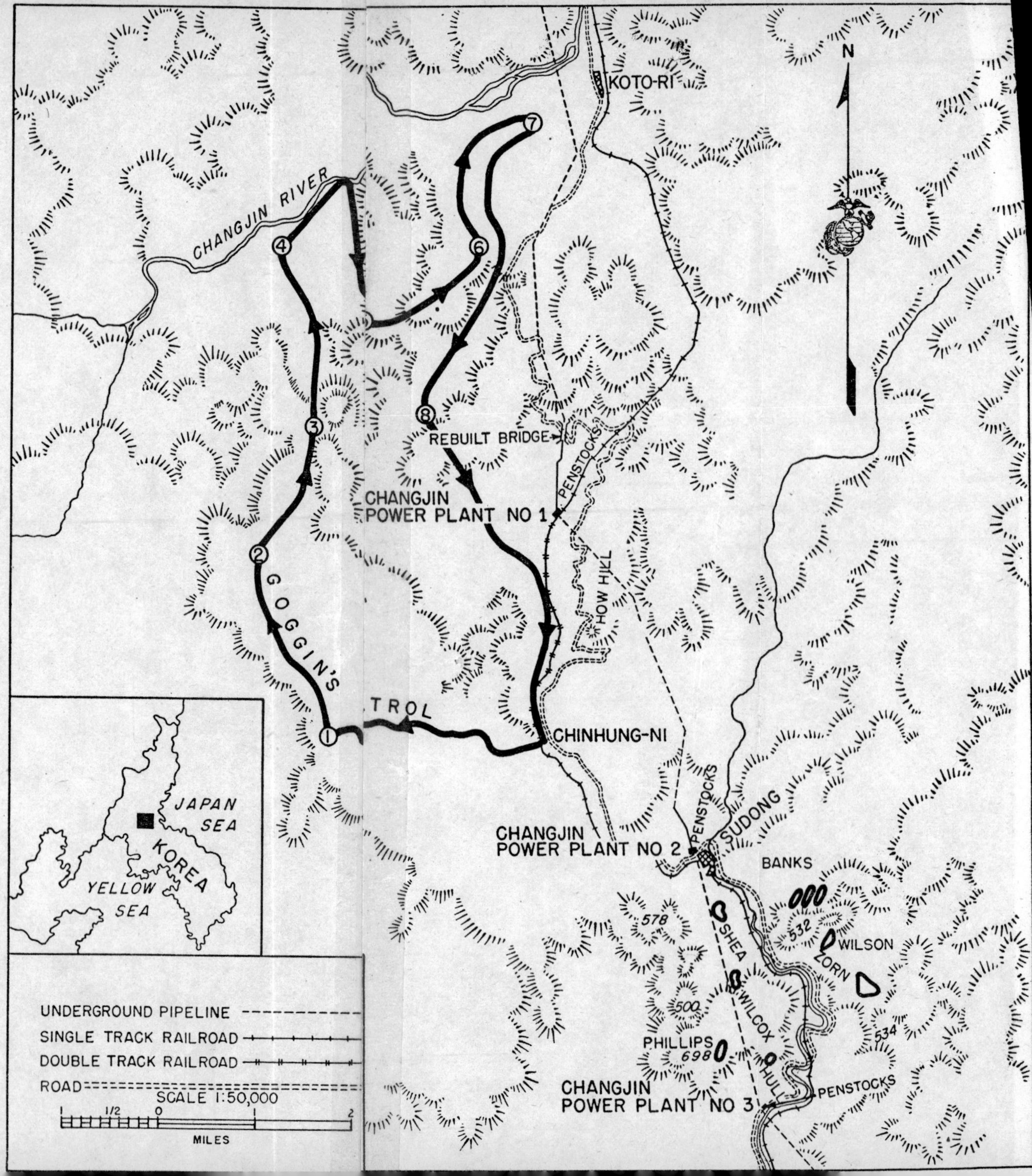

N
KOTO-RI
CHANGJIN RIVER
REBUILT BRIDGE
PENSTOCKS
CHANGJIN
POWER PLANT NO 1
HOW HILL
GOGGIN'S
TROL
CHINHUNG-NI
JAPAN
SEA
KOREA
YELLOW
SEA
PENSTOCKS
SUDONG
CHANGJIN
POWER PLANT NO 2
BANKS
578
SHEA
532
WILSON
ZORN
500
WILCOX
534
PHILLIPS
698
HULL
CHANGJIN
POWER PLANT NO 3
PENSTOCKS
UNDERGROUND PIPELINE
SINGLE TRACK RAILROAD
DOUBLE TRACK RAILROAD
ROAD
SCALE 1:50,000
1
1/2
0
1
2
MILES

the east coast of Korea—a distance of over forty miles. To the west the Eighth Army was over seventy miles away. What lay in that vast corridor of mountainous terrain between was not known.

To establish maximum flank security compatible with the forces at hand, Litzenberg ordered First Lieutenant Ralph Crossman (now commanding the Division Reconnaissance Company) to send a patrol into the area. Accordingly, First Lieutenant Ernest Hargett took a four-jeep patrol from his platoon and the trip began in late afternoon. Hargett returned at two o'clock in the morning with the report that only a few camp fires in the hills had been seen.

Early the following morning (November 1) Litzenberg ordered Crossman to take a company-sized patrol into the same area to determine if an east-west road leading into the Hamhung–Koto-ni road was more than an ox-cart trail. Crossman moved his unit to the top of the pass northwest of Chigyong and held up there for the night. A three-man enemy demolition patrol attempted to infiltrate the Marine lines during the night. One of these was killed and the other two fled into the hills discarding their explosives and clothes as they ran. The next morning Second Lieutenant Charles Puckett took his platoon down the mountain and set up his machine guns to fire on the houses in the valley below where enemy troops were seen. A company-sized enemy force attempted to envelop Puckett's unit and Crossman ordered a withdrawal.

Because of the distance Crossman had been out of radio contact with the 7th Marines since entering the hills the previous day. Concern was being felt over the welfare of the unit. First Lieutenant James Mariades went in search in an observation plane. He found the patrol and reported its position.

While Crossman's unit had been patrolling the area to the left flank of Litzenberg's regiment, Davis' battalion had effected the passage of ROK lines. The ROK's were in a highly nervous state and were eager to leave the area. They reported to Davis: "Many, many Chinese up here . . . an Army of Chinese."

Davis reported to Litzenberg: "It is rumored Chinese troops in strength are in the area."

The advance northward continued during the day against moderate resistance and when positions were consolidated for the night Davis and Sawyer were a few miles south of Sudong. By midday the ROK rumor was confirmed: the Marines were in contact with the 124th Division of the Communist Chinese forces. Litzenberg's prediction had come true. Before dark the Marines were to have met and defeated the Chinese in a bitter battle.

Late that afternoon (November 2) Davis set up his battalion defenses with First Lieutenant William Shea's company assigned to the high ground sixteen hundred yards south of Sudong and west of the road. Shea attempted to reach his positions by passing through Captain Myron Wilcox's lines and following the ridge line to the north. This was the logical route of approach, but steep terrain, threat of darkness and two enemy machine guns so hampered the move that Shea was forced to move into position from the river approach. It was dark before he had his men in position. (See map facing page 228.)

Captain David Banks' company took the high ground overlooking the bridge and directly across the road and river from Wilcox. Banks placed his unit on three fingers of terrain with a platoon on each of the land mass features. The company CP was in a draw between the 1st and 2nd platoons. Wilson's platoon of Wilcox's unit was east of the road and directly above the 2nd Battalion CP as was First Lieutenant William Graeber's unit. Thus, as night came on Davis had two companies west of the river and road and one to the east in addition to two platoons borrowed from Wilcox.

Sawyer, moving his battalion immediately to the rear of Davis, placed Captain Elmer Zorn's company on the high ground east of the road and south of Wilson's platoon. During the day Captain Milton Hull's company had climbed and fought to secure Hill 698—the commanding piece of ground west of the road. It was slow, costly fighting in which the Marines suffered fifty-two casualties. Late in the afternoon, Sawyer ordered Captain Walter Phillips to take his company into the hills, relieve Hull and continue the attack.

Hill 698 lies a distance of two thousand yards west of the tunnel and bridge which was of concern to Litzenberg. To have the tunnel blasted or the bridge destroyed meant the severing of the supply artery and dividing the regiment into two segments. There were no by-passes or secondary roads. Hill 698 had to be taken.

Militarily the hill was a natural fortress. The face of it was nearly perpendicular with but one narrow route of approach which would accommodate no more than one platoon in the assault. At three o'clock in the afternoon First Lieutenant William Schrier took his 3rd Platoon into the attack along this sharply rising finger of land. Schrier and his men reached the foot of the approach; halfway up they came under heavy fire and grenades shaped like Coca-Cola bottles hurtled down on the scrabbling, crawling Marines.

Depleted by casualties, Schrier's attack stalled halfway to the plateau. First Lieutenant John Yancey was ordered to take his 2nd Platoon into the battle. Yancey briefed his men on the assault: Sergeant Rugierre Cagliotti would take his squad along the right side of the finger of land; Corporal Lee Phillips would attack on the left side. Platoon Sergeant Allen Madding would go with Phillips' squad while Yancey went with Cagliotti.

Yancey told his men: "When we get within grenade range, throw two grenades. As soon as they've blown, get in close before the enemy can do what they did to the 3rd Platoon."

Yancey's men prepared for the attack by shedding their heavy, cold-weather parkas and loading up with extra ammunition and grenades. The machine guns opened up with overhead supporting fire and Yancey shouted: "Okay, let's get th' bastards. . . ."

Thirty-two men in the assault. Thirty-two men clambering upward. Almost at once the Chinese enemy opened fire with machine guns and small arms; then their mortars began blasting along the narrow spine. Phillips' squad came to a halt in the face of the mortar fire.

"Get moving. Run through it," Yancey bellowed. The thin line began to move again.

On the right Cagliotti had been wounded. Private Stanley Robinson took command of the squad. Pfc. Billy Appleby was killed, as was Connoly, Groh and Keeth. The depleted line of Marines now came into grenade range; they hurled the first grenade. Fifteen yards further up the hill the second was thrown. The Marines followed the last onto the top of the hill.

Robinson was the only man on the right who made the top. Ignoring the enemy he stood upright hurling grenade after grenade down the reverse slope where the enemy were forming for a counterattack. One of his phosphorous grenades fell in the middle of an enemy machine gun-position. That strongpoint was erased in a shower of burning phosphorous and flame.

On the left Phillips and three men made it to the top; one of his men, Pfc. Arvid Hultman, was wounded almost immediately. Yancey grabbed Hultman's BAR and began firing at the enemy from the hip. Though painfully wounded in the groin Hultman crawled down the slope collecting ammunition from fallen Marines and delivering it to Yancey.

Robinson, Madding, Yancey, the wounded Hultman and two unknown Marines fought off the enemy counterattack. As the fire fight slackened, Yancey got Lieutenant Raymond Ball, company executive officer, on the radio.

"We're on top—there's only six of us. You'd better get some help up here."

"Clements is trying to get through to you now—hold on."

On the western slopes of Hill 698 the enemy began to form; Yancey and his men could hear them shouting and yelling and then the bugles began to blare. To meet the attack the six men of the 2nd Platoon had three grenades and less than a hundred rounds of ammunition.

Much in the manner of a movie hero racing to the rescue, Private James Gallagher came charging over the lip of the plateau; he carried a machine gun and two boxes of ammunition—a normal load for two men. Soon after this the other men of First Lieutenant Leonard Clements' platoon came onto the hilltop and Hill 698 was in possession of the Marines. The enemy counterattack was beaten off with heavy casualties to the Chinese.

When night came on the first two battalions of Litzenberg's regiment held the high ground on either side of the road and river to a depth of twenty-five hundred yards.

In a well-co-ordinated night attack the enemy struck shortly after midnight. Shea's company, holding the most northern positions, was the first to sight and hear the approach of enemy tanks. Shea thought it was a bulldozer; Corporal Alfredo Mancillas was equally certain it was an enemy tank. A few minutes proved Mancillas correct. Shea rushed his two rocket launchers to the base of the hill to take the vehicle under fire but the range was too great and the tank passed on. A wire-laying jeep, driven by Staff Sergeant Clayton Vondette, with two wiremen, was stringing wire along the road north of Davis' CP area. Vondette saw a tank with its light on. Thinking it was a Marine vehicle not obeying the black-out regulations, he drove the jeep up to the armored vehicle.

"Turn off your —— light," he shouted.

A north Korean head popped from the turret and a machine gun opened fire. Vondette slammed the jeep into reverse; the two wiremen took to the hills to the right. Vondette cleared the area in a hail of machine-gun fire. The tank continued along the road until it entered Davis' CP area where it came under fire from Banks' unit on the high ground to the north. The sandbags which the tank crew was using to augment the armor plate on their vehicle, began to burn and the tank turned about. As it withdrew, it brought the roadblock under fire and five of the six Marines manning the obstruction were casualties.

While the tank was creating this diversion from the north, an enemy infantry attack was placed on the left rear and flank of Wilcox's unit. Before long the battle became general throughout the length of the two battalions. The 4.2 Mortar Company, in position astride the road midway between the command posts of Davis and Sawyer, was partially overrun.

Pfc. Billie Bradshaw remained in position with his mortar until the enemy came to close range. He rushed to meet them in hand-to-hand combat. While the 4.2 unit was battling against overpowering odds, Sawyer established an emergency defense line from his command post tent to the river. First Lieutenant Leslie Davenport and Sergeant Richard Oly took command of this final position and further enemy penetrations along this line were halted.

Captain Dave Banks' company, on the three fingers of high ground north and east of the road and river was hit hard. The enemy attacked from the high ground and struck between Mitchell's 1st and Bradley's 2nd Platoons. Sheer weight of numbers forced Bradley to shift his unit along the spur and into the zone occupied by Stemple.

In Mitchell's zone the fighting raged with the enemy closing to grenade and bayonet range. Sergeant James Poynter, commanding the 2nd Squad in Mitchell's platoon, coolly directed the fire of his men until the Chinese had surrounded his unit. Shouting encouragement to his men, Poynter engaged the enemy with his bayonet killing three and forcing several others to flee. When he saw Chinese machine-gun crews setting up their weapons he collected grenades from dead and wounded Marines and rushed the enemy positions. His fearless attack destroyed two gun crews and put the third weapon out of action before he fell with wounds that were fatal. Poynter's action disorganized the enemy and the rest of the squad moved to more favorable positions.

Across the road and river, Wilcox's company came under a heavy attack. In this area the enemy formed on the high ground west of the positions held by Baker Company and pushed their attack toward the road. For some time the Marines could hear the Chinese working up enthusiasm for the coming battle by joining together in a strident chant; once aroused, flares, bugles and whistles gave the signal and the battle was on.

The initial attack, under the cover of darkness and a devastating barrage of automatic weapons and grenade fire, forced a penetration in the lines of Baker Company. Staff Sergeant Archie Van Winkle rallied the men of his platoon and led a counterattack through the withering fire being laid down by the enemy. Van Winkle and every man who made the attack with him was wounded; despite his wounds he rushed across forty yards of heavy fire to assist a squad that had been cut off. Severely wounded for the second time, Van Winkle continued to shout encouragement and directions to his men until he collapsed from loss of blood.

First Lieutenant Chew Een Lee, commanding the machine-gun platoon in Baker Company, saw a vastly superior force overrun his left flank positions. Exposing himself to the intense small-arms fire, Lee carried out a reconnaissance in advance of his positions in order to properly redeploy machine guns in the defensive perimeter. Under cover of fire from his men, Lee moved up the enemy-held slope in order to draw fire and reveal their positions to his gunners. Seriously wounded, Lee led the counterattack which drove the enemy from the sector.

Despite these temporary penetrations Wilcox's company fought back tenaciously and the positions were held.

Directly to the east of Baker Company on the high ground in the vicinity of Hill 534, Zorn in command of Fox Company came in for heavy fighting. The initial Chinese attack on Zorn's position was overwhelming. The enemy moved around the flanks of the Marines and for a time had the company completely surrounded. Sergeant Earl Peach of the 1st Platoon saw the enemy setting up machine guns which would enfilade the Marines. He stormed the positions with grenades and destroyed two guns and killed twelve of the enemy. As the fire fight continued Peach saw a wounded Marine mortarman lying in an exposed position. Dashing across a fifty-yard strip under heavy fire, Peach was killed while attempting to assist the wounded man.

Major William Vorhies, weapons company commander in Davis' battalion, had set four heavy machine guns on the road covering the river and rail line. As the first sign of daylight approached an enemy company formed on the railroad track and began to move north toward

Sudong. Vorhies cautioned his men to hold their fire as he wanted to wait until the last possible moment to give the gunners the best shooting light.

The enemy unit began moving slowly to the north; a bugle blared a signal.

"Fire!"

The four machine guns opened up and the bugle died in mid-note. From the west Wilcox and Shea joined in the shoot. The enemy unit was annihilated.

The tactics of the Chinese commander were obvious as he made the most determined effort from both the east and west to drive a wedge between the two forward battalions and the regimental train and Roach's battalion.

Heavy fighting raged throughout the night. At daylight the enemy commanded the bridge at the rear of Sawyer's positions and the MSR was cut. With the arrival of daylight First Lieutenant John Theros (FAC) brought the Corsairs down on the enemy troops in the area of the bridge and heavy casualties were inflicted on the Chinese. Blasingame's air delivery section made an air drop of critical supplies before the road was reopened.

During most of the day the valley was swept by sporadic enemy fire as the Marines consolidated positions and eliminated pockets of resistance. The battalion aid station was hard hit by sniper fire and several Marines were wounded as they lay in their holes awaiting treatment. Lieutenant (jg) E. W. Clark, 1st Battalion medical officer, was shot in the leg. Pfc. Richard McChesney, ignoring the enemy fire, drove his bulldozer into the area and scooped a protective revetment about the hospital. Pfc. Eddie Alfaro attempted to run the gauntlet of fire with seriously wounded Marines, Staff Sergeant Carmine Delgandio, Pfc. Ralph Jaeger and Staff Sergeant Joseph Jagiello, who required the facilities of a field hospital. Alfaro was killed and the rest of the group was rescued by a patrol from Zorn's unit.

At the regimental command post six men (Pfc. Joseph Rushlow, Corporal Jack Becker, Corporal Loren Weilman, Sergeant Allan MacLeod and Sergeant Nathan Smith) volunteered to drive six trucks of supplies along the fire-swept road and over the disputed bridge to the beleaguered battalions. For protection the drivers piled sandbags over the engines and around the cabs.

"Let's hit it!" MacLeod yelled, and his truck roared off. The rest followed closely. Under a hail of small-arms fire the hazardous journey was completed successfully. Loading the trucks with wounded, the same men made the return journey. En route they were stopped by men from Zorn's company and Lieutenant Rollin Vancantfort was loaded aboard in a serious condition from a chest wound. Sixty-six wounded were returned to the rear without further injury.

To clear the enemy from the commanding ground above the critical bridge, Hull took his unit up the left of Hill 534 while Crossman maneuvered the Reconnaissance Company to the right. The enemy was forced into a withdrawal.

During the night and day of the third of November, Marine ground and air units killed 696 of the enemy troops in the 124th Chinese Communist Division. Total casualties to the Chinese division came to nearly 3,000.

At daybreak on the morning of the fourth, Davis sent his battalion into the assault on Sudong. Wilcox's company took the road approach, Shea's unit stayed on the high ground to the left and Crossman's Recon Company moved through the hills to the right. The attack developed against pockets of resistance. Hargett's platoon seized the high ground overlooking power plant number 2 of the Chosin Reservoir hydroelectric system. Sharon's platoon took the point and proceeded through the town and pressed on toward Chinhung-ni.

Sharon, in the lead jeep with Staff Sergeant Richard Twohey and Corporal Walter McDermott, made a sharp turn in the road near the Samgo railway station and came upon four T-34 tanks in well-camouflaged positions on the east side of the road. The enemy armor was so well dug in and concealed that Sharon and his group very nearly passed them by. There were no signs of life about the vehicles as Sharon, Twohey and McDermott clambered onto the second tank in line. The turret cover was down and locked. After working on the hatch without success the periscope tube was knocked off and a grenade dropped inside. This had instantaneous results; the engine started and the tank charged from its camouflaged revetment.

By this time Elledge and Sergeant Jim Thompson were on the scene with 75 mm. Recoilless guns and 3.5 rocket launchers. In addition to this armament there were two Corsairs overhead. The attack on the enemy armor became general with all available weapons employed. Three tanks were destroyed under blistering fire (much to Shea's relief). At the time of the discovery of the T-34's, Shea's company was in the process of crossing the river by the way of the railway bridge and the men of Charlie Company were strung out in vulnerable formation.

Davis arrived on the scene with First Lieutenant Danny Holland, FAC. Holland called down a Corsair on the fourth tank. After making a spot check, Davis ruled as to who was to get credit for the "kills." An assist was given Sharon and his group with Elledge and Thompson getting credit for three. The fourth tank went to the rockets of the Corsairs.

One of the imponderables in the whole affair was the unexplainable lack of alertness and aggressiveness displayed by the enemy tank crews. Had they opened fire with the appearance of the Marines they would have inflicted heavy casualties, especially to Shea's unit. Instead the tankmen chose to lay doggo until their vehicles were destroyed. Two factors entered into the final evaluation; the point of Davis' advance was covered by low-flying Corsairs and it was known that the enemy armor was prone to panic when the gull-winged planes were overhead. It was obvious that the tankers, upon hearing the Corsairs, buttoned up tight to escape detection only to be surprised by the swift advance of the Marines on the ground. Litzenberg and Davis were more than willing to give the major credit to the air half of the team.

During the afternoon enemy artillery laid down a barrage in Davis' CP area. After the first few rounds, however, deflection was changed and the remainder exploded harmlessly in the flats across the river. Later that day the Corsairs reported destroying a battery of artillery west of Koto-ni. No further artillery fire was received that day from these positions.

The advance continued to the north of Chinhung-ni and the enemy was seen moving into position in the hills to the left of Samgo-ri. It soon became obvious the Chinese had established their main line of resistance in this area. Puckett's unit came to action and was pinned down under superior fire. Hargett took a patrol into the hills to the east of the road and was soon engaged in a heavy fire fight. The enemy attempted an enveloping movement to cut off the patrol; Corporal Dick Moore ran into position with his BAR and, opening fire, discouraged the maneuver. The patrol was able to withdraw to more favorable ground.

During the encounter several Marines had been wounded. Corpsman Walter Hunter went forward to an exposed position to assist Pfc.

Alfonse Ladete. After dressing Ladete's wounds Hunter went still further forward in search of others who had been injured. Hunter was hit and seriously wounded. In the confusion of the fire fight and the effort of the enemy to envelop the patrol, Hunter was not missed until the unit had disengaged and were back within friendly lines.

Just before darkness Davis ordered his forward units to break contact with the enemy and to get into defensive positions for the night. During the twenty-four hour period Crossman's Recon Company had taken seventeen casualties. Pfc. Bernard Beriau was wearing an experimental bulletproof vest. He received a shoulder wound just outside the protective rim of the vest. His friends accused him of judging it that way.

As Beriau walked down the road to the aid station he passed Crossman. He grinned and pointed at the wound. "That's my liberty card, Cap'n. See you later."

In this advance Litzenberg was employing a formation which would be widely followed in later phases of the Korean war; the depth from front to rear of the regiment never exceeded six thousand yards with the regimental headquarters, Major Fox Parry's battalion of artillery, the medical installations and train between the two lead battalions and the one bringing up the rear. With the flanks strongly patrolled the 7th Marines moved into enemy territory as a solid, cohesive force ready to fight in any direction. Parry's 3rd Battalion of artillery from the 11th Marines supported and fought with the 7th Marines in so many engagements the unit began to call themselves the 4th Battalion, 7th Marines.

During the night Litzenberg ordered Roach to take his battalion through Davis and continue the assault on the following morning. Davis was directed to hold his present positions and to protect the flanks of the regimental column. Sawyer was to follow Roach at five hundred to a thousand yards. Roach made the passage of lines and his unit went into the assault at nine o'clock. Heavy small-arms and mortar fire was encountered and the assault slowed.

The enemy had made the decision to defend in strength a high piece of ground which was to become known as "How Hill"—some seven hundred fifty meters in height. The road northward from Chinhung-ni was bordered by the Changjin River and the Sinhung rail line. A thousand yards north of Samgo station the road bent in a northeasterly direction for another thousand yards. At this point, also, began the sharp incline of mountain road which led to the top of the mountain plateau of Koto-ni.

"How Hill" commanded this road and the Marines took heavy fire each time a unit attempted to move around a sharp turn.

Captain Thomas Cooney's G Company was assigned the mission of seizing this key terrain feature while First Lieutenant William Johnson's unit, to the left of the road, had the mission of taking the high ground north of Samgo station. Johnson's unit had trouble with the third finger projecting from its assigned target while Cooney's unit was stopped cold at the turn in the road.

Shortly after noon, Johnson's unit was hit by a platoon-sized counterattack. Second Lieutenant Joseph Mordente's platoon was heavily involved and hand-to-hand fighting ensued before the counterattack was repulsed with heavy loss to the enemy. A Chinese officer was killed. A map was found on him which gave the disposition of enemy troops facing the Marines. This information indicated that the Chinese had a reinforced battalion on either side of the road to oppose the advance of the Marines.

Roach established an observation post on the slopes of Hill 726, twelve hundred yards south of How Hill. From this point Lieutenant Colonel Fred Dowsett, executive officer for Litzenberg, and Roach planned the maneuver to get How Company onto How Hill. Dowsett and Roach came to the decision to send Harris' unit along the east-west ridge line until the commanding piece of ground could be taken in assault from the southeast. Cooney's unit would furnish supporting fire to Harris from their positions to the south.

At six o'clock the next morning Harris took his unit up the ridge for the long march into position. Attached to Harris' Company for the operation was First Lieutenant Ewald Vom Orde's platoon of engineers. It was the mission of this unit to rebuild a bridge which would allow a free flow of supplies to Harris in case How Company came to a protracted engagement. Vom Orde's men came across Corpsman Hunter who had been wounded and had lain in the hills since he became lost from the recon patrol.

Hunter was in a serious condition, having been wounded by friendly artillery as it placed preparatory fires on the hills. In addition to receiving wounds from Marine artillery he had been severely burned by Corsair napalm attacks. The Chinese had found him but had not harmed him. They had taken his carbine but had left his medical pack with which Hunter had treated his own wounds and burns and was able to exist until Vom Orde found him.

Because of the gallant spirit Hunter had shown with the 7th Marines since the landing at Inchon, it was a sad ordeal for the engineers to carry him down the steep hill to the road where Vom Orde had an ambulance waiting. Later that day Ladete, whom Hunter had treated before being separated from the patrol, made his way back into Marine lines.

While the rifle platoons were scrambling over the tortuous hills, artillery and mortars began working over the objective. It was four o'clock in the afternoon before Harris reported to Roach that his unit was in position for the assault. Roach, in turn, reported to Litzenberg that Harris was ready to jump off. The regimental commander wanted to know if air strikes had been called onto the target. Roach replied in the negative because there had been no planes available up to that time.

Litzenberg directed that an air strike be made on the target before the riflemen were sent into the assault. The FAC, First Lieutenant John Morgan, was fortunate in contacting two Corsairs as they came down the valley fully armed. The gull-winged planes were equipped with a napalm tank apiece. The pinnacle top of the mountain did not offer much of a target and one napalm tank burst a bit short and the other slightly long. The planes wheeled and placed their fragmentation bombs on the bull's eye. At 4:30 the preparatory fires had been laid on and the rifle platoons were ready for the assault. Second Lieutenant Minard Newton's platoon would attack from the left while Second Lieutenant Robert Reem's unit made the assault from the right.

"Okay, move out."

The skirmish line of the two platoons moved from the assembly area down the slope to the valley floor. Crossing the open ground at the base built a certain tension but no enemy fire was received. The Marine line entered the foothills which led to the sharp, precipitous rise of ground to the crest. About two hundred yards up the hill both platoons came under heavy enemy machine-gun fire. Casualties were being taken as enemy outposts were overrun or driven back. The assault line continued to surge forward.

As the Marines crawled and scrambled upward the enemy machine-gun fire was augmented by mortars and grenades. Throughout the advance the two units had remained abreast with Newton, and Reem in voice contact as they sought to co-ordinate their efforts. A combination of terrain, heavy enemy fire and a counterattack forced the line to halt. Harris reported the situation to Roach; he was ordered to continue the assault. Reem was notified of the order and the two leaders began forming their men for the final sweep to the crest.

Reem gathered his squad leaders, Sergeant Carrozo, Sikora, Edgar and Staff Sergeant Ricciardi, about him to outline the plan of attack. An enemy grenade fell on the ground among the group. Unhesitatingly Reem hurled his body over the explosive and was killed. Newton assumed command of both platoons and the assault was ordered.

Three times the thin skirmish line made the final assault on the crest; three times they were beaten off. On the fourth attempt Sergeant Charlie Foster, a most resolute leader, sprang forward.

"C'mon, first platoon, we're going forward. . . ."

Hurling grenades and firing his carbine as he made the final surge upward, Foster reached the crest. His men regarded it as a miracle that he was able to advance as far as he did through the withering fire. He was killed as he prepared to hurl his last grenade into the face of the enemy. For the fourth time the Marine line had failed to take and hold the crest.

Harris reported to Roach that enemy activity (bugles, flares and deployment of troops) indicated a counterattack in some strength could be expected.

The first assault on How Hill began at 4:30 in the afternoon. It was now growing dark and a decision had to be made on what orders to issue Harris for the night.

With darkness and terrain against the Marines and the capability of the enemy to mount a heavy counterattack, Roach called Litzenberg and suggested a withdrawal. Litzenberg replied instantly: "Withdraw them. We'll soften them up with artillery tonight and air tomorrow."

Roach asked Harris to spot a marker round of 4.2 mortars so that the hilltop could be interdicted while the unit was moved down into the floor of the valley. The mortarmen were skeptical of their ability to hit the target in view of the darkness and the fact that the target had not been properly registered in previously. The first round was fired.

Harris' voice over the radio was jubilant: "Right on—right on."

With the heavy mortars plastering the top and reverse slope, Harris got his unit off the hill and through Cooney's lines.

While the battle had been raging for How Hill, Johnson had taken his company forward on the left side of the road and onto Hill 611.

This land mass was due west of the objective Harris had been attempting to seize. Enemy resistance was light facing Johnson and the high ground was occupied with little or no difficulty. During the night Parry's artillery battalion fired on forty-five concentration points. Joining the howitzers were the 4.2 and 81 mm. mortars; the 81's fired a regimental unit of fire—eighteen hundred rounds.

As Harris was withdrawing, the enemy moved the reserve regiment of the 124th onto How Hill. This unit was so hard hit during the night by artillery and mortars that it was forced to withdraw.

At daybreak the next morning, Roach directed Second Lieutenant Arthur Mooney of Cooney's unit to take a lightly equipped, fast-moving patrol to How Hill and scout the area. Mooney was on top of the embattled crest before noon and reported the enemy had evacuated the position leaving behind several wounded and many dead. On the left side of the road Johnson continued to push northward rapidly and was in possession of the village of Pohujang by midafternoon.

From Chinhung-ni to Pohujang the incline was steep with the road constantly turning on itself in the ascent, yet the narrow-gauge railroad could function over the grade without too much difficulty. From Samgo station to Koto-ri, however, the conventional type rail locomotion had to be abandoned and was replaced by cable cars. The cableway had been severed and experts from Japan were ordered in to repair it.

From Pohujang northward the ravaged hills of Korea would play an increasingly important part in the actions and counteractions of the Marines as well as their Chinese enemies.

It is six air miles from Chinhung-ni to Koto-ni; by road it is ten. The plateau on which Koto lies has an elevation of four thousand feet. Puk-San Mountain to the northeast lifts its crest another twenty-one hundred feet above the plateau—the valley of Chinhung-ni is slightly under a thousand feet. Thus, the change in elevation is three thousand feet in six air-line miles. The road itself was narrow and gutted with many bridges. It was obvious to Smith and Litzenberg that this unsurfaced road could not stand the pounding of a vehicular military train. It was equally obvious that Lieutenant Colonel John Partridge's Engineer Battalion could not maintain and improve the road and still perform the priority tasks of building projected airstrips at Koto and Hagaru. At the moment tanks could not negotiate the road north of Chinhung-ni. Partridge was confident his engineers could improve the roadbed until it would carry tanks, but it would have to be closed to other traffic on the days the Pershings used it. This meant the loss of one day—or more—in transporting supplies into the dump at the top of the mountain and Smith did not propose to push the Marines forward until a substantial base of supplies had been established. Smith gave the order to improve the road but withheld his decision on sending the tanks forward.

In addition to the concern Smith and Litzenberg felt over the tenuous road, both remained sensitive to the unprotected flanks of the 7th Marines. Although Roach reported loss of contact with the enemy, Litzenberg was determined to reconnoiter his left flank before he committed his regiment to the mountain passes north of Pohujang. The attitude of the Marine staff at this juncture was "Little is to be gained by gaining time."

The tension was magnified by the wide dispersal of the division: Puller was still at Wonsan and Majon-ni; Murray was in a valley north of Hungnam with two battalions attempting to find a nonexistent road to the Fusen Reservoir while Newton's battalion was in Chigyong. It was a situation to be treated with caution. By tacit agreement none of the Marine units were pressed to the maximum.

Litzenberg asked for volunteers to make a hazardous foot patrol to the west in an effort to uncover enemy intentions and strength. Sixteen men were selected from the several hundred who requested to go. First Lieutenant William Goggin, machine gun platoon leader in Dog Company of Sawyer's battalion, was chosen to lead the unit. The men came from all three battalions. Corpsman James Walsh was to accompany the Marines.

The volunteers were: Sergeants Stephen Zivko and James Schifsky; Corporals Richard Woodly, Terry Lyles, Robert Mandich and Donald Hamilton; Pfc.'s Edsel Forrester, Eugene Garner, Jerry Nigh, Bernard Ashcraft, Joseph MacKenna, Homer Welch, Ralph Boelk, Theodore Walker and Donald Stonum.

The youngest Marine in the patrol unit was Pfc. Jerry Nigh who was eighteen; the oldest was Sergeant Stephen Zivko at thirty-three. Zivko had been a prisoner of the Japanese during World War II. The unit was to be armed only with rifles and carbines and was to carry enough rations to last two days. It was left to the individual what he would carry in the way of food. The only additional equipment to be carried was three radios—two 536's (Walkie-Talkie) and one 300. Corporal Donald Hamilton was the 300 operator. He was to be spelled off in carrying the heavy instrument by Corporals Richard Woodly and Terry Lyles.

Shortly after noon the patrol gathered at the 1st Battalion CP and was briefed by Davis. It was to move along a valley which lay to the west of Chinhung-ni. Three miles from the departure point Goggin would check in with Davis by radio and report his findings. At this point Goggin would turn north into the most rugged type of terrain. (See map facing page 228.)

In addition, there would be seven other checkpoints with the most important one being number four which was on Hill 1413. From this coign of vantage Goggin was to observe an east-west road which bordered the Changjin River. This road was to be placed under observation for an hour and a half. From this point the patrol would move still further north until checkpoint seven was reached which overlooked Koto-ni. The final point was the high ground overlooking the immediate flank of Roach's battalion north and west of Pohujang. Distance to be covered: twenty-five miles. As the unit made ready to move out Davis told Goggin: "If you get lost all you have to do is to turn east until you come to the big ravine. Follow it down to us—good luck."

Goggin led the patrol along the valley floor at a brisk pace. It was four in the afternoon when he reached the first checkpoint and attempted to contact Davis. Because of the shield of mountains it was impossible to get through. Goggin turned from the valley and began the stern climb into the heavily wooded high ground. It was a misty, cold day and darkness came early. After four hours of exhausting climbing the patrol reached the second checkpoint—Hill 1145. Contact was made with Davis: No enemy sighted.

Goggin set up a perimeter defense with two-man outposts on the pathway above and below the main body. Wet with sweat from the long climb the unit settled down for a cold, uncomfortable night.

At 2:30 in the morning Corporal Robert Mandich, in charge of the lower outpost, reported movement on his front. He had challenged a group of people but they had turned and run upon hearing him. The other outpost also reported contact at this time. After checking with both outposts Goggin decided to move out of the area. It was too cold for the unit to obtain much rest and movement might throw the enemy off if they were building up for an attack.

By 7:30 the patrol was on the southwestern rim of the plateau. The day had come bright and clear and the patrol stepped out at a mile-eating pace. For purposes of speed Goggin kept to the low ground. When the point came to native houses, flankers were put out and the stiff pace continued. Mandich, at the point, gave the signal that he had sighted enemy troops and the patrol took cover. Slowly the unit worked its way to the east and gained Hill 1413. Hamilton, a small youngster, was having difficulty negotiating the steep hills with the radio and was changing off with Woodly and Lyles more frequently.

This was the point from which the patrol would observe the road. Below them the Marines saw civilians sluice-mining for gold along the river banks. The miners sighted the Marines and after much shouting and yelling, Chinese soldiers spilled from the houses in the village. They opened fire on the patrol and Goggin was hit in the right hand. Corpsman Walsh bandaged the wound and the unit took cover on the reverse slope of the hill. Despite the enemy fire the road was kept under observation. After the first return of fire by the Marines, Goggin passed the word to conserve ammunition.

After a certain amount of desultory firing the sluice miners went back to work and the Chinese soldiers, numbering about forty, formed up and marched off into the hills. In the meantime Pfc. Edsel Forrester climbed the high ground to the east of the unit; he reported finding emplacements on the crest but no enemy troops.

After remaining in position an hour and a half, Goggin reported to Davis that there was no further enemy activity in the area and that the road was not being used for the transport of supplies. The patrol moved on and was on checkpoint five at ten o'clock; an hour and a half and two miles up-and-down later, the unit was at point six. The noon meal was eaten at this spot. At 12:45 (between points six and seven) Hamilton received a message over the 300 radio. He gave it to Goggin. "Driftwood Item will move to high ground northeast of checkpoint 8 this p.m. Davis."

Surrounding Koto-ni is an extensive plateau through which the Changjin River and tributaries cut rude corridors. Crossing this tableland became somewhat confusing to Goggin inasmuch as there were no outstanding landmarks upon which to chart his course. Between points six and seven, unwilling to take his patrol into a possible ambush with enemy troops in the Koto-ri area, Goggin turned to the east. As he gained the high ground commanding the ravine and the road he notified Davis he was going to show himself on the skyline. Davis in turn warned Roach to be on the lookout for the unit. Goggin went to the crest line and received a waving salute from Roach's Marines on Hill 1457—three thousand yards to the east.

First Lieutenant William Nietschmann, leader of the 2nd Platoon in Shea's company, brought his unit up the mountain and relieved the fast-moving patrol. Goggin's volunteer unit had moved twenty-five miles in twenty-six hours over the most tortuous terrain imaginable. The only casualty suffered was to Goggin. Their swift and accurate reports materially influenced Litzenberg in sending the 7th Marines over the mountain and onto the plateau. First Lieutenant Elmer Krieg, who had taken command of Reem's platoon, followed in trace of Nietschmann and occupied the high ground south of Koto-ni.

Goggin brought his weary volunteers down to the road where they waited for trucks to take them back to the regimental CP. Roach sought out Goggin. Unaware of his wounded hand, Roach grasped it in a hearty handshake of congratulations on a fine effort. Goggin very nearly collapsed from pain.

While the patrol had been searching out the left flank, the 7th Marines had conducted extensive patrolling. Roach's battalion had sent patrols through Pohujang and Hill 891. Davis had sent units to the northwest along the slopes of Hills 487 and 1225. Sawyer had moved his battalion into position to extend the perimeter behind Davis. Johnson's Item Company was in the rugged terrain to the west of the road and not more than two hundred yards from a bridge which was to play such an important part in the withdrawal. The unit was in need of a resupply of ammunition and rations and an attempted delivery was made by helicopter. Flown by Captain Eugene Pope, the craft came to grief in the turbulent wind sweeping down the mountain pass as Pope attempted to land at an altitude of thirty-one hundred feet. The helicopter crashed but Pope escaped serious injury. First Lieutenant Charles Ward landed with supplies but developed starter trouble on his 'copter and remained overnight at the 7th Marine CP. The extreme weather was having an adverse affect on the "egg beaters" and it was thought at the time that they would not be operable above Chinhung-ni; this line of thinking, however, vanished under the pressure of the crisis which was to develop.

During the ninth of November (the second day of the volunteer patrol) the 7th Marines advanced thirty-five hundred yards with active patrolling being continued. Second Lieutenant Paul Denny's platoon from How Company sized Hill 1457—the tallest hill on the southern rim of the Koto-ni plateau. When Roach asked Denny what could be seen from this high point, Denny replied, "Can see lots of snow and aircraft flying below me. . . ."

During the day General Almond visited the regiment. As he was about to award a Silver Star to Captain Thomas Cooney it was discovered the aide had forgotten to bring the medal along. With some asperity Almond told the aide to turn around. Using the young officer's back as a writing stand the general wrote on a bit of scrap paper: "This officer is entitled to wear the Silver Star medal." Attaching the paper to Cooney's parka with a paper clip Almond directed Roach to prepare the citation.

Interrogation of prisoners captured during this period indicated that Litzenberg's regiment had mauled the 124th Chinese Division so badly as to make this organization militarily ineffective. The next time the Marines came to heavy action it would be against General Sung's 9th Army Group.

Litzenberg's unit was on the Koto plateau in strength by the tenth of November—the Marine Corps' birth date. Litzenberg reported to Smith: "Have occupied Koto-ni this date." The time date on the message was ten o'clock in the morning on the tenth of November.

CHAPTER XVII

The Marines Are Introduced to Frozen Chosin

To keep the MSR open between Wonsan and Hungnam it was necessary to employ the division tank battalion as infantry and to assign the amphibian tractor battalion to the duty of guarding the railroad trains traveling between these points. The Hamyong main line follows the coastal plain avoiding the foothills by a devious roadbed. Along this route moved the supplies to support Litzenberg and Murray as their regiments moved northward. The enemy began a series of attacks on these supply trains and several of the train guards came to heavy and costly action.

First Lieutenant Gerald Anderson had his platoon aboard a northbound train when it stopped at Kowon, thirty-five miles north of Wonsan, to take on water. It was ten o'clock at night. The train was made up of two coaches and a string of gondola-type freight cars. Both coaches were hooked on behind the engine, with the cars to the rear.

The night was dark with flurries of mist and light snow hampering the visibility of the Marines on guard. As Private Richard Foster went to the front of the forward coach to relieve Pfc. Frank Wallace, a group of natives came into view from behind a railside building. Foster thought them to be civilians trying to hitchhike a ride into Hamhung until he saw they were armed. Stepping back inside the car and closing the door, he slipped a cartridge into the chamber of his rifle.

"What's up?" Corpsman Thomas Christensen asked.

"I don't know for sure, but I think we've got some unfriendly Gooks around."

The coach door was flung violently open and a North Korean soldier burst into the coach. Foster killed him and closed the door. This was the signal for the general assault by enemy guerrillas. Burp gun and rifle bullets began to stream through the wooden sides of the coach. The Marines in the coach sought cover as best they could and returned the fire; the guard on the gondolas were in better position to answer the attack.

Anderson was in the rear of the car and firing his pistol from a window. Above the uproar, Pfc. Frederick Markland shouted to the officer, "Can I try getting this train running?"

"Go ahead."

Foster stepped onto the platform and jumped to the ground to afford covering fire for Markland. They found Staff Sergeant Nile Wells lying wounded beside the engine. The two Marines carried Wells into the coach and turned him over to Christensen. Foster returned to the side of the engine and opened fire on a squad of enemy moving toward them from the village. Markland found the Korean engineer under the engine; he hauled the man into the cab.

"Get it going, Mac." Markland reinforced his order by waving his arm. The engineer waved his arms also indicating the tracks ahead were blown out. Markland motioned to the rear and the engineman nodded. Markland dropped to the ground and returned to the coach.

While Markland was in the cab of the engine, Foster had seen a man staggering along the roadbed. He went to assist him and found it to be Kong the Korean interpreter who was attached to the unit. Foster assisted him into the coach where Christensen was working over the wounded Wells.

Markland, on entering the coach, yelled at Anderson who was firing from the rear door. "The track is blown up forward. The engineer thinks it's alright in back. Okay?"

"Back it up."

Markland returned to the engine and waved to the rear of the train. Two of the enemy clambered up the steps and into the cab. Markland killed both of them as the train began to move slowly backward. Upon seeing the train in motion the enemy redoubled their fire; grenades were thrown under the engine and the train came to a sudden halt. The engineer was killed. Markland fought his way back to the coach.

The enemy, having established fire superiority, rushed the train. Foster shot one as he came through the door while Markland was killing one at a window. The fury of the attack died away for a moment. The only sound came from a scattering of bullets tearing through the wooden walls. The fire increased and the Marines in the coach took cover under the seats. Christensen moved Wells into the center of the car and placed sea bags around him.

A North Korean burst through the rear door. Anderson killed him with his pistol. A grenade exploded inside the coach; a second followed closely. Wells was killed and Private Olin Taylor was wounded; Anderson went down. Christensen went to Taylor's side and began dressing his wounds. Another grenade wounded Christensen and Markland as well as Pfc. Raymond Short. Although wounded a second time, Christensen continued to tend the wounded Marines.

A North Korean kicked open the front door and sprayed the interior of the coach with a burp gun. Taylor was wounded again and Pfc. Harold Keller was shot through the arm. Every Marine in the coach was now a casualty. Enemy troops entered the car and began to shoot into the bodies of the wounded. Markland and Foster feigned death. Nonetheless, one of the enemy shot Foster in the back and the bullet came out his chest; another clubbed Markland about the head and face with a rifle butt.

In the meantime the rest of the guard under Technical Sergeant Matthew Doetsch had withdrawn from the second coach and gondolas to more defensible positions west of the tracks. The enemy robbed the train of clothing, rations and weapons and retired into the hills.

When Markland and Foster recovered consciousness they found their comrades in the coach dead. Making their way into the village, they were guided to a Korean doctor who cared for their wounds and put them on an oxcart which started south. Six Marines and Kong, the interpreter, had been killed and eight Marines wounded.

While the train was under attack, another raiding force was attacking the truck park of the 56th Field Artillery to the East of Kowon. The enemy destroyed a number of guns and vehicles. At Yonghung, a few miles to the north, a truck convoy dropped off a battalion of the Army 65th RCT and began the return trip to Wonsan. An enemy ambush destroyed most of the trucks and inflicted heavy casualties on the personnel in the column.

A second train under the guard of Captain John Paul came to a halt four miles south of the train under attack. They were advised by natives that the rails ahead were blown out. Paul set up an all-around defense and waited out the night. From these positions the fighting about the forward train and in the Army truck park could be seen by the flashes, flares and explosions occurring in the dark.

At daylight Paul's train remained stalled because of the blown-out tracks. While waiting for a section crew to make repairs small groups of Army men began to come into the area. Most of them required medical attention and reported they had been in the convoy ambush. The 1st Medical Battalion, which was aboard the train, set up an aid station to care for the wounded and injured.

At 9:15 in the morning the track was repaired and Paul's train proceeded toward Kowon. About six hundred yards from the ambushed train a switch had been blown and the second train was again halted. Staff Sergeant Charles Kopp took a patrol forward to inspect the blown-out switch and the stalled train ahead; he reported that he had found the cars shot up and the personnel in the forward coach dead. The medical personnel removed the bodies and Paul ordered his train to back up to Chon T'an for water.

En route the train was flagged down by Army personnel; they told Paul there were two wounded Marines in an oxcart on the road. Markland and Foster were found. Their condition was serious. Blood plasma was administered at once by Hospital Corps officer, James Dean. Paul got through by telephone to Wonsan and requested a helicopter to evacuate the two men. After waiting for a time for the airlift Paul, on the advice of Dean, backed the train into Wonsan where Markland and Foster were rushed aboard the hospital ship *Consolation*.

Doetsch and his men made it safely back to Wonsan by road. It was two days before the trains began to run with any regularity again. Trips at night were no longer attempted.

While Litzenberg was pushing north to the Chosin Reservoir and Puller was occupied in the Wonsan–Majon-ni sector, Newton's battalion was detached from the 5th Marines and ordered to make a reconnaissance in force into the Huksu-ri area. This area had been previously scouted by Crossman's Recon Company. Sending this additional force into the area was further affirmation of the continuing concern the Marines felt over their left flank.

At seven o'clock in the morning on the seventh of November Major Merlin Olson, executive officer for Newton, took the two-company patrol into the hills west of Chigyong.

First Lieutenant John Hancock's Company (formerly commanded by Tobin and Fenton) led off in this reconnaissance in force. Corsairs were to cover the patrol during the daylight hours. Because of an insufficient number of trucks, Stevens was unable to move his company forward until late in the afternoon. Two and a half hours after departure the point was fired upon by enemy troops in the hills. Hancock detrucked his unit and disposed of the small enemy force; from this point on the column proceeded by foot. A destroyed bridge prevented vehicles from going further forward and a night perimeter was set up. In the late afternoon Stevens brought his unit into the area and the two joined for the night. On the following morning Stevens was to push his unit over the twelve miles of mountainous terrain into Huksu-ri. Local patrols were sent out by Hancock until nightfall.

At seven o'clock the next morning Stevens had his company in an approach march toward his objective. Attached to his unit was a forward air controller and an antitank section. An hour later two platoons from Hancock's unit moved out in trace of Stevens. Until midmorning the point advanced with occasional contact being made with enemy foraging groups. From overhead Marine pilots warned Stevens of a concentration of enemy troops. An air strike was called down on the enemy positions, and Stevens swung two platoons to the left of the road and secured the hilltop which was above and to the right flank of the enemy force. Another air strike was called and this time the Corsairs were led to the target by Captain William Parker in an observation plane. Parker marked the target area by dropping a red smoke grenade. After napalm and strafing attacks the enemy force began to retreat. Stevens' unit occupied the high ground without opposition. A North Korean officer and two men were captured.

On the road south of the enemy positions the enemy had prepared a series of roadblocks consisting of burned bridges, destroyed culverts and stone blocks placed across the road. With Hancock in reserve, Stevens sent his unit forward with one platoon on each side of the road. North of the village of Yong-Min, the unit began to receive automatic and small arms fire from the hills to their front and right front. As the unit took up firing positions additional enemy fire came from the left front.

The enemy was taken under fire by the company machine guns and mortars and an air strike was called down. The force opposing Stevens' unit was in battalion strength with seven machine guns on the hill to the left and five on the hill to the right. The fire fight continued until after dark at which time Stevens was ordered to disengage and bring his unit back into the assembly area. He was forced to use rear guards on his retraction and did not completely disengage until 2:30 in the morning. Hancock was waiting and the two units joined.

First Lieutenant Harold Javins' platoon of engineers rebuilt the destroyed bridge to the rear of the rifle companies and the truck convoy was able to proceed and join the units at the assembly area. This effort was especially commendable because the work was done under fire.

About this time orders were received and Hancock was directed to return to Chigyong immediately because of the enemy raids on the supply dumps along the rail line. Pedersen brought Charlie Company into the zone occupied by Hancock.

On the following morning Pedersen sent out two patrols from the bivouac area. Both units met and engaged the enemy in fire fights. The patrols returned late in the afternoon having accounted for twenty-four enemy dead and seventy-five wounded. Pedersen's unit suffered two killed and four wounded.

The next morning Stevens sent out a patrol with Second Lieutenant Nicholas Trapnell in command. This was followed shortly by a patrol from Pedersen's company under Second Lieutenant Robert Corbet. Captain Jack Jones, in the process of taking over command of Pedersen's company, went on the patrol as an observer.

Contact with enemy troops was made within three hours. By utilizing artillery and air support the high ground about the village of Tongchon was seized. Late in the afternoon Corbet's patrol became engaged in a heavy fire fight with a force of enemy troops which clearly had the patrol outnumbered. Olson ordered the unit to return to the battalion perimeter. The patrol, however, was pinned down and unable to disengage. Second Lieutenant Robert Kiernan, forward observer, was wounded and artillery support was called for by Corporal Jack Sheehan. Because of terrain and communications the system of getting fire directions back to Captain James Jordan's A Battery had to be improvised hurriedly.

Sheehan would call the fire mission verbally thirty-five yards to Corbet, the patrol leader. Using a 536 radio, Corbet would relay the mission three miles to First Lieutenant Loren Smith, executive officer for Pedersen. Smith would then relay the message to Major Albert Hartman, operations officer for the battalion. This message was then transferred to Jordan by direct wire communications and the mission would be fired.

Despite the supporting fires, the patrol continued to be pinned down and were taking fire on three sides. The enemy moved troops from the high ground north of Tongchon in an attempt to close the route of withdrawal of the unit. With considerable difficulty the patrol disengaged after darkness and began working its way back to the battalion perimeter.

While the patrol was moving back orders were received for the battalion to move to Majon-dong the next day when they were relieved by the 3rd Battalion of the 26th Korean Regiment. Newton requested permission to delay his withdrawal in order to make an attack on Tongchon on the following morning to assure that no members of the patrol be left in the hills. This permission was granted.

Plans were formulated for the attack and Hancock's company was ordered in from Chigyong. During the night seventeen men of the cut-off patrol worked their way into battalion lines and at daylight Stevens and Pedersen took their companies into the assault toward the village. By 8:40 the Marines had occupied the high ground overlooking Tongchon and air strikes were called on Hill 463. An hour later another air strike of napalm and bombs was placed on Hill 500. Throughout the advance Jordan's battery was delivering supporting fire.

Stevens and Pedersen swept the slopes and village recovering all the wounded and dead from the patrol and relieving thirty members who had held out in the hills throughout the night. The two companies then returned to the battalion perimeter. Three Marines had been killed and ten wounded, including Jones and Corbet who both remained in action. Preparations were made at once to begin movement to Majon-dong.

For purposes of orientation the deployment of the 1st Marine Division will be given at this time. Litzenberg was in Chinhung-ni and Goggin's patrol was being organized; Puller was in Wonsan with Ridge's battalion at Majon-ni. Murray, with Roise and Taplett, was attempting to find a passable road onto the plateau surrounding the Fusen Reservoir. Because of the distance separating Murray's CP and Newton's zone of action the 1st Battalion was placed under the control of the division for this operation.

On the west coast the Eighth Army had a serious setback when the 1st Cavalry Division was counterattacked and one of its battalions was cut off and largely destroyed. The cavalry unit had come to grief when a ROK Corps on its right flank had fled the area. These events had a sobering influence on the X Corps staff and there was guarded talk of "evacuation."

General Lowe arrived from the Eighth Army front and his report was pessimistic. Smith had a conference with Almond and the Corps commander issued the order for the concentration of the Marines as soon as Puller and Murray could be relieved by other troops. This information was received with considerable jubilation by all Marine units.

During this phase Sawyer and Roach, both of whom were majors, were relieved of their commands as more senior officers came into the Korean theater. Lieutenant Colonel William Harris took command of the 3rd Battalion, while Lieutenant Colonel Randolph Lockwood took over the 2nd. Sawyer remained as executive officer of the 2nd while Roach went to the regimental staff.

Also at this time Seaman Taylor "rejoined" the 7th Marines. Taylor's tug had been transferred from Inchon to Hungnam. Once in the area Taylor could not resist the temptation of fighting with his friends. He hitchhiked a ride north. As happy as the Marines were to see the fighting sailor Sawyer was forced to turn him over to the MP's for return to his ship. It was a sad parting.

As soon as Litzenberg had his regiment on the plateau of Koto plans were formulated to insure the stock-piling of sufficient supplies to support two regiments further to the north. Captain Lester Harmon's Charlie Company of engineers was assigned to build an OY strip. Because of the altitude the field would have to be twenty-five hundred feet. Later, when R4D's (two-engine transport planes) had to be landed to evacuate wounded, another field would have to be built. Three days later the first Grasshopper landed on Harmon's strip.

Throughout this period of consolidation aggressive patrolling was carried on to the front, flanks and rear. A patrol from Davis' battalion came across a battery of horse-drawn artillery which had given them trouble at the foot of the mountain. The guns had been destroyed by Marine air.

On the night of November 10 all personnel of the 7th Marines received a piece of birthday cake, such as it was.

The following morning Wilcox and Shea were sent out to patrol the hills to the northwest of Koto. Wilcox had to negotiate a sheer rise of ground towering above the Changjin River. Without contacting enemy troops Wilcox's unit occupied the high ground above the river and road leading to Hagaru. Shea had a longer approach march to gain his objective. The night positions of Charlie Company had been west of Koto; at first light the unit was in movement with First Lieutenant George Kliefoth's platoon at the point. Two miles west of the village, Shea's unit began the climb onto the hills to the north. Nietschmann took his platoon along the corridor of approach to the left of First Lieutenant Chester Penney's unit.

It was not long before the Marines came under fire from an estimated company of enemy troops. The artillery preparation was ineffective because the terrain was such that the radio equipment of the artillery observer could not be transported forward in pace with the infantry. Shea attempted to direct the artillery over his infantry radio but the targets could not be pinpointed and the preparatory fire was ineffective. Shea then ordered the 61 mm. mortars to work over the area and an air strike was called.

Soon after the assault began, Penney's platoon was pinned down by heavy fire. Going forward alone, he reconnoitered the enemy positions to find the key features of the enemy defense and the safest approach. Returning to the unit Penney briefed them on the plan of attack and then spearheaded the assault. Armed with a pistol and a knife, he charged up the slope and the men of his platoon saw him kill seven of the Chinese before he was killed by a grenade. The position was overrun and the high ground occupied.

The final objective was obtained late in the afternoon and when the order came for withdrawal to the regimental perimeter the sun was sinking. Rather than to risk an ambush by returning through an exposed valley, Shea decided to withdraw through the positions held by Wilcox on his right flank. It was dark before Shea's unit moved down the precipitous cliffs with their dead and wounded. Eight Marines had been killed and sixteen wounded during the patrol. The Marines named Hill 1305 "Penney's Hill."

That night it was four degerees below zero and the Marines were to suffer their first casualties from frostbite.

As Litzenberg consolidated at Koto and pushed patrols northward, Murray began to bring his regiment onto the reservoir road and close in behind the 7th. By the thirteenth Taplett had his battalion at Chinhung-ni and Puller was withdrawing Ridge's unit from Majon-ni and moving north from Wonsan.

Enemy opposition had virtually vanished. Occasionally patrols came across scattered groups who would withdraw upon contact. At one o'clock in the afternoon on the fourteenth of November Lockwood's battalion (formerly commanded by Sawyer) occupied Hagaru.

The weather had turned bitterly cold and the march northward was slow as units were forced to stop and build warming fires.

"Hey, Mac, your nose is froze."

"Th' hell it is."

"Okay, you guys, check your pardner's face—if it begins to turn white, tell him."

"Kee-rist, what this weather wouldn't do to a brass monkey."

Davis brought his unit north in trace of Lockwood and occupied commanding Hills 1162 and 1276, while Harris' unit (previously under Roach) remained in Koto guarding the supply dumps. To all intents and purposes, Litzenberg's regiment was moving into a military vacuum. The enemy had vanished into the barren hills of Korea. By late afternoon on the fifteenth of November, the 7th Marines were consolidated on the southeastern shore of the Chosin Reservoir. Davis occupied the northwest sector, Harris the northeast and Lockwood with Parry's artillery battalion defended the south-southwest zone.

That night the temperature dropped to minus fifteen degrees Fahrenheit. With this subzero weather came a sudden increase in nonbattle casualties. On this date (November 15) the division had suffered no casualties to the enemy, yet two hundred Marines became ineffective because of illness or frostbite.

The Marines were to experience two types of weather on Chosin. From mid-November to late in the month it was a wet cold with warm, sloppy days and cold nights. During the last week of November until the withdrawal it became dry cold with temperatures of minus twenty-five degrees Fahrenheit being experienced. During the early days of December there were days of stormy winds with heavy snow. Always it was cold.

The immediate effect on Litzenberg's men when they first experienced subzero temperatures was one of shock. Medical officers reported many to be in a dazed, stunned condition. A number of cases reported with low respiratory rates. Stimulants were required in addition to warming in order to restore the men sufficiently to return them to duty. After the initial reaction the Marines became accustomed to very low temperatures. After the first few days the shock reaction did not reappear.

The troops were affected indirectly in other ways by the extreme cold. Canteens had to be carried inside clothing to prevent the water from freezing while the wet components in the rations froze. When eaten in a frozen state, intestinal disorders resulted. Thereafter, only the dry portion of the ration was eaten with a consequent low caloric intake. In the next ten days riflemen were to lose from fifteen to thirty pounds per man—and this from men already trained to muscle fineness from running the ridges.

Riflemen, BARmen and machine-gunners were using Wildroot and Vaseline hair oil on the working parts of their weapons because it was thinner than the lubricant being issued. As it grew even colder the weapons were wiped dry with just the barest touch of oil. The extreme temperature was also affecting the artillery. The big guns could not fire as rapidly as under normal conditions because it took the piece longer to return to battery. Also, atmospheric conditions were shortening the range.

At Marine Corps Headquarters, Washington, the first reports arrived on the failure of the Shoe-Pac. For several years the Navy had been working on a cold-weather boot built on the vapor barrier principle. The Marine Corps obtained a number of these from the Navy and the Hood Rubber Company and sent a detachment of men to Churchill, Canada where the boots were tested in subzero weather. This footgear was found to be far superior to the Shoe-Pac. Contracts were let immediately and the Marine division was the first unit in Korea to be equipped with the new boot.

With the knowledge and concurrence of General Smith, Litzenberg adopted a policy of proceeding with deliberation. While a firm base of supplies to support a further advance was being built up at Hagaru, the 7th Marines patrolled aggressively in all directions in an effort to determine enemy strength and intentions. While these activities were going on, Captain Craig Turner's company of engineers was building an airfield and Captain Orville Bibb's company was improving the road up the mountain.

Not many days later these precautions were to save the lives of thousands of men—if not a Marine Division.

The next days saw further movement and consolidation of the scattered elements of the divison. On the nineteenth of November, Puller ordered Sutter's battalion into Chigyong and sent Lieutenant Colonel Donald Schmuck's battalion (formerly commanded by Hawkins) on a reconnaissance patrol into the Huksu-ri area to determine the positions and installations of the 26th ROK's. While this was in the process Puller was relieved of the mission of assisting the ROK's and the patrol was recalled. Puller was free to join the rest of the division.

Murray, under orders to take his regiment to the east coast of Chosin Reservoir, moved his CP to Chinhung-ni. Lieutenant Colonel John Stevens (in the process of relieving Newton) sent the 1st Battalion on patrols from Majon-dong. Roise took his unit to Sasu-ri, on the east coast of the reservoir, and sent out patrols while Captain Gilbert Powell's supporting battery of artillery registered in on avenues of approach forward of the infantry positions. Taplett remained at Chinhung-ni guarding the railhead.

At Hagaru, Litzenberg directed Harris to return to Koto to relieve elements of Murray's regiment and to protect and patrol the supply base and MSR. Davis was to conduct security patrols to the north and west to a distance of a thousand yards. Lockwood sent a patrol south to Toksu-Bong, then north to Hill 547. It returned to Hagaru by a southwesterly route. No enemy were contacted.

From Chigyong (Puller) to Hagaru (Litzenberg) and Sasu-ri (Murray) is a distance of seventy miles; despite the vast area covered by the Marines in patrolling no organized enemy was encountered. The weather continued bitterly cold and indoctrination lectures were given all units on how to live and fight in subzero weather. Each man was to carry an extra pair of heavy socks next to his body and they were to be changed once in twenty-four hours. Commanders were directed to see that this was done. Any officer experiencing frostbite had to make an explanation to his senior. The reservoir was to receive its Marine name—Frozen Chosin.

Thanksgiving Day lived up to the best traditions of the Pilgrim fathers—cold weather with snow. At this point, however, any similarity between New England and North Korea ended.

Puller moved his CP to Chinhung-ni and Schmuck relieved Taplett. Murray moved Stevens' battalion north of Roise on the east coast of the reservoir. Taplett, relieved of guarding the railhead by Schmuck, brought the 3rd still further north than the positions occupied by Stevens. Litzenberg ordered Davis to move into blocking positions in the vicinity of Yudam-ni.

For this movement over Toktong Pass, Hull's Dog Company, a section of 81 mm. mortars and Captain John McLaurin's battery of 105 howitzers reinforced Davis. Beyond Toktong Pass, Wilcox's unit made contact with an estimated enemy company on the high ground to the left of the road. Utilizing artillery and air support the Chinese were forced to withdraw. That night Davis had his unit in position at the head of the valley leading into Yudam-ni.

Most of the Marines (excepting Davis' battalion) received what the mess sergeants labeled "Thanksgiving Dinner." Here again, there was a vast difference between the customary American fare and field expediency. Yet the Marines appreciated the effort and had many things to be thankful for—the division was together again and in the past ten days but thirteen Marines had been killed and twenty-four wounded.

Inasmuch as the roads about Hagaru were to play such a vital role in the future operations of the Marines they should be described in detail. Hagaru lies twenty-five hundred yards south of the southern tip of Chosin Reservoir and to the west of the Changjin River which flows into the vast storage basin.

A road runs north of Hagaru along the east shore of the reservoir passing through the villages of Sugnong-ni, Pokko-chi, Sasu-ri and on to Sinhung-ni. This road follows the shoreline on a level journey until north of Sasu-ri where it bends east into the hills. Further on it rejoins the shoreline twelve hundred yards south of Sinhung-ni. From this point it generally borders the reservoir until it marries the road from the western side. Once joined the two continue along the watershed to the Yalu.

The road from Hagaru to Yudam-ni is considerably different than its east shore counterpart. This route follows a northerly course for some fifteen hundred yards and then swings to the west (away from the reservoir) and twisting and turning in tortured fashion leads into the rugged mountains forming Toktong Pass. The altitude of the pass is forty-seven hundred feet and slips by Toktong-San Peak on a southern shoulder.

Beyond the pass the road twists downward through Sinhung-ni (not to be confused with Singhung-ni on the eastern shore of the reservoir) and drops rudely into the valley of the Munon-ni River. Here it turns northward. The Munon-ni compartment cradles a gentle floor between steep walls of hills and carries northward to a confluence with two other river valleys. The village of Yudam-ni is built on the flatlands formed when these hills fade out and the valleys join on their approach to a protruding arm of the reservoir. It is eight airline miles from

Hagaru to Yudam-ni; hairpin turns increase the road mileage to fourteen.

This road continues to the north of Yudam-ni and forms the union already mentioned with the east shore road. From the village there is also a road leading to the west which joins the north-south artery between Kanggye and Pyongyang.

With Murray established on the east coast of the reservoir and poised for an advance to the north, X Corps issued a warning order directing Smith to be prepared to shift Murray to the opposite side of the water basin when relieved by units of the 7th Army Division. Smith canceled Murray's previous mission and directed him to remain in position until relieved.

The reason for this change in plan became apparent to Marines when further orders from Corps were issued at midnight on the twenty-fifth of November; the Marines were to atttack to the *west* from Yudam-ni and sever the enemy's line of communication to the Eighth Army front at Mupyong-ni—fifty-five miles distant. From this point the Marines were again to turn northward and proceed to the Yalu through Kanggye.

This plan, characterized as a "massive compression envelopment," came as quite a shock to the division when they learned they were to be the right arm of the "compressor." The zone of action of the 7th Army Division on the east coast of the reservoir took this unit northward. With the left flank of the Marines already exposed their right would rapidly become so as they moved west and the 7th pushed north.

This order heightened Smith's concern over the MSR. The rear boundary of the Marine division had been moved forward to Hagaru. The 3rd Army Division was to protect the road from Hamhung to Hagaru. Guerrilla operations around Wonsan, however, kept the 3rd committed to that area. Smith requested permission to retain units at Koto-ni and Chinhung-ni to protect his lone supply route. Almond approved this request and the 3rd Division was made responsible for the protection of the MSR only from Sudong to Hamhung.

On the night of the twenty-fifth of November the Army 1st Battalion of the 32nd Infantry moved north of Roise on the eastern shore; on the following day the remainder of the 31st RCT closed on Murray and the 5th Marines were free to move on Yudam-ni. On the morning of the twenty-sixth Litzenberg was ordered to seize the junction village and to take blocking positions and protect the MSR while Murray passed through and continued the attack to the west.

Litzenberg came against increasing resistance as he approached Yudam-ni. Late in the afternoon of the twenty-fifth Davis and Harris had their units on the high ground where they could look into the village and surrounding valley. Once again the enemy had resisted and retreated. Captain John Morris' unit (formerly commanded by Shea) occupied "Turkey" Hill and Shea led a patrol to the outskirts of the town without contacting enemy troops.

"Turkey" Hill was so named because Shea's patrol returned after dark and found that the short ration of Thanksgiving turkey (a day late) had been eaten by others. Canned shrimp (boiled) was substituted.

Late in the afternoon, three Chinese prisoners were taken. Upon being interrogated, they informed Captain Donald France, intelligence officer for Litzenberg, that the mission of the CCF 29th Corps was to move south of Yudam-ni and to attack the Marines from the south and the west. However, there were to be certain conditions under which the attack would be made: first, no general assault would be initiated until two regiments of the division had passed to the north of Toktong Pass; secondly, attacks were to be made only at night. This last condition was made out of respect for Marine air. Shortly after this the diary of a Chinese officer was recovered in which it was stated that the mission of General Sung's Army was to "destroy the Marine Division numbering in excess of 20,000 troops."

France was convinced the information was correct. Litzenberg was impressed and became even more wary of entrapment or surprise.

As Davis' battalion was moving north of Toktong in the direction of Yudam-ni, friendly natives informed his men that there were "many, many" Chinese at Hagsang-ni, a small village in the adjoining valley which led into Yudam-ni from the southwest. On the following day Davis directed First Lieutenant Eugenous Hovatter to take his company on a patrol into the area. Hovatter assigned First Lieutenant Frank Mitchell's platoon to take the point; in trace came Bradley's unit, the company march CP, First Lieutenant William Davis' 60 mm. mortar platoon, Stemple's riflemen and a section of 81 mm. mortars. This latter unit was sent on the patrol by Davis as an experiment to

---

Chosin Reservoir. *Koto is seized and a base of supplies built up. Litzenberg pushed on to Hagaru and the Marines get their first glimpse of "Frozen Chosin."*

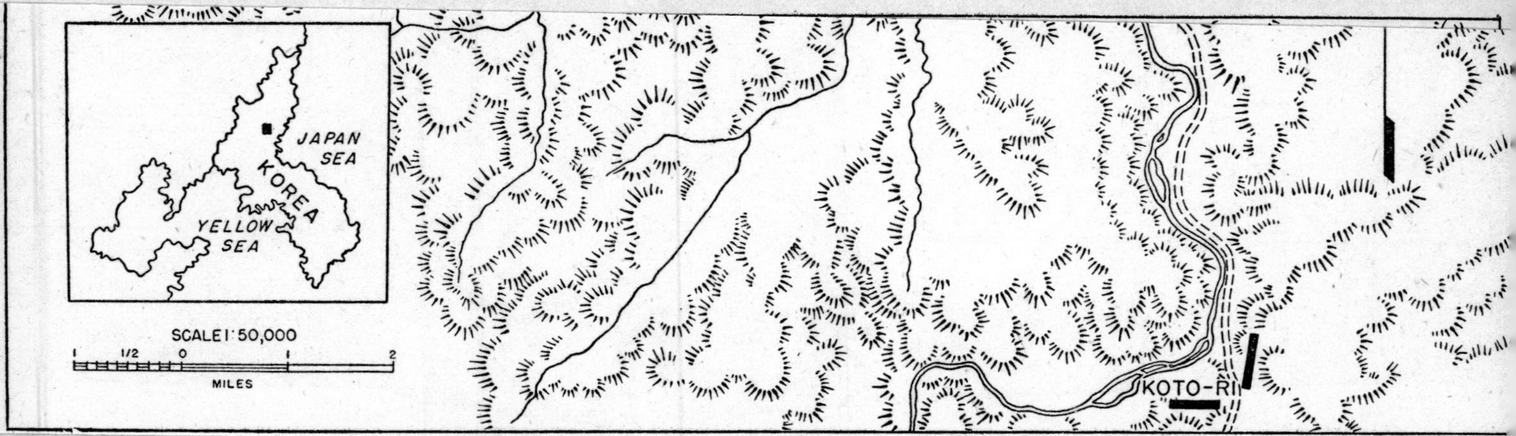
JAPAN SEA
KOREA
YELLOW SEA
SCALE 1:50,000
1 1/2 0 1 2
MILES
KOTO-RI

determine how fast such an organization could move over the rugged terrain with their heavy equipment.

Upon leaving the outskirts of Yudam-ni the patrol worked slowly to the high ground and followed the ridge line to the southwest. It had snowed during the night and movement to and along the ridge was a punishing ordeal. Mitchell set a stiff pace, however, and by four o'clock in the afternoon the point was opposite the village of Hansong-ni where they began to work down the spur to the valley and the village. Corporal Jewel Coquat had his fire team at the point.

The sides of the hills were covered with scrub brush and rank weeds which afforded excellent cover and concealment for an enemy ambush. Suddenly, the point came under small-arms fire. Swiftly the fire grew in volume. Coquat was killed and his BARman, Pfc. Dionicio Gorena, seriously wounded. Mitchell ran forward and, retrieving the BAR, put the weapon in action while directing the rest of his men into position.

At the rear of the company formation Stemple rushed his platoon onto a spur to the north of where Mitchell was pinned down; supporting this move was Davis' 60 mm. mortar platoon. From this point a base of fire was built up to assist Mitchell.

Under cover of the brush the enemy moved reinforcements up from the village and it soon became obvious to Hovatter that with night coming on his unit was in an untenable position; he gave the order to withdraw.

Under extremely heavy fire Mitchell moved among his men organizing a counterattack so that the wounded Gorena could be reached by litterbearers. Running out of ammunition for the BAR, Mitchell discarded it and led the assault with grenades. The enemy withdrew sufficiently to get the wounded to safety but Mitchell was killed as he closed hand-to-hand distance with the Chinese. Sergeant Jesse Swafford and Corporals Plasson and Janeway organized the rear guard and the unit slowly retracted.

The trek back to the Yudam-ni perimeter was slow and it was two o'clock in the morning before Hovatter was able to regain the Marine lines and deliver his wounded to the medicos; at daylight Gorena was evacuated by helicopter to the *Consolation* but died of wounds later. During the fire fight Corporal Walter O'Day became separated from his squad and could not be found in the heavy brush. He was listed as missing in action.

The reaction to Hovatter's attempt to enter Hansong-ni convinced

Davis the enemy were in some strength in that neighborhood. Wilcox was ordered to take his unit into the same area by a different route; the patrol went south on the Hagaru road for three miles then turned into the hills to the west. Once again enemy troops were engaged on the high ground above Hansong-ni. Ten Marines were wounded in the action with Wilcox receiving a painful face wound. He remained in action, however, and brought his unit back within the perimeter late that night.

Litzenberg felt considerable relief when Wilcox regained his defensive positions in the perimeter; while the patrol was out the sector had been thinly held by Kliefoth's platoon with elements of H&S Company and artillerymen.

This aggressive, long-range patrolling was to pay dividends. When the enemy began their "assault of annihilation" against the perimeter the thrust from the southwest had neither the strength nor fury of the attacks from the north and northwest. This was due to the fact that the enemy had been kept off balance by Hovatter and Wilcox and were not given time to build up their troop strength or to get into favorable positions of attack.

While Wilcox was patrolling to the southwest, Cooney took his company onto the high ground west of Yudam-ni. The unit moved out at 8:30 in the morning. Hill 1425 was seized by midday. Harris then directed Cooney to continue to the west and secure the adjacent hill mass which commanded the road leading into the village from the west.

Cooney's unit soon came to heavy action with an enemy force in considerable strength. The leading element deployed and pushed forward. The attack was held up by a well-positioned machine gun. Sergeant John Hamby asked for volunteers to knock it out. Six men volunteered. Slowly the group began working its way up the steep hill utilizing cover where it could be found. Heavy fire drove the men to cover but Hamby continued his attack alone. Exhibiting cool skill with his rifle and hurling grenades at intervals he closed on the enemy position and destroyed the gun, killed three of the Chinese and captured two. In the final assault Hamby was shot through the right shoulder. Despite the pain and loss of blood he returned with the prisoners and requested more men to assist in holding the forward position he had taken.

Hamby remained with the unit until loss of blood made him so weak Cooney ordered he be evacuated.

The advance was continued but soon again the Marines became heavily engaged. After a prolonged fire fight the patrol began to run short of ammunition. Harris ordered Johnson to take his unit onto Hill 1425, establish a base of fire for Cooney and to get ammunition forward. Johnson accomplished his mission, but the enemy pushed reinforcements into the zone and Cooney was forced to retire.

In addition to Johnson's supporting fire the artillery began to blast the enemy-held positions. With this assistance Cooney attempted to disengage and retract to Hill 1425. Despite heavy casualties the Chinese held their terrain advantage and maintained fire superiority. Cooney went forward to direct the final effort. Slowly, with fire teams affording cover fire for one another, position after position was given up. The final breakoff was nearing completion and Cooney was checking positions to assure that none of his men were being left behind when he was killed. He never did receive the medal awarded him by General Almond.

First Lieutenant William Buckley took command of the unit until Captain Eric Haars could come forward from Battalion. Buckley completed the withdrawal and the unit tied in with Johnson on Hill 1425 for the night. The engagement had cost the Marines eighteen wounded and five killed.

Again this patrolling was to be of great benefit. The enemy, engaged until dark, could not regroup in time to join in the general assault on the perimeter later that night.

These daylight actions were but the prelude to a night of bitter weather and savage and costly fighting. As soon as darkness came two divisions of enemy troops began streaming over the mountains and along the trails into positions surrounding the positions held by Litzenberg and Murray. Before daylight the Marines would suffer 95 killed, and 543 wounded.

On the twenty-sixth Murray brought elements of his regiment into the assembly area within the perimeter and prepared for the next day's attack. The following morning, with the 7th Marines protecting the flanks, Roise initiated the advance to the west.

That night it snowed lightly and the temperature dropped to minus twenty-five degrees Fahrenheit, and the skin of ice over the reservoir became thick enough to bear the weight of a man. The riflemen suffered greatly and squads were rotated from the lines to the warming tents. It soon became obvious to commanders that the cold would gravely affect the performance of the men. Litzenberg estimated that for every degree of temperature below zero a man would lose two per cent of his efficiency.

It took twice the normal number of men to perform the routine task of putting up tents and other camp installations. Although the vehicles had been winterized drivers had to take turn-about watches and start motors periodically to prevent freezing. This preventive action increased the consumption of gasoline and shortened the periods of rest for the personnel.

To the south the Marines were grimly concentrating the remainder of the division to support Murray and Litzenberg and protect the supply route. Ridge moved his battalion (less Sitter's company) from Chigyong to Hagaru where he was given the mission of defending the perimeter defenses in that zone. Sitter remained in Chigyong to guard the supplies that had to be left behind until shuttling transportation could bring them forward. Puller set up his CP at Koto with Sutter's battalion defending the perimeter.

In the movement north of the 1st Marines there was a shortage of motor transport. Puller gave priority on the trucks to tentage in order that warming havens could be set up for his riflemen. This decision, initially, caused a shortage of ammunition at Koto, but Puller's reason was basic; "I'll take care of my men first. Frozen troops can't fight. If we run out of ammunition we'll go to the bayonet."

Colonel James Brower shifted his artillery CP to Hagaru and deployed his units to support the infantry. Lieutenant Colonel Harvey Feehan's battalion (commanded by Wood throughout the southern campaign) was attached to Murray. When the 5th Marines shifted from the east to the west of the reservoir Feehan's battalion moved with the regiment and were in Yudam-ni by the twenty-seventh. Lieutenant Colonel Merritt Adelman's battalion was divided into three segments; Strohmenger's battery was ordered to Hagaru to support the perimeter and Ridge's unit; McClelland's unit went into firing positions at Koto-ni, while Blancheri's battery remained in the Chinhung-ni area to support Schmuck.

Parry, continuing to support Litzenberg, moved the batteries of Payne and McLaurin to Yudam-ni with Captain Ben Read's unit remaining in Hagaru to support the perimeter and Captain William Barber's company which was to take up positions on Toktong Pass.

Major William McReynolds' 4th Battalion arrived in Yudam-ni on the twenty-seventh. First Lieutenant Robert Messman's battery, already in the area due to detached duty with Feehan, reverted to McReynolds' control. Shortly after the artillery units closed on Yudam-ni an artillery groupment was formed with Feehan assuming command. This step was necessary because of the separation of the units from the regimental CP and to insure co-ordinated artillery support.

To lend further support to Litzenberg and Murray in their attack to the west, Smith ordered the Provisional Tank Platoon to join the two regiments beyond the pass. The attempt was made with four Sherman tanks. The ice-coated road caused the tanks to slide about considerably. Four miles west of Hagaru the tanks slid from the road; one threw a track. Three of the vehicles were able to regain the road and return to Hagaru. Unable to extricate the fourth it was left until a retriever could be brought forward the following day.

First Lieutenant Richard Primrose brought his platoon of Pershings into Hagaru. It was thought that the heavier Pershing might negotiate the narrow, icy road where the Shermans had failed. Primrose decided to make a test run. Dismounting the crew save for the driver, Sergeant Clyde Kidd, Primrose started out on a one-tank attempt.

With Primrose standing in the turret and Kidd sweating it out at the controls the big tank began the nervy trip. Impeded both by ice and heavy traffic the armored vehicle clawed its way carefully up the narrow highway. It passed the spot where the abandoned Sherman lay; Primrose waved the members of Barber's Fox Company digging in on the pass and the descent began. Three hours later the Pershing was inside the perimeter at Yudam-ni.

Primrose and Kidd returned to Hagaru by helicopter to begin preparations to bring the rest of the platoon over the road on the following morning. That night, however, the enemy cut the road between Hagaru and the pass and no further armor was able to get through. Staff Sergeant Russell Munsell volunteered to fly into the junction village by helicopter, man the Pershing and fight it in support of the infantry. This was accomplished.

While Primrose was making his test run, Litzenberg had ordered Barber's Company (formerly commanded by Zorn who had been injured) to place his unit on Toktong Pass and to hold this vital mountain gap midway between Yudam-ni and Hagaru.

The disposition of the Marines on the night of the twenty-seventh of November was this: Litzenberg and Murray were in Yudam-ni with two reinforced regiments. At Hagaru Ridge's battalion (minus Sitter's Company), reinforced by artillery, tanks and service personnel, was assigned the task of holding that sector. Puller was at Koto with a reinforced battalion while Schmuck was at the foot of the mountain at Chinhung-ni.

Two regiments were concentrated and the balance of the division was at vital points along the MSR. These positions had been gained but hours before the Chinese initiated their attack.

Lieutenant Colonel Olin Beall, commanding the 1st Motor Transport Battalion, had taken a long train of supplies into Yudam-ni during the day. Late that night Beall collected all available vehicles to return to Hagaru for a quick turn-around with more supplies on the following day. As the vehicular column departed all the wounded were taken aboard the trucks. Beall led his convoy through safely but it was the last friendly unit to pass over the road until the Marines fought their way back.

In the late evening, as the last trucks were departing for Hagaru, Second Lieutenant Nicholas Kavakich of the 2nd Battalion Weapons Company, called Pfc. Charles Kaylor to him.

"Kaylor, word has just been received from Division Rear at Hungnam that your request for release from active duty has been approved. Pack your gear and grab a ride back to Hungnam and report to the Casual Company. Here are your orders. Good luck."

Kaylor grinned, saluted and ran back to his machine-gun section. While packing he bade his comrades good-by. In return he received envious congratulations and skeptical questioning.

"How'n hell did you do it?"

"I've got two kids and a business. I wrote a letter to the commandant."

"That ain't enough. You must know Truman."

"S'help me, that's all I did. Just wrote a letter."

"Who'n hell's got a pencil and paper?"

"At least you're one of us who'll be home by Christmas."

Kaylor distributed three candy bars, a carton of cigarettes and two packages of gum among his friends. He shook hands all around and ran down the hill to the road leading to Hagaru. A six-by-six truck came rolling up to him.

"Where you goin', Mac?" Kaylor shouted.

"Hungnam." The truck stopped.

"I've got orders home. How about a lift?"

"Hop in."

Kaylor threw his gear into the back and crawled into the cab alongside the driver.

"My name's Kaylor."

"Mine's Holcomb."

The truck started toward the Toktong Pass and Hagaru. Kaylor told Holcomb about his great, good luck.

"It's the twenty-seventh of November. I ought to make it to Minneapolis by Christmas."

"Gimme your orders an' I'll swim it in that time," Holcomb told him.

CHAPTER XVIII

The Attack to the West

Roise assigned Captain Uel Peters' company to lead the advance into the bitter mountains of north-central Korea. Before the assault infantrymen had moved five hundred yards west of the Yudam-ni perimeter it was obvious the enemy had come to the decision to stand and fight. Throughout the area there were signs that enemy troops were in position in force. Peters met roadblock after roadblock and with each yard of advance the enemy fire increased. By midafternoon the advance stalled and Roise was ordered to consolidate positions for the night.

Peters occupied the high ground to the right of the road and Captain Samuel Smith's Company (formerly commanded by Finn-Hanifin-Zimmer and "H. J." Smith) went into positions astride the road. Jaskilka placed his unit to the right of Peters. On the Yudam-ni map the positions assumed by Roise's battalion are at numbers 2, 3 and 4.

The first day's advance to the west had netted the Marines less than two thousand yards. In the 2nd Battalion CP, Major John Hopkins, executive officer to Roise, carefully divided a small ration of brandy into two canteen cups. He handed a cup to Roise. "It's my birthday, Hal. I bummed this from the doc."

"To your health."

"To the longest fifty-five miles we'll ever travel—if we get there."

Because of the problems involved in describing the actions and counteractions on the night of the twenty-seventh of November de-

Yudam-ni and Hagaru. *The enemy onfall is delivered against the Marines. Defensive positions are marked as the fourteen-day battle begins.*

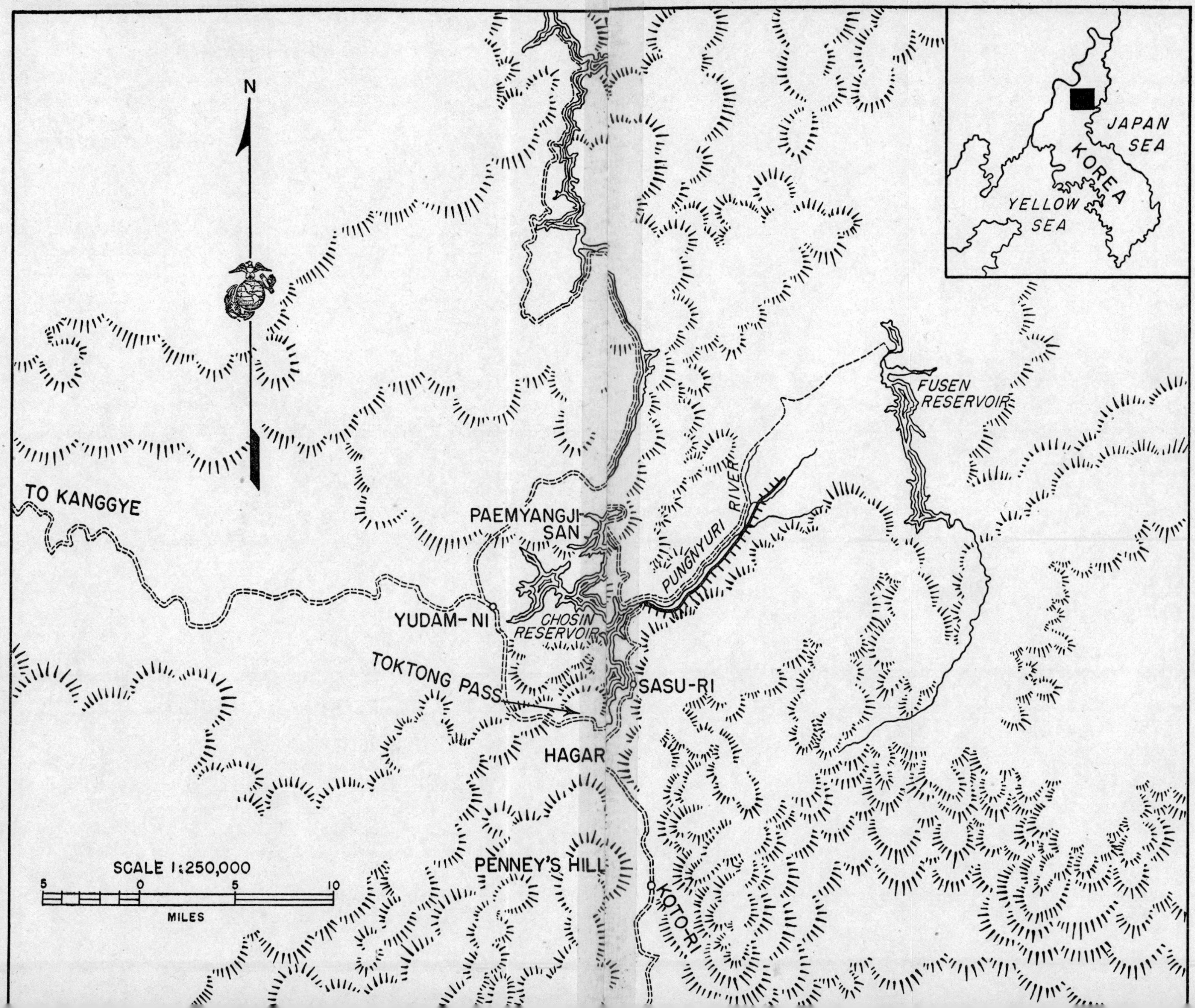

N
JAPAN SEA
KOREA
YELLOW SEA
FUSEN RESERVOIR
TO KANGGYE
PAEMYANGJI-SAN
PUNGNYURI RIVER
YUDAM-NI
CHOSIN RESERVOIR
TOKTONG PASS
SASU-RI
HAGAR
PENNEY'S HILL
KOTO-RI
SCALE 1:250,000
5 0 5 10
MILES

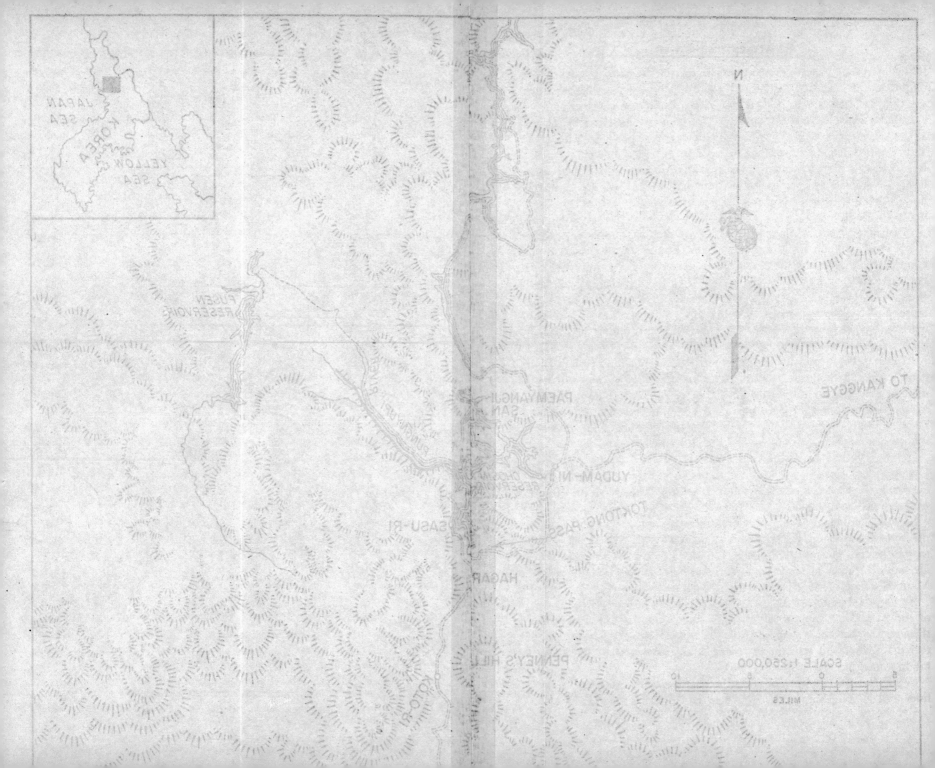

fensive positions have been numbered on the Yudam-ni map. Most of the actions occurred concurrently as the Chinese struck from three sides in their attempt to destroy the Marines north of Hagaru.

Captain LeRoy Cooke's company (formerly commanded by Harris at the battle for How Hill) was assigned a defensive sector on Hill 1402. This is position number 5 on the map. Denny's platoon dug in to the left of Krieg's unit. Krieg was supported by a section from Fitzgeorge's mortar platoon and was on the extreme right flank of the company line. Newton was to the left rear in a blocking position on a trail leading to the MSR.

It was ten o'clock at night when Krieg reported to Cooke that enemy troops were probing his front lines; a few minutes after this a strong Chinese force attacked. At the same time telephonic communications between Krieg and Cooke went out as they did between Cooke and the battalion CP. The enemy overwhelmed Krieg's right flank and the balance of the platoon was forced to withdraw into Denny's positions where a final defensive line was formed. A 60 mm. mortar was lost to the enemy.

Extreme enemy pressure continued to be exerted on Denny's right flank and Staff Sergeant Walton Watson was killed as he rallied his men to hold against the onrushing Chinese. Sergeant Kenneth Hoffie, machine-gun section leader, took over a gun when the gunner was killed. Despite severe wounds in the legs from grenades he remained with the weapon until dragged from it and evacuated.

A lone Chinese had worked his way well to the right and rear of Denny's unit. Armed with a burp gun, he began hosing the flank whenever attempts were made to reorganize and move to better positions. Casualties were being taken.

Second Lieutenant James Mitchell, executive officer for Cooke, came up from the company CP to join Denny. A burp gun burst drove him to the ground. He rose and charged in the direction of the infiltrator. He found his man, a Chinese captain, and killed him. The hard-pressed Marines suffered no further interference from this quarter.

As Second Lieutenant George Caridakis began to call down the fire of the 81 and 4.2 mortars his radio was shot out. Improvising a relay through the battalion switchboard to Captain John McLaurin, he directed, "Search and traverse in reverse." The howitzers of Parry's battalion joined in.

While the mortars were blasting the enemy Cooke came to the front lines and joined Denny. "We have to retake that ground," he said.

The counterattack was quickly formed. "Let's go," Cooke shouted as he charged forward. He was killed by a blast of automatic weapons fire. Denny was wounded but remained in action. In the face of the superiority of the enemy the attack failed. Fitzgeorge went forward under fire and brought Cooke's body back into the Marine lines. Fitzgeorge was wounded. Mitchell assumed command until Harris (just returned from hospital) could come forward from the battalion CP. All the officers of How Company had been wounded but Newton.

When the wounded began coming down the hill Pfc. James Hester and Corpsman Joseph Pancamo took their ambulance jeep forward from the battalion CP. The next day the jeep was found riddled by bullets. Neither Hester nor Pancamo was found. They are still listed as missing in action.

The enemy attack slackened for a time and Harris came onto the high ground and took command. Before reorganization could be completed, however, another furious enemy attack came on the front and flanks and Harris, under orders from battalion, directed his depleted unit to sideslip to the rear of positions held by Jaskilka. Denny covered the withdrawal.

At position number 4 on the map, Jaskilka occupied ground to the left of Cooke's company. These two units, however, were not tied in physically because of distance and a sheer shoulder of ground between them. Because of this intervening land mass it was impossible for either unit to support the other by fire.

Jaskilka was assigned the mission of protecting the battalion rear and a dangerous avenue of approach along the right flank which cut between Jaskilka and Cooke and led directly to the MSR into Yudam-ni. Jaskilka was confronted with defending a north-south corridor on the floor of which was a frozen stream and a few native huts. Vegetation was in the form of stunted trees and moderately heavy brush. Two hundred yards up the corridor was a natural contour of land upon which Jaskilka decided to form his defensive lines.

Before the night was over this corridor was to be known as "Easy Alley" for two reasons: first, in tribute to the stout defense put up by Jaskilka's Easy Company, and second, the ease in which staggering losses were committed on the enemy.

Jaskilka (who had just received orders to return to the United States) made a reconnaissance of the area and assigned positions to his platoon leaders. During the short meeting in which he issued orders for the night Jaskilka came in for some good-natured joshing over his return home.

"Who'n hell do you know?" Deptula asked.

"Didn't you know that Cates and me are buddies? He needs me at Headquarters."

"Just a pogue at heart," Jack Nolan grinned. "Let us hear from you from time to time, old boy."

"If you guys will button up and stay alert tonight I'll get a good night's sleep before shoving off. Maybe I'll get back before Norma has her baby."

The group broke up and the platoon leaders went to rejoin their units. Twenty feet from where the meeting had taken place, Deptula fell to the ground.

"Hey, skipper, I'm hit," he yelled.

"Knock off the grab-ass," Jaskilka yelled back. "Don't pull a phoney like that."

"I'm really hit—take a look."

A "look" was taken and it was found that a stray rifle bullet had passed through the lower part of Deptula's leg. As they placed the platoon leader on a stretcher to carry him to the rear he waved at Jaskilka, "See you stateside, skipper."

"With that scratch you'll be lucky to make Japan. That's as far as I got," Nolan reminded.

Staff Sergeant Russ Borgomainero assumed command of the 1st Platoon.

Night defenses were set up in the corridor with Borgomainero on the left and Nolan on the right. Second Lieutenant Donald Marchette's 3rd Platoon was placed in reserve. Both of the front-line commanders exercised good judgment and considerable skill in placing their men and attached guns from Uskurait's machine-gun platoon. Excellent fields of fire were obtained by all weapons. Borgomainero tied in his left flank with Christofferson's platoon (Peters' company) which was on the high ground to the west.

It was dark by six o'clock. At ten Nolan reported to Jaskilka that his men could hear the enemy talking a short distance forward of their positions. He requested that illumination from the 81 mm. mortars be made ready. Jaskilka directed Nolan to withhold fire until the last possible moment.

Immediately after this the enemy assault was made against Cooke, Jaskilka and Peters. The action of Cooke's company has been dealt with. Borgomainero's platoon came to action first as the enemy drove a wedge between him and Christofferson. Jaskilka committed a squad from Marchette's unit to assist in refusing the left flank. Over unfamiliar, treacherous ground this squad moved into the line with an alacrity not believed possible. Marchette chose to lead the unit personally.

To replace these men in the battalion reserve, Roise ordered an attached engineer platoon into position.

During the early phase of the enemy attack Nolan did not receive the requested illumination because Roise gave priority to the heavily engaged Christofferson. In addition, there was a critical shortage of illuminating mortars. Exercising splendid fire discipline Nolan's men waited until the enemy troops were but a few feet from their positions before all weapons opened up. As the enemy bore in closer the Marines met them with a hail of grenades.

When it was possible to provide Nolan with illuminating mortars the enemy dead could be seen in uneven rows along the entire front. For the first time the Marines knew how much damage they had inflicted.

Marchette was directed to bring the balance of his platoon forward to seal off the penetration effected by the enemy. The fighting continued in "Easy Alley" for nearly two hours until a light machine gun in Nolan's platoon set fire to a native house two hundred yards forward of his positions. This burning house lighted up the valley to both Nolan and Borgomainero. From then on the Marines settled down in their holes and began "shooting for record." Casualties among the Chinese were extreme; few if any of the initial force attacking along the "alley" escaped.

The first attack ended shortly after midnight and Jaskilka hurriedly reorganized his unit in order that a rotating system could be set up whereby men could return to the heated tents in the battalion command post; others huddled in their holes and pulled sleeping bags up to the knees. This was as much as any man would relax for all hands knew another attack would be made.

At 2:30 in the morning the enemy came back for more. This attack, however, was not pushed with resolution and it was stopped with further heavy casualties. The next morning Jaskilka counted over three hundred enemy dead; the closest was fifteen feet from Marine machine-gun positions (attesting to the fire discipline of Nolan's men), the farthest away was one hundred yards. Beyond that distance the Easy Company commander stopped counting.

As already indicated, Peters' company was to the left of Jaskilka. Throughout the day Peters had led the attack for Roise's battalion and had been the most heavily engaged. After an advance of five thousand yards in which nine roadblocks were overcome Peters was ordered to set up his night defenses. Because of the length of his front all three platoons would be put into the line. Belbusti placed his platoon on the left, McLaughlin in the middle with Christofferson on the right.

Peters' defensive sector is shown as number three on the Yudam-ni map.

As with all the ground in the frozen Chosin area it was most difficult to dig in. Some of the men had acquired Chinese picks and shovels in previous engagements and with these were able to hack shallow pits from the unrelenting earth. The entrenching tools carried by the Marines proved to be too light and fragile for such heavy work. By dark Peters had his unit as well prepared as possible and the long, bitter wait began. Tension and cold were as great a threat as the enemy.

After a series of probing attacks the enemy found the weakest link in the line—the point of contact between Borgomainero and Christofferson. Once discovered, the enemy struck Christofferson's flank with a furious assault of over three hundred troops. The positions of light and heavy machine guns were overrun and the gate was open to the enemy which led into Roise's CP and cut the road behind the rest of the battalion.

Knowing the dangers inherent in the situation, Christofferson ran to form Sergeant Richard Ederer's squad for the counterattack. While in the process of moving these men from the line, Pfc. John Meade gathered together Pfc. Donald Kjellman, Corpsman Leland Arntz and two others and rushed to fill the breach. Shouting encouragement, Meade got the others into positions where they could pour fire into the advancing enemy. When ammunition and grenades began to run low Meade ran stumbling and falling through the snow and over the rough ground to the company dump for a resupply. Staggering back to his comrades through a hail of small-arms fire Meade distributed the ammunition and took his place in the line. He made three such trips to the ammunition dump. On the fourth he was seriously wounded in the leg. Arntz was forced to hold him down while he cared for the wound.

During this time Peters was pouring 81 mm. mortars into the breach while Christofferson formed his counterattacking force. Armed with a submachine gun Christofferson led the assault toward the positions of the two lost machine guns. Enemy troops were in the process of turning these weapons about to use on the Marines. In a savage, close-in fight where Marines and Chinese grappled in the snow seventy-five of the enemy were killed and the two machine guns recaptured. Christofferson was credited by his men with killing twenty with his fast-firing weapon; Meade accounted for fifteen with his rifle and grenades.

As soon as the breakthrough occurred, Second Lieutenant Peter Osterhoudt, battalion communications officer, formed a group of fifteen men from his section and headquarters personnel and rushed up the hill to lend support at the critical zone. In addition to this reinforcement, Roise ordered Macho (reserve platoon of Smith's Dog Company) to bring his unit from battalion reserve to back up Christofferson.

At daylight Jaskilka formed a counterattack to regain the high ground in Christofferson's sector. While Borgomainero and Marchette formed their platoons for the assault, Jaskilka requested mortar support from Roise. This was denied because of a critical shortage of mortar ammunition; Jaskilka decided to supply his own support behind a grenade barrage.

Arming every man in the skirmish line with as many grenades as could be carried the assault troops moved forward behind their own grenade explosions. Good progress was made until an enemy machine gun on the right flank opened fire. The advancing line was pinned down.

Pfc. "R. A." Jackson spotted the position of the gun. Crawling through the snow he gained a position where he could reach the enemy gun with a grenade. Rising to his feet he took aim and threw. The grenade landed in the middle of the gun position and killed the entire crew. The line of Marines charged forward and the position was taken.

Jackson was hit by a burst from the machine gun as the grenade left his hand. He died a short time later.

There were over six hundred enemy dead lying in the snow before the combined weapons of Roise's unit.

Smith's Dog Company (position number 2) at the roadblock was subjected to containing fire and light probing attacks. For the first time since arrival in Korea, Dog Company came from a battle without being the hardest hit of any unit in the line. To Roise this was a great relief. It meant to him, and many others in the 5th Marines, that perhaps Dog Company had overcome the tragic jinx that had followed it from Pusan. Kelly, Kennedy and Mateo were the members of the "Hollywood Squad" still with the unit. Baker had been evacuated to Japan earlier with pneumonia.

At position number 1 the units of Haars (Cooney) and Johnson had no contact with the enemy.

Thus far we have considered the attacks placed against the Marines to the west and northwest of Yudam-ni. To summarize: The enemy endeavored to break through Cooke's unit and cut off Roise from the rest of the Marines at Yudam-ni; this effort was complemented with a second attack which would split Peters and Jaskilka and in this manner fractionalize the 2nd Battalion. Once divided the fractions could be destroyed at will. Against How Company the enemy was partially successful in taking the commanding terrain and pushing troops through the gap and into the valley below where Taplett's CP (position 11) was taken under fire. The counteraction against this breakthrough will be dealt with later.

Peters and Jaskilka stopped the second plan with bloody losses.

Two of the most savage battles fought on the night of the twenty-seventh of November were waged on the hills to the north of Yudam-ni, Hills 1282 and 1240. The reference points on the map are numbers 6 and 7. These two hills, less than a thousand yards apart, were to be fought over with a savagery unmatched in the annals of small unit warfare.

Hill 1282 (point six) was occupied by Phillips' company on the afternoon of the twenty-sixth. The Marines of Easy Company of the 7th Marines (not to be confused with Jaskilka's Easy Company) trudged up the steep, snow-covered approach ridges in silence. Many were footsore from frostbite; all were bone-tired and the effects of dietary denial were beginning to show in faces as well as reactions. Hacking holes in the iron land of Korea was slow, painful work. Officers and NCO's had to growl at the men to get them to expend the necessary effort to properly dig in. The next day was spent patrolling to the north. Light contacts were made.

A Chinese officer was killed. On his body the Marines found papers which identified his unit. He also carried a plotting board, an alidade and a tape measure to plot the Marine positions.

"Thorough, to say the least," Lieutenant Ray Ball, executive officer to Phillips, observed. "This slant-eyed gentleman wasn't satisfied with reconnaissance—he had to measure things."

The Chinese officer was a member of the 79th Chinese Division; this was the unit General Sung had assigned to crush the northern rim of the Yudam-ni defenses.

As a military organization Phillips' company was in no sense veteran, but it was rapidly becoming so. Seoul had been the indoctrinator and Hill 696 south of Sudong (Robinson, Gallagher and Yancey) the catalyzer. Those who survived that battle taught the replacements and twenty-one days of patrolling and skirmishing had welded them into a hard-cored company who boasted, "Easy for us, tough for others. That's Easy Company, Mac."

Phillips prepared his positions with care. Yancey's platoon was placed on the top of the hill facing to the northeast. Clements was in the same relative position on the ridge but faced northwest. The two units were occupying crescent-shaped positions with their points touching. In the center Phillips placed his CP and mortars. When Bey's 3rd Platoon arrived from detached duty with the Regimental Headquarters, Phillips placed them on a spur which ran generally north and south. The southern flank of Bey's unit was down the ridge line in the direction of the Yudam-ni valley; the northern flank tied in with the southern crescent tips of Yancey and Clement.

Phillips and Hull (commanding Dog Company) occupied positions about a thousand yards apart; the two commanders arranged to have patrols meet midway along the connecting ridge line hourly during the night. Second Lieutenant Richard Wells, machine-gun platoon leader, and four men were sent into the valley near the Regimental CP so that if the need arose someone familiar with the terrain would be available to guide ammunition bearers or reinforcements to the hill.

Heavy machine guns with a field of fire sweeping the broad saddle to the northeast were emplaced. Near by Yancey put the reliable Gallagher with a light machine gun. All along the front trip flares were planted for illumination. Schrier registered in his 60 mm. mortars to pound the ridge lines leading in from the north. As night came on the wind carried the faint, eerie sound of Chinese bugles.

"Those bastards talk different than we do and they blow their bugles different too. I haven't heard one of our calls yet."

"I wish Kate Smith would get that moon over the mountain, Mac, we could sure use it."

Some of the Marines foraged for twigs and brush that would burn so that they could warm their canned rations. Others, overcome by the lassitude brought on by excessive physical exercise, altitude and low caloric intake, lay in their frozen pits jabbing with a bayonet at a can of rocklike pork and beans. When a segment did break off the teeth were unable to grind it smaller until the mouth had warmed it. Yancey, who had been watching Robinson hobble along on frostbitten feet for several days, ordered the BARman to the hospital. Robinson protested vehemently. He finally turned over this weapon and cursing to himself, limped painfully down the hill. The moon, four days past the full, rose at 6:10 but a misty overcast cut off much of its welcome, helpful light.

The preliminaries to the Chinese assault followed a pattern to which the Marines were becoming accustomed—light probings by squads and platoons in an effort to determine points of joining between platoons and positions of machine guns and flanks.

After the first sporadic attacks the enemy began to exert greater pressure. Suddenly it became quiet save for the sound of hundreds of feet shuffling through the frozen snow. Gallagher crouched over his machine gun hoping it hadn't frozen on him. Yancey cranked the handle of the field phone. When Ball came on, he said, "They're building up for an attack—get the 81's to give us some light and then lay in on the ridge and work back toward us."

"There's a shortage of 81's—we can't give you many," Ball answered.

Yancey cursed.

The Marines waited until they saw the moon-shadows of the enemy in the snow before the trip flares were pulled; then they saw the first wave, then a second fifteen yards behind the first and still a third behind the second. As far back as the flares lighted the scene they saw Chinese at open intervals moving forward.

As soon as the flares came on bugles, shepherd horns and whistles made a witches' conference of the night with the wailing minors of Chinese singing added to the bedlam. As the first wave came closer the Marines could hear them chanting in English:

Sonofabitch, Marines
We kill
Sonofabitch, Marines,
You die.

"Let the bastards have it," Gallagher shouted, as he pressed the trigger. The near-by heavy machine gun opened up with him and all along the line the Marines began to fire and lob grenades.

"Lay it on, Ray, lay it on," Yancey yelled over the telephone to Ball.

The mortars began blasting closer and closer to the Marine lines as Schrier closed the range on his weapons. To the immediate front the 60's and 81's began mushrooming snow and torn bodies into the air. The machine guns and BAR's fired in long spurts and the riflemen rose to lob grenades.

As soon as it became clear that the main attack was being hurled against Yancey's platoon, Phillips left the CP and ran to the ridge top. He found his platoon leader moving from position to position with Sergeant Allan Madding at his side; each was carrying extra ammunition and grenades which they distributed with words of encouragement and advice. A grenade fragment had cut through Yancey's nose and excessive bleeding was forcing him to cough and spit continually in order to breathe.

As Yancey and Madding went along the line, Phillips moved to the opposite flank. He saw to the evacuation of several wounded and called up replacements from his company headquarters. He was hit in the shoulder and leg by rifle fire. Ignoring the wounds and enemy fire he continued to move among the Marines in the line.

"You're doing well, men," he told them. "Stay loose, you're doing well."

The enemy attack faltered and those in the assault waves still living withdrew on the racketing signal of bugles. Suddenly it was silent save for the occasional burst of rifle and machine-gun fire along the northern rim of the perimeter. Under the glare of the illuminating mortars Phillips' men could see windrows of dead and wounded Chinese in the snow before their positions. Some were within ten feet of the Marine line. Positions were reorganized, the wounded evacuated and dead removed. Wells could not be contacted to bring up a resupply of ammunition.

Because of the congestion of the single road and lack of transportation Lockwood had been unable to move his 2nd Battalion CP forward from Hagaru. Until this move could be made, control of Phillips and Hull was given to Davis. Thus, on the night of the all-out Chinese assault Davis was burdened with the command of five rifle companies.

While a corpsman dressed his wounds, Phillips got Davis on the telephone. "We broke up the first attack, Colonel, but we've taken a lot of casualties. We may need some help."

"Okay, I'll get it to you."

The command situation at Yudam-ni at this time was one of interest to military students. Smith was at Hagaru with but a small segment of the division. Radio communications between him and his two regimental commanders was difficult and slow because of the intervening mountains. Telephone wires had been cut by the enemy. Normally this was a situation where the ADC (Assistant Division Commander) would have flown in and assumed command but Craig had been ordered back to the United States under emergency conditions. At the moment Smith was without an assistant. As soon as it became evident the two forward regiments would be forced to fight with the minimum of control from division, Litzenberg and Murray brought their regimental staffs together to facilitate co-ordination. Murray moved into the same tent with Litzenberg while the two regimental executive officers, Dowsett and Stewart teamed up.

Litzenberg (about to be promoted to brigadier general) was considerably senior to Murray who was still a lieutenant colonel. With a unity of action worthy of the highest commendation the two regimental commanders solved the grim problem confronting them by mutual agreement and decision.

Thus, when Davis called the joint CP and informed the commanders of the situation facing Phillips, two platoons from Heater's company were instantly ordered onto Hill 1282.

In a warming tent of the medical battalion Robinson lay on a stretcher listening to the cascading sound of a fire fight to the north. It was not long before the ambulance jeeps drew up outside. Litterbearers brought in a stretcher and placed it alongside Robinson.

"What outfit you from?" Robinson asked.

"Easy, 7th," the inert figure mumbled.

"Did we get hit?"

"Clobbered. Mr. Yancey's wounded—so's the skipper—everybody is, I guess."

Robinson sat up. In the darkness he got into his clothes and parka. He stifled a moan as he pulled the shoe-pacs on over his swollen feet.

"Be seein' you, Mac," he whispered.

Robinson stumbled to the entrance and lurched through the opening. The cold night air made him gasp. He was selecting a weapon from a discarded stack of rifles when a corpsman came to him.

"What'n hell you doin', Robinson?"

"What does it look like, Doc?"

"Get back in your sack."

"Get out'a my way." Robinson slung the rifle over his shoulder and headed for the hill mass to the north. When he came to the steep hillside he had to crawl. The blisters on his feet had broken and his socks were wet with blood and pus. Robinson found his way to Easy Company, he found Yancey.

"What'n hell you doing here?" Yancey asked hoarsely.

"Looking for a job."

Yancey spat blood in the snow. "You got one. Over there."

In the meantime the enemy had been building up for a second attack. Once again the Marines heard the shuffle of hundreds of feet through the snow as bugles and horns began to blare; once again the strident chant came floating in on the north wind. The second attack struck with even greater fury than the first. Under heavy fire Trapnell (1st Platoon of Heater's company) took his unit onto the right flank of Clements'. Snyder moved up in trace of Trapnell and integrated his men with the depleted ranks of Easy Company.

Sheer weight of numbers forced a penetration of lines and separated Trapnell and Clements; an envelopment movement by the enemy forced Trapnell to withdraw to the higher ground to his rear.

Clements was wounded as the Chinese plunged through the gap and into the Company CP area and Schrier's mortar positions. Schrier was wounded. As Yancey tried desperately to form a final defensive line a grenade exploded in front of him and a fragment tore into the roof of his mouth. He continued in action. Phillips rushed forward shouting to his men and hurling grenades at the onrushing Chinese.

"Hold on, men!" Phillips roared. "This is Easy Company." He grabbed a rifle from the snow and plunged the bayonet into the frozen ground.

The butt of the up-ended weapon swayed back and forth. "We hold here."

He was struck by a burst of small-arms fire and killed. Ball, already wounded twice, assumed command. Unable to move Ball shouted instructions and encouragement as he continued to fire his rifle from a sitting position. He was hit again and again yet he continued to shoot into the enemy until he collapsed. He died shortly afterward.

What was left of Sergeant Kenneth Keith's squad was cut off from Yancey's platoon. Keith had four men left. He led them down the hill to Bey's unit where he contacted Staff Sergeant Daniel Murphy. Until this time the heaviest attacks had been against Yancey and Clements. Keith told Murphy of the breakthrough; Murphy hurried to Bey and requested permission to lead a squad of twelve men to the critical point. Bey agreed.

Corpsman James Claypool volunteered to join the group. Murphy (with Keith and his four men) formed the unit and led them to the right and up the hill. As they neared the breakthrough area the enemy took them under heavy fire. Without hesitation Murphy charged forward hurling grenades and shouting to the Marines to follow him. They fought their way into the CP. While Claypool attended the wounded, Murphy went in search of Phillips only to find the company commander dead and Ball dying.

Murphy got his squad into a defensive line and rallied others to take up points of vantage; he shifted a machine gun to a new position so that it would bear more effectively. When the Chinese resumed their attack he passed out the few remaining grenades; when rifle ammunition began to run low he loaded clips from BAR magazines.

On the other side of the gap Yancey was attempting to form a counterattack with the nine men left in his platoon. He rallied his men with the battle cry he had learned while with the Raiders in World War II. Through a blood clogged throat he shouted: "Gung ho, Marines, Gung ho!"

"Gung ho," Robinson answered.

"Gung ho," Gallagher echoed.

The thin line of ten men started up the hill with fixed bayonets but it was not to be; Yancey was hit in the right cheek and blinded. He went to his knees and began to crawl forward. The thin line of Marines melted away and the enemy formed for the final attack which would sweep Hill 1282 of Marines and open the way to Yudam-ni.

At four o'clock in the morning Stevens (1st Battalion 5th Marines) was ordered to send further assistance to Easy Company as well as Hull's Dog Company to the east. It will be remembered that two platoons of Heater's unit had been sent to Hill 1282 earlier. Further reinforcements were necessary if the northern defense line was to be saved from total collapse.

As the situation deteriorated to the north Jones was ordered into action with his company. The 3rd Platoon, under Lieutenant Harold Dawe, was directed to support Hull who was heavily engaged on the hill mass to the east of Phillips. Jones, with his remaining two rifle platoons, was ordered to move onto Hill 1282 and to seal off the enemy penetration in that sector.

Jones had arrived in Yudam-ni from the east shore of the reservoir after dark. There had been no opportunity for him to observe the terrain features of the area nor to make a reconnaissance of the route of approach to the presently assigned objective. Displaying excellent judgment and great energy, Jones led his unit in the black of night over the treacherous terrain without a false turn or wasted moment.

Two hundred yards from the crest the unit came under heavy fire. Jones deployed his troops and pushed on into the CP area where he found remnants of Easy Company still clinging to the reverse slope. Snyder was the only officer left. Jones took command of all the Marines in the area and began to organize the attack to regain the crest.

Because of the detachment of Dawe's platoon, Jones lacked the capability of performing an enveloping maneuver. He decided to make a frontal assault on the crest. Once the salient was secure he would eliminate the enemy from the crest by continuing the attack to the left. Jones assigned Corbet's 1st Platoon to the assault while Magness' 2nd Platoon was to move up immediately and begin the attack to the left.

Before ordering the attack Jones organized litterbearers and began the immediate evacuation of the wounded of the hard-hit Easy Company and Snyder's platoon. In the intense cold the wounded could not long survive.

Day was breaking over the cold, white mountains of the reservoir when the order for the jump-off was given. With a fury that could not be denied the salient was retaken; the spirit of Jones' men reached fever pitch when they saw their leader in the forefront of the attack bayoneting and clubbing the enemy. Two platoons of Chinese were killed as they fought to hold the vital ridge. Corbet was wounded and First

Lieutenant Robert Richter took command of the unit. By virtue of their speed Marine casualties were light.

Before the ridge to the left could be cleared, however, a determined group of thirty Chinese began an enveloping movement which put them to the flank of the CP; these troops opened fire on the litterbearers and wounded.

First Lieutenant Loren Smith, Jones' executive officer, gathered together Sergeants Wallingford and Owens and four men from the mortar section and led the attack on the flanking force. Although wounded in the face from grenade fragments Smith continued to press the attack with his small group. The fighting came to close quarters. The enemy force faltered in the face of the determined fire of the seven Marines; they began to withdraw, some broke and ran. Ten of the thirty Chinese were killed and several wounded. Smith established a line and went to the crest to get a squad from Jones to insure that the care of the wounded would not again be interrupted. Smith refused evacuation.

With the assistance of Marines from the 1st Battalion CP over two hundred wounded were taken from the slopes of Hill 1282 in the next few hours.

In the meantime the high ground was occupied and defensive positions established. The remnants of Phillips' company were put under the command of First Lieutenant James Lichtenberger and placed on the left flank of Jones while Heater's unit moved into right flank positions. Throughout the day the entire line was engaged in a continuous fire fight in order to retain the hard-won salient. Although wounded in the legs by mortar fragments, Jones continued to direct his unit; on six occasions, under the heaviest fire, he went forward of his lines to carry wounded men of Easy Company to safety.

At four o'clock in the afternoon Taplett sent Williamson's company onto the hill to relieve Jones and the other Marines. Heater's unit had suffered five killed and thirty-seven wounded; Jones had ten killed and thirty wounded. Of the one hundred seventy-six men of Phillips' unit who marched onto Hill 1282 only thirty were able to march off. Robinson and Gallagher were among those present.

On the afternoon of the twenty-seventh Hull took his company on a patrol to the north of Hill 1240 which is position seven on the Yudam-ni map. First Lieutenant Paul Mullaney had his platoon at the point. Three hours out he came in contact with about twelve enemy troops. These were quickly dispersed. At this stage First Lieutenant Thomas

Thomson passed through Mullaney and turned east in the direction of the village of Kyodong-ni on the shore of the reservoir. By two o'clock in the afternoon Hull's unit had covered over three thousand yards of the most precipitous terrain in the vicinity of the reservoir.

The village had been burned out by Marine air and was abandoned. As Thomson was crossing the low ground to enter the village he came under heavy fire from a well-entrenched enemy occupying the high ground to the north and west of the native hamlet. Four Marine Corsairs were overhead, but contact with the planes had to be improvised because a TAC was not on the patrol. First Lieutenant Edward Easter was the forward observer and his radio was linked with the artillery; by relaying through Parry's CP to Davis to the ground controller to the planes the four-Corsair strike was called in.

As Mullaney swung his unit into line abreast of Thomson he was hit and seriously wounded in the left arm. It was Mullaney's third wound in less than sixty days.

Shortly after the unit left their defensive positions Hull had been directed by the battalion adjutant to return Mullaney to Hungnam for rotation because of two previous Purple Hearts.

At this point the Marines came in contact with a strong enemy force which was well dug in and supported by heavy machine guns and mortars.

Thomson deployed his platoon and notified Hull. A second air strike was brought in by Easter.

The fire fight became general all along the line and it was not long before the Chinese had gained fire superiority; they held terrain advantage from the beginning.

It was obvious the enemy had given up the tactics of fighting just long enough to delay the advance before falling back for another stand on ground of his choosing. Now it was stand and fight and give no more ground. Thomson spotted an enemy machine-gun position and taking a fire team moved forward to knock it out. Thomson was killed.

Hull notified Davis of the situation and was ordered back to the perimeter.

The enemy continued to exert pressure on the Marines and clearly indicated they wished to prolong the engagement until darkness. While laying down a heavy fire to pin down the patrol, a platoon-sized force began to move into a flanking position. Seeburger brought his 60 mm. mortars into action. Despite these countermeasures the Chinese increased their volume of fire and the cry of "Corpsman" was heard along the line.

Hull rushed forward under heavy fire to supervise the breaking off and the evacuation of the wounded. Hull ordered the Marines to hold their fire, thinking the Chinese might also stop. This artifice only increased the enemy fire. Easter called in another air strike. While the Chinese sought cover from the savage air attack leapfrogging fire teams broke final contact. Sixteen casualties had been suffered.

As the Marines withdrew the enemy pushed forward. Prepared to fight a rear-guard action, Hull's unit carrying the dead and wounded conducted a slow movement back to his positions on Hill 1240. The wounded were evacuated to the hospital in the village and Hull made final preparations for the night attack he was certain the enemy would launch. Corpsman Fred Hardy had his wounds dressed and returned to duty.

As with the other units on the perimeter the Chinese made light probing attacks in the early evening. Shortly before midnight a small group of infiltrators were destroyed. At this time the intercompany patrols between Hull and Phillips were stopped. Enemy troops slipped through this gap and working their way down the hill took the Litzenberg-Murray CP under fire. Mullaney's platoon (now commanded by Seeburger) was occupying the crest with Sota's unit to the left and Sergeant Othmar Reller's platoon (vice Thomson) to the right.

To the cacophonous accompaniment of bugles, horns, whistles and the chanting and cursing of the Chinese the attack was launched shortly before midnight. The full force of it struck Reller's unit. Casualties suffered on both sides were exorbitant with the Marines accounting for ten to one. Still the enemy came on. Weber was wounded as he went forward to contact Reller. Seeburger was wounded and evacuated.

Hull, seemingly oblivious to the deadly fire, ranged the line hurling grenades and directing his men. Despite a stubborn defense the center platoon was forced off the high ground; the two flanking platoons in turn were impelled to withdraw to prevent being enveloped. This phase of the battle had lasted nearly three hours.

Halfway down the hill the withdrawal was halted by Hull. Quickly he began to reorganize his depleted unit for a counterattack. Sota's 2nd Platoon had sustained the fewest casualties and was assigned to lead the assault. The remaining members (not more than twenty) of the 1st and 2nd were combined into one and placed in reserve.

When the skirmish line for the assault was formed Hull shouted: "Okay, let's get the bastards." Well in front of the line he charged up the hill; no man behind him wavered.

The enemy, not prepared for such fast counteraction, were driven from the crest but quickly rallied and brought the Marines under intense fire. A platoon-sized group slipped around the flank and took the Marines under fire from the right rear with a machine gun. Sota was wounded. Reller was evacuated because of wounds. A feeling of despair swept the Marines.

"Hold fast," Hull shouted. "It's only one gun—it can't kill all of us." Grenades finally put the weapon out of action.

The Dog Company commander presented an awesome sight as he moved among his men. A grenade fragment had slashed open his forehead and his face was bathed in blood; a short time later a rifle bullet hit him in the shoulder. He continued in action.

Hull placed the few men he had remaining in a small circle on the topmost crest. The circle was so small that Corporal Walter Menard, Hull's runner, could toss grenades from the center to any Marine on the line who required a resupply.

As daylight came Hull and his Marines could see Dawe's platoon fighting their way up the hill toward them. The first Marine into the small perimeter approached Hull. "Sir," he said with a grin, "it looks as if you all have been having your troubles."

Hull and sixteen men were all that were left of Dog Company when reinforcements arrived. Daylight also brought to light the price paid by the Chinese. Hill 1240 was littered with their bodies. Menard (wounded) and Sergeant Walter Hathorn were the only two NCO's remaining of the original unit leaving the United States.

To the south of Yudam-ni Morris' Charlie Company (less Kliefoth's platoon) was in position number 10. The ground taken over had been occupied by Davis' battalion CP on the advance of the 1st into Yudam-ni. Morris utilized the holes previously dug out by bulldozers to set up his defenses. First Lieutenant Jack Chabek was assigned the right sector with Staff Sergeant Early Payne's 2nd Platoon on the left. In a middling position behind the two rifle units First Lieutenant Frank Donohue set up his mortars.

The ground occupied was on the southwestern slope of Hill 1429 and commanded the road between Hagaru and Yudam-ni. To the rear of the crescent-shaped line the boulder-strewn hill rose sharply. To protect the rear Corporal William Brown took his squad from Payne's platoon onto the top and dug in. It was midnight before the final dispositions were made and the unit settled down to wait out the night and for the enemy.

Morris was in contact with Wilcox as the wounded commander withdrew from the long patrol into the Hansong-ni area. Immediately after the passage of Wilcox to the Yudam-ni perimeter enemy activity was marked on the road. It was 2:30 in the morning when the enemy launched a sharp attack on Chabek's right flank squad. The swiftness with which these positions were overrun indicated the unit had not remained alert. Chabek committed his reserve squad and with the help of headquarters personnel and mortarmen from Donohue's unit was able to restore the line. The effort, however, was costly to the Marines.

Gradually the enemy attack swung to the right and onto Payne's front and then to his left flank. First Lieutenant Joseph Glasgow, forward observer, brought in artillery fire. Pfc. Bobby McElhanon was having trouble with his 60 mm. mortar tube. The base plate was broken and the tube could not be attached. He improvised by holding the tube in his hands while the rest of the crew fed in the shells. Good results were obtained.

The enemy, however, continued to exert heavy pressure on the left flank and Payne was unable to cope with the situation due to the fact that he was short Brown's squad. Every available man from the headquarters platoon and Donohue's mortar unit was thrown into the line. After heavy fighting the enemy attack was repulsed. Every man in the headquarters platoon was either killed or wounded. During this attack the enemy were placing two grenades in a sock and hurling two at one time.

Due to the aggressive patrolling by Wilcox the assault on Morris' lines did not begin for several hours after the Marines on the northern and western perimeter were struck. It was long after daylight before the enemy attack on Morris slackened. When there was time to reorganize and to take stock of the situation Morris attempted to get in touch with Brown but the radio had been shot out of order and contact could not be made by shouting.

Corporal Curtis Kiesling volunteered to scale the hill in search of the squad. Working his way through the boulders Kiesling disappeared over the crest. After a short time he reappeared. He shouted down to Shea: "No sign of them." Kiesling swung to his left to continue the search on another section of the crest. As he worked his way around an outcropping of boulders to his left an enemy machine gun opened fire. Kiesling was instantly killed.

Due to excessive casualties already suffered Morris and Shea agreed that further attempts to contact Brown were beyond an acceptable risk.

It was now ten o'clock in the morning and the situation facing Norris was bordering on the hopeless. His unit was surrounded; there were but six mortar shells left; rifle and machine-gun ammunition was critically low; fifty-four men had been wounded and fifteen killed; because of radio failure he was out of contact with Davis.

While the Marines took what steps they could to strengthen their positions, Corporal Leonard Delesky went to work in quiet desperation on the radio. His hands were numb from the intense cold and he had to constantly pause to warm them but he never left the instrument. So intent did he become with his task that he would not even look up when enemy fire swept the area.

On the line the riflemen could see the Chinese moving into position on both flanks and working to the high ground to their left rear. Overhead there was ample Marine air support available but there was no way to call the Corsairs down on target.

Davis was aware of the gravity of the situation through Glasgow's earlier reports to the artillery CP. As soon as the enemy attacks against the perimeter were stabilized to the point where the entire defense would not be jeopardized by the removal of two companies, he ordered Wilcox and Hovatter to effect the relief as soon as possible. Hovatter was to lead the way out of the perimeter. When he had reached a point about three thousand yards along the Hagaru road he was to swing into the hills to the east and come onto Morris' positions from the crest occupied by Brown. From there he would swing west toward the road. Wilcox would move in trace of Hovatter but would remain on the road until past the positions of the beleaguered unit. At this point Wilcox would swing east and tie in with Hovatter. Once this movement was effected Morris would be surrounded by friendly troops.

Shortly after ten o'clock the plan was put into operation. Bradley's platoon took the point and moved out at a rapid pace. An enemy roadblock was met and overcome with dispatch. The point turned into the hills and the long, rugged climb began; Stemple's platoon was in trace of Bradley. Contact with the enemy was made shortly after entry onto the high ground was begun and from then on the advance was slower.

Bradley moved around the crest held by Brown while Stemple occupied it. As the point moved onto the southeast slopes of the hill Davis' mortar section took a company-sized group of Chinese under fire with telling effect.

In the meantime Wilcox had moved south along the road and was getting into position to become the bottom arm of the pincer. The enemy dispersed by Davis' mortar fire were caught between Wilcox and Bradley and were cut down. First Lieutenant Robert Wilson called an air strike down on another group of Chinese to the west of the road. One napalm landed in the middle of thirty to forty enemy. Few survived its flames.

While the relief units were moving from the perimeter and into position Morris and his unit were holding sporadic firing and probing attacks. Delesky continued to work over the radio. At noon he let out a shout as the instrument grumbled and growled and came to life.

"Able and Baker Companies are on their way out to us."

The news was a stimulant to the weary Marines of Charlie Company and Morris laid plans for a rapid evacuation. The final relief was not effected until it was growing dark.

Litzenberg had directed Davis to make the relief and return to the perimeter with all possible speed because the Yudam-ni perimeter would be unduly weak on the southern rim while the two companies were on their mission. Additionally, Davis' battalion would be vulnerable to attack by vastly superior forces while in movement to and from the position held by Morris.

Hovatter's unit was deployed as a covering force while Wilcox saw to the evacuation of the wounded. Morris had but fifteen men who were able to leave the hill without assistance; of the twelve men who went with Brown to the crest only four came back. Kliefoth brought his platoon south along the road to meet Morris and assist in the final movement into the perimeter.

It was ten o'clock at night before all units were back within the defensive lines.

While the rifle companies in the northern and western sectors were fighting to retain the integrity of the perimeter local penetrations caused periods of anxiety and heavy fighting in various CP's on the valley floor. Litzenberg's CP was taken under light small-arms fire on several occasions during the night in question. Interior defenses were manned but the threat developed into little more than night-long harassment. Several of the artillery positions came under fire from infiltrators and the "cannon cockers" had to fight back with rifles as well as howitzers.

The hardest hit of the unit command posts was Taplett's at position 11 on the Yudam-ni map. Arriving in the area from the eastern shore of the reservoir in the middle of the afternoon, Taplett placed his three companies in positions of defense of his assembly area with Williamson's How Company occupying a sector facing to the west and Hermanson's George Company (formerly commanded by Bohn and Mize) facing northeast. Schrier's Item Company was faced to the north between Williamson and Hermanson. On Schrier's immediate front was the canyon which was an avenue of approach between the hills occupied by Cooke at map position 5 and Phillips at 6. A platoon-sized outpost was placed well forward in this canyon to check enemy movements and to warn of an attack from that direction.

Williamson came to action first as the enemy pushed through the gap left open with the turning of Cooke's flank and resultant withdrawal of that unit. Williamson, however, was never put to heavy pressure and when two native houses took fire and lighted his field of vision heavy casualties were inflicted on the Chinese. Williamson's lines also provided a haven for men of Cooke's company who had become lost in the darkness.

Schrier's canyon outpost was hit hard and driven in shortly after midnight. An enemy force in company strength moved swiftly along the corridor in an attempt to breach Taplett's lines and overrun the CP area. A fire fight of some intensity ensued with the battalion area heavily engaged. Major John Canney, Taplett's executive officer, rushed to place the headquarters personnel in positions of defense. Under heavy fire Canney moved from position to position in directing the defense. He was killed as he moved from the right flank to the center where the enemy were building up for an attack.

Hermanson left his positions lightly held and passed the platoons of Cahill (returned to duty from wounds suffered in the Pusan perimeter fighting) and Cashion through the CP area in a counterattack to the north. The impetus of this attack cleared the immediate area of enemy and carried up the draw and onto the ridge to the right. When daylight came Taplett had stabilized his positions and once again occupied the canyon and the ridge to the right.

The situation facing Litzenberg and Murray on the morning of the twenty-eighth was serious. Less stout-hearted commanders could well have termed it desperate. Hopeless might have been an acceptable word.

The position of the Marines at ten o'clock in the morning after the first all-out attack of annihilation was this:

To the west Roise was in the same relative positions as the night before; Jaskilka's early morning counterattack had restored the ground lost with the turning of Christofferson's flank; the three companies of the 2nd Battalion were fit and ready for more. Harris' company (vice Cooke) had been driven from the high ground and had lost heavily. Replacements and reorganization would be required to fit this unit for further action. Phillips' Easy Company had suffered such staggering losses in its valiant stand that it could no longer be considered. The same situation pertained to Hull's Dog Company. To the south Morris' Charlie Company was surrounded and fighting for survival. At Toktong Pass Captain William Barber's company was surrounded and had taken heavy losses. Barber might hold his lines against enemy assault but Litzenberg knew that time, attrition and subzero weather would defeat him.

At sundown on the night of the twenty-seventh Litzenberg and Murray had at their disposal eighteen rifle companies; at sunrise on the twenty-eighth three of these units were so depleted that they could not be considered militarily effective. Additionally, two companies were surrounded and their future effectiveness and employment in doubt. It took all day to relieve Morris.

To add to the gravity of the situation there was a shortage of artillery and mortar ammunition. Of greater concern, however, were the 450 battle and 175 nonbattle casualties in the tents on the valley floor. Immediate evacuation of many was necessary if they were to live. The helicopters of Gottschalk's VMO-6 could afford some relief but aerial evacuation by plane would be necessary to save the lives of many. An order was issued to build an airstrip which would take observation planes.

Fully aware of the serious situation facing them, Litzenberg and Murray made their plans. Murray, still under orders to drive westward, prepared his attack orders with misgivings. Litzenberg ordered the relief of Morris and began re-forming his regiment against the assault he was certain the enemy would throw against Yudam-ni the second night.

General Smith arrived at Hagaru by helicopter on the morning of the twenty-eighth and set up an operational CP. Fully aware of the heavy fighting and losses suffered by the Yudam-ni forces he awaited a change in orders from X Corps. If these orders were not changed Murray would continue the attack to the west. Obviously this was impossible.

The order sending the Marines into the attack to the west was, in effect, a wide envelopment. To be successful such a maneuver was based on the assumption that the holding force (in this case the Eighth Army) would hold. When Murray jumped-off on the morning of the twenty-seventh, the Eighth Army was already falling back. By the next day a retreat was definitely on. For the Marines to have continued the attack would only have involved them in a disadvantageous battle which would have had no effect on the fate of the Eighth Army.

When Smith did not receive orders from Corps to withhold his advance to the west, he assumed the initiative and directed Murray to consolidate his positions on Yudam-ni. Litzenberg was directed to open the road between Yudam-ni and Hagaru.

Had Murray pressed his attack on the twenty-eighth it would have broken the cohesion between himself and Litzenberg and would have strung the 5th Marines along a narrow, mountain road surrounded by two divisions of Chinese. Litzenberg's casualty-depleted force could not have held Yudam-ni the second night alone.

Once again the Marine division commander was displaying a realistic approach to battlefield problems. Throughout the campaign he displayed the rare gift of knowing when to refuse battle as well as when to deliver it and push forward. Smith's decision to hold Murray in place was to save his division from annihilation.

During the night of the twenty-seventh the Hagaru force had been free of enemy attack. Puller at Koto had spent an easy night but a convoy attempting to gain Hagaru from Koto had been attacked and was forced to turn back. Thus, the enemy had achieved two major steps in his over-all plan of defeating the Marines: Murray and Litzenberg were isolated from Hagaru by roadblocks, while Puller was similarly separated from Hagaru. Smith directed Puller to open the road north of Koto.

On the east coast of the reservoir the 7th Army Division had moved a task force into the general area formerly occupied by Murray's 5th Marines. This force was composed of two battalions of infantry and elements of a field artillery battalion. They were hard hit during the night of the twenty-seventh and their exact condition could not be determined because radio communications went out shortly after reporting they were under heavy attack. Brigadier General Hodes, unable to get through to the Army unit, set up his command post within the Marine lines at Hagaru.

CHAPTER XIX

The Enemy Strikes: The Marines Are Surrounded

Up to this point the engagements of the various units in the Yudam-ni area have been treated in detail through the night of the twenty-seventh of November and into the day of the twenty-eighth. In the case of Morris' company the action was carried through until the unit returned to the safety of the perimeter at ten o'clock on the night of the twenty-eighth. In other engagements the account was ended when the crisis was overcome by the arrival of reinforcements or the enemy ceased attacking.

In the case of Barber's Fox Company defending Toktong Pass it would be confusing to the reader and a great disservice to continuity to interrupt the valiant battle waged by Barber's men. For five days and five nights two hundred forty Marines fought off twenty times their number; wounded Marines died because blood plasma froze and could not be thawed; other wounded crawled from the warming tents to the freezing holes on the perimeter when the line became so thin another attack would breach it. Over two thousand Chinese died before the combined weapons of Fox Company, Captain Ben Read's artillery battery (emplaced at Hagaru) and planes flown by Marine and Australian pilots.

The men of Fox Company wrote a great chapter in Marine Corps history. This is their story.

At 11:30 in the morning on the twenty-seventh Barber was ordered to take his company from their positions on the perimeter of Hagaru to Toktong Pass. Here he was to set up defensive positions at this critical point on the Main Supply Route and to patrol and hold until relieved. This step was taken to insure that supplies could get through from Hagaru.

It looked for a time as though the unit would have to march the seven miles to the pass inasmuch as truck priority had been given to transporting Murray's regiment to Yudam-ni. While the company was forming to start the move First Lieutenant Donald Campbell, forward observer attached to Fox Company, came rushing up with good news. He had arranged for nine trucks from Read's artillery battery. It took considerable crowding to get twenty-seven Marines with their packs, sleeping bags, weapons and ammunition into one truck.

The trip to the pass was slow because the unit was in trace of McReynolds' 155 mm. Howitzer Battalion and the tractors towing the big howitzers made slow headway. It took over two hours to make seven miles.

Barber went ahead and made a reconnaissance of the ground. When the unit detrucked he was waiting for them.

The hill Barber had chosen to defend rose sharply from the road. Between the road and a sheer ten-foot cut-bank which introduced onto the hill were two native huts. The lower portion was covered with small trees; the rest of the way to the top was covered with a light blanket of brush. A broad saddle led from the hilltop to a ridge. This ridge (nine hundred yards distant) formed a crescent from the northwest to the east of the land mass that was to become known as "Fox Hill." The northwest portion of the crescent ridge was extremely rocky and slightly higher than the topmost positions occupied by the Marines.

Barber assigned First Lieutenant Robert McCarthy's 3rd Platoon to the top facing on the saddle; to the right First Lieutenant John Dunne's 1st Platoon went into position. Dunne's lines faced to the east and extended down the hill to the trees and bank. First Lieutenant Elmer Peterson's 2nd Platoon faced the west with his back to Dunne. The positions assigned resembled an inverted **U** with McCarthy's platoon at the arch, Dunne's unit on the right leg and Peterson's on the left. At the base of the hill was an interval between the piers of the **U**. This was closed by the 3.5 rocket unit and First Lieutenant Lawrence Schmitt's headquarters section. Barber located his command post with Staff Sergeant Robert Kohls' 81 mm. mortars and Lieutenant Joe Brady's 60 mm. mortars near the two native houses at the base of the hill.

It was dark before the unit was dug in. The men of Fox Company could look forward to a bitter night because Barber had ordered that foxholes and positions were to be prepared before the erection of warming tents.

Campbell was unable to register in Read's artillery battery. It was six miles from the artillery emplacement at Hagaru to "Fox Hill." This is very nearly the extreme range for 105 mm. howitzers. Due to the fact that subzero temperatures and altitude were affecting ammunition and the range of artillery pieces, it was not deemed an acceptable risk to fire over the traffic-jammed road between the two points. Kohls' 81 mm. mortars, however, were able to register in on the rocky ridge to the northwest. Sergeant John Henry set his heavy machine guns in position well down the hill so that his fields of fire would cover the road from either direction.

At the top of the hill McCarthy placed two squads on line facing north; the right and left flanks were tied in with Peterson and Dunne. McCarthy placed his third squad in a longer line to the rear of the first two. Because of the terrain and distance to cover, Peterson and Dunne were forced to place all their squads in line. There was no reserve.

Fox Company was in position by nine o'clock when Barber made his final round of inspection. With fifty per cent of the unit ordered to remain alert, the balance crawled into sleeping bags to face a long, bitter night. All was quiet save for the roar of trucks along the road. That noise died away too as Beall brought the last convoy of empty vehicles back from Yudam-ni.

The Chinese opened their assault from the north, northwest and south. The first warning McCarthy received of the attack came as the leader of his 1st Squad, Corporal Thomas Ashdale shouted, "Here they come."

The enemy struck in company-sized strength along the saddle. McCarthy's forward squads met the attack with courage and resolution and the fighting became close with grenades from both sides making a devil's rim of fire on the hilltop. The Chinese appeared to be armed with nothing but fast-firing burp guns. Of the thirty-five Marines in the forward line fifteen were killed and nine wounded. Corpsmen Morrissey, Jones and Bongartz went forward and evacuated the wounded. A machine gun jammed and the gunner rose to meet the charging Chinese and killed six with his pistol.

Despite the valor of the defense McCarthy was forced to abandon the forward positions and withdraw his men to the secondary lines established by the reserve squad. Only eight of the thirty-five came back. Three were missing.

Despite exorbitant casualties the enemy came on. Ashdale's squad on the left flank became heavily engaged. Pfc. Harrison Pomers was knocked unconscious when a concussion grenade exploded as it hit his helmet; he recovered and continued to direct his fire team. On the extreme left flank of McCarthy's shortened line Pfc. Gerald Smith's fire team was fighting against heavy odds to hold their positions and to prevent the enemy from turning the flank.

At the point where the two platoons (Peterson and McCarthy) joined, Private Hector Cafferatta and Pfc. Kenneth Benson of Peterson's platoon were sole remaining members of the right flank fire team which tied in with Smith's team.

Knowing that a penetration would jeopardize the entire unit Cafferatta exposed himself to the marching fire of the enemy by standing upright and emptying his rifle into their ranks; a wounded Marine reloaded a second weapon and handed it to him. This weapon was also emptied with telling effect. When he wasn't firing his rifle he was hurling grenades.

Cafferatta ran to his right and joined Smith; from this position he continued to fire his rifle from the standing position. An enemy grenade landed on the parapet and he kicked it away; he did the same with a second. A third fell in an elongated trench where wounded Marines were sheltered and he pounced upon it and threw it back at the enemy. It exploded as it left his hand, wounding him. He remained in action.

Smith's fire team killed sixty Chinese while Pomers' men accounted for forty-five. Cafferatta was credited with killing twenty.

Peterson's platoon was heavily engaged with the enemy at the same time McCarthy's front was being driven back. The crew of the light machine gun and two men of the right flank fire team (Cafferatta's) were casualties. Peterson rushed to the critical spot and was shot through the shoulder as he attempted to plug the breach in the line. He had his wound dressed and returned to duty.

While McCarthy and Peterson were heavily engaged the enemy struck from the south and Barber was forced to displace his CP and mortar sections up the bank and beyond the trees to the open ground midway up the hill. Brady and Technical Sergeant Alfred Phillips (60 mm. mortar section chief) were both hit by grenade fragments; six others of the mortar sections were wounded and two were killed. Pfc. Lloyd O'Leary took command of the 60 mm. mortars and opened fire on the saddle in front of McCarthy.

Peterson pulled the lower end of his line into the trees some fifteen yards above the bank and tied in with Schmitt's headquarters section. This line held and the enemy attempting to scale the bank were killed by the grenades tossed over the bank or by Henry's heavy machine guns. Dunne's platoon on the right flank was not as heavily engaged as were the others and no shift in positions occurred on this line. During the attack Barber moved from critical point to critical point under the heaviest kind of fire.

By daybreak the attack became disorganized and the Chinese could be seen withdrawing. A few continued to crawl forward and throw grenades or make one- and two-man assaults but they were killed. Shortly after daylight a flight of Corsairs passed over on the way to Yudam-ni and the Marines on the ground cheered them on their way. The enemy continued sporadic rifle fire and Cafferatta was seriously wounded in the arm and chest. When he was carried to the first aid tent in the trees the wound he had received hours before from the grenade was discovered.

There were three hundred fifty dead Chinese before the positions of Peterson and McCarthy; Dunne's platoon and the headquarters section had accounted for another hundred. Twenty Marines had been killed and fifty-four wounded. The three missing men were not found.

Shortly after daylight Dunne organized a counterattack to retake the high ground lost the night before. Sergeants Daniel Slapinskas and Kenneth Kipp led their squads in the assault. Under light opposition the Marines gained the top and saw several enemy soldiers attempting to get a light machine gun into position. These were killed. Pfc.'s Wilson and Turnipseed, and Corporal Charles North grabbed the gun, two boxes of ammunition and ran along the saddle on the heels of the retreating Chinese. Many of the enemy threw away their weapons as they ran. The machine gun was set up and opened fire with excellent results. Positions were once more occupied on top of the hill and Dunne's men returned to their lines.

Though the attacks had ceased Barber was concerned over the shortage of ammunition. There were very few grenades left and O'Leary had but ten rounds of mortar shells remaining. Barber requested an air drop and an air strike on the rocky summit to the northwest. At 10:30 eight P-51's arrived over Fox Company and were directed to the target by a relay through Hagaru. Barber did not have the required radio equipment to speak directly to the pilots.

Again the Marines gave a cheer when they found out that the pilots overhead were Australians. After bombing and rocketing the ridge the Australians strafed the valley south of the road. Enemy fire ceased almost entirely after these air attacks.

Campbell got Read's battery registered in on targets about Fox Hill and throughout the day a harassing fire was put on suspected enemy concentrations and positions. While this was going on Dunne took a patrol to the high ground east of the hill. The unit came under sniper fire but returned without casualties.

The corpsmen, James Morrissey, James French and Mervyn Maurath, with the assistance of Technical Sergeant William Bunch and a detail of Marines from the headquarters section had set up two tents in the trees to use as an aid station. With nothing but the supplies in their field packs these men were to work the night through attending the wounded. During the night they had nothing but a guttering candle to work by and it was impossible to build a fire to warm water or rations. They had to hold morphine syrettes in their mouths to warm them sufficiently for use. The plasma was frozen and could not be thawed; several Marines died from its lack. Corpsmen Edward Jones and William McLean roamed the front lines seeing to the evacuation of wounded to the tents.

Soon the tents were filled. Holes were dug in the snow outside and men were placed in sleeping bags near the tents. A rotation system kept any from freezing to death. Those seriously wounded remained inside.

When the enemy fire died away after the air strike and artillery fire, the Marines on the line began to collect ammunition and weapons from the enemy dead. Before long most of the men in the rifle platoons were armed with extra weapons, either 03 Springfield rifles or Thompson submachine guns.

During the early afternoon Marine transport planes came overhead and dropped supplies and ammunition into the open space near the two native huts below the cut-bank. The drop was excellent.

Sergeant David Smith, company supply sergeant, took a detail to collect the bundles. As he was cutting the first bundle from its parachute a sniper hit him in the leg and broke it. Schmitt went out to rescue Smith. He too received a broken leg from the same sniper. Dunne took a fire team from his line and eliminated the enemy sharpshooter.

First Lieutenant Clark Wright, Barber's executive officer, formed a detail with Staff Sergeant Wayne Watson and the supplies were brought into the shelter of the trees.

As the second night came on Fox Company lines were substantially the same as the first though more lightly manned due to casualties. Many of the wounded left their sleeping bags in the aid tents and went to the lines to join their fire teams. Campbell, in constant communication with Read in Hagaru, called in harassing fires throughout the night. O'Leary, now in command of both the 60 and 81 mortars, directed the 60's onto the saddle and the 81's onto the rocky ridge.

The early part of the evening was quiet. Shortly after two o'clock in the morning enemy activity began. A spray of mortar shells landed in the Marine lines. Corporal Ashdale was wounded and two men were killed. Ashdale had his wounds dressed and returned to his squad. O'Leary opened up with his mortars and the enemy fire ceased.

The Chinese ground attack began with light probings on McCarthy's front; then they hit with great force on both flanks of his platoon. A penetration was effected and forty to fifty enemy troops moved down the hill and into positions behind Peterson's lines. There appeared to be some confusion among the Chinese. Instead of exploiting their success they congregated in a tight group and began talking and shouting. To add to the bedlam bugles were being blown. Peterson turned a light machine gun around and opened fire; McCarthy joined in from his direction. Few of the Chinese survived.

Barber came rushing up the hill to the critical spot and joined McCarthy as the 3rd Platoon was being shifted to new positions thirty yards down the hill. Both officers were hit in the legs by a burst of fire from the right flank. Staff Sergeant John Audas took command of the 3rd Platoon. Barber had his wound dressed and remained in action.

Peterson's platoon was under heavy attack along the length of its line but was able to keep the enemy from closing with the assistance of Read's artillery and O'Leary's mortars. Peterson was wounded for the second time. Once again he received first aid and returned to his unit. Corpsman Jones was killed as he helped a wounded Marine to safety.

Dunne's platoon had a comparatively easy time of it. The Chinese never pushed the attack in this area and when a squad did move through a gap in the upper end of the line between Dunne and McCarthy a light machine gun was turned and the group was annihilated.

At first light Audas led the 3rd Platoon in the attack and the top of the hill was reoccupied. Pomers was seriously wounded in the neck during the assault but remained with his fire team until the crest was secure. The second night of battle had cost Barber five killed and twenty-nine wounded.

Chinese casualties for the night were in excess of two hundred killed. The rest of the night was made hideous by the cries of pain from the enemy wounded. This continued until the early morning hours as one by one they froze to death.

Sniper fire continued throughout the early morning but despite this Barber (limping badly from his leg wound) saw to it that the open portion of Fox Hill was circled with the colored parachutes from the previous air drop. At 10:30 Marine transport planes were again overhead and began dropping supplies into the marked-off area. Their aim was nearly perfect.

Shortly after the air drop Engelhardt brought his helicopter into the circle with batteries for the radios. Immediately the enemy opened a heavy fire on the plane; a round went through the cockpit just missing the pilot; several other rounds hit the fuselage. To save the plane from further damage Engelhardt unloaded his cargo and took off. He got back to Hagaru without further incident.

During the afternoon further supplies were dropped by Flying Boxcars of the Air Force Cargo Command. To the dismay of the Marines they saw many of the 'chutes drop five to six hundred yards to the west of the perimeter. Peterson formed a recovery detail. Though wounded twice, he led the unit outside the lines. They arrived at the bundles without incident and were cutting the parachutes free when a heavy fire from the rocky ridge pinned them down.

O'Leary went into action with his mortars while Audas' platoon (vice McCarthy) brought down heavy fire on the Chinese positions. These countermeasures, however, did not halt the enemy fire. Peterson ordered his men to run back to the perimeter individually. Brady, who had been wounded in the hand the night before, had gone out with Peterson. When his turn came he clutched two rounds of 81 mm. ammunition under his sound arm as he would a football and began running a zigzag course back to the perimeter. To lustier cheers than he had ever received while playing football for Dartmouth he made a touchdown run to safety.

The rest of the detail made it back without suffering casualties. Barber decided that the supplies would have to remain outside the perimeter until dusk when another attempt would be made.

Previous drops had supplied enough blankets and stretchers to get the seriously wounded off the frozen ground. C rations were issued to the entire unit and Bunch (wounded in the hand) got a fire going and coffee was served to all hands. Those men who were lightly wounded returned to the lines while those who could move about the aid station assisted the corpsmen.

Dunne led a patrol to the south and east of the perimeter; two Chinese were killed and three escaped. No one on the patrol was wounded. In the late afternoon (forty-eight hours after arrival) Barber called a meeting of his platoon leaders and key NCO's.

He told them: "Here's the latest dope from division. The 5th and 7th Marines are heavily engaged at Yudam-ni. They've taken a hell of a lot of casualties. Last night the perimeter at Hagaru got hit hard. They're surrounded and cut off from Koto. Because of this there is no possible way that we can be relieved. We can expect even heavier attacks than we've had. Let's get booby traps and trip flares out front and button up. We have nothing to worry about if we fight like Marines."

The wounded on the stretchers heard the news and asked for Barber to come to them.

"Give us rifles and grenades, Cap'n. If the going gets tough we can make the line."

At dusk Barber borrowed Slapinskas' squad from Dunne and brought them to the rear of Peterson's lines.

"We've got to get that ammunition," Barber told the unit. "The rest of the outfit has been alerted that you're going out. They'll give you cover fire if you get in trouble. Pass through the lines as silently as possible and there'll be no talking. You'll go out unarmed so you'll have two hands for carrying. Return individually once you've got your bundle. If you get fired on hit the deck and stay doggo. If it's only sniper fire go on with your mission. If the fire becomes heavy work your way back at once."

Barber co-ordinated the movement through the lines with O'Leary's mortars blasting the rocky ridge and Read's artillery firing to the west of the parachutes. The detail received no enemy fire as it moved slowly beyond the lines. Ten men searched out ten bundles and returned. A second trip was made before all the ammunition had been retrieved.

Most of the bundles contained 60 mm. mortar shells, in addition to a supply of 81 mm. mortar illuminating shells and three cases of fragmentation grenades.

O'Leary was jubilant. "Let the bastards come on now—we'll light the area up like a county fair and really clobber them."

The early part of the night was quiet until two o'clock in the morning when the Marines on the lower part of the hill heard a voice calling in English: "Fox Company, you are surrounded. I am a lieutenant from the 11th Marines. The Chinese will give you warm clothing and good treatment. Surrender now!"

A machine gunner yelled, "Send up a flare so I can talk to the son-of-a-bitch."

O'Leary's mortars fired a brace of illumination shells and the gun opened fire. This was the last attempt the Chinese made to talk the Marines into surrender.

Thirty minutes later the Chinese attacked from the south. Two companies came from the valley across the road with fixed bayonets, satchel charges and concussion grenades. For the first time there was little or no firing as they advanced. Henry's heavy machine guns and the light guns from Peterson's unit turned the attack into a slaughter as O'Leary's illumination shells lighted the field of fire. As Staff Sergeant Wayne Watson called adjustments to O'Leary, Campbell brought Read's artillery down on the attackers with the fuses timed to explode overhead. Those of the enemy who gained the road sought cover under the bank; the Marine riflemen at the base of the hill rolled grenades into the huddled groups. Very few of the Chinese recrossed the road to the safety of the valley.

The morale of Fox Company rose with the sun. Technical Sergeant Charles Dana built a large fire and coffee was made for everyone. Most of the Marines were able to heat their rations over individual fires. There was considerable joking and good-natured joshing among the men on the line.

"This is a hell of a war! Didn't fire my rifle enough last night to even warm my hands."

"Those Chinks have shot their load. Look at 'em out there—I counted fifty dead without moving my head."

By this time Barber was hobbling about the perimeter with the greatest difficulty. When he sat down he had to be helped to his feet, yet he continued to make his rounds and direct the action of the unit. When sniper fire started again from the rocky ridge he requested an air strike. Four Corsairs from Coles' Checkerboard Squadron arrived a few minutes later.

Once the target was identified to the satisfaction of the flight leader the Corsairs began the strike; the first plane strafed and rocketed the ridge, the second planted a five-hundred-pound bomb onto it while the third burned it out with napalm. In a matter of minutes the ridge was covered with a pall of smoke and flames.

The ground Marines gaped at the low-level attack. "Look't those guys —they all must be bachelors."

"If they ain't their wives'll be widows."

"If that one guy comes in any lower he'll be chopping kindling with his propeller."

Later the same planes worked over the valley to the south from whence the previous night attack had come. When the Corsairs were emptied of armament they flew in tight circles about Fox Hill while the pilots waved and waggled the wings of their planes. Every man of Fox Company able to get to his feet stood and cheered.

Another drop was scheduled for late afternoon. While the unit was waiting for this, Farish brought his helicopter in with replacement batteries for the radios. As with Engelhardt, the enemy opened fire on the plane. Farish delivered his cargo and took off.

The air drop was not made until just before dark. As the cargo plane circled overhead the Marines were requested to turn on their flashlights to guide the pilot. This was done but the drop was made too soon and the supplies landed some eight hundred yards east of Dunne's positions. Once again Slapinskas' squad went out on a retrieving mission which was accomplished without incident. For the first time since establishing positions on Fox Hill, Barber was free of concern over his ammunition reserve.

It began to snow heavily shortly after the air drop was secured; in the next four hours three inches of fresh snow blanketed the hills. The temperature continued to remain in the neighborhood of twenty degrees below zero. There were ample medical supplies and blankets now, and the wounded began to joke among themselves that if they didn't get evacuated soon they would be returned to duty before they got to a hospital.

During the heavy snowfall the enemy moved four machine guns onto the rocky ridge. Shortly after one o'clock these guns opened fire. Barber took instant and effective countermeasures.

Campbell was directed to make arrangements with Read to deliver fire on the ridge. O'Leary was to co-ordinate his mortar fire so that he would illuminate the area as the artillery shells exploded. Sergeant Clyde Pitts, of Audas' platoon, was to make the necessary adjustments for the battery from a forward position. All was in readiness; Pitts had his binoculars fastened on the target; O'Leary had illuminating shells ready to drop into the mortar tubes; Read reported to Campbell: "Four guns ready to fire."

Campbell looked at Barber and the unit commander said, "Okay."

Campbell spoke into the radio. "Fire."

Read answered back, "Four rounds on the way."

Barber told O'Leary, "Fire."

Two rounds of illumination burst as the artillery shells exploded. O'Leary fired four more rounds. The ridge was bathed in a brilliant light. Barber waited for Pitts to request an adjustment but all he heard was "wonderful, lovely, beautiful."

Barber shouted over the phone, "What about those machine guns?"

Pitts curbed his ecstasy over the sight before him. "They're gone. Beautiful shooting. Wiped 'em out."

Campbell told Read, "Cease fire, target destroyed, mission completed."

Read answered, "Say again all after 'cease fire.'"

"Target destroyed, mission completed," Campbell repeated.

It was difficult for Read to believe that his battery had wiped out a target on the first salvo at a range of six miles. There was no further enemy action that night.

After a night of comparative ease Barber had no desire to see his troops become slack from inaction. The day of December 1 was spent cleaning up the company area; ration cans and trash were buried in holes and the equipment of the casualties was placed in a central area to the rear of the headquarters section. The dead were placed in rows on the top of the bank and covered with ponchos.

During the morning eight Corsairs from Wyczawski's squadron arrived on station and began working over the rocky ridge again. It appeared to the ground Marines that these planes were attempting to outdo the squadron of the day before. Once again the ridge was a mass of flames. The strike was called off temporarily to allow an air drop by Air Force Flying Boxcars. Most of the bundles hit the target inside the perimeter but a few floated to the front of Dunne's positions.

At the request of Barber the orbiting Corsairs strafed and rocketed the hills to the south and east of the company positions while the supplies were recovered. Under this low-flying air cover the bundles were retrieved without an enemy shot being fired at the detail.

Dunne took a patrol to the ridge north of Fox Hill in the early afternoon. As the unit began to move west toward the rocky ridge they came under heavy fire; despite supporting fires from the mortars and Audas' 3rd Platoon Dunne's unit could not move forward. Wright, who was directing the supporting fire, was hit twice by small-arms fire. Dunne was forced to withdraw. One Marine was killed and four wounded on the patrol.

Despite the constant air-artillery-mortar fire poured into the ridge the enemy was able to remain in position due to the fact they had dug deep caves in which they hid during the heavier attacks.

That night (December 1-2) the enemy action was limited to long-range sniper fire. By now the morale of the beleaguered unit had reached such a pitch that it was a disappointment when the enemy failed to attack.

In the meantime Barber had been alerted that Davis' 1st Battalion was moving overland from Yudam-ni to effect a relief. As Davis neared the area Barber warned him that the rocky ridge was still held in considerable strength. Reflecting the spirit of his men Barber added that if the 1st Battalion required assistance Fox Company was ready and willing.

At 11:25 in the morning the 1st Battalion 7th Marines came onto Fox Hill. This epic, cross-country move will be dealt with later.

During the five days and nights Barber's unit held out against overwhelming odds, twenty-six Marines had been killed and eighty-nine wounded. Three Marines were missing in action. Though a search was made of the area their bodies were never found. Six of the seven company officers had been wounded.

Upon reading the accounts of these small unit actions of the Marines from Pusan to Chosin, the civilian (and many in the military who have not experienced battle) may well ask what held the men of Barber's company to the line in the face of hopeless odds. What force was capable of instilling within each man a spirit where "uncommon valor became a common virtue?"

The unthinking will say it was love of home and country. The stupid politician will say they were fighting for a free world. The sheltered clergyman will say they were fighting to preserve the Christian way of life. None of these pat phrases come close.

The fire of patriotism dies quickly. It is cold by the time the band stops playing and the flags are furled and the voice of the cheering multitude are faint in the distance. By the time the rifleman gets to the battlefield all the fanfare and cheering is forgotten. About all that remains is a suspicion that the hysteria of the send-off was manufactured so that the stay-at-homes would buy another bond or give another pint of blood.

The men of Barber's company were not kept in the line of fire by patriotism.

Loyalty to their military legion kept the men of Fox Company to the stern task of killing when death to themselves was close and almost certain. It is the only force potent enough to overcome the instinct of self-preservation. *Esprit de corps* held the Marines to their posts though the phrase has been vulgarized and the services robbed of much of it by meddlers who don't know its meaning.

The news of the Eighth Army defeat and the crisis facing the Marines was received by the American civilian population with shocked dismay. The newspapers were filled with black headlines and the word "trapped" was constantly used. The Marines resented the word when applied to the division for it had a connotation of having been caught unawares. In Washington long-distance lines were flooded with calls to Headquarters Marine Corps by worried parents: "What is the true situation? —I haven't heard from my boy for over two weeks!—Is it true the division has been annihilated and the news is to be let out slowly?—Why don't you do something about the situation?—If the Army won't help them why don't you send the 2nd Marine Division over and get them out?"

To these thousands of calls Marine spokesmen answered: "The situation is serious but not hopeless!—The Marines have been in precarious positions before but they have always gotten out!—There are over twenty thousand Marines on the reservoir and they will fight their way back!"

In Tokyo Admiral Joy prepared a dispatch to the chief of naval operations: "Request General Shepherd be ordered this theater earliest . . ."

The day before this dispatch arrived in Pearl Harbor, Colonel Victor (Brute) Krulak, operations officer for Shepherd, departed for Washington. Arriving in San Francisco at noon, Krulak was in Washington the following day. A dispatch was waiting him from Shepherd: "Join me earliest Korea."

Four hours later Krulak was on another plane headed for the west. Flying by the way of San Francisco, Honolulu, Wake Island and Tokyo, Krulak joined Shepherd in Hungnam seventy-two hours later. Elapsed time from Honolulu to Hungnam, Korea via Washington: one hundred and six hours.

At Camp Del Mar, Oceanside, California, Headquarters for the Training and Replacement Command, Brigadier General Merrill Twining was at his desk when his aide entered the room.

"General, a flash has just come over the radio that the Chinese have the 1st Marine Division surrounded."

Twining looked up from his papers. "All I can say, young man, is that I'm damned sorry for those Chinamen."

In Korea General Smith relieved the anguished minds of thousands of parents and millions of Americans when he said, confidently, "Retreat, hell! We're only attacking in another direction."

CHAPTER XX

The Battle for Survival: Every Man a Rifleman

The engagements around Yudam-ni on the night of the twenty-seventh of November have been dealt with to the exclusion of the activities at Hagaru and Koto. On the night of the onfall against the Marines north of Toktong Pass, there was little or no enemy activity at Hagaru or Koto. General Sun had intended to place all three sectors under attack simultaneously but was thwarted by time and space and Marine air. The Chinese troops assigned to attack the two southern perimeters were unable to get into position in time. Numerous roadblocks, however, were set up between Koto and Hagaru as well as Hagaru and Yudam-ni.

As far south as Chinhung-ni Schmuck's unit contacted a platoon-sized enemy patrol, but the Chinese withdrew as the Marines opened fire. At Koto Fredrick's company sighted enemy units on the high ground to the north. A platoon-sized patrol engaged the Chinese. A second platoon had to be dispatched to assist the first before the fire fight was resolved. More enemy troops were sighted moving on Koto from the south and west. Air sightings reported numerous groups of twenty-five to thirty enemy troops moving south on either side of the perimeter.

Air strikes in conjunction with McClelland's artillery fire were brought down on these troops with excellent results yet the encircling movement continued. An Army observation plane reported that two bridges had been destroyed and eight roadblocks established between Koto and Hagaru.

In the early afternoon a motorized patrol was formed from Cronk's company. The mission of this unit was to open the road to Hagaru. Fifteen hundred yards north of the Marine positions the patrol came under small-arms and mortar fire. Cronk sent two platoons into the assault to clear the ridge east of the road of enemy troops. The assault was supported by artillery fire and air strikes.

By three o'clock in the afternoon Cronk was heavily engaged with his entire unit. Fredrick sent a platoon forward to assist in evacuating Cronk's wounded. When it became apparent the enemy were in such strength that they could not be routed by one company Sutter ordered the patrol to withdraw. Cronk had suffered five killed and twenty-nine wounded.

The road south to Chinhung-ni was still open and during the day friendly units came up the hill. Among these were three companies from the Army 185th Engineer Battalion; Company E of the 1st Medical Battalion; Baker Company of the 31st Army Infantry Regiment; the 41st Royal Marine Commando; Sitter's George Company and the Division Recon Company. Puller utilized these units to strengthen the Koto perimeter. As darkness came the enemy established roadblocks between Koto and Chinhung-ni.

At a meeting with correspondents Puller told the newsmen: "We've been looking for the enemy for several days now. We've finally found them. We're surrounded. That simplifies our problem of finding these people and killing them."

At Hagaru, Ridge was faced with defending a large perimeter with only two companies of infantry. While at Majon-ni the commander of the 3rd Battalion had screened and selected twelve South Koreans to serve as counterintelligence agents. Upon arrival at Hagaru, Ridge sent these men into the surrounding territory. They returned within twenty-four hours and their reports were uniform: "A division of enemy Chinese are moving south and will attack the Hagaru perimeter at 9:30 on the evening of the twenty-eighth."

Ridge went to Bowser (division operations officer) and reported his findings. Immediate steps were taken to form a perimeter defense with a heterogeneous mixture of troops manning positions on the line which could not be covered by Ridge's two rifle companies. The general emplacement of these bobtailed outfits can be found by referring to the Yudam-ni–Hagaru map. Points A, B and C were positioned by H & S Company of the 3rd Battalion; H & S Company of the 1st Marine Division; TAC Reconnaissance Group of the 1st Marine Division; the Motor Transport Battalion and Regulating Detachment of the 1st Service Battalion filled in the rest of the line to C. How Battery of the 11th Marines and the Antitank Company of the 7th Marines occupied positions to the juncture of C and D. The hills to the east of the town (D) were manned by Army detachments from X Corps made up of units from H & S Battalion, Engineer Battalion and the Signal Battalion.

Manning the roadblock and bridge at the juncture of sector D and E was the Weapons Company of Ridge's Battalion. First Lieutenant Joe Fisher's Item Company covered H sector and to his left was Corley's How Company.

Due to the terrain and intelligence information received, Ridge reached the decision that the enemy attack would come from the south. He placed his two rifle companies in line where the expected attack would strike the hardest.

It was a complicated and difficult task to form the noncombat troops into line units, establish sectors of defense, zones of fire and set up communications, distribute supporting weapons and place reserve stocks of ammunition. By nightfall on the twenty-eighth the perimeter had been established, a mobile reserve formed, and the troops settled down to await the onfall.

Ridge's counterintelligence natives were correct to the day and strength of the enemy. The attack began one hour later than reported. Second Lieutenant Richard Carey (Ridge's intelligence officer) explained the time differential by stating that perhaps the Chinese, being night fighters, were not on daylight saving time.

Because of the front to be covered by the rifle companies Corley had to place his three platoons in the line. Barrett's unit was positioned on the right flank, Goss in the middle with Endsley on the left. With Betts' machine guns and Snelling's mortars in support and the artillery registered in so they could fire in any direction, the riflemen crawled into their holes.

It began to snow shortly after dark and by nine o'clock two inches covered the icy crust of previous falls. Visibility was hampered but the riflemen gained a certain warmth from the snow covering. Twenty minutes before the ground attack the Marine lines were taken under heavy fire by enemy artillery and mortars. Considerable numbers of white phosphorous shells were used and heavy casualties were being taken. Even while the Marine lines were under fire the enemy infantry crept within grenade range and as the artillery and mortars lifted the hand explosives began to blast.

The attack which followed was heavy and violent. Goss' line was driven back and his right flank turned. A penetration was made which threatened Corley's CP. Goss rushed to the threatened flank with five men; he was killed. Barrett's line held except for his left flank positions. Two of these were overrun and Pfc. Charles Monroe was blown from his hole by a grenade. Knocked unconscious by the shock, Monroe quickly recovered and retrieving his BAR opened fire from an exposed position. Dazed and bleeding he continued to pour fire into the enemy ranks and the further penetration in this sector was stemmed.

As soon as Ridge was notified of the breakthrough he dispatched a fifty-man unit to Corley under the command of First Lieutenant Grady Mitchell. The reinforcements dulled the initial drive but only after heavy casualties. Mitchell was killed. By now the enemy held fire superiority and their buildup of strength was rapid.

First Lieutenant Horace Johnson (Corley's executive officer) ran across a field of heavy fire to the battalion CP for more reinforcements. To the extreme left Endsley's platoon came to heavy action especially on the flank which tied in with Goss. Endsley rushed to the squad in trouble and called down mortar fire which stemmed the enemy tide temporarily. While reorganizing his unit into new positions he was fatally wounded.

When the initial enemy attack broke through First Lieutenant Harrison Betts was at the company CP unloading ammunition for his machine guns from a jeep trailer. A white phosphorous shell landed near by and many of the Marines were wounded. With the help of Technical Sergeant Robert Barnes, Betts re-formed the group and led them in an attack on a native house in the zone held by the remnants of Goss' platoon. Thirty Marines began the attack with Betts and Barnes. Two more white phosphorous shells wounded all but eight. Betts continued the attack. By the time he reached the native hut all had been wounded but himself. Dragging the men inside Betts began to rove the outside to protect the Marines within. He held this position until the daylight counterattack restored the lines. During this three-hour vigil he killed nine Chinese and wounded several others.

It was apparent from the first artillery and mortar shelling that the enemy were aware of the positions held by Second Lieutenant Edward Snelling's mortar platoon. Despite the savage fire poured onto his unit, Snelling continued to direct the fire of his weapons in support of the hard-pressed riflemen. Assisted by Sergeant Nicholas Federspiel, Snelling moved his weapons to new positions and continued to fire.

A jeep and trailer loaded with mortar shells came forward from the central dump. In the darkness and confusion of battle, the driver of the vehicle overshot his mark and drove into enemy-held territory. Taken under heavy fire he was forced to abandon the jeep. Hampered by the snow, Snelling ran, in the face of the heaviest sort of enemy fire, to the vehicle and drove it back to his mortar positions; during the engagement Snelling's men fired twelve hundred rounds.

Johnson, who had gone back to the battalion CP for reinforcements, was given another fifty men by Ridge. Quickly organizing a small force into squads, Johnson led them forward. Contact was made with Corley and limited objectives were taken to seal off the penetration. A piece of shrapnel struck Johnson's helmet knocking him down. Dazed, he regained his feet and continued to move from position to position as he sought to strengthen the line. Corley was also wounded but continued in action.

On Corley's right flank, Fisher's company met the attack with stubborn resolution. Second Lieutenant Robert Needham's platoon became heavily and closely engaged. Wire communications with the supporting tanks were severed. Needham's runner, Pfc. Ronald Levasseur ran across an open stretch of ground to deliver a message to the tankers. He returned to Needham. Both crossings were made under heavy fire. When not delivering messages, Levasseur remained in the lines firing at the Chinese. So that he could detect the enemy better, he fired from a standing position. He saw a Chinese rush forward and drop into a vacated foxhole. Levasseur killed him with a grenade.

Once again it became imperative that another message be delivered to the tanks. Levasseur volunteered. He was killed as he crossed the fire-swept ground to the rear.

Throughout the savage attack, Fisher roved the front lines calling down mortar fire and encouraging his men by a fearless example. His unit held their positions without allowing a penetration.

Three hours after the enemy launched their attack on the southern and western rim of the Hagaru perimeter, the attack withered as the Chinese sustained exorbitant losses; at daybreak seven hundred fifty dead were *counted* before the positions of Fisher and Corley. A later counter-attack regained the hut where Betts was on his lone vigil guarding the wounded.

East of Hagaru in sector D the hills rose sharply from the road. Ice and snow covered, it was very nearly impossible to scale them. Ridge had stationed detachments from three Army units on this line. To oversee and report from that sector, Captain John Shelnutt was assigned to the Army unit. The radio operator with him was Pfc. Bruno Podolak. At two o'clock in the morning, Shelnutt reported to Ridge that the Army Engineer Unit was under heavy attack and being forced to withdraw. Thirty minutes later Podolak reported that Shelnutt had been killed and that due to his heavy equipment he had been unable to get down the hill with the Army unit. Podolak told Ridge he would hide out in a hole and report from time to time on the enemy strength and intentions.

Ridge directed his executive officer Myers to form the remaining men from the mobile reserve and to retake the hill at all costs. At this time there were but twenty Marines in the reserve. Gathering these men together Myers led them to the road and ditch at the base of the hill. Considerable confusion existed among the troops which had been expelled from the crest line, and it was some time before Myers could effect a reorganization for the counterattack. Accompanying Myers as a radio operator was Corporal J. D. Mitchell. While forming a skirmish line, tank and mortar fire was laid down on the hilltop. Podolak informed Myers the enemy held the hill in battalion strength.

With energy and resolution, Myers instilled in his composite group a spirit that would make them face the almost impossible task of retaking the hill. It was 3:15 in the morning before the preparatory fires had been registered in and the word for the attack given. Slipping, falling, crawling, the thin skirmish line began the steep six-hundred-foot ascent of the icy hill. Again and again Myers and Mitchell moved back and forth along the line, with Myers shouting encouragement to the leaders and prodding the laggards. Lieutenants Burke, Dunning and Miller followed his example and kept the line moving upward.

Of the three hundred fifteen men who began the attack, but seventy-five reached the crest. En route Podolak was picked up and he continued to serve Myers with his radio until he was shot in the back. The bullet penetrated the radio set before it struck him, thus saving his life. In spite of his wound, Podolak continued in action. A thin defensive line was formed just below the crest of the hill as a cover against an enemy machine gun which was positioned on their left flank. Shortly after daylight, a Marine air strike was brought in and the enemy machine-gun position was destroyed. Myers informed Ridge he had but sixty Marines and fifteen Army personnel on the hill. Ridge attempted to relieve the pressure on Myers by directing Lieutenant Norman Foster (Signal Battalion officer) to lead an attack up a draw to the left of the positions held by Myers' group. Foster got his men nearly to the top when they were pinned down by heavy fire from the north. Another attack group was formed and sent up another corridor to the left of Foster's. This attack also failed.

As the day wore on and no further reinforcements had reached Myers on the top of the hill, he was forced to move his unit back and down on the reverse slope where they dug in at the edge of the brush above the road. These positions were maintained through the day and night.

The morning of the twenty-ninth found the Hagaru defense line intact in all sectors save for the new line established by Myers at the base of the hill. During the night-long battle, the Hagaru defenders had suffered in excess of five hundred casualties. It was obvious reinforcements would have to be gotten in from the south if the perimeter was to be held.

One of the imponderables of this engagement was the enemy use of mortars and artillery. With the interior of the perimeter jammed with trucks, supplies, hospital and service personnel, the Chinese could have inflicted terrific damage and casualties had they lifted their fire. Instead they continued to pound the immediate front lines where the units were dug in. The casualties, as a result, were much lighter than they would have been. Two hospitals were in operation inside the perimeter. Commander Streit had his medical company established in a school building not more than three hundred yards from the front lines. Throughout the night small-arms fire came through the wards. Streit took steps to keep the wounded in his building at a minimum by evacuating them to Halloway's hospital in the center of the town.

To clear the road between Koto and to reinforce Hagaru, Puller organized "Task Force Drysdale," named for Lieutenant Colonel Douglas Drysdale, Royal Marine Commando, who was to command the composite unit moving north.

The 41st Independent Commando, Royal Marines, was formed in August and flew from England to Japan on the first of September. The unit went into training at Camp McGill and subsequently made three raids on enemy rail lines along the east coast of Korea. As the United Nations forces advanced along both coasts in November, targets for

Commando raids became scarce. In mid-November Drysdale received orders to report for duty with the 1st Marine Division. It was the intention of the Marines to use the Royal Marines as an additional reconnaissance company.

The Drysdale unit arrived in Hungnam in the middle of November. After a short period of cold-weather training the Commando was ordered to join Litzenberg. Drysdale departed Hungnam in advance of his unit on the twenty-eighth of November. North of Kojo he found the road blocked and a convoy under fire. He returned to Kojo and reported to Puller. Smith was contacted and Drysdale was given the assignment of breaking from the Kojo perimeter and fighting through the enemy roadblocks to Hagaru.

"Task Force Drysdale" was to be made up of the 41st Commando, Sitter's George Company and Captain Charles Peckham's Baker Company of the 31st Army RCT en route to join its parent battalion on the east shore of the reservoir. In trace of the combat units would be a truck convoy under Major Henry Seeley and odds and ends of other units moving north. The vehicular train would number more than a hundred units.

Drysdale made a recce along the road to the north just before dark. Returning to the perimeter he called a meeting of unit commanders and gave his orders. The next morning, at first light, Drysdale made another reconnaissance along the road. Upon returning he gave his final orders for the breakthrough.

The 41st Commando would take the first hill to the east of the road; Sitter would take the second; the Army unit would remain on the road and parallel the progress of the two Marine units as the high ground was secured. The attack on the key terrain features would be preceded by a thirty-minute artillery bombardment followed by an air strike.

The day was misty with flurries of snow cutting down visibility which delayed the arrival of the planes. The artillery preparation was laid on as scheduled and the Corsairs came in just before nine o'clock; the Commando departed the Kojo perimeter at nine and took the first objective against light opposition.

Under orders from Drysdale, Sitter followed in trace of the Commando by three hundred yards. Once the British Marines had secured their objective Sitter pushed on past in the attack on the second. With Hopkins' platoon abreast of Jaeger's, the two assault units moved from the high ground into a valley and began the climb to their objective. The Marines came under enemy fire from the right front. Staff Sergeant Gerald Tillman was seriously wounded, as was Corpsman Dan Clark. In a short time, fourteen casualties had been suffered.

Chaplain James Lewis and regimental dentist, Lieutenant (jg) Charles Fain took charge of evacuating the wounded back to Koto. Before Hopkins and Jaeger could seize the second objective, rocket launchers had to be brought forward to be fired against an enemy machine-gun emplacement. When this position was destroyed the ridge was seized. The Commando passed to the left of Sitter and secured the next ridge to the north. At this time radio communications between Drysdale and Sitter failed.

It soon became apparent that the enemy were entrenched along the route in far greater numbers than had been anticipated. Three and a half hours after the jump-off the task force had advanced but two miles with eight more to go. Drysdale reported to Puller by radio and was informed that tanks were on their way to reinforce him.

At 1:30 in the afternoon Captain Bruce Clarke arrived with eight tanks. It was Drysdale's idea to feed the tanks throughout the column of trucks but Clarke resisted this plan. Inasmuch as the command relationship between the task force commander and the tank commander had not been established Drysdale acceded to Clarke's wishes and the tanks took to the head of the column in a group.

Four hours had now passed with but two miles gained. It was obvious that hill-by-hill attack could not be made. It was decided to depend on the tanks and close air support to keep the flanks clear while the task force shoved through as rapidly as possible on trucks.

Drysdale sent a runner to Sitter with instructions to bring his unit from the high ground and entruck them. The new formation for the advance along the road would have the Army unit behind the tanks with Sitter in trace and the 41st Commando covering the rear.

It was two o'clock before the column moved out again; almost immediately it began receiving fire from the right side of the road. The tanks halted to answer. When the column stopped the Army troops deployed in the ditches alongside the road. Casualties were being taken. Sitter worked his way by the column of stalled vehicles and joined the tanks. A bridge had been destroyed to the front and the enemy were covering the roadblock from a group of native houses to the right of the road. The tanks destroyed the houses and the fire subsided.

In the meantime, First Lieutenant Charles Merrill (Sitter's executive officer) had brought George Company forward and passing through the

Army unit assumed the lead in the column. The tanks made a foray up the road by using a by-pass around the destroyed bridge. They returned and Clarke reported to Drysdale that the tanks could make Hagaru but he did not believe the trucks could get through. Drysdale decided to push on.

The tanks refueled and once again the column began to move northward. The alignment behind the tanks was this: Sitter's unit, the Commando, the Army company and Seeley's transport vehicles.

A short distance south of Pusong-ni (a village less than four miles from Koto) the road passed through a narrow defile. A high bluff commanded this restricted passageway and the enemy had selected this site to block further movement northward; besides a debris block in the road, machine guns and mortars were positioned on the bluff. Once again the tanks halted to take the enemy under fire and once again the vehicular train was forced to stop and the troops detruck. Mortar fire began blasting the area and casualties mounted.

By this time all the radio in the column had been shot out and control was being lost because of lack of communications. To add to the plight of the force it began to grow dark. Clarke's tank radio was still operative and he informed Puller of the situation; Puller in turn got in touch with Smith. Because of the critical need for reinforcements in Hagaru, Drysdale was directed to push through at all costs.

Lieutenant Dennis Goodchild, Drysdale's adjutant, was wounded as he went along the side of the road under heavy fire to contact Clarke. Second Lieutenant James Crutchfield, Sitter's machine-gun officer was wounded. Sitter's jeep was knocked out and Merrill was wounded. Drysdale was hit. As Pfc. William Baugh's squad from the Anti Tank Assault Platoon was disembarking to assume defensive positions, an enemy grenade was hurled into the truck. Baugh shouted: "Grenade!" and threw his body over the explosive. None of the other Marines in the truck was injured, but Baugh died a short time later from his wounds.

As the column formed to move again, Drysdale's original plan was followed by feeding the tanks into Sitter's vehicular train at intervals. By now it was dark and the Marines could look to the north and see the lights on the air strip at Hagaru. The lead tank destroyed an enemy machine-gun position on the railway embankment, and with the other tanks firing their machine guns to the right and left movement was restored.

The tanks and Sitter's unit forced a passage and after suffering heavy casualties gained the Hagaru perimeter. Once the Pershings and Sitter had slipped by, the enemy closed in on the Commandos. A mortar shell hit an ammunition truck at the end of the Commando column. The resultant blast formed a roadblock which separated the Commandos from the Army company and Seeley's convoy. The enemy had achieved their basic aim—to fractionalize the column. The next step was to destroy the fractions.

Lieutenant Douglas Knock, Royal Marine surgeon, was killed and Captain Parkinson-Curnine, with twenty-two of his troop, was cut off and surrounded. Captain Leslie Marsh, Commando troop leader was wounded as was Major Dennis Aldridge. Both men remained in action.

Taking extreme casualties the Royal Marines continued to fight through the narrow cut. The Commandos cleared the road and pushed on. Three more roadblocks were met and overcome. At 1:30 in the morning (sixteen and a half hours from Koto) the Royal Marines entered the perimeter at Hagaru. Corporal Cruse and six Commandos had been cut off at the last roadblock but gained friendly lines by fighting their way through three enemy positions.

Drysdale's Marines had lost fifty per cent of their number. Later, when there was time, Smith wrote Drysdale: "I can give you no higher compliment than to state that your conduct and that of your officers and men under your command was worthy of the highest traditions of Marines."

The exploding ammunition truck to the rear of the Commando forced the long train of vehicles to halt. The troops scrambled out and took up defensive positions. There was excessive confusion because of the mixed nature of the men in this section of the convoy; there were the drivers from Seeley's trucks, a detachment from the Division Military Police Company, mail clerks, liaison groups and odds and ends of other sections from division headquarters.

The roadway where the vehicular train came to a halt formed a gentle S and was approximately halfway between Koto and Hagaru. To the left (west) was a shallow ditch and beyond the ditch rice paddies to the banks of the Changjin River. From the road to the river was a distance of three hundred yards. Beyond the river were the sharp-rising mountains.

Bordering the road on the right (east) was a deep ditch. Beyond this drainageway was a level space of ground of one hundred fifty yards and then the Sinhung railroad track. East of the track was another ditch and beyond this a plateau some twenty to thirty feet higher than the road. Upon this plateau the Chinese had taken positions with machine guns and mortars. The mountains rose sharply at the back of the plateau.

With such a heterogeneous group, control and cohesiveness was virtually impossible. Certain officers and NCO's rose to the occasion and, acting independently with the men immediately available, set up hurried defensive lines. Warrant Officer Lloyd Dirst and Technical Sergeant Kubiak of the Military Police Detachment formed a group and occupied positions in the ditch facing on the plateau. Ignoring the enemy fire Dirst and Kubiak walked the road along the lines handing out ammunition and directing the fire of the MP's.

At the north end of the line Lieutenant Colonel Arthur Chidester and Major John McLaughlin formed a line which covered the road leading down from Hagaru. Major James Eagan collected some men and got them into position on the railway embankment. Eagan was wounded and captured with most of his men. Chidester was wounded. McLaughlin took command of all troops, including Peckham's Army unit, in his sector of the hastily formed perimeter. First Lieutenant Herbert Turner had swung his platoon of tanks into line behind Seeley's trucks. When movement forward ceased Turner left his tank and went forward to investigate.

On the southern circle of the perimeter Seeley rallied his truck drivers into a line which tied in with Dirst. The road between Seeley's position and Koto was cut. The convoy was surrounded. The enemy then pushed across the road separating Seeley and McLaughlin.

As the casualties began to mount an interior perimeter was set up in the larger ditch to the right of the road to haven the wounded; Sergeant James Nash went across the open space and across the railroad tracks to bring back several wounded. By this time it was dark and a ring of fire encompassed the beleaguered unit.

In the meantime the Chinese had brought up more machine guns and had emplaced mortars in the rice paddy near the river and another on the plateau on the right. Strangely enough the enemy made no concerted attempt to destroy the vehicles in the long line. A jeep and three trucks at the head of the column were set afire. After that enemy mortar fire was desultory. Positions were taken by Chinese riflemen on the right and left rear flanks which permitted firing into and along the ditch where the wounded lay.

At the beginning there had been much promiscuous firing by the defenders until the ammunition began to run low and certain control had been established. The enemy appeared in no hurry to press the attack and wipe out the unit. Rather, they remained within medium small-arms range while individuals and small groups of two and three worked in close to hurl grenades.

At the rear of the perimeter Seeley's men were withstanding the fight and infiltrators in better condition than the rest of the sector. This is explained largely by the fact that Seeley knew most of the men and NCO's in his sector and his orders were followed with more resolution. When the Chinese forced a penetration between Seeley and McLaughlin, Seeley moved his men from the road to more defensible positions along the river bank.

By three o'clock in the morning many of McLaughlin's men were out of ammunition and there was a constant redistribution of the remaining rounds. Dirst, walking the road to oversee the defenses, received a serious head wound. Nash, who was already wounded, rushed from the shelter of the ditch and pulled Dirst off the road. Two unknown Marines turned a jeep about and attempted to run the gauntlet back to Koto for more ammunition. They were captured; the Chinese took them east of the road where there were more Americans.

A Chinese officer who spoke English told the prisoners he wanted someone to go to the perimeter and tell the officer in charge that surrender terms would be discussed.

Sergeant Guillermo Tovar, who had been captured with Eagan, volunteered to carry on the negotiations. Accompanied by three Chinese officers Tovar approached the lines in the area controlled by McLaughlin.

After considerable shouting back and forth Tovar identified himself and passed through the lines and talked with McLaughlin. The Marine officer told Tovar to return to the negotiators and bring them to the railway for a parley.

Another huddle while an answer was reached. Finally the interpreter said: "You surrender. You lay down your arms and the wounded can go back."

"I'll have to talk to my people." McLaughlin returned to the ditch where the wounded were collected. He found Chidester. "The Chinese have told me they'll let us send the wounded back to Koto if the rest will lay down their arms."

"Do you think we can trust them?" Chidester asked.

"It's a chance we'll have to take if we decide to give up."

"How much ammunition left?"

"Not much. Not more than two clips a man."

"I don't see what else you can do, Mac."

"We'll have to contact Pop Seeley."

McLaughlin returned to the Chinese. "I'll have to talk to the officer commanding the southern sector."

The negotiators showed a certain impatience at the delay but finally agreed. McLaughlin turned to Tovar. "Contact Major Seeley. Tell him to come up and talk with these people. Take your time."

Tovar walked along the shoulder of the road past the long line of vehicles. Toward the end of the column he began to shout: "Major Seeley—Major Seeley."

McLaughlin's final instructions to Tovar were: "Take your time. Stall as long as you can. Maybe we can hold out until daylight and get some Marine air in to help us."

As Tovar went back over the railroad embankment McLaughlin passed the word to cease fire. Slowly the order was transmitted from position to position and the cold, bitter night became silent save for desultory firing from Seeley's sector.

Tovar returned with the Chinese and the English-speaking officer told McLaughlin: "We have you surrounded. There are many of us. We have killed and wounded many of you. We will kill all of you if you fight on. You must surrender."

McLaughlin took his time in answering. Finally he asked, "What about my wounded? What happens to them? We must get them out of the cold or they will die."

The Chinese huddled over the question. After a time the English-speaking one said, "We will take care of your wounded."

McLaughlin shook his head. "We must send our wounded to Koto." He pointed to the south. "We are not surrendering because you can beat us. We are surrendering to get our wounded cared for. If we can't get our wounded evacuated we will fight on."

"Hold your fire," Seeley shouted. After some time the Marine fire subsided. "Who are you?"

"Sergeant Tovar—MP Company—Major McLaughlin sent me."

The two met in the rice paddy and Seeley was informed what had transpired at the head of the column. Seeley had forty-four men left and enough ammunition to hold out until daylight. Before departing for the conference he instructed two junior officers, "Hold fast in these positions. I'll stall as long as I can. If we can hold out until daylight, we can chase these bastards out of here with Marine air."

Seeley moved across the road with his guide and joined the Chinese to the north of the road where Eagan lay.

"How are you, Jim?" Seeley asked.

"They got me in the legs, Pop."

"What do you think of this surrender business?"

"We've got our wounded to think of," Eagan answered. "They can't live out here very long in this weather."

"I don't believe they'll ever send them back to Koto. My unit's not out of ammo. I think we can stall and hold out until daylight. I'm not going to surrender."

Seeley joined the Chinese. The surrender terms were explained in sign language inasmuch as the English-speaking officer had remained with McLaughlin. The sign language used by the Chinese was simple, graphic; one of them pointed at Seeley, threw his weapon onto the ground and raised his hands above his head. He then pointed at his watch and held up three fingers.

Seeley appeared not to understand. The gestures were repeated with some impatience. At the conclusion of this demonstration the officer held up two fingers.

"I don't think you can stall much longer, Major," Tovar said.

"Hold them off as long as you can while I get back to my outfit and get dug in better. Tell Major McLaughlin that I'm not going to surrender."

Seeley made motions to the Chinese that he was going to return to his unit. After a moment's hesitation they allowed him to depart but kept Tovar with them.

Before Seeley regained his own unit the Chinese troops had entered the lines to the north and the disarming of the northern group began. Other Chinese troops began to vulturize the trucks.

Seeley held a hurried consultation with the officers and men of his unit. He came to the decision that once McLaughlin's men had been disarmed and their positions occupied by the enemy his small group would have small chance of holding out. Collecting the wounded the unit crossed the river and began climbing the nearly vertical mountain to the west of the road. It was slow, painful work as the wounded had to be dragged over much of the distance. Seeley's group regained friendly lines at Koto five hours later.

The Chinese did not keep their promise to McLaughlin and the wounded were not returned to Koto. A few were left in the native hut between the road and river, but most of them were taken into the hills with the rest of the prisoners.

Among those captured were Kaylor and Holcomb. Kaylor, after receiving his orders to return to the United States, had climbed into the truck driven by Holcomb at Yudam-ni. In a convoy going south to Hungnam, Kaylor and Holcomb had been caught in the ambush of the McLaughlin-Seeley group moving north. Six months later Kaylor and Holcomb and sixteen other Marines escaped. Kaylor arrived in Minneapolis in June, 1951 instead of Christmas, 1950.

Of the combat units starting out for Hagaru, Sitter arrived after suffering 63 casualties. Drysdale's Commando lost 90 of 255. Twenty-two of the Royal Marines became prisoners. Baker Company of the Army 31st Regiment was particularly hard hit. But one officer and 69 men found their way back to Koto; 140 were missing in action. Forty-four Marines were missing in action. Tovar escaped from the Chinese three days later and returned to Koto.

Upon Sitter's arrival at Hagaru his unit was placed in reserve where he reorganized and prepared to relieve Myers and recapture the high ground to the east of the town. At nine o'clock on the morning of the thirtieth, Sitter effected the relief, and with Hopkins and Jaeger's platoons in the assault, the high ground was retaken. All through the day Sitter's unit consolidated positions and dug in for the expected night counterattack. The entire perimeter was subjected to intermittent mortar and artillery fire during the day.

The enemy resumed their attack at 9:30 that evening. Fisher's company heard bugle calls to the west of their positions and a short time later a green flare was seen. Small groups of the enemy made probing attacks against Fisher's line, and by 11:30 a full-scale attack was launched. This attack was supported by mortar and artillery fire, and once again Item Company fought back with savage resolution and the Chinese were beaten back with heavy casualties.

At the same time that Fisher was under attack, a large enemy force came from the hills to the northeast and struck Sitter's left center. Rushing to the critical area, Sitter rallied his men as an enemy penetration threatened to overrun his CP. During this close-in fighting, Sitter was wounded by a hand grenade but refused evacuation as he continued to lead his men in repelling the attack.

A platoon from the 1st Marine Engineer Battalion was on Sitter's left flank. When a machine gun was put out of action the unit leader (First Lieutenant Ermine Meeker) called for volunteers. Pfc.'s James Ogden and Richard Welch rushed forward. Ogden manned the gun as Welch supplied him with ammunition. Ogden received a head wound, but refused evacuation. As he resumed fire, he shouted, "Get more ammo and grenades up here—if these bastards want a fight, we'll give 'em one."

In spite of the heavy toll taken by the Marines, the Chinese closed and Ogden was killed. Welch took over the gun.

Heavy fighting continued throughout the night and George Company's left flank was bent back. Ridge rushed reinforcements to Sitter and the line was stabilized.

At daybreak, when the enemy attack subsided, Sitter's line was in the form of a **V** with the point on the high ground, and the left arm of the **V** extending back to the road. The right arm maintained its position and tied in with 3rd Battalions Weapons Company at the road junction.

During the period in which the actions at Koto and Hagaru have been reported, Murray and Litzenberg were heavily engaged at Yudam-ni. It will be remembered that the initial Chinese onfall on November 27 has been covered in detail. Morris' Company has been rescued and brought back into the defensive perimeter. On the morning of the twenty-eighth Litzenberg and Murray received instructions from Smith: "Until present situation clarifies remain present positions in lieu of mission assigned." It was on receipt of this message that Murray withheld his attack to the west and began to plan with Litzenberg for the consolidation of all Marine forces around Yudam-ni.

A composite unit under the command of Major Warren Morris was formed. It was composed of a company each from the 1st and 3rd Battalion 7th Marines and Able Company 5th Marines. Morris was directed to push his unit to the south and to relieve Fox Company at Toktong Pass. Morris moved south at 9:30 on the morning of the twenty-eighth, but soon came in contact with an enemy force which greatly outnumbered his, and his movement was halted. Air sightings also revealed that additional enemy were moving along the high ground into flanking positions. Upon receipt of this information Litzenberg ordered Morris to return to the perimeter.

In the meantime considerable reorganization had to be effected among the hard-hit units who had defended the perimeter on the night of the twenty-seventh. Because of excessive casualties Hull's Dog Company was disbanded and combined with the remnants of Phillips' Easy Company. Total effectives of these two units were but seventy-five Marines. Additional reinforcements were received from Parry's Artillery Battalion, (one hundred fifteen men), and Captain Robert Polson's Weapons Company. Roach (formerly commander of 3rd Battalion 7th Marines) was placed in command. When some organization had been effected, Roach reported to Dowsett: "This is Damnation 6, formerly Driftwood 6." With that introduction the new unit promptly became Damnation Battalion.

Because of the heavy losses suffered, this reshuffling and reassignment posed a morale problem for Roach. The men appeared to delight in their new unit name. In the space of hours the entire unit had green kerchiefs made from parachute cloth, wrapped about their necks and were asking when Damnation Battalion went into action.

The mission of this unit was to move to the left of Davis on the perimeter and to hold the shoulders of the high ground through which the 7th would have to move in the attempt to open the MSR to Hagaru. As Roach marched his unit into position, Hull came from the hospital tent and asked that he be allowed to join. Because of the seriousness of Hull's multiple wounds Roach was forced to deny this request.

Litzenberg's concern for Barber's unit increased when Morris was turned back. In the later afternoon of the twenty-ninth Litzenberg called Davis to his tent and outlined a plan for relieving the beleaguered Marines at the pass. The scheme was bold in that it meant Davis was to move overland with his battalion, with much of the journey to be made at night. Litzenberg told his battalion commander: "It's obvious we can't bull our way down the road. I don't think the Chinese will expect us to move overland. Barber has to be relieved and Toktong Pass held. Prepare to move out tomorrow morning."

Davis returned to his unit, and began preparations for the long march. Every man physically able was to make the trip. The sick and walking wounded would be left behind and it was their mission to bring the battalion vehicles and other equipment with them when the road was open. Each man was to carry four meals, a full canteen of water, and an extra bandoleer of ammunition. Crews were doubled on the 60 mm. and 81 mm. mortars so that these units could move with the same speed as the riflemen. The choice of rations was left to the individual. Most of the men chose tins of bread and fruit. By carrying the canned fruit next to their bodies, it would prevent the contents from freezing and the sugar would be a nutritious stimulant. Additional stretchers were taken along and mortar ammunition was strapped to them. In addition to this each man was to carry one 81 mm. shell and his sleeping bag—making a total of approximately one hundred twenty pounds per man. Lieutenant Chew Een Lee escaped from the hospital and, with his arm in a sling, joined his unit.

The plan was for Davis to move out in column behind Newton's How Company. Newton was assigned the mission of taking Hill 1419. Once this land mass was secured, Davis would pass on through and begin his overland trek.

Just before issuing the order to move out, Davis was told by Navy Lieutenant Peter Arioli (Regimental Surgeon) that Navy Lieutenant (jg) Robert Wedemeyer (Davis' Battalion Surgeon) had been running a high temperature for several days and he (Arioli) had ordered Wedemeyer into the hospital. Arioli volunteered to make the trip in Wedemeyer's place.

Davis was concerned about the condition of his men. Since the tenth of November they had been living in zero and subzero temperatures, and dietary deficiencies and lack of hot food were taking their toll. Many had suffered mild cases of frostbite, and nearly all had cut and bleeding hands from digging foxholes in frozen ground. The morale of the unit, however, was sound and the spirits of all rose when they were informed the mission of the 1st Battalion was to relieve Fox Company.

The line of advance was to be Hovatter's company at the point, followed by Davis' command group and in trace Kurcaba's unit, with Morris' company bringing up the rear.

Hill 1419 was a thousand yards east of the Yudam-ni–Hagaru road. A series of fingers ran from the knob in the general direction of the MSR. The enemy was entrenched on this hill mass and had been since engaging Morris' company three days before. After a concentration of artillery fire and air strikes. Newton took his unit into the assault. The approaches were steep and the snow was a great hindrance. The Marines had to resort to climbing on their hands and knees. With each succeeding yard gained, enemy resistance became more stubborn. The attack of How Company stalled.

Before further progress could be made Davis had to commit Hovatter and Kurcaba. Second Lieutenant Leslie Williams took his platoon into the assault. Good progress was made until the right flank unit was pinned down by heavy enemy fire. Williams had reached an abutment on the hill about five hundred yards from his objective and heavy fire began inflicting casualties in his unit. Hastily reorganizing his men under fire, Williams led them in a direct assault on the high ground to his front where they came to hand-to-hand combat with the enemy. This action had much to do with relieving the pressure on How Company to the right, and Hill 1419 was captured. In a subsequent action Williams was killed.

The wounded and dead were passed down the line through Charley Company to the road where they were evacuated to Yudam-ni. Once the tail of the column moved off the road, Davis had the problem of carrying his dead and wounded with him.

Anticipating that Davis would require additional forces to make his march to the Fox Company positions, Litzenberg assigned How Company to continue with him. It was seven o'clock in the evening before the land mass was secured and Davis' main concern at this time was the condition of his men. They had been climbing and straining on the hill for most of the day and were wet with perspiration. He feared the subzero temperature that they would face that night. He set up a defensive perimeter on the hill crest and sent Kurcaba's company on a patrol to the southeast. This was to check on enemy activity and intentions in that direction. There was no enemy contact.

The temperature at this time was twenty-four degrees below zero and it was not long before Davis was aware that to remain in position overnight would be disastrous. Covering himself with a poncho, he turned his flashlight on the face of his compass and oriented himself and made the plan for his further advance toward the pass. For further orientation he called on the artillery in Yudam-ni to fire white phosphorous on the hills to his front. Due to the snow and darkness this did not prove an effective guide as it was impossible to see the shell bursts.

In the new line of advance Kurcaba's company was to take the point, followed by Hovatter, Morris and Newton. Davis instructed Kurcaba to place the direction of march on a bright star on the southern horizon rim. In order that he could be close to the point, Davis established his command group at the rear of Kurcaba's company. It was nine o'clock at night when the order was given for the column to move out.

On the top of boulder-strewn Hill 1419 a narrow path wove through brush and two chimneys of rock. At this narrow passage Davis posted guides to inform the Marines as they came by that the star was their marker. Accompanying Davis wherever he went was his runner, Pfc. Michaels, and Corporal Leroy Pearl with the radio.

Baker Company moved out with Chew Een Lee at the point, and Kurcaba had instructions to hold up on the next mass (fifteen hundred yards) where further orientation of direction could be made. As long as the Marine point remained on the high ground the star served as an adequate beacon. However, once the path led them into the valleys, they would lose their marker. As the point plunged into the second valley Davis sensed that the line of march was veering to the right. Radios had frozen and communication with Lee was impossible. In order to get word to Kurcaba to halt, Davis resorted to passing the word from man to man along the column. But because of the exhausted state of the men and their being heavily shrouded about the face and ears by the parka hoods, it was impossible to get the command forward.

Davis began to run through the heavy snow. As he ran he berated the men along the line for not remaining alert. The Marines, not knowing in the darkness who this shouting person was, told him "Pipe down, you're making too damn much noise." Finally Davis caught up with the point and halted it.

Unaware that the unit in front had stopped, the men in the rear continued blindly forward until they bumped into the man ahead. Then, with a long, gasping sigh, the Marines collapsed in the snow like dominoes in a child's playroom. The direction of march was corrected. Then came the task of getting the exhausted men to their feet and on the move. Officers and NCO's roved the line, manhandling and, in many cases, kicking and belaboring the men to their feet. Slowly the column was formed and moved forward as so many fatigue-drugged automatons.

The route chosen by Davis for his night march was to the east and generally paralleled the Yudam-ni–Hagaru road. Of considerable comfort to the marching column was the sight of Marine artillery bursts on the road to the west and below them. This diversionary fire, planned by Litzenberg, would cause the enemy to believe a night approach march was to be made on the MSR. As a result, Davis was not to come in contact with the enemy until he reached the high ground north of Sinhung-ni. Due to the deviation in the earlier line of march, the unit was now fifteen hundred yards west of the position he wished to attain.

At this point a small fire fight broke out with an enemy force to the east. Lee and Kliefoth worked their platoons around the Chinese and attained ground as well as fire superiority. It was now three o'clock in the morning and Davis ordered his four companies to dig in on their present holdings. As had happened before, when the column came to a halt the men fell to the ground completely spent. When the enemy opened long-range machine-gun fire from the south, there was little or no response from the Marines. Long windrows of men lay inert in the snow oblivious to all else save the demand for rest. The high ground upon which Davis decided to set up his defenses was too small an area to adequately hold four rifle companies. But Davis knew his men had reached the state where further advance was impossible. The tail of the column (Charlie and How Companies) was brought up from the valley and placed in perimeter defense with Able and Baker. Placing so many men in such a small area was a considered risk which Davis was forced to assume. The riflemen slowly got into position and the enemy fire was returned.

The TBX radio was set up and for the first time in eight hours Davis was able to contact Litzenberg. The regimental commander was informed of the position held and of Davis' intention to move out at daybreak to effect the relief of Fox Company.

Gradually the enemy fire subsided and each company formed two-man patrols which moved from position to position to make certain that twenty-five per cent of the men remained alert. Throughout the remainder of the early morning hours the Marines were under sporadic long-range sniper fire. As Davis crawled into his sleeping bag in the shelter of a boulder, a bullet passed through the hood of his bag, but he was not hurt.

The positions taken by the relief battalion were fourteen hundred yards northwest of Fox Company positions. At first light Davis went forward to Kurcaba's lines and consulted with the company commander on the approach to Barber's position. Kurcaba's unit moved out in the assault at daybreak. The initial move was without enemy contact for the first thousand yards. Then the Marines came under enemy fire from the "Rocky Ridge."

It was the mission of Baker Company to take the high ground directly north and looking down upon Rocky Ridge. When this area was secure Hovatter was to move to the left and on to a hill mass still higher than that occupied by Kurcaba. Newton's How Company was bringing up the rear with the wounded who were under the charge of Arioli. The two-hour rest and the feeling that their task was soon to be ended had given a life in spirit to the riflemen. Good time was made in the passage of the cross corridors of the mountainous terrain, until a messenger came running from the rear with the information that Newton was under attack and the wounded were in danger of being captured.

As Davis was preparing to meet this new threat, a second messenger arrived saying that the enemy had been beaten off and the situation at the rear of the column was stabilized. Davis then ordered the wounded to be brought forward into Morris' company's positions, and the approach to Barber was resumed. Kurcaba's unit drove the enemy off the hill directly north of Barber, but as the column continued to advance it came under long-range fire from all four directions.

As Davis climbed the hill occupied by Kurcaba, Pearl came running to him in great excitement. He said, "Colonel, I've got Fox 6 on the radio!" His voice shook with emotion. As Davis talked to Barber both men became emotionally inarticulate. Finally, Barber informed Davis that an air strike was coming in and asked him to hold off his attack to the south until the Marine Corsairs had bombed and strafed Rocky Ridge. Barber further informed Davis that if he needed assistance, Fox Company was ready and willing to send a patrol to the north.

The air strike was delivered and Kurcaba attacked to the south. At 11:25 in the morning Davis and his men moved into Barber's lines. The men of Fox Company began to cheer; their vociferous greeting was of short duration as they saw the haggard faces of the Marines who had come to their aid.

"Good God! These guys have been through more than we have."

Arioli went immediately to the wounded at the base of the hill. Later, as he stepped from one of the tents, he was shot and killed by a sniper.

Morris and Newton placed their units in position in the immediate vicinity of Barber's company, while Kurcaba and Hovatter continued to the east to clear the enemy from the pass. Davis reported to Litzenberg, "Mission accomplished. Fox Company relieved."

CHAPTER XXI

The Attack to the South

It will be recalled that on the twenty-eighth of November Smith, in view of the situation on the Eighth Army front and the heavy attack placed on Murray and Litzenberg, had issued the order withholding the attack to the west. On the twenty-ninth of November, when no change in plan had been received from X Corps, Smith ordered Litzenberg to employ his entire regiment in opening up the road between Yudam-ni and Hagaru. Late in the afternoon of the twenty-ninth Smith received a telephone call (radio link) from Almond stating that the scheme of maneuver was changed. Smith was given the command of and responsibility for extricating the Army units on the east coast of the reservoir. In addition, Smith was directed to withdraw the 5th and 7th Marines and consolidate positions around Hagaru. The Marines at Hagaru had not the strength to mount a relief unit to the assistance of the Army Task Force. Ridge had but three depleted rifle companies with which to defend a perimeter. To have sent any portion of this force out to relieve the Army would have placed Hagaru in jeopardy.

General Hodes, who had set up his CP near Smith, reported that the cut-off Army battalions had suffered four hundred casualties and it appeared impossible for them to fight their way out of the entrapment. Smith ordered that the priority for air cover and support would be given to these people and that they should make every effort to improve their position by fighting southward toward Hagaru.

On the morning of the thirtieth of November General Barr, commanding the 7th Army Division, flew into the perimeter for a conference with Smith. Later in the day Barr flew by helicopter to the positions of the cut-off Army battalions. Upon his return, Barr agreed with Smith that it was possible for the army units to improve their situation with the help of Marine air support. Smith directed Hodes to prepare a dispatch to Colonel Faith (Army Task Force Commander) that every effort should be made to fight his unit to the south, but that he should do nothing which would jeopardize the safety of his wounded.

Almond flew into Hagaru for a conference with Smith. The idea of consolidating positions in the vicinity of Hagaru had been given up. Almond directed Smith to fall back on Hamhung, and stressed the necessity for speed in this withdrawal. Smith was authorized to burn or destroy any equipment or supplies which would hamper his movement. Smith in turn informed Almond that his withdrawal would be governed entirely by the ability of the Marines to evacuate the wounded. Smith further declared it was his intention to fight his way to the sea and he could not afford to discard or destroy equipment.

When Murray and Litzenberg received the order on November 30 to withdraw from Yudam-ni to Hagaru, a joint plan was drawn up and flown to Smith by helicopter. The plan called for Litzenberg's regiment to lead out from Yudam-ni with Murray's unit covering the rear. The artillery and the regimental train were to be in the middle of the column. The walking wounded were to be given weapons and marched in a column along the road. The more seriously wounded were to be loaded in trucks and such ambulances as were available. Smith approved this plan and directed his regimental commanders to put it into effect immediately.

As soon as the plan for withdrawal was approved by Smith, Litzenberg and Murray began to readjust their forces within the perimeter so that the 7th Marines could expand to the south while the 5th Marines fought the rear guard. To accomplish the heading-out of the attack, it will be remembered that Litzenberg would have but two battalions inasmuch as Davis was already on his overland trek. To augment the casualty-depleted rifle companies, twenty-six provisional rifle platoons were formed from the artillery battalions and small detachments from headquarters and service personnel. In most cases these units were led by artillery officers.

It will be remembered that on the night of the twenty-seventh of November, when the enemy onfall was placed against Phillips and Hull to the north of Yudam-ni, these units were reinforced and later relieved by Jones and Heater. (Positions 6 and 7 on the Yudam-ni map.) In the general reassignment of positions following the enemy attack, Taplett's battalion was assigned the mission of holding the northern rim where the enemy still continued to exert the heaviest pressure. Schrier's Item Company occupied the sector formerly held by Phillips and Jones. Schrier was under constant attack and finally Taplett ordered Hermanson on to the hill to relieve Schrier.

The enemy immediately placed a heavy counterattack on Hermanson's right flank. The platoon commander (Price) and the platoon sergeant (Gilbert) were killed, and the platoon guide and two squad leaders were wounded within a few minutes of the attack. Pfc. Edmund Orsulak, who was acting as a platoon runner, took charge of the right flank and by his decisive action and leadership steadied the line.

Pfc. David Alley, a BARman of the 3rd Squad, took command of his unit when the squad leader was killed and his aggressive tactics put an end to the confusion due to the heavy casualties. George Company held their positions on the northern rim.

By noon of the first of December Litzenberg began to expand the perimeter south along the MSR in conformance with Smith's order to withdraw to Hagaru. During this movement priority to air and artillery support was to be given to Murray's regiment as it withdrew from the high ground to the north and west of Yudam-ni. This southern movement was made in conjunction with Davis' relief mission and the capture of Hill 1419.

In the assault to the south, the movement of Davis and his battalion has already been recorded. Paralleling Davis' movement, Harris launched three attacks during the night to break an enemy roadblock along the MSR without success.

The Chinese, in regimental strength and under orders to maintain the cloture at all costs, fought with great tenacity. Reinforced by provisional platoons of artillerymen, Harris pressed the attack, but each advance was met by an enemy counterattack. Sergeant James Johnson was an artilleryman assigned to infantry duty in "Jig" Company. During the attacks on the roadblock, Harris kept this unit in reserve to give all the time possible for organizing and orienting the "cannon cockers" to their new role.

When positions were somewhat stabilized, Harris ordered "Jig" Company into the line. Shortly thereafter the enemy struck in a counterattack. Johnson's platoon became heavily engaged. Assuming command of the unit, Johnson directed the defense with remarkable skill. The vast numerical strength of the enemy prevailed, however, and the attack could not be contained. Johnson was ordered to withdraw. Exposing himself to the Chinese fire, Johnson directed a position-by-position withdrawal of his men. As the enemy closed, Johnson faced them alone, firing his rifle and hurling grenade after grenade into the advancing line. When last seen Johnson was in hand-to-hand combat. His action made it possible for his men to establish a new offensive line. By seven o'clock in the morning the enemy counterattacks on Harris' front lessened and were believed to be contained.

Taplett was directed to displace from the high ground to the north, pass through Harris and spearhead the assault to the south. At the time Taplett received the order two of his companies (George and How) were on the high ground previously fought over by Hull and Phillips. Item Company, hard hit the day before, was in reserve in the valley. Under the cover of a devastating attack by air and artillery, Taplett withdrew his two forward units without casualties. The air and artillery laid down such a blanket of fire that the enemy were unaware of the withdrawal until the ground units were several miles to the south. George Company was the last Marine unit to leave Yudam-ni and the bridge was destroyed as the last elements crossed over.

During this withdrawal Roise moved Peters' Company on to Hill 1276, south of Yudam-ni and east of the road. Jaskilka had the mission of covering Taplett's withdrawal with long-range machine-gun fire. Smith and Jaskilka remained in position until two o'clock in the afternoon.

With Williamson's How Company in the lead the attack was made to the southeast with the mission of seizing the high ground to the right of the road. Schrier's Item Company was assigned a similar objective to the left of the road.

To the right of the road Williamson's How Company had seized its objective under intense small-arms and automatic weapons fire and were securely emplaced by seven o'clock in the evening. In a night attack Schrier was partially successful in seizing his objective, but was forced to withdraw due to heavy casualties sustained.

During the night a heavy enemy counterattack developed along the entire battalion front with the brunt being borne by Schrier's unit. Staff Sergeant William Windrich led a squad of the 1st Platoon to positions which would meet the enemy assault. Seven of the twelve men were wounded before they attained their positions. Windrich received a serious head wound. Refusing to be evacuated, he returned to the company CP and organized a group of volunteers to evacuate the men who had been wounded in the assault. Assuming command of the platoon at this time and reorganizing them, he led them into positions on the company left flank. Windrich was again wounded, this time in the legs. Again he refused evacuation. When Sergeant Charles Pearson approached him and asked if he could dress his wounds, Windrich replied, "There isn't time. They're only small holes anyway." For over an hour he continued to direct his platoon by moving from position to position and shouting words of encouragement to his men. About this time he collapsed from loss of blood and pain and died a short time later.

On the opposite flank from Windrich, Technical Sergeant Dale Stropes directed the fire from his sector. Under intense enemy fire, he saw to the redistribution of ammunition until he received a serious back wound. In spite of his wound, he formed a group to evacuate other wounded to the aid station at the rear. While in the process of moving the wounded off the hill Stropes received a chest wound which killed him.

First Lieutenant Dorsie Booker, artillery officer from the 1st Battalion 11th Marines, brought a provisional platoon forward to reinforce Schrier. Composed primarily of artillery men, Booker's unit moved into line where it came under a series of heavy attacks. Recognizing the inherent danger in the loss of the left flank, Booker led a counterattack which regained the commanding ground in his zone. He directed the efforts of his men with skill and when casualties had depleted his unit he supplied himself with weapons and ammunition from the dead and wounded and manned the most hazardous positions. Throughout a period of five hours he continued to lead his men in a fearless manner until he was killed.

Combined with the efforts of Booker were the actions of Pfc.'s Palmer Bratten and Amon Harvey. Bratten was acting as squad leader of a machine-gun platoon during the enemy counterattack and constantly moved from one gun position to the next in repairing the weapons and supplying ammunition to the gunners. When not occupied with this task he saw to the evacuation of the wounded. When the order was given to withdraw to better defensive positions, Bratten volunteered to man a machine gun in order that the rest of his men could withdraw. This he did and his unit was able to retreat under his covering fire. Bratten was killed by grenades as he fired the last of his ammunition.

Harvey, an artilleryman hurriedly changed over to a rifleman, met the enemy onslaught by constantly exposing himself in firing upon and directing the fire on the enemy. When the Chinese overran several positions in his sector he voluntarily led the counterattack which regained them. Harvey was wounded early in the engagement, but continued in action until subsequent wounds made it impossible for him to stand. He then crawled to an exposed position and continued to shout words of encouragement to his men.

At ten o'clock in the morning (December 2) Hermanson took his unit through Schrier and continued the attack. Schrier's company had suffered such heavy casualties that the remaining men were combined into one platoon and attached to Hermanson. Schrier was wounded and evacuated. An accurate count of the enemy dead in this zone was three hundred and forty-two.

The advance along the MSR was slowed by considerable enemy small-arms and automatic fire from prepared positions. By eleven o'clock at night the intermediate objective of Williamson's company had been reached. By 2:10 in the morning a spur running from a high ridge to the southeast was secure. During the day Hermanson had been wounded and was replaced by Mize who once again assumed command of the unit he had led through Seoul. After constant air strikes and 81 mm. mortar missions, Mize had seized the assigned objective of his unit. These actions cleared the roadblock to the south and a composite company from the 7th Marines continued another six hundred yards where it was halted by enemy fire.

Fighting the rear guard, Jones' Charley Company was attacked from the north by an enemy force estimated to be in battalion strength. The lone tank (Munsell) had been assigned to the rear guard. Under a concentration of rifle and machine-gun fire, Jones ran to the tank and directed it into a position where its fire could be brought to bear to support his troops. The enemy attack was finally repulsed at two o'clock.

Roise's battalion had remained in the same relative positions occupied on the previous day. Later it displaced to successive delaying positions as rear guard of the entire force.

Peters' Fox Company moved on to the high shoulders of ground south of Yudam-ni and east of the road. It was their mission to protect the regimental train as it moved southward. Assuming hastily prepared positions, the unit dug in and shortly after dark the enemy launched the counterattack in battalion strength. Christofferson's 3rd Platoon became heavily engaged at grenade range. Pfc. Walter George was manning a BAR when the attack began. George's weapon went out of action and, realizing the seriousness of the situation, George left his position and ran to the assistance of Pfc. Waldon. Without seeking cover, George supplied Waldon with ammunition, and when the magazines were depleted he reloaded them with his bare hands in the freezing weather.

Seeing a number of his squad wounded and in exposed positions, George rushed forward and dragged them to places of cover. Once again he turned to assisting Waldon. He was hit by a burst of machine-gun fire and refused evacuation. He continued to crawl from position to position, seeking ammunition for the automatic weapon until he died of his wounds.

Peters was forced to withdraw across a saddle of high land to positions southwest of Hill 1276. Night fighters were called in and the hill was placed under attack from the air. At dawn an unsuccessful attempt was made to recapture the high ground. Once again the hill was placed under aerial bombardment preceding a second ground attack. For the second time the Marine attack was repulsed by four well-emplaced machine guns on the reverse slope. At this time orders were received to withhold further attacks inasmuch as the roadblock had been broken and movement to the south was possible.

While the Marines were fighting to overcome the roadblock south of Yudam-ni, Davis had been active in the Toktong Pass area. Immediately upon relieving Fox Company, Davis had ordered Hovatter and Kurcaba to clear the enemy from the pass east of Barber's positions. The Chinese were well entrenched and under orders to hold at all costs. First Lieutenant Harrol Kiser was committed to the assault by Kurcaba. By this time Kiser's platoon could muster no more than twenty-one men. Against heavy fire, Kiser gained his initial objective. The rest of the company came under heavy fire as it began the attack to seize the high ground to the east. Kiser reorganized his unit and led an inspired attack on the flanking ridge line which reduced the enemy fire on the remainder of the company. Forty Chinese were killed and five captured. Although wounded, Kiser continued in action throughout the day.

Materially assisting Kiser and the rest of the unit was Private James Beard. Armed with a BAR, Beard advanced from one enemy position to another firing his weapon, in many cases, from the hip. Advancing on a heavy machine gun, he killed the crew with a grenade and promptly turned the weapon around and opened fire on the retreating enemy.

Beard killed seventeen with this weapon before he ran out of ammunition.

Once the pass was cleared, Davis directed his operations officer, Major Tom Tighe, to take Hovatter's and Kurcaba's units into the valley to the south of Barber's positions while Davis led the units of Morris and Newton to the northeast. The attack of Tighe into the valley caught the Chinese by surprise. Upon withdrawing in the face of Tighe's assault, the enemy found themselves trapped by Taplett's 3rd Battalion, which was moving up the hill. Marine air and artillery were called in. Tighe and Taplett closed the trap and the enemy force was annihilated. During the final fire fight, a Marine had been seriously wounded and Taplett requested evacuation by helicopter. First Lieutenant Robert Longstaff responded. He was shot down and killed. Taplett sent a patrol to the scene of the crash and recovered the body.

At one o'clock in the afternoon Munsell's tank came up the road with elements of Mize's company and the Marines of Yudam-ni and Fox Hill joined. At this time Davis received orders to assume the point and led the way into Hagaru.

Directing Barber to remain in position, Davis formed his column for the final attack in clearing the road into the Hagaru perimeter. Hovatter led off, followed by Kurcaba, Newton and Morris. At each critical point along the road Davis placed outposts to cover the long train and units behind it. Overhead two Marine observation planes squirrel-caged above him, informing him of enemy concentrations and positions. To the front and on both flanks Marine Corsairs strafed and rocketed the hills and ridges, and the ground Marines could see the Chinese breaking and running under the air attack. The only personnel to ride were the badly wounded and frozen. With his jeep filled with wounded, Litzenberg walked alongside.

As the outposts were placed in the hills, the walking wounded continued down the road to the haven of the perimeter.

Due to the long pauses necessitated by fire fights and the breaking of roadblocks, the vehicular train in the Litzenberg-Murray column began to run out of gasoline. A pinpoint air drop was made to the head of the truck column. Motor fuel was distributed. Unfortunately, Diesel fuel was not dropped and a number of tractors towing 155 mm. guns had to stop several miles from their final objective. At 7:35 in the evening of December 3, Dowsett and the advance party of the 7th Marines arrived at the Hagaru roadblock. The first battle in the advance to the sea had been won.

As the news spread in Hagaru that the 5th and 7th Marines had finally fought through, many hurried to the roadblock to watch the arrival. Naval Lieutenant (jg) Robert Harvey, who had served as battalion surgeon for Taplett throughout the southern campaign, went to meet his old friends as they came into the perimeter. He found several hundred Marines already waiting. They saw the point come into view and the snake-line of following trucks. Six hundred yards from the perimeter entrance the point halted and the trucks ground to a stop. Those of the wounded and frostbitten who could walk crawled from the vehicles and formed on the bleak, frozen road. There, in silence, they began to march; with no word or count the cadence was picked up and the Marines at the perimeter entrance heard the frozen Shoe-pacs on the frozen road pounding in rhythm.

The Marines of Hagaru watched the Marines of Yudam-ni march toward them, march by them—haggard, bearded and hard. The men of the 5th and 7th received their tribute from the tears in the eyes of the Marines awaiting them. Overcome by the sight of the depleted ranks, Harvey wept with the others. He whispered over and over, "Look at those bastards, those magnificent bastards—"

Ridge felt a great relief as the two regiments came into his thinly-held lines. From General Smith to Pfc. Bruno Podolak the feeling was the same—"We've got it made; there aren't enough Chinese in all of China to beat us now."

During the period from the Chinese onfall on the twenty-seventh of November to the third of December when Litzenberg and Murray gained the perimeter at Hagaru, the Marines had suffered 2,260 battle casualties. Of these, 358 had been killed, 153 were missing and 1,749 had been wounded. In addition to this, 1,072 men had become non-battle casualties.

While the Yudam-ni Marines were fighting their way to the south (December 2-3), Hagaru had suffered no heavy attacks upon its lines. After the first attack on the twenty-ninth, Ridge had divided the perimeter into two sectors. Lieutenant Colonel Charles Banks (commanding officer of the Combat Service Battalion) assumed command of the northern half. A Raider in World War II, Banks proved a bulwark in organizing and directing his service personnel. Within the perimeter, however, there was considerable activity as preparations were made for the arrival of the Litzenberg-Murray force.

With inadequate equipment to work the frozen ground, Marine engineers had completed the air strip. A ninety-thousand cubic yard cut and a sixty-thousand cubic yard fill had to be made in the frozen soil to form a runway thirty-two hundred feet long. Scarifier blades were welded to bulldozers in an attempt to break the frozen surface; demolitions were used. In between, the engineers manned a section of the perimeter at night and were under fire during the day. At first the runway was only fifty feet wide with no taxiways, and it was possible to accommodate only two planes at one time. The engineers continued to expand the facilities until it would accommodate six planes without blocking the runway. Without lights and a ground control system, the use of the field was limited to daylight hours.

Captain "Bud" Hering, senior medical officer for the division, was in charge of evacuating the wounded. On the first of December, in the later afternoon, the first two-engine cargo plane landed successfully. It took off almost immediately with twenty-four wounded. One hundred fifty casualties were evacuated before darkness set in.

Navy pilot B. J. Miller, Chief Aviation Electronics man, had flown his four-engine plane (R5D) onto Yonpo Airfield from Japan. In the operations tent he heard of the critical state of Marine casualties at Hagaru. He consulted with his copilot Powell and the plane's crew and all volunteered to fly to Hagaru for a load of wounded. Miller returned to the operations tent and informed the Marine officer that he had a plane available for the evacuation of wounded. The Marine assumed that it was a two-engine affair and Miller saw no reason why he should mention that he was piloting a much larger four-engine aircraft. With a load of stretchers, Miller took off and in a few minutes was circling Hagaru.

Runways of four to five thousand feet are normal for handling four-engine planes. Miller was confronted with a strip considerably shorter and, due to the surrounding hills, would have to go in "hot." A successful landing was made to the astonishment of the Marines on the ground. The stretchers were unloaded and thirty-nine wounded were placed aboard. Miller taxied the aircraft to the extreme end of the rough runway. He gave it full throttle. In a carrier-type take-off the plane cleared the first ridge line by thirty feet. It was the first and only four-engine plane to use Hagaru airstrip.

On the second of December, nine hundred nineteen men were flown out.

The medical care of casualties in Hagaru was being provided by Companies E and C of the 1st Medical Battalion. Surgical teams from each of these units had moved into the reservoir area with a team from Company C attached to Murray and the other attached to Litzenberg. When orders were received to attack to the west from Yudam-ni, Hering decided to detach these two teams from the regiments and consolidate and reinforce them so that a divisional hospital could be established in Hagaru where there were buildings.

Hering felt that the MSR was too long for proper evacuation and that hospital facilities should be established in the operating area. Because of the lack of proper housing, Puller was to evacuate his wounded north to the hospital at Hagaru. With the onfall of the enemy on the perimeter at Hagaru, Hering further reinforced his medical unit by having two additional surgical teams flown in by helicopter.

Though the casualty load greatly overburdened the available medical facilities, Hering and his staff met the challenge with a skill and energy the Marines will long remember. In a period of forty-eight hours fifteen hundred Army and one thousand Marine casualties were treated, processed and evacuated. Certain troops did feign wounds and illness and escaped the ordeal of Hagaru by being flown out. This occurred only once, however, and Hering began a closer supervision over personnel boarding the planes.

Shortly before dark on the night of the second, Lieutenant Colonel Olin Beall (commanding the 1st Motor Transport Battalion) received a message from his troops defending the northern sector of the perimeter that a large group of people were approaching his lines. Beall immediately joined Captain James Camp at the edge of the minefield. Many figures could be seen on the ice of the reservoir. Beall formed a squad which went forward and, upon identification that the men were American soldiers, began to conduct them into the Marine lines. Most of the men coming off the ice were wounded and frostbitten and in a state of shock from exposure. The Marines were informed that they were the "sole survivors" of the Army Task Force on the east coast of the reservoir. Throughout the night stragglers continued to come off the ice and were immediately conducted to the hospital.

Before daylight the next morning, Beall had organized a rescue group to go out onto the ice and recover those too badly wounded to make the

Marine lines. With Pfc. Ralph Milton and Corpsman Oscar Biebinger accompanying him, Beall drove onto the ice. Opposite the village of Pokio-chi (two miles from the southern tip of the reservoir), they came upon six wounded. They were loaded into the jeep and returned to Hagaru. These men told Beall they had crawled onto the ice from a convoy that had been ambushed in the neighborhood of the sawmill close to Pokio-chi. Beall informed the division that he was forming a rescue party to search out any other men who might be in the village or on the ice. Second Lieutenant Robert Hunt brought trucks to the shoreline and built fires and set up warming tents.

On the second trip onto the reservoir, a native sled was attached to the jeep. As the vehicles came opposite the village, Beall instructed Milton to head for shore. Almost immediately they came under automatic weapons fire. Milton slewed the jeep about and headed toward the center of the ice. The Chinese fire died away. Leaving Milton and Biebinger in the vehicle, Beall walked toward the shore. The enemy did not fire upon him.

Biebinger joined Beall and together they dragged seven wounded across the ice and loaded them onto the jeep. While Milton returned to Hunt's evacuation point, Beall and the corpsman continued getting the wounded from the shore to the center of the reservoir. Corporal Andrew Contreras brought a second jeep onto the ice, followed by Hunt. An attempt was made to bring the three vehicles closer to shore, but they were immediately brought under mortar fire. Beall ordered them out to the center of the ice and the fire once again died away.

During this time Beall had been studying the actions of the enemy and he noted that when he approached the shoreline with a rifle slung over his shoulder, the enemy would fire upon him. Thereafter he left his weapon in the jeep and could approach shore without drawing fire from machine guns. All were subjected to sporadic sniper fire. However, this too died away once a wounded man had been reached and was being assisted across the ice. Hunt joined Beall and both men, feigning wounds, crawled across the ice and to the shore. They found a soldier with a compound fracture of both legs as well as a serious arm wound. Beall took a sling from an abandoned rifle and slipping it around the wounded man's sound shoulder, tobogganed him out across the ice.

In the meantime, Hunt had penetrated inland some distance and returned with other wounded. Milton and Contreras joined the two officers to assist in the evacuation. With the sleds attached to the jeep, twelve to fourteen wounded could be brought off the ice at one time. During the middle of the day Beall was joined on the ice by a stranger.

Beall told him, "I don't want too many people out here because it draws fire from the enemy. What's your rank?"

The man replied, "No rank; I'm just John Q. Civilian."

"What'n hell are you doing out here then?"

"My name is LeFevre. I'm the Red Cross field director in this area."

Beall allowed LeFevre to remain on the ice and told him that he could direct the walking wounded to the evacuation point at the foot of the reservoir. A strong wind began to sweep in from the north and it became more and more difficult for Beall and his party to stand or move on the ice.

Throughout the day Beall and his small group continued to go ashore and return with wounded. LeFevre stayed at his job until he collapsed from fatigue and had to be taken ashore.

During the late afternoon, Beall and Hunt observed the enemy moving into positions on a finger of land which flanked their entry onto the shore. Inasmuch as there were still a large number of wounded to be evacuated, Beall ordered a platoon to come onto the ice with automatic weapons. Chief Warrant Officer Russell Waggoner brought several jeep-loads of men forward and set up machine guns. The final evacuation was made under cover of the fire laid down by Waggoner's men. After spending twelve hours on the ice with the temperature at twenty-four degrees below zero, Beall and his group returned to Hagaru. During the day they had evacuated three hundred nineteen men.

The following morning aerial observers reported more wounded on the ice. Beall responded immediately in a jeep with Corporal William Howard and Milton. Four soldiers were found huddled in an old fishing boat that had been frozen in the ice. Under heavier fire than had been received at any time on the day previous, the men were hauled to the vehicle. They told Beall they had been held prisoners by the Chinese for several days. Two enemy soldiers had taken them from a hut and out onto the ice. As they began to walk away, the Chinese opened fire on them and all were wounded. They dragged themselves to the boat and kept alive during the night by huddling together under the two blankets they had with them.

Beall sent the jeep to Hagaru. Leaving his weapon on the ice, he went ashore. This time his approach to land was unopposed. A short distance inland he came upon a line of trucks which had been halted by a destroyed bridge. The trucks were filled with dead. Many had been killed by grenades as they lay wounded in the vehicles. He searched through the long line without finding anyone alive. Without being fired upon, Beall returned to the ice and was picked up by Milton. The last of the wounded of the Army Task Force had been rescued.

It took nearly twenty hours for the troops and regimental trains of Murray-Litzenberg to pass into the Haragu perimeter. The rear guard was under constant enemy pressure. On one occasion the artillery unlimbered and fired point-blank into the enemy; on another, an artillery ammunition truck was set afire and Pfc. Russell Sedel of Powell's battery rushed through heavy fire to the vehicle and beat out the flames. His action prevented an explosion which would have inflicted heavy casualties and blocked the road.

The final elements of the Yudam-ni forces entered the Hagaru perimeter at one in the afternoon of the fourth of December. Throughout this period all available warming tents and galley facilities were utilized to house and feed the new arrivals. In most cases this was the first hot food the Marines of the 5th and 7th regiments had enjoyed in eight days.

Captain Wallace Blatt, helicopter pilot of VMO-6, took part in a grim and tragic rescue attempt at this time. During the day the pilots had worked to get their craft operating in the subzero weather. They had about given up and decided to become ground Marines when Blatt got his engine running. About the same time a report came in that a Navy pilot had crashed on the reservoir. Blatt took off, but returned; covering Navy planes had informed him that an ax and a fire bottle should be taken along.

Securing this equipment, Blatt flew to the scene of the crash. In the meantime Lieutenant (jg) Thomas Hudner had crash-landed his plane near the one that had been shot down and was attempting to extricate the pilot from the burning plane. Blatt landed and joined Hudner in trying to put out the flames and rescue Lieutenant (jg) Jesse Brown. It was an impossible task with the equipment at hand to put out the fire or release Brown from the crushed cockpit. Both men were forced from the plane when the flames reached the fuel tanks.

General Smith based his future plans upon the ability of Herring to evacuate the wounded and to grant a short period of rehabilitation to the Marines of Yudam-ni. A thousand casualties were evacuated on the fourth of December. About nine hundred of these were personnel from the east shore Army Task Force. Herring estimated that by nightfall of the fifth he would have all casualties evacuated that the medical department would be free to move.

On the morning of the fifth General Tunner, commanding general of the Air Transport Command, flew into Hagaru. Smith thanked Tunner for the supplies his planes had dropped. Tunner informed Smith that he was prepared to send in planes as fast as the small field could take them and to evacuate the Marines by air. This proposal surprised Smith and he informed Tunner that instead of flying men out, the Marines had flown in six hundred fifty replacements in the past twenty-four hours, and that no able-bodied man would be evacuated by air.

On the afternoon of the fifth, Smith called his unit commanders together for a final conference to go over the orders for the advance on Koto. The order provided for an advance in two regimental columns. Litzenberg would lead off and in his command would be a provisional Army battalion made up of the survivors of the task force. This unit numbered three hundred eighty-five men and was under the command of Lieutenant Colonel Anderson. Colonel Faith, the task force commander, had been killed. In addition to Litzenberg's combat troops, he would have in his column his own regimental train, as well as division train number one.

Murray's 5th was to do the rear guard and follow Litzenberg out of the perimeter. Ridge's battalion and Drysdale's Commando were attached to Murray. In his column Murray would have his regimental train and division train number two. Over twelve hundred vehicles were involved in the move.

Murray was directed to hold the Hagaru perimeter until Litzenberg had gained sufficient distance along the road south to permit the rear guard to move without undue crowding.

At first light on December 6 Litzenberg was to attack south astride the MSR and cover the advance of the remainder of the division to Hamhung.

With the exception of vehicle drivers, relief drivers, radio operators, casualties and personnel specifically designated by commanders, all personnel were to proceed on foot to the flanks of motor serials to provide close-in protection. A secondary purpose of this provision was to reduce frostbite casualties by keeping men active. Perimeter defenses were to be established around all serials of the motor convoy at all halts.

It was further directed that vehicles breaking down be pushed to the side of the road and, if not operable by the time the column passed, that they must be destroyed.

The artillery plans for support of the movement to Koto provided, generally, for continuous support by displacing a part of each battalion as early as practicable while holding the remainder in position at Hagaru for initial support. This was to be accomplished by having two batteries of Parry's battalion and one battery of McReynold's unit move at the head of Litzenberg's regimental train. Parry's batteries were to occupy initial positions midway to Koto to support the attack south from that vicinity to Koto. McReynold's battery was to proceed into Koto and take position to provide support back toward Hagaru. McClelland's battery at Koto was also capable of firing north about halfway to Hagaru. Initial support for the movement was to be provided by the battery remaining at Hagaru. When the other two batteries of Parry's battalion were in position, it would displace forward. The remaining battery of McReynold's battalion would provide general support for the movement until ordered to move out. Priority for movement on roads was given to the artillery. The plan for support of Murray was similar with two batteries of Feehan's Battalion moving out at the head of Murray's regimental train to positions midway to Koto, where they would fire to the north in support of withdrawing units of Murray's regimental train. Parry's remaining battery and Strohmenger's attached battery would displace south when the other two were in position.

A plan for air support of the withdrawal was prepared by Major General Field Harris, who directed all supporting air operations. Aircraft employed were from 1st MAW and Task Force 77 (fast carriers) and Marine squadrons aboard carriers. An umbrella of twenty-four close support aircraft was to be maintained above and covering the head, rear and flanks of the column during daylight hours while search and attack aircraft covered the ridges flanking the MSR and approaches leading into it. Support was also to be provided at night by night-fighter aircraft.

A plan was prepared for the destruction of all supplies and equipment which could not be moved by motor transport or evacuated by air. A directive by General Smith provided that the absolute minimum of supplies would be destroyed and that a maximum amount of supplies, equipment and vehicles would accompany the division out of Hagaru. Only equipment that was obviously inoperative or could not move without the use of tracked prime movers was to be left behind and destroyed. Excess ordnance items were to be evacuated by air.

At this time Colonel Bankson Holcomb (division intelligence officer) estimated that the 58th, 59th, 70th, 80th and elements of 79th and 89th Division's CCF had been committed against the Marines in the Chosin Reservoir area. Although these units had been badly hurt by ground and air action, they still retained sufficient strength to continue attempts to destroy the division. He further estimated that CCF ability to launch a co-ordinated attack was dependent upon the rapidity with which they could reorganize their battered and demoralized forces. Reports received indicated that the enemy was concentrated in several localities along the MSR south of Hagaru and that his activities had been confined to the construction of roadblocks and the blowing of bridges along the MSR.

Smith requested a force to relieve Schmuck's battalion of its mission of protecting the MSR at the base of the mountain. On the evening of December 5, X Corps issued orders providing for the 3rd Army Division to organize Task Force Dog. This force was to be commanded by a general officer and was to consist of one infantry battalion, one artillery battery, an engineer detachment and a Tactical Air Control Party. The mission of the force was to facilitate the movement of the Marines from Koto to the Hamhung-Hungnam defense area. At a date and time to be announced by Almond, Task Force Dog was to advance from Majon-dong to Chinhung and relieve Schmuck. Upon relief by Task Force Dog, and when directed by Smith, Schmuck was to attack north to assist the division advance to the south from Koto.

During the night of December 5-6, McReynold's battalion fired heavy concentrations of medium artillery on critical areas along the MSR to the south. These fires, in addition to softening up possible enemy areas of resistance, served the purpose of expending excess artillery ammunition on hand.

Litzenberg's plan provided for Lockwood's 2nd Battalion with one tank platoon attached, to cover a frontage of four hundred yards astride the MSR. Davis' battalion, on a frontage of five hundred yards, echeloned to the right rear and Anderson's Army Provisional Battalion on the same frontage echeloned to the left rear. As Davis moved along the high ground flanking the MSR on the west, Anderson's Army Battalion was to move along the high ground to the east. Harris' 3rd Battalion was to follow along the road in regimental reserve behind the regimental train, with one company along the flanks of the train. Artillery units and division train number one were to follow Harris.

Early in the evening Litzenberg began forming his units in the shallow interior of Hagaru to begin the attack to the south. By 4:30 in the morning, Davis had his battalion formed in a column and Kurcaba's company began the attack on the first objective. Fifteen hundred yards south of Koto, in the vicinity of the village of Tonae-ri, a group of twenty-four enemy were surprised as they slept in their positions. They were killed and the first objective secured. Lockwood's battalion jumped off as the advance guard at 6:30 A.M.

In the reorganization of Fox Company following its battle of Toktong Pass, Barber was evacuated because of wounds, and command of the unit was taken over by First Lieutenant Welton Abell who had been a public information officer for the 7th Regiment.

Reinforced by artillerymen and Marines flown into Hagaru, Abell was to spearhead the attack to the south. The initial advance was made without opposition for a distance of approximately two thousand yards. The enemy, having allowed Fox Company and the tanks to pass by, opened fire on the rest of the column. A co-ordinated attack by Bey (commanding Easy Company), supported by tanks and mortar fire, neutralized the resistance and the column continued. Bey and Sawyer were wounded. Both continued in action. This action had been time-consuming inasmuch as it was noon before the advance could be resumed. During this battle Dunne, the sole remaining officer of the Fox Company battle of the Pass, was killed.

In the meantime, on the right flank, Davis had sent Hovatter's company forward on the high ground. Davis' battalion continued to move to the south with all three of its companies being sent out at various intervals to sweep the flanks. There was constant enemy contact throughout.

The drive down the road was halted by fire again from Hill 1162 to the east. Once again Abell deployed his unit and took the target under fire. Bey took his unit forward and assumed the point. The column continued its movement at two in the afternoon. However, the enemy continued harassing the column with sniper fire, which increased until the movement forward was again halted by heavy fire. Bey rushed his unit into the assault and cleared the strongpoint.

After advancing along the road for another thousand yards, once again the column was halted by heavy fire. The position was neutralized by mortars and the advance to the south continued.

Along the route the Marines, under orders from Litzenberg, were destroying by fire all huts and houses. He told his unit commanders, "We'll leave no warming pens for the enemy behind us."

At eight Davis began to bring his unit down from the long ridge on the right flank and thereafter followed the west edge of the valley. Bitterly contesting every yard of advance, the enemy continued to bring fire on the Marines from the left flank and to hamper their progress by destroying bridges and placing physical blocks across the road. These blocks usually consisted of destroyed vehicles which had been lost in the Drysdale ambush.

Progress was again stopped after a fifteen-hundred-yard gain when enemy machine guns opened fire from Hill 1182, which commanded the road from the east. Artillery and mortar fire knocked out the gun shortly after midnight and the advance continued. After progressing twelve hundred yards, movement was halted by a blown bridge.

Lieutenant Ewald Vom Orde brought his platoon of engineers forward and repaired the bridge. The column began to move again. One thousand yards farther south another destroyed bridge halted the column. The enemy fire from the east increased and brought the train of thin-skinned vehicles under heavy fire.

The regimental command group, in trace of an Army tank, became separated from the forward elements. Litzenberg had gone forward afoot to join the advance guard in their attempt to overcome the enemy in this zone. Behind the tank were the jeeps of Captain Donald France, First Lieutenant Clarence McGuinness, Dowsett, Major Henry Woessner and Roach. The area was illuminated by a burning house to the left of the railroad track. France and McGuinness were killed, Dowsett was wounded and Woessner's driver was killed.

Still farther to the rear the division train was also halted and under fire. Major Frederick Simpson, Headquarters Battalion, deployed his men, consisting of clerks, cooks, drivers and bandsmen, as best he could. Master Sergeant William J. McClung assumed charge in one sector and, by constantly exposing himself to enemy fire, was able to organize and direct the fire of his small party. He collected other personnel and was able to build up a solid base of fire. When two of the trucks in the column caught fire and illuminated the scene, he directed his men to new positions offering better concealment. He returned to the immediate area of the burning trucks and began to remove wounded Marines from the lighted area. He was successful in dragging Corporal Figg to safety. He was killed as he carried a third Marine to cover.

During the height of the battle Chaplain Cornelius Griffin, Lieutenant (jg) Robert Wedemeyer and Sergeant Matthew Caruso ranged the road in search of wounded to attend. Wedemeyer, surgeon for the 1st Battalion, told Griffin of a seriously wounded Marine in a field ambulance farther along the road. Accompanied by Caruso, Griffin entered the ambulance and began to give the last sacraments to the wounded Marine. Machine-gun bullets tore through the side of the ambulance, killing Caruso immediately. One bullet struck Father Griffin's chin, shattered his jaw, passed on through his face and entered his right shoulder. Wedemeyer entered the ambulance before the enemy fire had ceased and began dressing Griffin's wounds.

Roach ran to the rear and contacted Newton, commander of How Company. Newton deployed his unit quickly and skillfully and overran the enemy positions. Due to the inability of Anderson's Provisional Battalion to eliminate the enemy from the high ground, Harris was ordered to furnish flank protection on the left.

During the confusion and darkness, Harris disappeared. Despite a thorough search by his men as well as by Staff Sergeant Robert Gault and his group from the Graves Registration Section, Harris' body was not recovered. Major Warren Morris assumed command of the unit.

In the meantime, Vom Orde, determining that the bridge was beyond repair, bulldozed a by-pass. Chaplain John Craven, by signaling with his flashlight, directed the tanks over the soft-shouldered strip of road.

The 2nd Platoon of Thomas' Item Company came under heavy fire as a following tank stalled on the by-pass. An enemy machine gun began sweeping the road. Sergeants Chambers and Goodrow deployed their squads along the west of the road, but the advantage of terrain and fire was in favor of the Chinese. Sergeant Leland Ehrlich got his squad into position and shouted to Chambers, "I'm going to get them."

With that he charged across the road and up the hill. When the enemy turned the gun on Ehrlich the other Marines were able to destroy the crew. Ehrlich was killed.

The forward elements of the column continued in the direction of Koto. At 5:30 in the morning, Bey and his company made contact with Puller's force. It had taken twenty-two hours to negotiate the nine miles.

Leading elements of Morris' battalion reached the Koto perimeter at seven. Litzenberg ordered them to return to the north and keep the road open until contact was made with Murray. To the rear, the batteries of Payne and Read were heavily engaged. As daylight began to break, the artillery column was placed under a heavy mortar attack and the enemy could be seen forming for an attack. The artillery pieces were hurriedly placed in direct firing positions and opened fire. By employing time fire, ranges were from one hundred to five hundred yards. The enemy force of eight hundred was slaughtered, but some forty to fifty escaped.

While the 3rd Battalion was fulfilling this assignment they received heavy fire from the high ground to the east of the road and about fifteen hundred yards north of the Koto perimeter. An air strike was called down which eliminated the enemy fires. Contact with the leading elements of Murray's Marines was made at 2:30 in the afternoon.

In addition to sending the 3rd Battalion to the north Litzenberg sent Lockwood on the same mission to aid units of the division in completing their movement into Koto. Lockwood took up blocking positions to the left of the road in the general area of where Drysdale's task force had been ambushed nine days previously. Drysdale's Commandos had a similar mission in knocking out enemy resistance to the north and west of Lockwood. Two days previously OY planes from VMO-6 had seen the word "Help" stamped in the snow. Air drops of food and medical supplies were made. Twenty-two Royal Marine Commandos had held out for nine days and were recovered. Ten had to be carried out on stretchers.

With Litzenberg closing on Koto, Murray was faced with a grim situation at Hagaru. The high ground to the east of Hagaru which commanded the road to Koto was of continuing concern to Murray. At ten o'clock in the morning of the fifth, Roise was directed to relieve Sitter's Company and elements of the engineer and service units who had assisted in the defense of this sector of the perimeter. By four o'clock in the afternoon, Roise's men had scaled the steep hill. In many cases ropes had to be used to assist the heavily burdened machinegunners and mortar men to the crest. At the completion of this movement, Roise was in line with Stevens' 1st Battalion on his left and Taplett's 3rd on his right. Because of the length of front to be covered by Smith's Dog Company, Peters was directed to attach one of his platoons to Smith.

In the early afternoon Murray called a meeting with his unit commanders. He outlined the plan for the move to the south by Litzenberg and then informed them of the mission assigned to the 5th Marines: "We'll hold our present positions until the 7th Marines clear the road to Koto, after which we'll move out. When we do move out we will come out as Marines and not as stragglers. We're going to take our dead, wounded and equipment when we leave. We're coming out, I tell you, as Marines or not at all. Any officer who doesn't think that we can get out of here will kindly get frostbite and go lame and I'll see that he's evacuated."

At ten o'clock that night Roise was called to Murray's CP where he received orders to seize the high ground northeast of his present positions. Murray felt that this step was necessary in view of the fact that this hill commanded the MSR and Litzenberg's force could be brought under fire. Roise returned to his CP and made plans for the attack. Lucy's 4.3 mortar company was to be in direct support and would provide a fifteen-minute preparation on Smith's objective. The following morning at seven o'clock the mortars began firing. When the scheduled aircraft did not arrive at 7:15 as planned, the mortars continued their preparatory fires. Ten minutes later Marine Corsairs came in and made bombing, strafing and rocket runs on the objective. Due to a shortage of napalm tanks, this weapon was not available to soften the enemy positions further.

On the ridge line Smith and the members of Dog Company awaited the time to jump off. As the final air strikes were brought in, First Lieutenant Manning Jeter, forward air controller, stood on the crest, the better to direct the Corsairs to their target. Jeter was wounded. He was replaced by Captain David Johnson. A total of seventy-six planes were used during the aerial assault.

Sorenson's second platoon jumped off in the attack. Before the unit had advanced fifty yards they were pinned down by withering enemy fire. Sorenson was wounded in the left shoulder and evacuated. First Lieutenant John Hinds assumed command.

Smith directed McNaughton to move into the assault. McNaughton's unit also was pinned down to the rear of Hinds. McNaughton directed the 3rd Squad under Gallagher to move into position facing the east and try to silence the heavy enemy fire from that direction. At this time Smith ordered Johnson to bring his platoon into position in a flanking movement. The three platoons charged forward into the enemy fire and the first objective was seized.

This initial attack was to the north. Once this high ground was secured, Smith ordered McNaughton to attack and seize the next higher piece of ground to the east, which Gallagher had engaged by long-range fire. McNaughton sent Sergeant Hughes back to get the 3rd Squad. Hughes did not return and Gallagher's squad did not come forward. Later McNaughton learned that Gallagher's unit had been hard hit and only two men remained unwounded.

McNaughton made his attack with twenty men. The objective was seized, and as the platoon was digging in Staff Sergeant Roger Lohsen killed two Chinese when they rose to hurl grenades at McNaughton.

Smith brought the rest of the company onto the high ground and the unit began digging in. These attacks consumed over four hours and Dog Company had been hard hit by casualties. The wounded were evacuated and the dead collected. McNaughton had but fifteen men left in his platoon, of which four were wounded.

Between the newly won positions and the Hagaru-Koto road, McNaughton observed one hundred fifty to two hundred enemy in a draw. Johnson (the FAC) called in an air strike and heavy casualties were inflicted. At this time Pfc.'s Hicks and Henry, both wounded, came forward from Gallagher's positions and joined McNaughton.

As Dog Company was digging in on its new position, Roise ordered Peters onto the first objective to secure and protect that flank. Hinds' 2nd Platoon tied in with Peters across the saddle.

Despite the air strike, the enemy in the draw above the road were showing indications of mounting an attack. Smith directed McNaughton to take a patrol down the hill and to eliminate the Chinese force. Leaving his wounded on the hill, McNaughton took Lohsen, Pfc. Daniel Edwards, Sergeant Frank Raponi and Corporal Paul Lea on the mission. Sergeant Jones and seven men were to provide flank and cover fire.

As the small patrol went down the hill, a further base of fire was built up by Johnson's platoon. Lea was hit in the foot and McNaughton placed him in a position where he could render supporting fire with rifle. After the briefest of fights, the will to resist evaporated and the Chinese surrendered en masse. One hundred fifty prisoners were captured. As defensive positions were resumed on objective two, Lea was wounded again. Corpsman Stanley Weaver was also wounded.

Shortly after nightfall enemy activity was heard between the positions occupied by Peters and Smith. A heavy enemy attack soon developed and the brunt of it was borne by Hinds' 2nd Platoon. The Chinese closed to grenade range and the entire area was subjected to a heavy attack by hand explosives.

Seydel, fighting desperately to save his machine-gun positions, killed seven of the enemy with his pistol. Honeycutt, executive officer to Smith, was wounded. Pfc. Warren Howard and Corporal Fred Walz, manning a machine gun in the support of Hinds' platoon, came to close and heavy action. While Walz fired the gun, Howard ran for grenades. Upon his return to the gun position, the grenades were largely instrumental in stemming the enemy attack. Walz and Howard alternated at firing the gun and throwing grenades. Many of the enemy were killed within ten feet of their position. Although wounded, Howard remained with his gun and assisted in carrying it to a new position when the order for a withdrawal came.

Smith's CP was forced to withdraw into Peters' line. Seydel was killed.

The first platoon, under the resolute leadership of Johnson and Staff Sergeant Leroy Dodge, fought with great stubbornness. Johnson and McNaughton combined their depleted units and fought a slow withdrawal back to the first objective. Staff Sergeant "Swede" Larsen (one of the leaders of the attack on Hill 88 outside Seoul) was killed. Upon assuming their new positions, Dog Company could muster but eighty men.

At daybreak, Dodge led a volunteer group of five men forward and the bodies of Seydel, Larson and fifteen other men were recovered. The enemy, well entrenched on the high ground, watched Dodge and his men, but did not take them under fire. Over one hundred seventy Chinese dead were seen in the immediate area.

Concurrently with the night attack on Dog Company, Jaskilka's unit came under a heavy attack which was preceded by a mortar barrage. Jaskilka's unit occupied positions at the base of the hill and astride the road leading in from Koto. The low ground was frozen and covered with ice and it was impossible for adequate emplacements to be dug. The enemy onslaught struck Jaskilka's line at ten o'clock at night. The initial fury of it was sufficient to carry into Borgomainero's lines. The left flank was in danger of being turned when the enemy captured a light machine gun and began to turn it upon the Marines. Corporal Jack Williams, manning a heavy machine gun thirty yards to the left, realized the enemy were in a defiladed position and he could not bring his weapon to bear upon them. Dashing across the open ground, Williams killed the Chinese in the immediate area, recaptured the gun and turned it over to a crew which had come forward. Williams was killed as he returned to his original position.

As the enemy pressure continued on Borgomainero's line, Sergeant Andrew Dunay, section leader in the antitank platoon, dashed forward when one of his gunners was knocked unconscious by a grenade. Manning a rocket launcher, he began to fire white phosphorus rockets into the Chinese. When the launcher failed to function, Dunay shouted for more rockets and began to hurl them by hand. His action saved a machine-gun position from being overrun and killed more than thirty of the enemy.

The enemy attack continued on Jaskilka's lines until 6:30 in the morning. As in the case of "Easy Alley" of Yudam-ni, Easy Company fought off the attack without allowing a serious penetration of lines. Daylight revealed over three hundred enemy dead in the snow.

Jones' Charlie Company received a heavy attack on the flank where it was tied in with Jaskilka. Eighty-one and 60 mm. mortar fire were utilized with maximum effectiveness on enemy troop concentrations. At one stage of the battle when the enemy had pressed to close range, Jones, under heavy fire, directed an Army Sherman tank into position where the weapons of the tank effectively supported the ground troops. The enemy attack withered and ended shortly before midnight.

About the time Jones had repulsed the attack on his front, Heater's company became heavily engaged. A penetration of lines was effected and the enemy continued to attack vigorously. Under a hail of enemy fire Lawson, Hodge and Carroll brought resupplies of ammunition and grenades to the hard-pressed front lines. Trapnell's platoon fought back with stubborn resolution. Lawson and Carroll were killed.

Stevens committed Hancock's company (which had been in reserve) to reinforce Heater. Hancock integrated his first platoon with Trapnell's unit on the right sector of the hill. Kohler's 2nd Platoon was sent forward to reinforce the left flank. Mortars of both companies were placed in position to the left rear of the high ground and they co-ordinated their fire missions. A bitter grenade and small-arms fight went on through the remainder of the night.

At dawn the enemy attack decreased in intensity. With better visibility supporting arms became more effective and Marine and Navy aircraft, coming on station, made numerous close air support attacks. Under the air assault the enemy became demoralized and ran for the hills. Three hundred forty enemy dead were found before Able Company's positions. Marine casualties for the night to the units of Heater and Hancock were thirty-three wounded and ten killed.

While the attack was underway against Heater, the enemy placed a second attack on Jones' front lines shortly after two in the morning. With skillful use of supporting arms and an Army tank on the left flank, Jones' unit quickly repulsed the enemy thrust. Throughout the remainder of the night small groups of the enemy attempted to infiltrate, but these were annihilated. At daylight Jones and his men counted two hundred sixty dead Chinese within two hundred yards of their company perimeter. Jones' casualties for the night were ten wounded in action.

In Taplett's sector of defense no enemy contact was made. As had occurred in the earlier attacks on Hagaru, the enemy had made their main effort from the east, northeast, south and southwest. In a period from darkness to daylight, the battalions of Stevens and Roise had killed over fifteen hundred of the enemy.

With the cessation of the Chinese attacks and with the leading elements of Litzenberg in Koto, Murray began to displace to the south. Taplett was directed to proceed to the head of the division train and search out and eliminate enemy activity which was holding up the advance of the vehicles. Mize and Williamson were directed to take their units forward and contact Lieutenant Colonel Joe Stewart.

A small enemy force armed with automatic weapons had the front of the column pinned down. Mize deployed his unit along the railroad embankment and took this force under fire. The enemy fire was neutralized and the column began to advance. At this time Taplett came forward and directed Mize and Williamson to assume the lead and protect the advance of the motor column. If enemy resistance came from the west of the road, Mize was to assault the positions under supporting fire from Williamson; if the enemy opposed the assault from the left of the road, Williamson would go into the assault under cover fire from Mize. Rapid progress was made with this arrangement until Williamson's company came upon enemy positions manned by a battalion of Chinese. Mize echeloned his unit forward along the railroad embankment and provided enfilade fire across Williamson's front as that unit went into the attack. The enemy force was caught in a withering cross fire and heavy casualties were committed. At five that afternoon Taplett's battalion and regimental train entered the Koto perimeter.

In the meantime, Stevens' 1st Battalion commenced withdrawal from the Hagaru perimeter at eleven in the morning. With Hancock's unit providing left flank security and Jones covering the right, the 1st Battalion arrived at Koto shortly after eight at night.

Roise's battalion displaced from the hills and acting as a rear guard, proceeded to Koto without further enemy action. As the last Marines departed the Hagaru area the town was put to the torch and the engineers destroyed the bridge. The last elements of Marines saw the enemy swarm from the hills and begin to vulturize the area in search of food. Roise entered Koto at 9:30 on the night of December 7.

The attack to the south from Hagaru to Koto had cost the Marines six hundred sixteen casualties.

CHAPTER XXII

March to the Sea

The large number of casualties pouring into Koto from the units arriving from Hagaru seriously overburdened the facilities. Besides the wounded, these included frostbite cases and many men suffering from intestinal disorders caused from eating frozen C rations and snow in lieu of drinking water. Many riflemen, suffering from severe diarrhetic conditions, had soiled themselves while straining over the mountains and there was naught they could do about it. Once again the Naval corpsmen and doctors performed miracles.

The runway at Koto was being extended, but at this time could not handle transport planes. Marine aviators First Lieutenant Truman Clark, First Lieutenant John Murphy and "Little Mac" McCaleb began to fly obsolete torpedo bombers (TBM's) onto the Koto strip. Although none of these pilots had flown such planes before, they assumed the risk in order to get the wounded out as quickly as possible. This type of plane could carry from six to nine wounded, depending upon the injury. On the first day, Clark and McCaleb evacuated more than eighty apiece. To facilitate the landings, Captain Malcolm Moncrief, a qualified carrier-landing officer, flew into Koto and by flag signals brought the three TBM pilots safely to the ground.

On the morning of December 8 a Marine two-engine transport circled the field in a heavy snowstorm. The Marines on the ground saw the plane and then lost sight of it as the storm increased. Visibility was cut to zero. When the storm let up for an instant, all concerned were astonished to see the plane on the ground. It took off shortly with nineteen casualties. Air operations were suspended for the day following this departure. The efforts of the Marine aviators had lessened the medical burden at Koto and only two hundred casualties remained to be evacuated.

Smith's plan for attacking down the mountain was simple and basic. Murray and Litzenberg were to seize and hold the commanding ground on either side of the canyon while the vehicular train moved south between them. While the Marines were moving south from Koto, Schmuck (having been relieved by the Army) was to attack to the north and seize the high ground halfway up the mountain. Puller, with a battalion of the 31st Infantry attached, was to hold the perimeter at Koto until the trains cleared the area. At this time he was to follow out and conduct the rear guard. As the trains cleared the road, the infantry would leave the high ground and move down in trace. The last vehicles in the column were to be the tanks. This assignment was directed in view of the fact that if a Pershing were to stall or throw a tread on the one-way mountain road, it would be most difficult to clear it out of the way.

Posing a serious problem in the plan, however, was the fact that the Chinese had destroyed a twenty-nine-foot section of the one-way concrete bridge a mile and a half below Funchilin Pass. Where the bridge had been destroyed, the drop-off down the mountain was sheer and there was no possibility of a by-pass. A bridge had to be rebuilt.

Lieutenant Colonel John Partridge, commanding the 1st Engineering Battalion, had made an aerial reconnaissance of the site on the morning of the sixth. After landing at Koto he contacted Colonel McGraw of the 185th Combat Engineering Battalion and one of his own officers, First Lieutenant George Babe. Preliminary plans were made at this time. Partridge was informed that Lieutenant Ward of the 58th Treadway Bridge Company was in Koto with several Brockway trucks. These trucks were especially designed to haul and place into position sections of a Treadway bridge. Ward had had considerable experience in Italy handling this type of equipment and his suggestions proved most helpful.

In the meantime, Blasingame of the Marine Air Delivery Section at Yonpo, was preparing to drop Treadway bridge sections into the Koto perimeter. Captain Cecil Hospelhorn and eleven of his Quartermasters Aerial Supply Company arrived from Japan to assist Blasingame in the aerial delivery of the bridge sections. These sections, weighing approximately twenty-five hundred pounds, were most difficult to handle. Rigging parachutes on them to carry them to the ground without damage was complicated.

Blasingame made a test drop over Yonpo and the section landed with such force it crumpled. A priority flight from Japan brought larger chutes. With a hundred-man work detail furnished by the 1st Amphibian Tractor Battalion, Blasingame and his men worked throughout the night in preparing for the drop. The Air Force furnished eight C-119's (Flying Boxcars) and by daylight all was in readiness to drop the eight sections of the bridge.

With the arrival of Murray and Litzenberg, the perimeter at Koto was packed with men and vehicles. Smith had directed Partridge that every unit and man would be informed of the drop so that casualties would not occur. Captain Guy Washburn was to direct the drop from the ground. It was Washburn's job to direct the planes and time the point of "kick-out."

Blasingame had chosen the plane flown by Air Force Pilot Manchester to fly the first section. Manchester had worked with the Marines for some time and Blasingame was impressed with his courage and skill. He was continually asking, "Am I loaded? Where do I go?"

The eight Boxcars took off and were over Koto at 9:30 in the morning. Manchester made a dummy run and on the second time over, when Washburn said, "Kick it!" the first section slid out, the 'chutes opened and a good landing was effected. Three of the sections were dropped in the eastern zone of Koto and the remaining five were dropped to the west. One section was off target and fell into the hands of the Chinese. Portions of the sections were slightly bent, but Ward was certain all could be repaired. With the sections loaded on his Brockway trucks all was in readiness for the final attack to the sea.

At eight in the morning on the eighth of December, Litzenberg moved his regiment forward to seize the first two objectives on either side of the road at the lip of the mountain. With the wounding of Dowsett, Davis had been assigned as executive officer of the regiment. Sawyer took command of the 1st Battalion. When the high ground on either side of the road was secured, it was Sawyer's mission to push down the MSR to the bridge site. The day was clear and bright as Hovatter took his unit to the point and began the move down the mountain. In trace of Hovatter were Kurcaba and Morris.

Less than two thousand yards from Koto Bradley's platoon came in contact with the enemy and was soon engaged in a heavy fire fight. Sawyer directed Kurcaba forward to the left of Hovatter while Vorhies' Weapons Company built up a base of fire from the road.

The weather had closed in and heavy flurries of snow made it impossible to call in the artillery or air support. The fire fight at the point grew in intensity rapidly.

Williams' platoon became heavily engaged to the right of Bradley and was pinned down by fire on three sides. Pfc. Frederick Stouffer, a platoon runner for Williams, ran across open terrain, gained the road and clambered aboard a Pershing tank. When the snowstorm let up, Stouffer remained in his exposed position and pointed out enemy positions to the tank commander. Though wounded, Stouffer remained atop the tank, continuing to direct the fire which allowed his unit to proceed in the attack. Williams was killed.

In the meantime, Kurcaba had moved his company to the left of Hovatter and attacked on a line adjacent to Able Company. Kurcaba's assault platoons came under extremely heavy fire and Chew Een Lee was wounded. His replacement, Second Lieutenant Joe Owens, was wounded within minutes of taking over the command.

Kurcaba pushed forward through heavy machine-gun fire and began organizing the men remaining in his assault platoons. He was killed and First Lieutenant Woody Taylor assumed command. With the fire from Morris' company sweeping the face of the hill, Hovatter jumped off. Morris joined the attack and both units cleared the enemy from the high ground.

These fire fights had been time consuming and it was three in the afternoon before the enemy positions were neutralized and the point could push on. Because of the early fall of darkness Litzenberg ordered Sawyer to tie in his lines and put the vehicles in a circle in the tank park on the edge of the plateau.

Progress during the day had been negligible. With his trucks and bridge sections, Partridge had moved forward at one stage and when Sawyer's advance was blunted, Litzenberg ordered the engineers back into the tank perimeter. In attempting to get the heavy trucks off the road, one of the Brockways was backed onto what appeared to be a flat bit of frozen ground. It proved to be a pond which was frozen over, but not heavily enough to sustain the truck. The truck was retrieved by a tank, but it was inoperative. Fortunately, this particular vehicle was loaded with spare and excess material.

While the leading elements were fighting to the south, Smith attended funeral services in Koto. Because of the lack of air facilities in the small perimeter and priority given to the wounded, one hundred seventeen

Marines were buried in a common grave. Both Protestant and Catholic services were held.

At the base of the hill Schmuck's 1st Battalion had been deployed at Chinhung-ni. Save for sporadic enemy action and patrol activities, the unit was fresh and eager to assist the division down the mountain. While holding his position at the base of the mountain, Schmuck had foresightedly reconnoitered the road and bordering mountains to the north. He had evaluated the situation correctly when he determined that Hill 1081 would be occupied by the enemy as the most likely land mass from which to inflict damage on the Marines. Due to its terrain features it could only be seized from the south. It was sheer and rocky and commanded a road both to the north and south for a distance of fifteen hundred yards. From these positions a well-entrenched enemy could deny passage in either direction. Upon being relieved by Task Force Dog, Schmuck immediately moved his troops to an assembly area north of the village. Under cover of darkness in the early morning hours of December 8, Wray's Charlie Company at the point moved north. The first objective was the southwestern nose of the ridge line embracing Hill 1081. The second objective was the hill crest itself and the fingers extending northward from it. This was the point which dominated the hairpin turn below Funchilin Pass.

The distance from Schmuck's assembly area to the first objective was six and a half miles. By the time Wray had moved his unit onto the road, the countryside was engulfed in a heavy snowstorm (the same storm which had hindered Sawyer). The snow was powdery and there was little wind to sweep it away. With previous snowfalls, the Marines were moving through snow from six to seven inches in depth. At 8 in the morning Wray was in the approach to objective one. Under the cover of the storm Wray was able to approach and seize the first objective without firing or receiving a shot. At this point Schmuck placed his 4.2 mortars.

With his first objective secured, Schmuck assigned Noren's company to the north astride the road. In trace, Barrow followed with his unit. Noren advanced as rapidly as the deep snow would permit his men to move, and his advance was opposed by erratic rifle fire as he rolled up surprised enemy outposts.

Despite the lack of opposition, Noren proceeded fully alert because the snow, showing the tracks of hundreds of feet, told him of recent occupation. The first roadblock, though manned by two machine guns, was easily overcome due to the gunner's inability to see in the storm. A second roadblock was taken and overcome just as easily and the sandbag bunkers were captured while they were still warm from enemy occupancy, and a kettle of rice was cooking on a small stove. These enemy bunkers were large, substantial affairs backed with rice bags filled with dirt. The entire structure was camouflaged with brush.

With objective one in the hands of Wray's Charlie Company and Noren in possession of the road and enemy bunkers at the south of the hairpin turn, Barrow was given the mission of seizing the hill crest. Because of the steepness, Barrow was compelled to make the ascent in a column of platoons. Jones led off with the second, McClelland followed and bringing up the rear was Staff Sergeant William Roach and the 3rd Platoon. Roach was commanding in place of Swords, who was deemed too ill by the battalion surgeon to participate.

Exhibiting considerable energy and physical stamina, Barrow and Technical Sergeant King Thatenhurst reached the top first. At this time the snowfall limited visibility to less than twenty-five yards. As Barrow and Thatenhurst made the last ascent on their hands and knees, they heard enemy troops chattering a few yards away. The storm lifted for a moment and they saw ten or twelve Chinese moving about on the hill crest. Thatenhurst slipped quietly down the hill to meet Jones and to caution him to make his approach in silence and from behind a spur which would conceal them from the enemy should the storm lift. It had taken two hours of the most arduous climbing to reach the top.

While waiting for Jones to join him, Barrow reconnoitered the immediate area of the crest line. There were sheer drops on the eastern and western sides. The crest itself was of a width where only a squad could be used in the attack. No envelopment tactics were possible.

Again the weather closed in, obliterating all but the immediate area and Barrow brought his platoon leaders, artillery and mortar FO's forward and briefed them on his plan of attack. Barrow attempted to prepare for the assault by calling in fire from the 4.2's. This was quickly abandoned when the shells began to explode close enough to shake the ground, yet could not be seen.

Jones led his platoon in the attack along the ridge line. Crawling along the tortuous footing, it was impossible for more than three or four men to form a skirmish line. Men fell, got up and fell again. Directly behind Jones, Barrow set the 60 mm. mortars. It was his intention to fire them as he would a cannon if the ground permitted.

McClelland was deployed in a partial perimeter facing the north and he was to hold this area as a base. Barrow went forward in trace of Jones and the mortars with Roach's 3rd Platoon. Jones had proceeded nearly one hundred yards when his forward fire team came under heavy automatic weapons fire. It was soon obvious the enemy were firing wildly at the sound rather than the sight of the Marines. By twos, threes and fours the Marines crawled forward with only a few being able to fire back at the enemy.

Barrow realized that such an advance would be disastrous once his meager skirmish line reached the enemy main line of resistance. He called a halt and Jones was directed to take two squads along the left face of the mountain. Once in position he was to swing to his right and come up over the top. On the right flank Barrow, with Roach's platoon, would approach the enemy strongpoint from a rocky draw.

Slithering and crawling on their hands and knees, Jones and his men attained their positions. Corporal Joseph Leeds placed his fire team at the extreme left flank. It took them the better part of an hour to crawl one hundred fifty yards. In the meantime the 60 mm. mortars were brought forward and set up so that they could be brought to bear on the enemy bunkers.

With all in readiness on both sides of the enemy knob, the mortars began to fire. Under the handicap of poor terrain and poorer visibility the mortar crews were unable to make a direct hit on the main enemy strongpoints. Barrow gave the signal and, with Jones on the left and Roach on the right, the attack was made. Scrambling hand over hand, falling and stumbling, but always moving forward, the Marines began to yell and shout at one another. Barrow, being a Southerner, was partial to Rebel yells. There were many of these, but there were also a good many "Kill th' bastards!"

Leeds located the focal point of fire about the same time as the enemy turned their guns in Jones' direction. Leeds ordered his fire team into the assault. Pushing ahead of them in the face of close and heavy machine-gun fire, he killed nine Chinese in the bunker and eliminated the weapon. Leeds was mortally wounded in the attack.

The sudden attack and the shouting of the Marines completely demoralized the Chinese defenders. They sprang from their positions and began to run, some to the north and some directly into the Marines. They were killed. The bunkers were eliminated by rifle fire and grenades. The final push had cost Barrow seven dead and eleven wounded.

Because of the early fall of darkness it was impossible to carry on the attack and Barrow formed a tight perimeter to wait out the night. To evacuate the ones wounded, it took a four-man stretcher team five hours to reach the base of the mountain.

In the meantime, Noren had been proceeding along the road. Under sporadic, inaccurate machine-gun fire the third roadblock was overrun. By now it was 4:30 in the afternoon and Noren received orders from Schmuck to dig in and hold for the night.

After a bitterly cold night the morning was bright and clear. Barrow ordered McClelland's 1st Platoon into the assault to clear the enemy from the rest of the hill. It was now possible to use all supporting weapons and the attack was preceded by artillery, mortars and air. The terrain was such that it was possible to envelop the enemy strongpoint from a shelf on the left flank. McClelland worked two squads into position here. Staff Sergeant Ernest Umbaugh took one squad along the military crest of the ridge to the right. A base of supporting fire was built up by Roach's platoon and when the preparatory fires had been delivered, McClelland jumped off in the attack.

The squads to the left came under heavy machine-gun fire. Umbaugh ran across the topographical crest of the hill and joined the squad receiving the heaviest fire. He assisted in organizing the attack from this position and the first enemy position was overrun. During the assault the attacking force was receiving heavy fire from the bare hill two hundred fifty yards to the north. Umbaugh again crossed the fire-swept crest to return to the right flank squad. He halted the advance of this unit and built up a base of fire directed upon the entrenched positions to the north. Once the field of fire in this squad was organized, Umbaugh recrossed the hill for the third time and rejoined the remainder of his platoon. The enemy in the immediate area had been eliminated and the attack on the final objective was formed. McClelland's platoon now could muster but twenty men.

For the final attack Barrow brought Roach's platoon forward to strengthen the advance elements while Jones was directed to set up a base of fire. With Sergeant Henry Noonkester, McClelland and Umbaugh in the front, the final assault was made over the bare ground. The initial strongpoints were overcome with Umbaugh tossing grenades through the embrasures of the enemy bunkers. Noonkester led his fire team into close fighting and his accurate fire and hurling of grenades eliminated two enemy emplacements.

The last stages of the battle of Hill 1081 ended in a battle of grenades and rebel yells as Corporals Flowers, Carter, Billy Webb and "Hand Grenade" Riley stormed about the area like mad men in their final elimination of the enemy. Umbaugh was killed in the final attack.

For the Koto forces the night passed without active enemy attacks. At 7:30 in the morning Sawyer prepared to push down the road to the bridge site. Considerable difficulty was experienced in getting the units into formation as the continuous strain of fatigue and battle was having its effect. As one observer remarked, the Marines appeared to be moving in slow motion.

For an orientation of time, Sawyer began to move south along the road at the same time Barrow was making his final attack on Hill 1081.

Because of the clear weather, all supporting weapons could be utilized. Once again the air umbrella of Marine and Navy aircraft was overhead and there was ample evidence that the enemy were becoming disorganized. Some concern had risen over the report of "over one thousand" Chinese running through the hills paralleling the advance of the Marines. These sightings had been made between snow flurries the day before. As Sawyer pushed down the road he was continually on the alert and searching his right flank for the possible appearance of this enemy unit. With little or no opposition being placed against the Marines either on the flanks or on the road, good progress was made.

Hovatter had his unit at the point with Morris in trace. Peppin and his engineer platoon accompanied the point, and holes and soft shoulders in the road were bulldozed and cleared as rapidly as the infantry could move forward. As Sawyer's main body approached the power house and the destroyed bridge, Partridge and Vom Orde joined him with the bridge sections. A patrol from Morris' company became engaged in a fire fight. Morris' unit was unable to clear the enemy from their positions overlooking the road east of the power plant. The fire fight continued until dusk, at which time the enemy troops came from the hills and walked up to the Marines and surrendered. These Chinese were stupid from fatigue and frozen to their weapons. When they were disarmed their fingers had to be broken from the rifles they carried.

Morris' company was formed into six outposts of eight men each and placed in position on the high ground overlooking the road from the power plant to the railroad bridge further south.

Upon interrogation it was discovered that the enemy were members of the thousand-man unit which had run through the hills the day before. With the sudden drop in temperature, they had, as Tighe put it, "frozen in their own sweat." These prisoners reported that many of their units had suffered one hundred per cent casualties due to subzero weather.

Upon arrival at the destroyed bridge it was discovered that the enemy had blasted the southern abutment. As a result, sandbags and timbers had to be used to build up a base upon which the Treadway sections could rest. This material was at hand and work on the bridge began at 1:30 in the afternoon. With Peppin, Vom Orde and Ward co-ordinating their efforts, it was completed by four in the afternoon.

From the plateau at Koto the long train of vehicles began to descend the mountain. The only impediment to the movement was caused by the icy road conditions and small enemy groups who attempted to block the road by sporadic fire from both flanks.

The next obstruction in the road was a railroad bridge which had been bombed; a section of it had dropped into a stream bed, blocking the thoroughfare. Vom Orde was concerned with removal of this. If the heavy girders had frozen in the river, its removal would take time. Fortunately, this was not the case and upon arriving at the scene a bulldozer placed its blade against the heavy steel and literally skated it out of the way.

During this time, Sawyer had been out of radio contact with Litzenberg. While Vom Orde was working over the girder and building a roadbed across the stream, Sawyer (who had been wounded in the leg two days previous) limped back along the long row of vehicles attempting to find one which had a radio in operating condition. He was unsuccessful. He returned to the head of the column and his radio operator, Corporal Ray Burns, excitedly reported he had made contact and had received a strange message. Burns said there had been no call sign— "As Moses was taken through the bullrushes, so lead him to the bottom of the pass."

Further radio contact was impossible and on further questioning of Burns, Sawyer was informed that the voice sounded like that of Davis. Sawyer assumed that these were orders for him to push on, although his original orders were to remain in position near the bridge site. At the time Sawyer had but seventeen mortar men from Vorhies' Weapons Company available to form a point and push on down the road. It was now midnight. As Tighe, Sawyer, Vom Orde and Vorhies were discussing the situation, Tighe sensed a person standing at his shoulder. He turned and grabbed him, exclaiming, "Why, the sonofabitch is a Chinaman." The enemy soldier, as the others, was slowly freezing to death and was seeking shelter and food.

At one in the morning Sawyer reached the bunker where Schmuck had established his CP. The Marines of the north and south had joined.

On the eighth of December General Shepherd met with Admirals Joy, Struble and Doyle aboard the U.S.S. *Mount McKinley* in Hungnam Harbor. At this conference plans for the evacuation by sea of all friendly units in northeast Korea were begun.

On the ninth of December Smith received orders from X Corps which revealed that all United Nations forces were to evacuate the Hungnam area. Involved as they had been with their own problems, this order apprised the Marines of the serious setback suffered by the Eighth Army.

With the bridge built and a fairly steady flow of traffic on the road, the folding-in of the infantry units on the protective ridges could begin. As planned, Puller began to relieve units of Litzenberg and Murray. Once relieved, these battalions gained the road and moved out of the mountains.

Civilian refugees gathered at the roadblock on the north of the Koto perimeter on December 9 numbered about thirty-five hundred and it was found necessary to drive them back by firing over their heads. Heavy enemy small-arms fire was received from the northeast during the day, but no attack developed. Much enemy activity was noted to the north, east and west of the perimeter and air strikes and artillery fire were placed on observed enemy groups. In several instances the artillery fired direct fire on close-in enemy groups. During the night of December 9-10, the air strip was covered by enemy fire. The covering force in Koto and trains waiting to move out fought a constant rear-guard action. About two hours before daylight a force of about three hundred fifty enemy attacked Ridge. This attack was beaten off by daylight.

During the day of the tenth, movement of the column south from the Funchilin Pass was hindered little by enemy action, undoubtedly owing to the heavy air cover and the increased efficiency of artillery fires during the daylight. Sporadic small-arms and occasional mortar fire were received. However, the column received fire from enemy positions commanding the MSR north of Hill 1081, which halted the column in that area. Artillery and mortar fires were called down by Barrow on a large group of enemy moving across his front north of Hill 1081 and a heavy toll of casualties was taken.

The tanks were to move south after the last wheeled vehicle, screened to the rear by Major Walter Gall's Reconnaissance Company. At midnight the tank column moved out. Gall placed Hargett's platoon at the rear of the tank column, with the remainder of the company being interspersed through the column.

As Gall was making his final disposition of troops to protect the tanks, he was approached by a civilian who spoke English well. This man asked for a doctor to attend a wounded member of his party. With an enemy probing attack building up and his line thin to the north, Gall told the Chinese there was not time to give him medical assistance. The Chinese asked if he could follow closely behind the column. Gall warned the man that he might be fired upon if the enemy should attack from the rear.

There were forty-six tanks in the column. Gall placed Shutler's 2nd Platoon with five, followed by Kraince's unit protecting five more. Hargett was to cover the rear. The tanks in advance of Shutler would be unescorted by infantry. First Lieutenant Jack Lerond commanded the platoon of tanks bringing up the rear. Gall sent his vehicles down the mountain in advance.

Along the icy mountain road south of the pass the tanks moved slowly with lights on and dismounted crew members acting as guides. With a high cliff on the left of the road and a sharp drop on the right, tank guns were useless for firing to the flanks. Only the leading and rear tanks could fire to the front and rear, respectively. The .50 caliber machine guns mounted on the turrets were also restricted as to their ability to fire. Furthermore most of the tanks were out, or nearly out, of machine-gun ammunition.

With frequent stops due to holdups in the column ahead, the Korean refugees with intermingled CCF troops kept approaching the last tank in the column. At about two in the morning, the ninth tank from the end had a brake lock holding up the remainder of the column. At this time the same civilian who had talked with Gall came forward from the refugees and informed Hargett that a large group of CCF troops had moved from the mass of refugees to the high ground above the column. The Chinese was excited. "There are many, many *Balu* (Communists) in the hills about you!"

Almost immediately the enemy began an attack from the high ground above Hargett. The men of the Recon Company deployed and answered the fire. Two men were wounded. Hargett had them placed under the rear tank as the fire fight grew in intensity. Sergeant Bland set up a machine gun and got it in operation, holding off the enemy who by then were attacking down the road. By this time the enemy on the high ground had closed and were within grenade range; hand explosives began to blast around the rear tank. Technical Sergeant LaMonte tried to warn the tank crew, but evidently they were confused by the noise and firing and would not open up.

Hargett's small platoon, hard hit by casualties, was forced to withdraw and form a defensive line to the rear of the second tank. Hargett sent Sergeant Hanson forward to contact Lerond and request that the tanks up forward open fire on the hills to the right and the left. In the meantime, Hargett sent his casualties to the forward end of the column. A satchel-charge explosive was thrown close to the second tank. Pfc. DeMott was blown over the embankment and into the ravine. Friendly natives found him later and cared for him. After the satchel-charge explosive, which inflicted more casualties, Hargett sent LaMonte, who had been wounded, back to the third tank from the rear. Hargett covered the second tank with four men. Hargett was wounded.

The enemy had set up a machine gun on the right flank and were sweeping the road with fire. With more than half his men wounded, Hargett, Sergeants Vickery and Bland, a corpsman, and Pfc.'s Strelow and Hedl attempted to return to the rear tank in an effort to rescue the wounded under it and the tank crew inside. The corpsman and Hedl were wounded. Faced with having his small unit wiped out, Hargett ordered the withdrawal and formed a line to the rear of the third tank. The enemy clambered aboard the last tank and set it afire. The crew of the second tank escaped by plunging from the turret into the ravine to the right.

In the meantime Lerond had ordered his crew to abandon the tank ahead of number three. The driver of the tank immediately behind the one that had caused the original block refused to leave his vehicle and after seesawing around, by-passed the stalled tank and drove it on down the road. Hargett collected his wounded and, fighting a slow withdrawal, backed down the road.

When tank number nine had stalled, breaking the column, radio communications failed and the forward elements proceeded unaware of the battle at the rear. It was not discovered until the tail of the column failed to cross the bridge.

Gall rushed back with Shutler's platoon and the enemy were driven off.

Hargett and his wounded reached the bridge just before it was destroyed by the engineers.

Due to a mistake in timing, Schmuck had withdrawn his battalion from its positions around Hill 1081 and proceeded southward in advance of Gall's company. As a result, the depleted Recon unit was forced to fight the rear guard into Chinhung-ni. They closed on this town at eleven o'clock the next morning.

Movement south of Chinhung-ni by division units was carried out primarily by marching owing to the shortage of trucks. At Majon-dong, rail movement was employed to supplement the limited motor transport. While Hargett was heavily engaged at the tail end of the column, Puller's regimental train was ambushed at Sudong. Captain George Petro's antitank company became heavily engaged. The attack stopped the column and heavy fire came from the front and both flanks.

In the darkness and confusion Petro rushed forward to organize his men into a firing line. He was accompanied by Pfc. Marvin Wasson and an Army Lieutenant Colonel Page. While Petro carried a seriously wounded Marine to cover, Page led an aggressive two-man attack into the enemy lines. Page was killed. Wasson was wounded but continued in action. Manning a 75 mm. Recoilless gun, Wasson fired white phosphorus into several houses, setting them afire, which illuminated the scene to the advantage of the Marines. Wasson then manned a light machine gun and killed many of the enemy as they were fleeing from the burning buildings.

Concurrent with this action, Warrant Officer Armon Sealey and Pfc. William Holt rushed reinforcements to the heaviest sector of fire. Holt, observing that the leading elements were pinned down by heavy fire, picked up his light machine gun and ran to the head of the column. He opened fire on the enemy. As supporting weapons adjusted their fire on the enemy positions, the Chinese began running from shell-struck buildings and emplacements. From an exposed position Holt brought heavy and accurate fire into the enemy ranks. When his field of fire became masked by a disabled truck, he picked up his machine gun and, moving around the truck, continued to fire from a standing position.

Petro had made a second trip into forward positions to rescue a wounded Marine. During this engagement eight Marines were killed and twenty were wounded. After the hazards that had already been surmounted, this was a bitter loss to the Marines, particularly since it was thought that the movement was being covered by protective forces.

By six in the morning of December 10, the division trains began to enter Hamhung. By early evening on the eleventh of December the final elements of the 1st Marine Division entered the seaport town. From the period November 27 through December 11 the 1st Marine Division had suffered 3,637 battle casualties and 3,657 nonbattle casualties, most of which were from frostbite.

The attack to the sea was ended and the Marines were gladdened by the sight of a vast armada of Navy ships waiting for them. As the men of the division began to go aboard ship there was no one among the ground Marines who did not speak with praise of the Marines who had flown over them day and night and in impossible weather.

Smith voiced the sentiments of his men when he wrote to General Field Harris: "During the long reaches of the night and in the snow storms many a Marine prayed for the coming of day or clearing weather when he knew he would again hear the welcome roar of your planes as they dealt out destruction to the enemy. . . . Never in history has Marine Aviation given more convincing proof of its indispensable value to the ground Marine. A bond of understanding has been established that will never be broken."

Epilogue

One of the fine unit histories written after World War II was titled *The Old Breed*. It was an account of the 1st Marine Division in the Pacific. *The New Breed* is about the same division, but few of the same people.

George McMillan, the author of *The Old Breed,* wrote of Marines who had fought in a dozen small wars and one or two large ones. He wrote of Marines who fitted Colonel John Thomason's description: "a number of diverse people who ran curiously to type, with drilled shoulders and a bone-deep sunburn, and a tolerant scorn of nearly everything on earth. They were the Leathernecks, the old breed of American regular, regarding the service as home and war an occupation, and they transmitted their temper and character and viewpoint to the high-hearted volunteer mass."

The new breed of Marine no longer answers to this description. The uniformity of size is no longer there, nor do they have the length of professional military training. There are few of the old breed left, very few. Most of the old ones were buried at Guadalcanal, Pelelieu or Okinawa. There is a similarity, however, between the old and the new—the will to win and curses on the man or unit who lacks it; the moral stamina to stand and fight when all seems lost; the courage to charge a hill when death warns to stay. Somehow the blood line has remained without taint or blemish.

A newsman asked Puller, one of the old breed, the difference between the old and the new. Puller answered instantly, "Old breed? New breed? There's not a damn bit of difference so long as it's the Marine breed."

INDEX

Set in Linotype Electra
Format by Katharine Sitterly
Manufactured by The Haddon Craftsmen, Inc.
Published by HARPER & BROTHERS, *New York*